Frameworks for Teaching

Frameworks for Teaching

Readings for the Intending Secondary Teacher

Edited by
Roger Dale, Ross Fergusson and
Alison Robinson
of the Open University

Hodder & Stoughton

A MEMBER OF THE HODDER HEADLINE GROUP

British Library Cataloguing in Publication Data

Frameworks for teaching: readings for the
  intending secondary teacher.
  1. Education, Secondary – Social aspects –
  Great Britain
  I. Dale, Roger   II. Fergusson, Ross
  III. Robinson, Alison   IV. Open university
  373·41   LC191.8.G7

ISBN 0 340 42421 4

First published 1988
Impression number 12 11 10 9 8 7 6 5 4
Year   1998 1997 1996 1995

Typeset by Latimer Trend & Company Ltd, Plymouth.
Printed in Great Britain for Hodder & Stoughton Educational, a
divison of Hodder Headline Plc, 338 Euston Road, London, NW1 3BH
by Athenæum Press Ltd, Gateshead, Tyne & Wear

Contents

Contents

Contents

'Frameworks for Teaching'
Course Team

Clem Adelman
Robert Burgess
Guy Claxton
Roger Dale (Chair)
Brian Davies
Rosemary Deem
Geoff Esland
Ross Fergusson
Mike Flude
Merril Hammer

Charles Hannam
John Head
Desmond Nuttall
Jenny Ozga
Alison Robinson
Philip Robinson
Christine Rose
Kathy Stredder
Mike Walker
Peter Woods

Preface

This Reader is part of the Open University course EP228, *Frameworks for Teaching*. The aims of that course are to assist students in:

a   coping successfully and confidently with their roles as new teachers in the classroom, the school and the wider profession;
b   developing a foundation for continuing professional development;
c   understanding the contribution of school both to the wider society and to individual growth.

The course also includes specially written units, original documents, a specially made 3-hour video of classroom activity, television programmes and audio tapes. This Reader is intended to complement these other parts of the course and in compiling it their contributions have been taken into account. Opinions expressed in articles are, therefore, not necessarily those of the Editors, the Course Team or the University.

However, while the Reader has been compiled with a particular set of aims in mind, those aims are widely shared throughout initial teacher education, and our hope is that the issues and approaches raised in this volume will make it of value to anyone interested in this field.

The EP228 Course Team is against the use of sexist language and gender stereotyping. We have tried to avoid the use of sexist language in this Reader but some examples of this may remain from the original articles, and for this we apologize.

Acknowledgments

We would like to thank all our colleagues on the EP228 *Frameworks for Teaching* course team. It is on their behalf and on the basis of their suggestions that we have compiled this Reader. We are also grateful to other colleagues in the School of Education at the Open University who suggested articles for inclusion, especially Madeline Arnot and Gaby Weiner, and to our secretaries, Diane Ward and Carole Dalton, for maintaining their patience and good humour throughout.

Introduction

When Merril Hammer suggested *Frameworks for Teaching* as the title for the course this collection is primarily intended to serve, she made clear the attraction of its double meaning – the frameworks within which teaching takes place, and the frameworks that guide teaching. That duality was very much in our minds when we set about putting this Reader together. Like the course it serves, we wanted the Reader to reflect the two key dimensions of the education of teachers. These dimensions appear in many forms – theory and practice, subjective and objective, content and context, technical and analytical, but whatever the form, we wanted the course and the Reader to reflect their separate and joint indispensability. We need both a 'problem solving' orientation that seeks immediate solutions to pressing problems and a 'critical' orientation that enables us to stand back and examine the construction of both the problems and their solutions. There are few, if any, pure cases of either orientation in this volume. Though the articles do differ along this dimension, as they do also on the associated dimension of value for short-term survival and value for longer term professional development, neither pole becomes an end in itself. So, for instance, while some of the articles describe what may be happening in the classroom and describe some way of coping, significantly, they all do rather more than this; they all ask, 'what else is a teacher doing when he/she is marking books, disciplining pupils or whatever?'

While we assume that everyone who uses this volume in an initial teaching course will have a subject specialism, none will find their specialism reflected here, except incidentally. This generic quality has some limitations; its strength is that it fosters an active reading. Readers need to relate the articles to their own subjects as well as to the schools and the locality where they work. This should encourage a critical and questioning stance towards each piece and enable them to set their day-to-day activity in a broader context.

The frameworks for teaching in secondary schools for the rest of this century are uncertain. The past dozen years or so have seen unprecedented changes in both the context and the content of teachers' work. And though in one sense teaching is still fundamentally a matter of the teacher standing in front of – or among – a group of pupils and having to control them, and trying to impart knowledge to them, in other senses even this has changed. The pupils and how they are to be regarded have changed; they are now recognized as a much more heterogeneous population, differentiated into sub-groups on other grounds besides 'ability', with each sub-group having a legitimate claim to an education suitable for them. The destinations of those pupils, too, have changed. The option of entry into work (in this sense of a freely contracted and normally paid for job) at the school leaving age – the assumption for most young people for 30 years after the Second World War – is no longer present for the great majority.

Indeed, the changes in teachers' work and its accompanying uncertainty have been especially evident in the secondary age range, and especially in the education of 14–19 year olds: with 16 the effective age of entry into work for a decreasing minority of young people a new upper secondary/tertiary phase of education may be in the process of being created.

The work of teaching itself is changing, too. Teachers' influence over how and why they teach what they do has been consistently eroded over the past dozen years or so. Their situation has moved steadily from one of a 'licensed' autonomy, where, within the fairly clear boundaries set by the recruitment demands of the relevant labour markets they were able to exercise considerable control over the content of secondary education, to one of a much more 'regulated' autonomy, where even the core professional act, the classroom transaction, is to be more closely scrutinized and appraised.

It is worth looking at these two features, the nature of the pupil population, and the context of teaching, a little more closely. For even if there is likely to be more change before a settled framework for teaching in the twenty-first century emerges, those involved cannot wait but still have to do the job; it is our view, and a key purpose of this collection of readings, that an understanding of the nature, causes and implications of those changes is the best way of coming to terms with them and building an effective professional response to them – which is, after all, what becoming a teacher means.

The heterogeneity of the school population has been much more clearly recognized over the past decade and a half. The 1944 Education Act required schools to provide an education suited to a pupil's ability. That requirement was essentially interpreted as meaning that *academic* ability was the criterion both for the division of the population into educational strata, and for the allocation of resources and prestige. And this largely survived the introduction (still incomplete) of comprehensive secondary education. More recently both the criteria for differentiation, and its educational consequences, have begun to change. The clearest example of the latter is the provision for Special Educational Needs. While groups of young people are variously identified as 'different' educationally (ESN, Maladjusted, Delicate), provision for them, how they were to be educated, has varied considerably. Crucially, they were not given the right of access to, or the support they would need to benefit from, the kinds of educational experiences enjoyed by their 'normal' peers. That right was enshrined in the 1981 Act, though it may be honoured as much in the breach as in the observance.

However, it is clear that even accepting academic ability as the criterion for the distribution of educational resources does not guarantee everyone receiving their fair share from education. For we know that this criterion 'selects out, but by no means succeeds in keeping in, for subsequent entry to higher education, the top layers of measured intelligence' (Glass in Douglas, 1964, p. 22). It has long been known that those, even of the same requisite IQ, whom the system has failed to 'keep in', have come in hugely disproportionate numbers from the working class, and we have learned from major sociological studies how the processes of schooling themselves contributed to that keeping out. Similarly, it has long been known that fewer girls than boys entered higher education. And although it has become evident that the process of schooling may contribute to gender, as to class, inequality, it is only recently that this recognition has been acted on and that responses to it have consisted of more than reiterating the existence of formal equality of opportunity. The same, of course, is equally evident in the case of ethnic minorities. Just as the consciously and unconsciously sexist practices of schools have denied girls the substance of equality, so have their consciously and unconsciously racist practices denied it the ethnic minorities. Without a clear recognition of class, gender and ethnic differences, of the contributions schools make to them, and consequently of what steps can be taken to mitigate them, formal equality of opportunity amounts to no more than the opportunity to remain in an inferior position in the labour market.

In 'treating everyone alike', as schools have been quite rightly proud to claim they do, there was a tendency to overlook the basis of the similarity of treatment. That basis was not, and could not be, 'neutral'; whatever basis is chosen for giving out prizes favours some above others. The meritocratic claim that sheer measured ability should be the basis for allocating resources and deciding treatment, for 'treating them all alike', may be the closest we will get to a 'neutral' or 'fair' basis, but it has not, as we have seen, proved possible to implement it successfully. And that evidence also points to the bright, white, male middle-class young person being the norm for equality of treatment. It was, and frequently still is, very broadly, his needs, and what was right for him, that were the basis for treating everyone alike. It was a norm for equality of treatment whose inbuilt biases guaranteed for the majority inequality of treatment and outcome.

The heterogeneity of the secondary school population is confirmed by their post school destinations. Rather than work or sixth form being the options, depending on qualifications and preferences, there is now an array of alternative destinations for young people, with youth unemployment having largely eliminated the work alternative in very many parts of the country. This all adds to the complexity of the teachers' task. Not only can they no longer 'treat everyone alike' in the way that used to be appropriate, but they cannot be sure of what their charges will be doing next. When it was 'work or the sixth form', they knew all about the latter and didn't need to know about the former. Now, all teachers, not just careers teachers, can be expected to know something about YTS, B/TEC, tertiary colleges, CPVE and so on.

The 'young people' that secondary teachers face are, then, in the course of being newly constructed. 'Recognizing and responding to differences' has become as important as 'treating them all alike'. Whom teachers teach is changing. So, too, are how they teach, what they teach, and the conditions under which they teach it.

We mentioned above that all the articles here look at 'what else' teachers are doing when they are marking books, dictating notes, or whatever. The key point about many of the current changes is that the 'what elses' that teachers do are being codified, whether as a requirement, a preference, or to be rejected. The clearest example of this is found at the level of pupils, where profiling as a form of assessment makes available to scrutiny and possible assessment aspects of the pupil previously not considered as part of what counts as school achievement.

Hardly perhaps by coincidence, much the same is promised for teachers themselves. It is intended that they should be subject to some form of appraisal of their performance, but even pending the formalization of a scheme of teacher appraisal, increasing emphasis is being put on local education authorities and head teachers 'managing' their teaching force much more tightly. This is just one aspect of the shift towards a 'regulated' autonomy for teachers. Appraisal could regulate that autonomy even in the classroom. Outside the classroom, heads are expected to manage their teachers, and outside the school new and more powerful influences are being brought to bear on the curriculum. While there have always been pressures on the curriculum, what is different about the current pressures is that they are of a piece with changes in other aspects of teachers' working lives. The thrust of these changes is in the same direction – towards an augmented control of the teaching force, more routinization of teachers' work and increased centralization of curricula. As we write (mid–1987) none of these issues is finally settled, but they can clearly be seen as part of the attempt to bring the position of the teaching force into line with the other changes that have affected the education system over the past ten years or so – increased central government control (with MSC as well as DES now involved in 14–19 education), a more instrumental role for education, close monitoring of the system, and more influence on education from outside the service (for example, from parents and 'industry'). It is not our place here to say whether these moves are to be welcomed or not – in fact, we think that in themselves they could be effective in promoting almost any kind of education system. Rather, we wish to draw attention to their consequences for beginning teachers and the kind of education system and conditions, problems and opportunities they are likely to find.

Our aim, then, has been to indicate to potential secondary teachers, as clearly as can be achieved through a volume like this, the changing construction of the young people they will face, some of the tools at their disposal, and the context and the content of their job. No such volume can provide answers. If we have succeeded in clarifying the problems and sharpening the questions, we shall be more than satisfied.

It is for these reasons that we have excluded pieces whose argument or research base are too closely tied to subject or circumstance to prevent extrapolation and generalization. We have also excluded readings solely concerned with prescribing (often inadequately grounded) 'best practice' or whose handy hints and tips beg fundamental questions about the ends and the best means of education; or whose concern with minutiae indulges the inexorable tendency to be blinded to woods by trees. These exclusionary criteria are largely mutually compatible, and produce a collection which we hope balances immediate relevance (ready for translation to subject and school) with more profound understandings through examining wider contexts. The former is ephemeral, the latter enduring. With experience in teaching the urgency of the former will fade, the longer term relevance of the latter become more evident.

The composition of the collection reflects these priorities. New teachers walk from the world into the school, from the school into the classroom; for them the gates which separate the school from the world are of less concern than the doors which separate the classroom from the school. Their first concern is to survive in the classroom; this is the subject of the first section, The Classroom Framework. With some confidence and understanding of the classroom, the school context takes on more relevance, as well as more meaning. Section 2 on the School Framework helps open the door. The Social Frameworks are in one sense the most familiar since they apply to the larger world which most of us know better than schools. But the world takes on a different and more complex meaning when viewed from the school gate for both pupils and teachers. Section 3 addresses this.

No collection of readings for so diverse an audience will be entirely successful in both remaining accessible and exploiting the knowledge, expertise and experience of all who read it. The pieces here represent a range of levels in terms of intensity and complexity. Some will stretch and challenge most students; some may frustrate students well-read in the area by their brevity and the removal of detail or elaboration. A few may overtax students new to writing in this area. None are intended to be read in isolation or to speak entirely for themselves by themselves.

Section 1:
The Classroom
Framework

Introduction

No writing better conveys the fusion of theory and practice, subjective and objective, content and context than teachers' own accounts of their early professional lives. Their recollections of their own pupilhood are sufficiently prominent to be rekindled by re-immersion in living classrooms. That they have 'crossed the line' is no inhibition to the exhumation of the whole range of their own experiences, behaviours, understandings and relationships. As beginning teachers, they also sit close to ideas and ideals about how education in schools could and should be; teacher education enables a more systematic and grounded consideration of theories of teaching, prescriptions and models. All teachers bring to their first school and classroom, then, an amalgam of deep-seated memories, personal priorities and inculcated guidance (and a unique array of other things) to re-experience the education system at work. The initial encounters trigger a wealth of questions, dilemmas and contradictions. Theory struggles to match practice. Subjective needs vie with objective requirements. Context constrains content. Principle is pulled towards pragmatism. Progressing competes with surviving. At their best these tensions are creative, at their worst destructive. But when they are captured in the everyday language of diary descriptions of recognizable and sometimes mundane incidents by a reflective teacher, their insights are potentially invaluable.

Such a diary is abridged in the first reading, 'The Whole Experience: Diane Elliot's First Year'. It is a fitting opening to this collection not just because of its great immediacy and accessibility, but because it embodies the duality of meaning of frameworks which underpins our title. In being so overtly concerned with problem-solving (as a personal collage it has no duty to be representative) it sets out an agenda of issues which confronts many teachers and whose roots spread far wider than any of their classrooms. As an account it is neither comprehensive, nor typical. But it is inspiringly illustrative both of the benefits of keeping a personal journal, and of the mutual dependency of the two kinds of frameworks for teaching with which we are concerned.

The extracts from Guy Claxton's 'Teaching and Learning' continue the overt concern with the personal experience of teaching, and the problem-solving orientation, but they move forward – on the one hand by generalizing the personal (Diane Elliot is quite visible here), on the other by looking towards the *personal* experience of learning. The obstacles to learning described are linked closely with people's beliefs about themselves as individuals, their survival, and the considerable array of defensive strategies which are voluntarily or involuntarily marshalled when belief or survival are perceived to be threatened. These may inhibit not only pupils' learning, but also teachers' own capacity to learn from experience and adopt suitable strategies and techniques.

The third reading views the process from the other end of the telescope. It scans the field for patterned understandings of what actually happens when a learner learns as a direct result of a teachers' teaching, and *how* the two are connected. Alan Tom ('Teaching as a Moral Craft') examines the connections between process (teaching-learning) and product (attainment of a learning goal) in teaching. He is concerned, for instance, with pupils' roles in mediating the process-product link where other studies have put teachers at the centre. This approach calls for flexibility, versatility and sensitivity which eschew attempts to technicize teaching, prescribe universally effective pedagogies or proselytize 'one best way'.

The contribution of pupils to determining learning outcomes is not confined to how they respond to teachers. It extends powerfully to the social dynamics of the classrooms in which they learn. For Measor and Woods' pupils, perception of what being in the classroom involves becomes central. This reading describes the pupils' view of first contacts with teachers and the negotiations of powers, rules and behaviours which occur.

A fundamental question in deciding the conduct of *lessons* is: which is more appropriate, whole class or group teaching? Evans' detailed study in science classrooms looks at the range of sometimes supposedly marginal factors which have direct bearing on the question. Among them are the respective extent and modes of teacher control in whole class and group teaching, the limits and possibilities of active pupil engagement and learning in each mode, the relative control exercised by teacher and pupils over the pace of work, and the kinds of regulative versus instructional talk which each mode engenders in teachers. In short, the choice pivots on questions of effectiveness of learning on one hand and classroom control on the other.

The last two contributions to this section take up two factors raised by Evans, but little explored: the effects of differences of gender and ethnicity in the classroom. Pat Mahoney's article discusses a wide range of ways in which being female – including being a female teacher – may be a disadvantage in the classroom. The daily patterns of movement, talk, relationships and teacher responses, Mahoney argues, all serve to marginalize girls and reinforce boys' superior roles. Cecile Wright's research in 'School Processes: an Ethnographic Study' cites instances of racist teacher attitudes (and black and white pupils' perceptions of those attitudes) which single out and discriminate against Afro-Caribbean and Asian boys and girls. The resultant disaffection produces counter-cultural groupings, relationships of entrenched conflict, a conviction that schooling is rigged against them. What is significant here is less the extent of disadvantage than its roots in attitudes communicated in classroom practices and verbal exchanges.

I

The Whole Experience: Diane Elliot's First Year

Charles Hannam, Pat Smyth and

Norman Stephenson

[. . .]

Diane Elliot
Mathematics and general subjects teacher
Mixed comprehensive school
South-West

First term: first week

Bright fourth year: 'Is this your first year of teaching, miss?'
  'What makes you ask that?'
  'You don't crack the whip like the others do.'
  HUH!
  Third year boy in my tutor group (yes, I have a form to register!): 'What's your first name, miss?'
  'Would you rather call me by my first name?'
  'Yes, and if you don't tell us we will find out anyway.'
  'You can call me Diane if you like.'
  . . . a few minutes later:
  'Please, miss'!
  So much to adjust to at once, so different from my practice school (thank goodness). This is for real, I can't run away from mistakes at the end of term and I'm the one responsible for the kids I teach. Getting used to open-plan and team teaching. Traditional skills learnt on practice aren't much use.
  Individualized learning instead of class teaching is ten times more work. Difficulty of team situation with another member of staff whose approach is much more traditional and authoritarian than mine. He thinks I permit far too much noise, wandering around, and 'time wasting'. So he walks over to my

area and tells the kids to 'settle down'. I am sure my face shows what I think of this – what effect does this have on the kids?

Feeling of general exhaustion ... the staff is extremely friendly and supportive though and on the whole the kids are fairly easy to get on with.

Last lesson in the afternoon. I am just sorting things out when I over-hear this conversation. The head walks in to a fourth year lesson, looking for someone. As he walks into the room:

' 'allo, sir.'

'Hallo, Susan.'

'Sir, do you know anything about computers?'

'Nothing at all.'

'That's useless. You can't help me with this then, can yer?'

How many schools are there where that conversation could take place?

Second week

How much cheek can I take from fifth form boys, who don't know whether to treat me as a teacher or a bird? I *don't* want to draw an arbitrary line which makes me an 'authority', but if I don't, then (*a*) no work gets done and (*b*) the girls get hostile ... this one will have to be worked out.

Once a week, lunch duty – half an hour of privacy in the corridors. So why do I do it? I wonder if it satisfies a perverse need? – half an hour a week of that and I am able to be permissive in the classroom without my ego suffering too much. It's a nice theory, even if it is not true.

Children, first years, eleven years old. I see such a mixture:

Cynthia, I see you, a child with the demeanour of a woman of forty. Always neatly dressed, hair immaculate. Taut, anxious, needing approval, worrying about your schoolwork. I could make a few guesses as to what your mother is like.

Jean, I see you doing drama, gay, untrammelled. I see you in maths lessons anxiously striving to get full marks, infuriated with yourself when you don't. What have your parents and teachers instilled into you already?

Lewis, I see you, well dressed, always looking washed and combed, working neatly, precisely. You are a sweet child, ingratiatingly attentive. In fact you are so 'good' that you worry me. I'd like to be able to give you permission to have your tie scruffy, your shirt dirty, splash in a puddle, flick ink pellets, get into a fight.

Colin, I see you fighting, running around, disturbing the others. I envy your freedom, I tell you to do some work: you finish your fight first.

John, I see you but do you see me? I ask you what your second name is and you don't know. I ask you what your dad is called, 'Just dad.' Your mum? what do other people call her ... pause ... 'Mrs Exton.' How can I help you to know who you are?

William, I see your need for love and caring, but there are thirty other children in the room as well. I hear you telling me you always have two helpings at dinner ('I've free dinners, miss') because it stops you being hungry at teatime. You are bring so many needs into the room with you. What hope have I of meeting even a fraction of them? What of the needs I bring? From whom do I need approval?

The staffroom: warm, relaxed, friendly – but there are tensions too. They show at staff meetings. Certain factions are already noticeable, certain roles thrust on to certain shoulders – willingly accepted, and unwillingly suffered. Problems and frustration in working in a group of this size. The head is a skilful chairman.

Departmental meeting: four established staff and three new ones. An interesting group, many differences, strong and possibly conflicting person-alities. But we have a well-defined and fairly urgent task to complete. I feel we work well. The task is satisfactorily completed. Our relationships have been maintained and cemented. We all go away with a sense of achievement. It will be a learning situation for me to be a member of this group as it develops during the year.

I find the work very demanding, enjoyable, exhausting, and at times frus-trating. It leaves me feeling drained – I have to replenish my own resources somehow. The support of the more experienced staff is marvellous in this respect. [. . .]

Fourth week

Second form lesson: 'please miss, can you come and see Jenny.' (Jenny has been sitting behind me so I didn't notice anything.) I go over to her – she is crying and looking very unhappy. I sit down with her and put my arm round her shoulders. She turns and cries on my shoulder. 'What is it Jenny?' 'I can't do these. I don't understand any of it.' . . . 'Is that so bad that you have to cry? I'm not going to get angry with you.' She stops crying. I sit with her for ten minutes or so and we work patiently. She understands far more than she thought. I leave her with some work to do and at the end of the lesson she comes to me looking happy, to tell me she has finished all the work and got it all right.

Who the hell has done that to this child? Who has made her cry? The parents? A former teacher? What event in her past makes her *that* unhappy when she fails to grasp a minor point first time? I feel angry. Adults ought not to make children cry. People are too precious to be put at risk by introducing artificial anxieties. There are quite enough real ones.

Fifth form lesson: I get on well with this group, only sixteen of them. They are rude and abusive in a friendly manner, and I respond in kind – and we all get some work done.

'How old are you, miss?'

'Twenty-two.'

'Come off it!'

'When did you start counting backwards?'

'Twenty-two squared more like.'

I am astounded! Generation-gap already? This is the last lesson in the afternoon and I am still thinking about it when I get home. Perhaps they 'can't' believe that I am as young as twenty-two (some of them have sisters of that age). If they did there would have to be a radical re-appraisal of their teacher concept. So perhaps they need to believe I am older than is actually the case.

The fourth form do pose problems – even the bright ones. Take Shirley for instance. Very good at maths: fine . . . but she started going out with Simon who is in the same group and she sits with him in lessons. Now the problem: she is considerably better at maths than he is – very bad for his ego – and is deliberately slowing her pace down to match his. Ray (head of department) suggests a talk on women's lib! I reply that I don't really think she'd be very receptive to it at the moment. She can afford to freewheel for a while and when she gets bored, she will start to work again.

Problem of my adjustment to what I am doing. Spending so much of my time with adolescents, learning to live with their behaviour. How great a capacity for adolescent behaviour is there still left in me? And how do I prevent the kids' actions eliciting a similar response from me? How accepting can I be? Two of the fourth year threaten a fight; one picks up a chair. I say 'If you want to fight, use your hands, not the furniture.' Excited, surprised 'Can we?' 'Not in here. Out there.' After a couple more threatening gestures to satisfy honour, they sit down and work. A little later in the lesson I am suggesting to Reg that he do some work. 'Why? What do you do anyway? You just wander around looking at what we have done and put red ink on it.' I get a little further round the room and say to Billy, 'What have you done this lesson?' He answers angrily 'A damn sight more than you have.' How seriously should I take the implied criticisms in these replies? I don't really expect the kids to appreciate exactly what the work is that I do, but, still, these answers disturb me a little. Are they, in fact, feeling neglected and left to their own devices too much? And why the blazes didn't I ask *them* this at the time? [. . .]

Ho, ho! A perfect example of displaced anger. Miss Claridge has just had her once-a-week lesson with Eric Burns's fourth year and they/she have left my work area in one hell of a mess. I resent running around after other members of the department, but I appreciate how she feels after a lesson with that lot, so I don't want to let off steam at her – especially as it's Friday afternoon. So I find Ray in the staffroom and moan at him as head of the department. Then the two of us have a go at Eric Burns as it is his group. So first Ray and then Eric bear the brunt of my unexpressed anger towards Miss Claridge! I point this out and apologize to them – we all laugh about it 'Let's go home. Thank God it's Friday.'

Fifth week

God I hate Mondays! Worst timetable day of the week and then a staff-meeting. I discover Miss Claridge *wasn't* responsible for the mess on Friday – it was Sylvia's fifth year the lesson before! There is a moral here some-where – like, ascertain your facts before complaining. I make abject apologies to Eric Burns.

Staff-meeting is particularly frustrating today. I come away feeling very wound up. We spent about fifteen minutes on one trivial item which reduced essentially to: this is a problem – this is not a problem – this is a problem – let the year teachers handle it. Is this sort of thing an inevitable consequence of making the full staff-meeting the decision-making body?

Four ways of looking at conflict:

The lion: there is conflict and I will win.

The lemming: there is conflict and I will lose.

The turtle: there is conflict but it isn't mine.

The ostrich: what conflict?

Can I remove the conflict from the classroom?

And is it desirable to do so? Can I remove it only by being an ostrich or a turtle? And how much 'success' can I hope for? Omnipotence is rather out of the question when dealing with adolescents!

My difficult fourth years again: they are not under my control, as a whole group, at all. As I deal with each small group all is fine, but as a whole set they definitely determine what is going to happen. I am unwilling to wield the big stick with them. But I have this silly feeling that I 'ought' to be controlling them more. But if Helen and her friends work (sometimes) and if that group of 'remedial' girls is working (sometimes), perhaps things aren't too bad. So why do I feel uneasy when they swear and I don't rebuke them, when they cheek me and I respond in kind rather than punishing? From whom am I anticipating criticism and does it matter? Why and from where do I still have hang-ups about that particular kind of classroom control – especially at a place like this where, in fact, there is a lot of support for my approach. Questions, questions! ... Perhaps I am my own worst critic and I am projecting these self-criticisms on to others. Perhaps it is merely ('merely'!) a matter of learning to live with my own feeling of insecurity in a relatively unstructured situation (unstructured when compared with traditional classrooms). If so, there could well be a tendency for me to look back to more established classroom norms for security – they provide a less stressful situation than carving my own way. Maybe this is the source of my unease. But it's not helped when, at change of lessons, a nicely spoken second year girl hears Maria swear like a trooper – at a friend but in my hearing – and asks me, 'Don't you mind when they swear, miss?' How am I supposed to answer that?

I am starting to get involved in extra-curricular activities now. A Very Good Thing! to play in the school orchestra alongside one of the fourth years I teach, when he is a considerably better clarinettist than I am. To have a part in this term's production when some of the kids are better singers and actors than I am. To make a mistake, and know that the rebuke of the member of staff directing the thing is directed at me and the kids. I feel this is very good for me, for the kids and for our relationship.

Eighth week

Walter Ellison and I are in the staffroom discussing my third year tutor group. I remark: 'I get on very well with them as long as I don't make them do anything they don't want to do.'

Walter: 'Well, what's *your* reaction when someone tries to make you do something you don't want to do?'

Hmmm ... good point. My reaction as usual is evasion. The kids' is invariably confrontation! [. . .]

I am talking to two first years after school on Thursday.

Fred: 'When you were young, miss (!!) what made you decide to be a teacher?'

Me: 'Oh, lots of things.'

Fred: 'Was it the long holidays?'

David: 'No, it's because of us lovely children!'

Fourth year top set lesson. There are five boys who habitually work together in a group. Two of them came to me about ten minutes after the lesson had started. 'You've got to do something about those other three, miss. We do all the work and they just copy it.'

'Why must I do something about it? It seems to me this is your problem, not mine.' Mutter, mutter, rhubarb, rhubarb. The two go off and the group of five have a good old ding dong for the rest of the double lesson!

At the end of the lesson I ask them if they have sorted it out. 'Yes, we do one day's work each!' I said this was OK! The following lesson, they did nothing at all, and since then they have all been working. I feel my approach to this group is slowly being vindicated. But it's slow and it's uphill all the way.

Ninth week

My fifth form CSE set have done no work over the week-end at all. I articulate my feelings to them as 'it's your exam not mine.' But this is dishonest even though ostensibly true. It doesn't explain the fact that I feel disappointed/ annoyed/let-down by the group. Why? Although I would strenuously deny that you can measure good teaching by exam results only, there is some level at which I am operating on the assumption that I am going to be judged by this group's CSE results. I am not at all sure who I think is going to do the judging. As with most other things, I am my own worst critic, and I'm projecting this (in anticipation) on to an undefined 'someone' in the school.

So what is the philosophy I am trying to work on? And how does it work with this group? Some of them are working well and are capable of getting a grade I. Some of them are plodding along, will get a comfortable III and meanwhile we are establishing a very good relationship. But there are three or four of them, to whom I am teaching nothing worth mentioning, with whom I have not established any sort of working relationship and for whom I am doing nothing as far as I can see. I am certainly not raising their levels of awareness at all. The whole of today has been harrowing ... a feeling of general depression, dissatisfaction, failure and everything else ...

I went out to the deputy head's place in the evening as I felt in great need of someone to talk to about the way I was feeling. It makes a tremendous difference that there are people on the staff who are understanding, sympathetic and supportive. Alan was most encouraging and (best of all) he *listened* – there's a moral in that too! Today things have been much better.

We've got some students in on practice and I have one helping me with my second form. I find this slightly ridiculous. As if I know anything about this game called teaching. But then, I *can* remember what it was like being on practice. What I find most strange is that Molly Denbury refers to me as a 'teacher' when I still have to remind myself sometimes that I am no longer a student! Because of a staff absence Molly finds herself thrown in at the deep end, taking a boisterous (but harmless) fourth year group. She said to me afterwards 'I was a bit scared at first, but I wasn't too worried as I knew you were next door.' Oh ha ha! Tickled my ego no end. [...]

Tenth week

First years submitting written comments to their representatives on the school council: 'TEACHERS THINK THEY RULE THE WORLD. THIS HAS GOT TO STOP.'

My fourth year group complaining about the way another member of staff treats them – saying to me in effect 'Tomorrow we will kick you again, but today we want you on our side.' I find it hard to resist going into collusion with them over this (in fact, I am not sure I did resist) as I feel they have a good case as far as this member of staff is concerned. This is their conflict, not mine – The turtle (ho ho): 'there is conflict, but it's not mine' – so I must keep out.

Amy Rivett is bemoaning the fact that stroppy fourth years don't understand the 'status' of a degree and don't give staff due credit for their abilities ... we have no status but what we earn. In theory this is good ... in practice? it's obviously bothering her. It hasn't worried me yet – but there is time.

First year group of six very difficult boys causing problems for all the staff who teach them. They go too far, my patience gives out and I really lose my temper with them, for the first time. I think they realized they had succeeded in making me angry, but I am not sure how they'll react. There are ways and ways of expressing anger.

Why does anger so often end up with the people who don't deserve it? A lot of the department's anger really belongs with Eric Burns, not just because he is away this week but because of his general attitude. But that is not where it ends up. It circulates round among the rest of us and ends up with the kids. I wonder how much of my resentment against Eric is subconscious envy? *If* I could treat kids the way that he does, *If* I could frighten them like he does. *If* etc., etc. – then I wouldn't be having the problems I am having. But I can't treat people like that, and I wouldn't want to. But it's bloody exhausting to have chosen (chosen?) the harder way. The problem with the fourth year is that I can *either* relate to them in the way I want to *or* I can teach them, but I don't seem to be able to do the two things simultaneously.

Oh, the devious ways we get the kids to do what we want! Like saying 'please' in a tone of voice which admits no argument.

Interesting the way the fifth form group I take is developing. The girls all call me Miss. The boys who seem to me to be secure in themselves are now calling me Diane. The other boys are embarrassed to call me Miss, embarrassed to call me Diane, and have resorted to calling me 'Oi, come 'ere' – presumably a temporary thing until they sort out what they are going to call me.

Why did I get stroppy with my tutor group during registration this morning? So, they were fooling around and making a row – so what? they've just moved – *we*'ve just moved! – into a new tutor base. They are exploring the possibilities of the new room, making it 'theirs'. So why did I stop them? If it was because I couldn't stand the noise, why didn't I just say 'I can't stand this row' instead of 'this is not the sort of behaviour . . . blah blah blah'? At times, the things I come out with disgust me! How long before this sort of analysis after the event turns into not making the mistakes?

Next day. Just before their lesson I'm held up, and arrive nearly ten minutes late. As soon as I walk in something about the feel of the group strikes me as odd. Within two or three minutes the whole group, and those boys in particular have conveyed to me that they were afraid I'd abandoned them! The six boys really work hard for the whole lesson and go out of their way to present their 'best' side to me. I take the opportunity of praising their work – it's not something I get a chance to do very often. The lesson ends with several spontaneous gestures of affection from them. I wonder how long this will last?

Had my 'fourth form thickies' for a double lesson today. For the first time with that group I positively enjoyed the lesson. I don't know why. Nothing was observably different from usual – perhaps we are at last settling and getting used to each other.

Last week of the first term

Damn all fourth years! I got so angry with them today: descended to being bitchy with the girls, bloody-minded with the boys and generally being as petty and adolescent as they are! One of the department is away so the rest of us are teaching ninety-seven per cent this week. We are all tired and we are all getting ratty with everyone. Of course the kids get the brunt of it. My reaction at the moment is to play 'Wooden Leg': 'This is only my first term, you can't expect me to cope with this,' etc., etc. In fact, like so many other things, this is a teacher problem and a pupil problem – lessons aren't a problem to a fourth year, but their lessons *are* a problem to me. Hell, I really *am* a teacher, not a student. They *are* my responsibility. The question is not 'What am I going to do about the fourth year?' rather, it's 'What am I going to do about me, about the way I react to them.' I know after the event that getting ratty with them doesn't help – but just as I won't fake annoyance I don't feel, I also won't repress anger I am feeling.

I have just finished writing fifth form reports. Me! writing reports. The whole idea is ridiculous. Writing reports is something real teachers do . . . oh yes! Maybe I'd learn more if they wrote reports on me.

Last lesson with the fourth year. What was it that Kohl said about his desire to run an 'open classroom' always being two steps ahead of his ability to do so?

Donald 'threatens' me with elastic band and a paper pellet. I laugh.

'Put it away, Donald.'

Donald (to friend): 'See?'

I raise my eyebrows.

'He said you'd take it off me. I said you wouldn't. He didn't believe me.'
The difficulty is that I *do* care what they think of me. [. . .]

Second term

First day back: the fourth year is in a 'the-first-day-of-term-don't-want-to-work' mood. Roger has been challenging a group of idle girls, one by one, to one-arm wrestling – and has flattened them all. Bridget: 'Go on, miss, you have a go.' Foolishly, I agree. I defeat him. Immediately that whole group of girls starts working. (I wonder what would have happened if I had lost?) On reflection I am not sure how 'foolish' it was. It accurately represents my relationship with that group – fighting all the time (well, most of the time) . . . These kids don't verbalize – they act out. And clearly my acting out *did* communicate with those girls.

One of the deputy heads is talking about a pupil's 'insolence' – which implies that he sees the kids as somehow inferior. There is no possibility of him being 'insolent' to a kid. Rude, yes. Sarcastic, yes. But, by definition not 'insolent'. Yet he wouldn't admit to thinking that the kids are inferior.

The fourth year again today. They highlight all the conflicts, all the difficulties, all the inconsistencies, all the stupidities in me, in the system, in adolescent groups. In any traditional sense I can't 'handle' them. There is only one person in the department who can – by being systematically nasty, rude, sarcastic and so on; holding people up to ridicule, using divide-and-rule techniques. If what we are trying to do with these kids is to keep them with noses down, working, then that seems to be the only way. I *cannot* treat kids like that. Perhaps I should have succumbed to the 'get them under your thumb first' philosophy? Nonsense! That's fundamentally disrespectful to their status as persons.

However, decided to get 'tough' with them today. After about five minutes: Kate said: 'What's the matter with you? you used to be ever so nice.' Me: 'Maybe, but I am getting very tired of you taking advantage of that.' And I promptly stopped being nasty! Towards the end of the lesson, as they were packing up, Patrick was flicking pellets. Out of sheer desperation at trying in vain to make him stop, I said: 'Can you hit that notice on the back wall from this side of the room?' We had a long talk (the first ever) about the merits of different constructions of pellets for range and accuracy. He did hit the notice – several times – and then picked up all the pellets and put them in the bin!

Second week

Giving a lift home to one of the staff. He is holding forth on teacher defences. He points out that Eric Burns's excessively authoritarian behaviour is a defence . . . but then goes on to describe his own conscious, deliberate system of defences: that of being 'enigmatic' – if no one knows where he is at, then they can't get at him. This saddens me. Am I being hopelessly naïve in thinking that I don't, for most of the time, employ teacher defences? If I don't, am I being hopelessly naïve in thinking I can maintain this state of affairs?

Fifth years: By what process of collusion have we managed to end up with the situation that 'we don't work last lesson on Tuesday'?

I am discussing with each person in my third year group the reports I have just written on them: e.g., Betty Skidmore. The essential content of hers is that she is capable, but has no confidence. Her immediate response is 'All my teachers have always said that.' So we've obviously done her no good by repeating the fact! Just reinforced her lack of confidence. How is it that we constantly reinforce 'undesirable' self images in kids? And I have just been guilty of exactly that. Mike Hart is a tough little skinhead. He doesn't work. He's very aggressive. Thursday morning during maths two of his mates from another group wander in, rattling money in an old yoghurt pot. They're 'collecting money for the old folk'.

Mike: ' 'ere miss, I'm doing that an' all. Can I go with them?'

Me: 'Do you think I am going to give you permission to go wandering all over the school, disturbing other peoples' lessons, rattling that thing? You've got another think coming.'

Mike: 'Yer don't believe me do yer? You go and ask Basher' (his form master's nickname).

Me: 'You go and ask him. If he'll give you a note then I'll let you go.'

Mike sits down and sulks for the rest of the lesson. His mates go on their way 'collecting'.

Later that day I checked up. It *was* genuine – it had arisen out of something in their assembly. They collected £1.50 altogether, and bought a large box of chocolates, which they are now raffling. The proceeds will be used to buy food parcels for local OAPs. So I have helped to confirm this kid's image of himself. It's useless me talking about what 'schools' do to people. Schools don't do anything. It's people – people like me who *talk* about the need to trust kids and then *do* exactly the opposite. The following day I apologized to him and bought some raffle tickets, but I still have to face the fact that when put on the spot my first reaction was one of mistrust.

Frank is a first year who clings, demands a vast amount of attention and looks like a beaten puppy if he doesn't get it. To start with I gave him as much attention as I could, but it's getting to be a strain with thirty others in the room and I find myself wishing he'd just go away. The trouble is, I suspect that people have been wishing he would go away for the past eleven years.

I am talking to one of the senior staff about the frustrations I feel with my 'difficult' fourth year and he will insist on turning the discussion to the pupils' problems, or the teacher's problem, or job satisfaction – anything but discuss the living relationship. I am *not* talking about job satisfaction. I am talking about Bob who has some brain damage from a car accident and is pathetically earnest about his work, to no possible effect; I am talking about Neil who would like to work if it weren't for his mates; I am talking about Peter – we get on very well but I can't teach him anything; I am talking about twenty other kids who find the school irrelevant. And I am talking about me who is trying to find something constructive in all this. An altogether much more important living, painful thing than 'job satisfaction'.

Third week

Mike (the one I didn't trust last week) saw me in the corridor today, said ''ello miss', and held the door open for me. There has been a subtle change in the way my other fourth form treats me. It must have been going on for some time, and I have only just noticed it. They have stopped trying to run rings round me – not because I got tough with them, but because, I think, they found it a most unsatisfying game. All that happened was that *I* laughed at them (how different from the others). They've stopped complaining that I don't fit their teacher image. They accept me as a person who has occasional 'off days'. The more sexually precocious boys are now able to ask for assistance without having to put on a big act of impressing me. And one of them complained today when the bell went! [. . .]

Fourth week

Discussing with Ann Scobie (one of the deputies) the attitude that some of the kids have towards me: basically 'one of the gang' who is a traitor if acting as a member of staff. Her comment was that maybe our loose structure doesn't eliminate the 'them and us' situation, but merely draws the boundaries in different places – the kids regard a small core of the senior staff as 'them' and everybody else as 'us'. I wonder?

The head makes his autocratic decision that the school shall be democratic, and appoints staff accordingly. I make the decision that the kids I teach should, as far as is posible, be self-directing. I make a decision for freedom and the kids are bound by it. As long as schooling is compulsory, I see no way round it. [. . .] In spite of our informality, the diffuseness of our hierarchy, our loose structure, there are unwritten expectations of the behaviour of probationary teachers. I am only aware of them because I have once or twice overstepped the boundaries. These expectations are by no means shared by every individual in the staffroom, but they seem to be there as a group norm – or maybe I am just being paranoid about it. I find it disturbing to have been labelled 'a radical progressive' by one of the senior people. A ghastly label, whatever it means. Interesting too that even at a school like this I find myself at that end of the spectrum (label or no label) in the things I am *trying* to achieve – and people who want to change the system are always likely to be seen as a threat, even in a system dedicated to change.

I wonder if my relationship with that fourth year is a kind of Laing knot?

'We are bad.

You ought to judge us as bad.

You don't judge us as bad.

Therefore you are bad.

So we don't like you.

But you are good.

Therefore we are bad . . . and so on *ad nauseam*.'

Sixth week

Middle-aged friend of my parents: 'How are you liking teaching then?' I mutter something about hard work. (How can I possibly *tell* her what it's like?) 'Well, yes, it will be for the first year. After that you'll have all your lesson notes prepared and you won't have that to do again.' I didn't bother to say anything – I couldn't even begin to use words like: mixed ability groups, team teaching, individualized work, open plan, etc., etc.

I think I shall give up trying to understand my fourth year. I've been discussing their reports with them:

'You can't write that. My old man would go up the wall.'

'Do you think it is unfair?'

'Oh no. It's quite true but you still can't write it.'

Perhaps I should see it as a compliment (of dubious worth) that they ask me to defend them from their parents, from other staff, from themselves?

Seventh week

Tensions inherent in the pastoral role of the group tutor. Two 'difficult' girls in my tutor group are beginning to trust me, to talk to me, to open up a little. They've been in trouble recently and there is about to be a general clamp-down on them and I am expected to do my share of it. This will completely bugger up any relationships I am forming with them. The year-master has agreed to a compromise whereby he will do my tutor's disciplining for them, to enable me to maintain and build up my relationship with them – but this has dangers in that they might well start to play us off against each other.

Disturbing how we let one member of the department carry all our authoritarianism for us – without acknowledgment. Yes, he is willing to do it – you can't force people into roles they don't want – but I am certain that it's not good either for him or for the rest of us for this to continue. This causes me to wonder what is the role I have in the department – established subversive, I think, with all the tensions inherent in describing it like that. [. . .]

Memo to myself: The improvement of my *relationship* with my 'unmotivated' fourth year does not necessarily mean that they are going to do any *work* for me!

I must be careful that my relationships with the kids are not at the expense of my relationships with other staff. Last night Ray arrived, we were clearing up at the end of the day, talking about something fairly seriously, when some of my first years burst into the room to tell us something. Some time later when they'd gone, I realized that Ray had left, that I hadn't noticed him go, that we'd been in the middle of a conversation . . .!

Eighth week

[. . .] Lunchtime: I am sitting in the library, chatting with some fourth years.
'We are not working this year you know, but we'll work next year. No one works in the fourth year.'
Me: 'Who decides that?'
Ernie: 'Did you work when you were in the fourth year?'
Dick: 'Of course she did. You had to in those days.'
Me: 'What do you mean – those days? – I'm not ninety!'
Andy: 'Well, you had to, didn't you?'
. . . later in the same conversation:
Noel: 'If you made me sit at a table on my own, and made me work, then I'd do something.' (In fact, this whole group of boys sit together and work quite well.)
Me: 'If you want to sit at a table on your own, no one is stopping you.'
Noel: 'Ah yes, if I wanted to, but I don't.'
Why and how can we assume that our system will suit everyone who comes to us at fourteen? By then they have so much 'background' that some of them might never adjust to our free and easy way of doing things – indeed why should they adjust? [. . .]

Ninth week

Away for the week-end, staying with some friends who have recently started being voluntary helpers at a local youth club. They have a group of the kids round on Sunday night. I am helping to lead the discussion on women's lib. I take a fairly non-directive role, only occasionally pressing for clarification of someone's contribution, pointing out inconsistencies. At the end of the evening one of the girls: 'Are you a teacher?' My God, am I already part of a recognizable breed? [. . .]

Signs that I am beginning to get somewhere with my fourth year bottom set. It's getting towards the end of term. I warn them that I am in no mood for their usual behaviour. They decide to test this, and I hit the roof. This is so rare that they are shocked into silence. A couple of minutes later, Nora comes over. (Nora can be very scathing, and has been on occasions. She's been known to reduce some women teachers to tears.) 'Are you all right, miss? You haven't had a row with your boyfriend?' I could have hugged her (why didn't I?). A month ago that would not have happened. I talk to a group of them – explain that it is the end of term. I've had reports to write, a parents' evening, rehearsals for the show ... and I've just about had enough. They are most sympathetic. Jimmy: 'I wish all the teachers were like you.' But one or two of the more senior staff, who are occasionally disturbed by the noise we make, are not very happy about the way I am working with this group. They say I should hammer them more.

It is noticeable how physical the kids' relationships with me is (not just me; I've discussed this and it is also true of *some* other staff):

first year who runs to me to tell me some good news;

second year who is upset and cries on my shoulder, wanting physical comforting;

fourth year boy apologizing for something, who puts an arm round my shoulder and says 'sorry';

another fourth year who has just cracked a joke at my expense, pats me patronizingly on the head, and says 'never mind, dear'; and so on.

Last week of second term

As I am leaving the room at the end of the lesson, Angela comes out of the room next door. (Angela is a second year, a plodder, not very bright, very worried about everything, and intensely serious.)

'Miss Elliot, Geoff is trying to kiss me under the mistletoe and I don't like it. Please make him stop.' Poor kid looks upset, so I go into the room: 'Geoff, come here a minute.' Geoff swaggers up to me, with a piece of mistletoe sticking out of his blazer pocket, and a supremely unconcerned, you-can-go-stuff-yourself expression on his face. I grin at him and say quietly: 'Hasn't anyone ever told you it's a waste of energy chasing girls who aren't willing? It's much more fun if you find one who is willing.' Geoff looks as though he has just had a revelation, ignores the girl and goes off in search of more willing prey. Now did I do the right thing or should I have told him off? To put it at extremes, have I solved all his future sex problems for him or will it be my fault when he gets syphillis? The answer of course is neither, but how *do* I assess the effect I have on the kids? Or is the only thing I can do to respond as person to person, as the here and now demands, and for the rest stop worrying about what I can't control?

As it's the last week and because this time last year a lot of kids got drunk, the staff meeting decided to have a clamp-down on drink in school this week. Wednesday afternoon, first lesson after lunch, I had the fifth form.

Charlie strolls in with a can of brown clearly visible in his blazer pocket. How do I tread that knife-edge of maintaining my relationship with the kids *and* maintaining relationships within the staff group? Several of the fifth form, and Charlie in particular for a large part of the time, choose to ignore the fact that I am a member of staff and show resentment when I act as a member of the staff group. They seem to be operating on the assumption that they can abuse me as much as they like, but I will still be their ally in their conflict with other members of staff. So what I actually do is to warn Charlie and then report him to the deputy head. As a result of this (he is caught drinking the stuff in the boys' bogs) a letter is sent to his parents, etc.

So what was I doing in this action? When Charlie walks in with his can of beer clearly visible, I feel my authority threatened. Shit. I try reason – try to explain the reasons for the prohibition of alcohol in the school. But Charlie is a difficult character – everyone finds this. Reason has no effect. So I gave him a veiled warning, which he chooses to ignore and then I report him to the deputy head at the end of the lesson. You're a coward, girl! In theory I approve of kids having the initiative to tell the school authorities to piss off. In practice, I don't like my own authority being challenged by a person like Charlie, whom I heartily dislike. Everything about him annoys me. So why is that? He is very intelligent and is more than prepared to use that intelligence to screw the system. Am I jealous? – I who plodded right through the sausage machine and am now part of the bloody system? Part of it is intolerance on my part. OK, so kids of fifteen-sixteen think it's clever to smoke and drink. These are particular kinds of social one-up-manship that I never felt the need to indulge in during adolescence – so am I just being intolerant of Charlie's need to be one up? Perhaps I should take the trouble to find out how this behaviour helps him? Instead of reporting perhaps I should have tried to discuss with him (*away* from the group) why he felt it necessary to bring beer into the school. Who was he trying to impress? I don't know if my relationship with him is good enough to work at all.

I'm being very hard on myself about all this. Hoping that the kids I teach will learn to see through the system, and helping them to do so does *not* imply encouraging them to be mindlessly irresponsible. In view of Charlie's general attitudes, behaviour, etc., maybe I didn't act too unreasonably. But what am I saying to them? In effect: 'You should be old enough and sensible enough to uphold the values of the school authority.' This is absolute crap. Or maybe: 'You should be old enough and sensible enough to question intelligently the values of the school authority.' That's a bit better. And Charlie certainly wasn't questioning intelligently. Is there any value at all in mindless rebellion? On balance, I feel that my basic action was justified – although I certainly could have handled it better. [...]

Third term: first week

First year lesson: they have come straight from cookery.

'Miss, would you like a jam tart?'

'Thank you, Judy. May I eat it now?'

Judy (with utter seriousness): 'I don't know if you should in a lesson ... but I suppose you can – it's yours.'

We were interviewing today for a new post in the department next year. The whole department was involved in the selection procedure – strange to find myself sitting in judgement on the candidates, some of whom have a lot more experience than I have (not difficult!).

Third week

The fourth years I teach seem to find it necessary to sustain a lot of sexual fantasies about me! (and, I discover, about other young unmarried female staff too). e.g.:

(a) that I used to be a go-go dancer;
(b) that I am having an affair with Eric Burns in our department;
(c) that I am having an affair with the male deputy head;
(d) that I am having an affair with the head of lower school;
(e) that I am living in sin with my boyfriend. (The group of girls holding this
    fantasy is completely thrown by my questioning the meaning of the word
    sin.) [...]

Fifth former to a visitor to the school: 'You don't do so much bookwork here but you learn, you learn more, if you know what I mean ...' – someone has got past the stage of seeing us merely as failed authoritarians!

Sixth week

The youth tutor and I took a bunch of the kids away youth hostelling for the week-end. I was a little worried as the crowd going were most of the rowdy fifth form lot. They were so different! They weren't being confined against their will in a classroom and they showed a degree of responsibility which, in school, would be unbelievable to the staff and impossible for them.

As exams approach, I find I am getting very stroppy with my CSE group – in fact, I am more worried about the exam than they are. OK, so it's the first group I have ever had who are going to take an exam, but even so ... And I know that what we are trying to do in this case isn't measurable just by exam results, but even so these kids are going to need these exams, and the world outside – just waiting to judge us – is going to come down like a ton of bricks if our results aren't as good as they 'ought' to be.

Maths CSE exam today. My group were amongst those taking it and I was helping to invigilate. It was a ghastly experience. After all we are trying to do as a school, after the inevitable 'let's work together to beat the examiners' game, there we are, the staff, acting as police while the kids actually take the exams. [. . .]

Parents: without going into all the sordid details, a group of the parents who are anti the school have banded together and are speaking through three local people who aren't parents. (The reason behind this is that the parents wish to remain anonymous 'in case our children are victimized' – the particular fear being our Mode III CSE marking.) Anyhow this group managed to get the chairman of governors to agree to a meeting. It was all very badly handled, and was little short of a kangaroo court. Hearing this reported to the staff in all its gory detail made me realize the extent of my institutional loyalty, in that an attack on the school feels like an attack on me. And it brings out all our old insecurities as a staff – are we going the right way after all?

Parents evening to discuss reports. Difficult being 'on show' in the present political climate, but there were some good things too – parents who took the trouble to come in to say they think we are doing a good job, they are behind us all the way, etc.

Last week of third term

Unwitting compliment from a fourth year I have just reprimanded. 'Oh miss – I didn't think you was looking. You must 'ave eyes in the back of yer 'ead.' It's called evolution for survival!

Another report to the staff on the current political climate – it's rough. How can we possibly run a free democratic school in a society which is demonstrably *not* free or democratic? and how can we make the kids realize that this is what they are up against when they jibe at the limits to their participation in our democratic set-up?

Found myself being quite unnecessarily nasty with a girl who was late for registration – ugh, end of term.

I have just discovered that next year's timetable will not allow me to continue with a particular first year group that I like very much. I feel excessively pissed off about this. They're a group of kids I enjoy teaching. They like me, and it would have been very good to keep them next year.

Next term will be different. I shall be going *back* to a new year, there will be other probationers, to the kids I will just be a part of the furniture. My pastoral post will mean that my involvement in my department will be considerably less. And I will be part of the 'hierarchy' (such as it is). [. . .]

2

Teaching and Learning

Guy Claxton

[. . .]

Beliefs prescribe domains of experience that are resistant to change. Some patches of our map of the world – both the maps of experience and of language and thought – are open to question, while others are not. Any experience within these latter areas that does or could controvert a belief is a threat, and must therefore be avoided. Thus are we surrounded by mental predators of our own creation. And because learning depends on attending to experience that conflicts with what is already known, learning in these domains is blocked or impeded. (It is more correct, of course, to say we have *degrees* of investment in our beliefs, and that this degree determines the force with which we resist their disconfirmation.) And so we come to threaten our own survival by refusing to keep up to date with a changing world. If the last time I stuck my head out of the window was ten years ago, I can't know now whether it is still raining or not. Or, as Mark Twain said, a cat that has once sat on a hot stove won't ever sit on one again – but it won't sit on a cold one, either. If you daren't risk getting burnt again, you can't discover whether the fire's gone out.

But things are even worse than this. There are four special beliefs that are widely held, though in varying degrees, and which have a debilitating effect *not just on the growth of certain areas, but on the whole theory, for they are beliefs that relate to the learning process itself.* They are:

1 I believe that my personal worth depends on the success of my actions. Therefore I must be *competent*.
2 I believe that my personal identity depends on being predictable to myself – that I am what I think I am. Therefore I must be *consistent*.
3 I believe that my survival and/or my sanity depends on my being able to understand, explain and predict what is happening in my world at all times. Therefore I must be in *control*.
4 I believe that it is possible and desirable to go through life without feeling bad – getting upset, anxious or guilty. Therefore I must be *comfortable*.

Now we can see the full scope of the problem, for these four 'commandments' about how I must be are the exact antitheses of the ways of being that are required of a learner.

Whenever we encounter a learning situation that is important then the struggle between hanging onto a theory that is demonstrably inadequate and plunging into the insecurity of not-knowing cannot be denied. To stand any chance of achieving an expanded competence, we have, like a snake, to slough off a familiar but constricting skin and risk the transitional nakedness and vulnerability. To take this risk requires not courage so much as a deep acknowledgment that if you do, you might die, or be hurt, or lose the gamble; if you don't, you will certainly lose because you have chosen to remain encased within a skin that becomes ever tighter and more uncomfortable. Thus it follows that only if you can risk failing, in the sense of not getting what you expect, and of allowing yourself to admit that your theory is inadequate, can you fully engage with the learning process. Learning is what happens when you take the risk of not being *competent*.

Three related risks also have to be taken if learning is to proceed unimpeded. You have to take the chance of finding out that you are not *consistent*. If you allow yourself to experiment with previously untried ways of acting and being, you may catch yourself doing things that don't fit in with your idea of yourself. As well as your theory about the world being in jeopardy, so may your theory about yourself. You may be surprised by yourself, because in order to find out what *works*, you may have to try out things that aren't 'you'. The third risk that learning may require is that of not being in *Control*. In the gap between giving up a bit of your old theory and discovering a better bit, you have to be prepared to tolerate not-knowing and not-being-able-to-predict. You may have to flounder, thrash about, seek help, and admit you can't do it on your own, clutch at straws of advice or intuition, before the

Figure 2.1

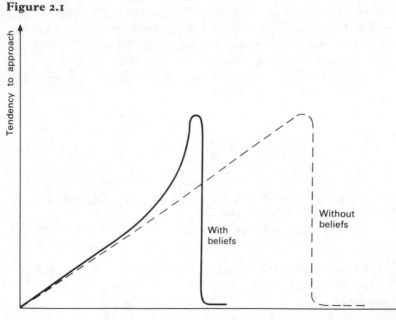

22

learning begins to come good, and a new, greater sense of control emerges. Finally, learning is often, as we have seen, accompanied by anxiety, so it is necessary to take the risk of not feeling *Comfortable*.

To the extent that I hold these as beliefs, therefore, *any* learning situation that threatens to make me incompetent, inconsistent, out of control, and uncomfortable appears to be a threat to me – to my survival as the person I think I am or hope I am or ought to be. When one of these triggers is pulled, learning is resisted, regardless of what the learning is actually about.

The mechanism whereby this happens is simple. [. . .] A person's tendency to approach and learn from a situation increase[s] as the degree of conflict between the demands of the situation and the current capacity of their theory increase[s] – up to a point. At that point 'challenge' flipped over into 'threat', and the dominant survival strategies became the nonlearning ones of fight and flight. Now what happens when you suffer from the Four Cs is that *other* conflicts arise. As soon as a significant disparity between theory and experience arises, instead of just dealing with that, you have to cope with the conflict between the effect that this disaparity is having on you (e.g. making you feel uncomfortable) and your belief about how if you were half the man you were supposed to be you could handle such a situation without turning a hair. Thus you become more anxious still, and challenge becomes threat all the sooner (see Figure 2.1).

Situations of slight but manageable stress will, if they activate the Four Cs, be immediately transformed subjectively into apparent threats to survival. The upshot is that *the degree of strangeness that one can tolerate, that is, engage with and learn about, is drastically reduced and the frequency with which one resorts to escape, defence and demolition, increases.* More and more I have to deny my fallibility, my frailty, my tenuous grip on reality, my fearfulness, in order to preserve an image of myself that I do not need but cannot drop. Every time these buttons are pushed, it becomes more important for me to Be Right than to Find Out What Works. I cannot do both at once. [. . .] So it is that people keep on sending their children to school, though that is not where learning is; they sit in traffic jams on sunny days getting hot and irritable and pretending they're on holiday; they keep on turning up at an office where people don't even know about cheese (or love, or laughter, or self-expression); and they keep on going home to a relationship that died ten years before. Anything rather than risk acknowledging an old failure in order to start on the road to a new success. Bertrand Russell once said that most people would die sooner than think – and most people do. By 'think' he meant not just cogitate, but actually dare to question their presuppositions about life.[1]
[. . .]

What All Teachers Ought to Know

If teachers do not understand what learning is, and how it happens, they are as likely to hinder as to help. Unless their intervention is timely and their exhortations appropriate to the learner, they will be unhelpful. They will upset her, undermine her confidence, distract her from what she is doing, and impede the development of her own learning strategies. Teaching *is* a subversive activity[2] but it is often the learner, not the system, that is subverted. Here are some things that teachers need to know in order to avoid making learning more difficult.

1 You can take a horse to the fountain of knowledge but you cannot make him drink from it

Teaching does not produce learning, any more than horticulture produces plants. Learning and growth are things that happen, and cannot be forced. They can be helped to happen more readily and more economically. But they cannot be *made* to happen. A gardener cannot 'make' a graft take, a heart surgeon cannot 'make' a body accept the transplant, and a teacher cannot 'make' a learner assimilate new knowledge and skill. Teaching is not like carpentry, where the carpenter can create the joint he wants, subject only to the limitations of his skill and ingenuity. He is working with dead material, so connections have to be produced, products *assembled*. But the surgeon, the gardener and the teacher are working with live material and connections in the living world are *grown* organically, not assembled mechanically. To put the cutting in the ground is not enough: it has to grow roots, and so does knowledge.[3]

If teachers do not understand that teaching is grafting, and that grafting is a slow and subtle business which requires much concern for the nature of the plant and which cannot be made to happen by force, then it will be 'hard graft' indeed, full of wasted effort and misplaced blame. 'Damn trees', they will fume. 'I keep shoving the twig in as hard as I can and it keeps dying. Last week they seemed to understand and this week it's gone again. Lazy trees! Stupid trees! Naughty trees!' And, because the teachers' mistaken understanding makes them angry, it is they who act stupidly by kicking the trees and shouting at them. This is the first and greatest insight into teaching. And the second is similar, namely this:

2 People learn best what they most urgently need and want to know[4]

Nothing is learnt that is not connected, however remotely, with the satisfaction of need or want and the avoidance of threat. Learning is the improvement of our theory about the world, and the only yardstick of improvement, the only 'motivation', is the quality and security of our survival. Learning is the search for an answer to a question that matters. Thrown in at the deep end, the question 'How to swim?' becomes urgent. Pupils who have been labelled 'less able' (or just plain thick) by their school may have vast stores of knowledge about cars, or skill at sport, acquired with great ease under the influence of such motives. But the answers that school kindly provides them to questions that do not concern them will not stick at all. The most likely reason, after all, that the horse will not drink is that he isn't thirsty.

An un-thirsty horse can be motivated to drink, however, if you hit him until he does. Now he has an urgent question: 'How to avoid the whip?' And if the answer is 'Drink', he will learn to drink. You can teach someone something that they don't want to know, in other words, by hooking the learning up to a reward that they do want, or a threat that they will seek to avoid. Whether this works, and for how long, depends on the shifting balance between the learner's needs. The threat of detention, for example, may not be sufficient to outweigh the need to impress his friends. That which is to be learnt gets used as a pawn in the battle between conflicting needs.

To use these goads may 'work'. But the beaten horse feels doubly uncomfortable, distended by the liquid and frightened by the whip, and he will not love either you or the fountain any the more for the experience.

This applies, it is important to know, when you offer a reward, as well as when you threaten a punishment. The learner may work for the reward, if he wants it, but he is still unlikely to be interested in either you or the learning as anything other than a means to an end. The doing or the knowing that he is acquiring will be pursued only for as long as, and to the extent that, they produce the reward.[5] Cutting corners, copying other people's homework and bluffing your way through become sensible things to do, because proficiency is not the point. Many pupils in school learn to 'get by' because getting by is what they need and want to do – whether that means winning teacher's approval, or just avoiding detention. Learning French and Physics are secondary, and it is appropriate for the majority of adolescents that Secondary Schools are so called, for they are full of secondary activities. Some children need and want to pass exams, and for them this primary goal requires more 'learning'. And some need to want to be good at swimming, or at Chemistry, or at Leadership. Only for these few is the learning both the means *and* the end.

3 When people feel threatened they stop learning

Teachers have to be sensitive to the difference between challenge and threat. When people feel challenged they can be prodded and pushed. Their learning can be encouraged and stimulated. Often there comes a moment, though, when it becomes too much, and they 'switch off' in one way or another. 'Switching off' means defending, for example, by going unconscious; and defending is not learning. Prodding and pushing are now the last thing that a person wants. Once they have 'gone blank', whether it is about reading or sums or how to hold the racket, previous attempts to 'stretch' them are counter-productive, creating a thicker and thicker fog of confusion, anxiety and hostility, and self-doubt. When you say 'Come on . . . you remember what that word is, don't you?' the fact that they don't is experienced as another nail in the coffin of their dislike of the subject matter and distrust of themselves as learners. Though from the outside it appears unjustified, defending is *always* appropriate, being the natural response to a perceived threat. If teachers do not spot the shift, and they keep on pushing when a learner is threatened, the learner can very quickly be turned off the teacher, the subject, the context (for example, school), learning in general, and eventually himself. Frightened horses have other things on their minds than drinking.

4 Teachers need to know the learners' signals of threat

It follows that, if teachers are not to make this mistake, they must know the signals that the learner uses to signify that he has had enough. One may say he feels bored, another may start playing truant, and a third may suddenly sweep the half-finished jigsaw puzzle off the table. Learners develop very different responses to such situations and they need to be decoded. Usually when a learner has had enough the appropriate reaction by the teacher is to leave him alone for a bit. If he is not too upset all he needs is time to cool off. He does not need a post-mortem on how come he finds maths so dificult, or soccer so threatening. The majority of long-term learning difficulties are created by teachers themselves who have persuaded learners that they have 'learning difficulties' – thereby adding to the uncomfortable weight of having failed the guilty burden of being 'not good enough' – a flawed person. Parents mostly have the time and inclination to learn their children's signals. Secondary school teachers, while they may or may not have the inclination, almost certainly do not have the time to get to know any of their students well enough. They are, therefore, unaware of how often and for how many students their teaching is threatening.[6]

Being constantly exposed to things that you cannot understand (like Maths) or required to attempt actions that you cannot do (like gym) is itself threatening for many people: unable to run away, every moment is fraught with the danger of being exposed, yet again, as incompetent. And this in its turn threatens to bring the public humiliation that we would do almost anything to avoid.

5 People cannot learn what they are not ready for

As we have seen, certain ideas and skills presuppose others, and if the skills are missing it is impossible to grasp and digest the more complicated ideas.[7] It's no use having a thirty foot ladder if the first eight feet of rungs are missing. The important question for teachers is: who knows best what the learner is ready for? Once you've acknowledged the necessity not to force people to study what they cannot grasp, there are possible ways to proceed. One is for the teacher to try to diagnose the learner's current state of competence, infer from that what he is ready to learn (i.e. what he is capable of learning; not necessarily what he wants to learn), and present it to him.

Educationalists currently favour this course, and are busy devising diagnostic tests of 'cognitive level' and structuring curricula according to their 'cognitive difficulty'.[8] Robert Gagné, for example, says that: 'One important implication of the identification of learning conditions is that these conditions must be carefully planned *before* the learning situation is entered into by the student'.[9] This method is expensive, crude and generally ineffective. The alternative is to have a rough, intuitive shot at what the next thing to teach might be, and *modify it according to the learner's response*. Let him tell you whether it feels right or not. This is the simple and trustworthy method whereby new parents learn to play with (i.e. teach) their babies successfully. If you are sensitive to how your teaching is going down, you will very quickly find the right level. A learner's readiness to learn from what you are presenting is indicated clearly by his interest. If he feels challenged, then he's ready. This in turn makes the teaching challenging and fun. When your Enid Blyton is rejected as 'kid's stuff', or your attempt to introduce 'the Classics' produces squirming and a flood of unrelated questions, like 'What's for tea?', then you know you've got it wrong.

The first approach separates motivation and ability: it attempts to discover the latter without regard to the former. The whole philosophy of this book is contrary to this: it says that what one needs to know is what one is ready to know, and readiness is therefore signalled by need or want or interest. This signal is occasionally mistaken: every so often we find we are 'out of our depth', or have 'bitten off more than we can chew'. But on the whole it is reliable. Learning is essentially a growth, not an accumulation, and it must always spring from and return to what is known.

6 Learners may lend their control to a teacher but they cannot give it away

When someone chooses to be taught, she is saying to the teacher: 'I want some knowledge, ability or quality that you have, and I am temporarily going to hand over to you the responsibility for deciding what, when, where, how, how often, and in what sequence I study it, because I trust that by doing so I shall learn better.' This is the nature of the teaching–learning contract, when voluntarily entered into by the learner. Remember the quotation from Jerry Bruner. [. . .] 'Instruction is a provisional state that has as its object to make the learner . . . self sufficient'. If teachers do not see that the power they are given is only on loan, and that they are hired to increase the learner's autonomy as well as her competence, they are liable to get an inflated idea of their own importance, and to resist the fact that teaching is an activity whose goal is to make the teacher redundant. Since most school teachers are hired not by the learner but by an intermediate agency, it becomes harder still to see that students and their families have only lent their power of self-determination and that they can, like an investor, withdraw their capital if it is generating neither growth nor interest.

Another way of saying this is that, in general, it is the learner's right and responsibility to decide what her 'end' is, and it is the teacher's right and responsibility, if the learner chooses to be taught, to decide on the best means of attaining that end. When I decide to have golf lessons, or driving lessons, or to study a book on psychology, or to become an apprentice stone-mason, or to become a disciple of a guru, this is what happens. I submit to you because I guess that the best learning-amplifier in this case is to be taught by you.

Just like other learning strategies, *being taught* is a technique for creating learning opportunities, and getting the most out of them. An experienced flaw or hole in my theory about the world determines *what* I need and want to know about. My accumulated learning strategies determine *how* I go about finding out about it. It follows that teaching is all to do with facilitating learning, and nothing to do with deciding what the object of learning shall be – or only to the extent that the teacher may set minor goals (like playing scales) which she knows are helpful or necessary to achieving the major goals (playing the piano) that the learner has set for herself. When one person takes it on herself to decide what another needs or ought to know, that is something different. It is *indoctrination* if the object is knowledge or belief, and *conditioning* if it is habits and manners. Indoctrination and conditioning are attempts to teach things whose values and appropriateness have been determined by the teacher, and which may therefore not be rejected by the learner. The indoctrinator/conditioner drives a wedge between need and want. Your own appetite is no longer to be taken as a trustworthy guide to your hunger and your diet. Somebody else Knows Best.

There are circumstances in which any parent or teacher or society thinks that they do Know Best, and that a child will ultimately benefit from being moulded. In certain basic cases, such as a baby's wish to investigate things that are physically dangerous, everyone would agree that her frustration is justified. In all other cases the justification is arguable. What is not open to question, however, is the effect that conditioning and indoctrination have in dividing the child against herself. [. . .] to be told that something for which you have no energy is Good, while things you like are Bad is to be fractured. You become split between a centre that discriminates between Challenge and Threat, Pleasant and Unpleasant, Successful and Unsuccessful, and another, often antagonistic one, that is based on a conditioned and indoctrinated sense of Right and Wrong, Good and Bad. Thus to be subjected to experiences – especially learning experiences – that are said to be Right but feel Nasty is to be systematically estranged from your own natural sense of what is right *for you*. The more such experiences one suffers, the more confused one becomes. Indoctrination and conditioning – choosing what someone else should become – are, therefore, sometimes necessary, sometimes justifiable, but never fail to leave unwanted chips and dents in the learner's developing identity. For many children, being at school becomes an endless nightmare (screenplay by Kafka; direction by Orson Welles) of being told that what feels wrong is right and what feels right is wrong.[10]

7 Whatever you are teaching, you are teaching 'yourself'

That is to say, the learner is learning *about* you as well as *from* you. Whether you intend it or not, you are a potential model of an adult and of a teacher, and if you are teaching children, it is likely that they will be as interested in you as in the subject matter. Children will learn, through observation and imitation, from who you are as well as from what you are saying and doing. You are on display. Your pupils' manners will be influenced by your manner – for good or ill. Albert Einstein once said, 'The only rational method of educating is to be an example.' And he added, 'If you can't help it, be a warning example.'[11]

Teachers model what it is to be a teacher – teaching style. The fact that pupils have picked up a very clear, though unconscious, model of teaching is indicated by student teachers when they start their teaching practice. Their first intuitive guess at how to teach reflects the way they were taught. Yet it is doubtful that any of them consciously intended to absorb those values and habits. Very often they don't even *like* the teacher that they discover lurking inside them, and often that model is inappropriate to the new situation. This off-the-peg teaching habit has to be unpicked, rewoven and remodelled into a more hard-wearing and comfortable style. This does not apply only to school teachers. Being a driving instructor is different from being a preacher; being a university lecturer in high-energy physics is different from training new recruits in the army, or from trying to interest a group of day-release apprentice butchers (called Meat One) in the subtleties of *Lord of the Flies*.[12] If you try to rehearse an orchestra the same way you are trying to train your daughter to keep her elbows off the table, it won't work.

Teachers may provide a good model of a learner – or they may not. Good learners take their time, don't mind asking questions, aren't afraid of saying 'I don't know' or of being wrong, can change their minds and enjoy finding out.[13] If a teacher does not model these attitudes, and thereby show that it is safe for the learner to learn, then all his preparations and exhortations will be undermined.

And as well as all these mannerisms of the teacher *qua* teacher, he is also a model of a grown-up person. A school teacher's accent, hair-style, clothes, and vocabulary, the car he drives and his political views – everything about him – is of intense interest to his pupils because it is a possible piece in the developing jigsaw puzzle of adulthood. How I feel about his attitudes, how they fit in with the rest of me, how my friends feel about them, are all important bits of data in my search for a suitable grown-up self.

8   Even water takes time to digest

When you show someone how to do something, or explain an idea to them, what you are doing is suggesting a solution to them. Your demonstration, instruction, or explanation, if it is to 'take' has to be assimilated by the learner into her existing scheme of things. She has to chew it over and, if necessary, modify it a little, or 'put it into her own words'. This may happen in seconds, or it may take weeks or years, but it is a process that takes time. However 'right' you know you are, however much you know that the learner could save herself trouble by taking what you say for granted, she needs to make it her own. Teaching is not like programming a computer. It is not just a matter of sliding a floppy disc into someone else's brain. In learning, *digestion* must always come between *ingestion* and *constitution*. If a teacher does not realize this she may be inclined to get impatient. [. . .]

9 'Teaching' is always part of the learning context

Remember that learning is, at root, the creating of an association between all simultaneous or consecutively active bits of your mind-theory. That means that what you learn will be tied to its context. To put it more concretely, if somebody learns something by being taught, 'being taught' becomes part of the context for what is learnt. In the most extreme case the concepts or abilities simply will not be reactivated unless the teacher and the class-room are present. In all other situations their relevance is not perceived. And these 'other situations' may include just those occasions when the knowledge is supposed to be available. Despite having being taught in college that shouting at a class doesn't work, a student teacher, faced with 4B, finds himself shouting. Despite having been taught in school that electricity is dangerous, a 14-year-old may still stick his penknife into a socket, not believing that he can really get hurt. Despite having done 'compound interest' in Maths, and passed the tests, it remains a puzzle that the Building Society interest gets bigger every time.

It is one of the jobs of a teacher to vary the nonessential features of the learning context so that they do not gain control of what is learnt. And, equally, she can help by drawing attention to those features that *are* relevant. If the learners are studying for exams, it helps to give them exam-like tests. If they are rehearsing a play, it helps to rehearse on stage, and to have at least one 'dress rehearsal'. If you will have to perform under pressure, practise under pressure.

People sometimes say they have forgotten everything they learnt at school. And it is true that some of it seems to be lost for ever. But some is not lost, but only buried in the archives, filed under 'School', a classification that nobody asks for any more. 'School' is the trigger, but the circumstances rarely arise to pull it. Take people back after twenty years to their old school, sit them down at their old desks, and you will, both of you, be amazed at the warehouse of memories that is unlocked. A teacher who wants to teach for real-life competence must be aware of this 'contextualization' problem.

Notes

1   For further reading I recommend Hamachek, *Encounters with the Self*, and Esther Harding, *The I and the Not-I*.
2   *Teaching as a Subversive Activity* is the title of a well-known radical education book by Neil Postman and Charles Weingartner.
3   There are particular learning strategies, like *remembering* and *repeating* [. . .], where the amount of integration that results is minimal. But these are special purpose strategies, to be used not from preference but in those circumstances

where integration is blocked. They are models not of learning in general, but of one specialized, limited, nonpreferred *kind* of learning. If the teacher wishes to optimize learning, he should always seek to avoid the circumstances in which these 'brute force and ignorance' methods are necessary. In schools often the very opposite seems to be happening.

4   This is, I think, an exact quotation of the opening sentence of a respectable Ed. Psych. text-book that I looked at five or six years ago. Unfortunately I forget the author.

5   There is some nice research by M. Lepper and D. Greene and others, on what is called 'the undermining effect' (see *The Hidden Costs of Reward*, Lawrence Erlbaum, Hillsdale, New Jersey, 1978). In many circumstances (though not all) when a person is externally rewarded for doing something that they have previously done spontaneously, the action becomes tied to the reward, and the apparent 'intrinsic motivation' is undermined. [. . .]

6   This point is well made by John Holt in *Teach Your Own* (Lighthouse, Brightlingsea, Essex).

7   This concern has been most influentially expressed in educational psychology by R. M. Gagné in *The Conditions of Learning*, 3rd edn (Holt, Rinehart & Winston, New York, 1977), where he develops an elaborate but psychologically dated hierarchy of learning processes.

8   See, for example, Michael Shayer and Philip Adey, *Towards a Science of Science Teaching* (Heinemann Educational, London, 1981).

9   From an article entitled 'Learning Objectives? Yes!' in T. Roberts (Ed), *Four Psychologies Applied to Education* (Schenkman, Cambridge, Mass., 1975).

10   For observational but compelling evidence of this, see especially the early books by John Holt, such as *The Underachieving School*, *How Children Learn*, and *How Children Fail* (Penguin, Harmondsworth, 1971, 1972, and 1973 respectively), and others like *Lives of Children*, by George Dennison, or Jonathan Kozol's *Death at an Early Age* (Bantam, New York, 1968).

11   Albert Einstein, *Ideas and Opinions*.

12   See Tom Sharpe's book *Wilt* (Pan, London, 1978) for advice on how to accomplish the latter.

13   This list is a condensation of a discussion in Postman and Weingartner. [. . .]

References

DE BONO, E. (1976) *Teaching Thinking*. London, Temple Smith.

DENNISON, G. (1972) *The Lives of Children*. Harmondsworth, Penguin.

EINSTEIN, A. (1973) *Ideas and Opinions*. London, Souvenir Press.

GAGNÉ, R. M. (1977) *The Conditions of Learning* 3rd edition. New York, Holt, Rinehart & Winston.

HAMACHEK, D. (1978) *Encounters with the Self*. New York, Holt, Rinehart & Winston.

HARDING, E. (1977) *The I and the Not-I*. London, Coventure.

HARRIS, T. (1973) *I'm OK – You're OK*. London, Pan.

HOLMAN, J. (1979) *Introduction to Psychosomatics*. London, Biodynamic Psychology Publications.

HOLT, J. (1971) *The Underachieving School*. Harmondsworth, Penguin.

HOLT, J. (1972) *How Children Learn*. Harmondsworth, Penguin.

HOLT, J. (1973) *How Children Fail*. Harmondsworth, Penguin.

HOLT, J. (1981) *Teach Your Own*. Brightlingsea, Essex, Lighthouse.

JULIEN, R. M. (1981) *A Primer of Drug Action* 3rd edition. San Francisco, W. H. Freeman.

KOPP, S. (1974) *If You Meet the Buddha on the Road, Kill Him*. London, Sheldon Press.

KOZOL, J. (1968) *Death at an Early Age*. New York, Bantam.

LEPPER, M. and GREENE, D. (1978) *The Hidden Costs of Reward*. Hillsdale, New Jersey, Lawrence Erlbaum.

LOWEN, A. (1976) *Bioenergetics*. Harmondsworth, Penguin.

MENZIES, I. (1970) *The Functioning of Social Systems as a Defence Against Anxiety*. London, Tavistock Institute.

POSTMAN, N. and WEINGARTNER, C. (1971) *Teaching as a Subversive Activity*. Harmondsworth, Penguin.

RYCROFT, C. (1971) *Reich*. London, Fontana.

SHARPE, T. (1978) *Wilt*. London, Pan.

SHAYER, M. and ADEY, P. (1981) *Towards a Science of Science Teaching*. London, Heinemann Educational.

VONNEGUT, K. (1968) *Mother Night*. London, Jonathan Cape.

WILBER, K. (1979) *No Boundary*. Boulder, Colorado, Shambhala.

WOLLHEIM, R. (1971) *Freud*. London, Fontana.

3

Teaching as a Moral Craft

Alan R. Tom

[. . .]

Contemporary research emphasizing the identification of effective teaching behaviors usually falls in a tradition called process-product research. In this tradition, effectiveness is defined in terms of relationships between observed teacher behaviors (processes) and student outcome measures (products). [. . .]

However, such a process-product correlation does not permit one to claim that the process is the cause of the associated product. As a result there have been recent attempts to design experimental studies on process-product variables so that teacher behaviors can be identified that are causes of desired student outcomes (Gage and Giaconia, 1981).

In 1971 Rosenshine and Furst conducted a comprehensive review of fifty correlational studies available at that time. While they acknowledged that 'we know very little about the relationship between classroom behavior and student gains' (p. 37), they did present five teacher behavior variables for which there was 'strong support' from the correlational studies and six variables for which there was 'less strong' support from the same studies. These eleven variables are: clarity of teacher presentation; variety of instructional procedures and materials; teacher enthusiasm; task-oriented or businesslike teacher behavior; student opportunity to learn what is subsequently tested; teacher recognition and use of student ideas; criticism of students (negatively related to achievement); teacher use of structuring comments; varied types of questions; teacher probing of student responses; and student perception of the difficulty of instruction. However, doubt was cast on these findings when Heath and Nielson (1974) demonstrated that Rosenshine and Furst's (1979) analysis of the subsequent research on the eleven variables resulted in his continued endorsement of only two: task-oriented or business-like teacher behavior and student opportunity to learn what is later tested. He also noted that 'recent work has shifted from studying specific variables to looking at larger patterns' (p. 31).

Is it reasonable to find nothing more than weak associations between student achievement and such individual teacher behaviors as teacher clarity or teacher use of varied types of questions? Medley, for one, argues that process-product research is based on a 'widely believed but almost certainly incorrect idea that there exists a single set of performance competencies – of skills and abilities – which all or nearly all effective teachers have, and which all or nearly all ineffective ones lack' (1973, p. 43). [. . .]

Aptitude-Treatment Interactions (ATIs)

One research strategy that introduces a second dimension into teacher effectiveness research is the study of the interactions that occur between treatments (one dimension) and student aptitudes (a second dimension). In ATI research the term *treatment* refers to style of instruction or some other type of teacher behavior while the term *aptitude* is defined as '*any* characteristic of the person that affects his response to the treatment' (Cronbach, 1975, p. 116). An ATI study tries to discover the relative effectiveness of treatments when combined with differing student aptitudes. In contrast to process-product research, which seeks to find out which teacher behavior is effective across a range of situations, ATI research attempts to discover what is the best method of instruction for learners having a particular characteristic.

An example of a typical two-group ATI study should clarify what it means to select the best method of instruction for a particular student characteristic. Domino (1971) hypothesized that an instructor who dominates a class would obtain poorer results from students who liked to set tasks for themselves than he would from students who liked to meet requirements set for them. He also hypothesized that an instructor who encourages independent activity by students would obtain the opposite results. Domino found that when the student's style of learning corresponded with the teaching style of the instructor, the outcomes were better for all but one of the dependent variables, that is, the treatment (teaching style) did interact with an aptitude (learning style).

Cronbach, who first called for ATI research more than twenty-five years ago, recently assessed the status of the study of ATIs. Cronbach and Snow conclude that while ATIs do exist, 'no Aptitude X Treatment interactions are so well confirmed that they can be used directly as guides to instruction' (1977, p. 492). Other analysts of the ATI literature concur with this negative assessment; Tobias, for example, states that 'there are few replicated interactions that permit prescriptions such as: "Use method X with this kind of student, whereas this other student should be instructed by method Y"' (1976, p. 63). At present there is consensus that ATI research cannot be used as a basis for instructional decisions (Snow, 1977, 1980; Tobias, 1981, 1982). [. . .]

Cronbach hypothesizes that interactions beyond first-order ones are the basic reason that he and Snow found many 'inconsistent findings coming from roughly similar inquiries' (1975, p. 119). For generalizations about instructional phenomena – that is, instructional theory – to reflect the true complexity of these phenomena, analysis must encompass interactions of the 'third order or fifth order or any other order' (p. 119). 'Once we attend to interactions,' notes Cronbach, 'we enter a hall of mirrors that extends to infinity' (p. 119). These interactions can be so complicated that even listing them becomes difficult. Further, these higher-order interactions are both time and place bound so that 'enduring systematic theories about man in society are not likely to be achieved' (p. 126).

Instructional theory, therefore, must be composed of highly qualified generalizations. These generalizations cannot necessarily be restricted to a single dimension of teaching style and to a single dimension of student aptitude. For example, such varied student aptitudes as social class, age, and sex may need to be taken into consideration. Neither can instructional theory exclude subject matter. Taking these multiple dimensions into account, Snow concludes that 'instructional theory may be possible . . . but it should concern itself only with narrowly circumscribed local instructional situations, relatively small chunks of curriculum for relatively small segments of the educational population' (1977, p. 12). A typical instructional theory, therefore, might apply to 'the teaching of arithmetic in grades 1-2-3 in Washington and Lincoln schools in Little City, but perhaps not to the two other elementary schools in that town' (p. 12). [. . .]

Direct Instruction

Recently several attempts have been made to work at a level somewhat more sophisticated than the search for generic teaching behaviors but not so complex as the multidimensional approach advocated by Snow (1977). Prominent within this middle range of teacher effectiveness research is the development of the model of direct instruction. According to Rosenshine (1979), direct instruction refers to instruction with the following dimensions: an emphasis on academic goals, student awareness of these goals, strong teacher direction of classroom activity, a stress on large-group instruction, questions typically at a low cognitive level in order to maximize correct responses, extensive coverage of content, and a task-oriented but not authoritarian classroom environment. This definition includes the two teaching behaviors that Rosenshine (1979) believes may still have general applicability: task-oriented or businesslike teacher behavior and student opportunity to learn what is subsequently tested. However, these two behaviors are now integrated with other behaviors into a pattern or teaching model rather than being individually considered.

Many recent reviewers of research on direct instruction imply that it is the most effective approach to teaching (Peterson, 1979, p. 58). For example, while Good (1979) grants that 'direct instruction ... may be *inconsistent* with the goals of certain subjects (e.g. social studies, art)' (p. 62), he nevertheless claims that 'in comparison to other available treatments (or at least those conventionally present in classrooms), direct instruction may have superior general effects for all types of students' (p. 60). In a similar way, Rosenshine (1979) reports that the direct instruction research he has reviewed is limited to the areas of reading and mathematics, but he also leaves the reader with the impression that this model is as good or better than other approaches for achieving a wide variety of cognitive and affective objectives.

Peterson (1979) argues that direct instruction is being oversold. She believes it may be effective for attaining some educational outcomes but not others. [. . .]

The results of Peterson's analysis of cognitive and affective outcomes are mixed. Direct instruction did fare better than open instruction in the case of mathematics and reading achievement, but the effect sizes were small: only about one-eighth of a standard deviation. In the areas of creativity and seven affective outcomes, the differences all favored open instruction, with the effect size ranging from one-thirtieth to two-fifths of a standard deviation. Thus, while few of the effect sizes were large, the choice of a teaching approach appears to be connected to the type of educational objective being sought. [. . .]

The lesson in Peterson's analysis is that we need to be cautious about embracing direct instruction. For certain purposes and types of students, direct instruction may be better than less direct approaches, but even in these cases the actual differences in effect size seem to be small. To claim that direct instruction is an important advance is to risk overestimating both its effect and its range of applicability. [. . .]

Can the Teacher Effectiveness Model be Saved?

[. . .]

In teacher effectiveness research there seems to be a trade-off between accuracy and generality, as well as accompanying issues of research-design feasibility. If we desire accurate and potent theories, we will want to build into our research designs such diverse contextual variables as social class, type of objective, age of student, type of subject matter, and so forth. But a systematic program of teacher effectiveness research that controls for the relevant contextual variables is of doubtful feasibility because it would be excessively expensive and impossible to complete. On the other hand, a more feasible research strategy is the development of a limited number of generic instructional theories, but these generic theories are likely to be weak. [. . .]

Selecting such a midpoint might provide the advantage of having each end point, accuracy and generality, without the problem of either developing a huge number of instructional theories or worrying about the potency of these theories. Once we settle at the midpoint, we are back to one of the options previously examined: direct instruction. I have already noted how the advocates of direct instruction tend to see this model as having wide applicability, thus emphasizing its generic potential (for example, Brophy, 1979; Good 1979; Rosenshine, 1979). But the direct instruction model has emerged out of research on a particular classroom context – mathematics and reading achievement, especially at the primary level – and there is neither a conceptual nor an empirical basis to support the generic potential of direct instruction. Instead of attempting to discover 'whether direct instruction is more effective than more indirect or open ways of teaching', we would be better off, according to Peterson, if we asked a less generic question: 'For what educational outcomes is direct instruction most effective and for what kinds of students?' (1979, p. 58). The answer to this question seeks a balance between generality and accuracy by focusing on the conditions under which direct instruction is most effective. At the same time, this research approach seems feasible because there is a limited number of instructional models besides direct instruction that are in need of examination.

In order for us to start matching instructional conditions with the direct instruction model, we must have insight into the reasons why direct instruction is, at times, effective. Without knowledge of the factors that contribute to, or inhibit, the success of direct instruction, we are literally unable to construct an informed research agenda for identifying the conditions under which it is appropriate to apply direct instruction. Unfortunately, the answer to the question 'Why does direct instruction work?' is, according to Good, 'largely unknown' (1979, p. 57).

While Good does speculate about the explanation for direct instruction's effectiveness, his three 'general reasons' why teachers experience success with direct instruction are ambiguous and not particulary informative. First, he claims that direct instruction provides 'a positive motivational source that encourages teachers to plan their days more fully, take their responsibilities more seriously, and thus fulfill their expectations' (p. 57). Second, Good believes direct instruction helps teachers decide to focus on a few of the 'vast array of goals' facing the contemporary teacher, a process he labels 'proactive stimulation' (pp. 57–8). Third, and somewhat more specific-ally, he suggests that 'the model provides a plausible, practical system of instruction', by which he means that large-group instruction, a central characteristic of direct instruction, enables the teacher to focus on detailed planning, obtain feedback from a large number of students quickly, and spend less time organizing for instruction than in the case of individualized and small-group instruction. The third reason seems to boil down to a contention that large-group teaching has instructional and managerial advantages over small-group and individualized teaching.

To assert that direct instruction has the capacity to motivate teachers, focus their energies on a few goals, and help them use their time more efficiently is not to offer a comprehensive and conceptually precise analysis of the success of direct instruction. This low-level explanation, however, does reveal the conceptual simplicity of the direct instruction model, a condition that is understandable when one considers the origins of this model. Instead of deriving the direct instruction model from a conceptualization of causative factors in children's achievement, the developers of the direct instruction model generated the model by examining which processes (teacher behaviors) were correlated with certain products (student learning), primarily in the areas of mathematics and reading. The model, therefore, specifies a pattern of teacher behavior (large-group instruction, specific goals, etc.) often associated with student learning in mathematics and reading. Such behavioral correlations, of course, are below the level of conceptualization, thereby severely limiting the explanatory power of the direct instruction model. [. . .]

The Teaching-Learning Link: its Strength and Directionality

Underlying the tradition of teacher effectiveness research is the assumption that teaching directly produces learning. Review carefully two sample quotations by prominent researchers:

> Since it may be assumed that whatever effect a teacher has on pupils must result from his [or her] behaviors, it is only necessary to identify the crucial behaviors, record them, and score them properly to measure effectiveness in process. (Medley and Mitzel, 1963, p. 258)

> If teachers do vary in their effectiveness, then it must be because they vary in the behaviors they exhibit in the classroom. . . . There seems to be no more obvious truth than that a teacher is effective to the extent that he [or she] causes pupils to learn what they are supposed to learn. (Dunkin and Biddle, 1974, pp. 13–14)

These two quotes, and similar ones, make clear that many teacher effectiveness researchers believe that teacher behavior can cause student learning to occur.

This behavior-to-behavior link – that is, teacher behavior to student learning – is what I call the billiard ball hypothesis. The pool player (the teacher) aims the cue ball (his [or her] behavior) so that it will strike the target billiard ball (the student) at exactly the right angle to cause the billiard ball (the student) to go into a pocket (the achievement of what the student is supposed to learn). Not only does the billiard analogy visualize how many teacher effectiveness researchers view teacher behavior as directly leading to student learning, but in addition the analogy suggests two subsidiary assumptions: the centrality of the teacher and the passivity of the student.

Just as the pool player and the cue ball are the focal points of billiards so do teacher effectiveness researchers concentrate on the teacher and his [or her] behavior. The centrality of the teacher and his [or her] behavior is obvious in the case of research emphasizing the identification of either effective teaching behaviors or potent instructional models, but even in the case of ATI studies the emphasis is more on the teacher's behavior (the treatment) than on the student's characteristics (the aptitudes). Remember that aptitude is defined as '*any* characteristic of the person that affects his response to the treatment' (Cronbach, 1975, p. 116), thereby defining aptitude in terms of treatment and making it clear that the conceptual focus in ATI study is on the nature of treatments and on matching treatments to aptitudes. So strong is the 'teacher' emphasis in the teacher effectiveness tradition that when it was popular several years ago to measure classroom interaction through observational systems, the best known system, Flanders Interaction Analysis, had seven categories of teacher behavior but only two categories of student behavior.

The billiard analogy also helps highlight the passive role attributed to the student by teacher effectiveness researchers. Just as pool players naturally think of how they can use the cue ball to move the other billiard balls to desired locations, so too do teacher effectiveness researchers think in terms of how teacher behavior can be manipulated in order to obtain the desired results, that is, student learning. Latent in teacher effectiveness research, especially in the dominant process-product approach, is the belief that teachers initiate behaviors and students respond either by learning or by not learning. Since the processes in the process-product paradigm refer entirely to teacher behavior and other teacher activities, the only role for the student in this paradigm is to be a receptacle.

The accuracy of the billiard ball and related assumptions – the hypothesized direct tie between teaching and learning and the subsidiary assumptions of teacher centrality and student passivity – are critical to the maintenance of the teacher effectiveness tradition, especially to the process-product paradigm which has become virtually synonymous with the concept of teacher effectiveness. For example, if there are significant factors which intervene between teacher behavior (process) and student learning (product), then the process-product paradigm must either be reconceptualized or abandoned; this paradigm currently cannot account for such intervening factors, a reason perhaps for its failure to yield substantial findings. Similarly, the process-product paradigm assumes influence flows from the teacher to the student so that any evidence that students affect teacher behavior tends to reduce the explanatory and predictive power of the process-product paradigm. Therefore, to the extent that the billiard analogy and related assumptions are inaccurate, doubt is cast upon the teacher effectiveness enterprise as it is currently conducted.

Analysis of the validity of the three interconnected assumptions is facilitated by their empirical nature. Their normative content – that is, assertions about what ought to be – is minimal. Rather than being statements about what is good or bad, they are statements about relationships that are thought to be true. To test their validity, I draw primarily on published research, but I also refer to personal experience and to commonsense knowledge relevant to these assumptions. After examining the validity of the assumed direct tie between teacher behavior and student learning – that is, the billiard ball hypothesis – I also evaluate the validity of focusing research on the teacher and his behavior and of construing the student as the passive recipient of teacher behavior. The discussion of these assumptions, while separated for the sake of conceptual clarity, in reality represents an interrelated set of issues. With that qualification in mind, I turn now to the assumed direct tie between teaching and learning. [. . .]

Initially there were attempts to find a linear relationship between teacher behavior and student learning, but later researchers conceived this relationship as being either curvilinear or situational. In all three conceptualizations, however, teacher effectiveness researchers see the tie between teacher behavior and student learning as being direct.

The linear approach assumes that there is a correlation between how often an effective teacher behavior is exhibited and how much student learning occurs. [. . .] Clearly, a research approach built on the premise that the more often an effective teacher behavior occurs the higher will be student achievement is a research approach which presumes a direct tie between teacher behavior and student learning. [. . .]

The search for teaching behaviors whose potency is proportional to the frequency of their use has not been particularly fruitful, leading some researchers to posit a curvilinear relationship between effective teaching behaviors and learning outcomes (see, for example, Soar and Soar, 1976). Under the curvilinear hypothesis, increasing an effective teaching behavior indefinitely does not necessarily lead to corresponding gains in student learning. Rather, for many teaching behaviors there is a point at which more of a potent teaching behavior leads to a flattening out of the learning curve and ultimately to a decrease in learning. The key question therefore becomes one of finding the optimal frequency of use for a particular behavior or teaching model, a balance that may need to take into account certain student aptitudes and/or the type of educational objective to be mastered. For example, when an indirect teaching style is being used to foster student creativity, the optimum level of indirectness may vary for low-anxiety as opposed to high-anxiety students (Soar, 1968). Since the curvilinearity of teaching behavior is interrelated with student aptitudes and curricular outcomes, we are once again back to aptitude-treatment interactions, including all the higher-level interactions needed to construct useful instructional theory.

An alternative to both the linear and the curvilinear assumptions is the belief that *when* a teaching behavior is used is more important than either *how often* it is used or how well it is *matched* with student aptitudes or curricular outcomes. Berliner makes a strong case for the situational appropriateness of effective teaching:

In our classroom observations we have become acutely aware of the difference between a higher-cognitive question asked after a train of thought is running out, and the same type of question asked after a series of lower-cognitive questions has been used to establish a foundation from which to explore higher-order ideas. We have seen teachers ask inane questions, or direct questions to what we believe was the wrong child. We have seen positive verbal reinforcement used with a new child in the class, one who was trying to win peer-group acceptance, and whose behavior the teacher chose to use as a standard of excellence. We watched silently as the class rejected the intruder, while the teacher's count in the verbal praise category went up and up and up. (1976, p. 372).

[. . .] In the example cited by Berliner, teacher praise was ineffective because of the youngster's desire for peer-group acceptance; teacher praise actually had the opposite effect intended by the teacher because the praise set the youngster apart from the very group with whom he wanted to be identified. The teacher's effectiveness, therefore, can be greatly dependent on his insight into a youngster's motives.

The potency of this example is with its capacity to reveal the simpleminded-ness of the billiard ball hypothesis. Instead of the cue ball (teacher behavior) striking the target billiard ball (the student) at the precise angle needed to deflect that ball into a pocket (a learning goal), we now see that the target billiard ball is a cause of its own movement in a particular direction. Student motives, for example, can act as an irregularly shaped barrier located just in front of the target billiard ball; this barrier absorbs the impact of the cue ball but does not necessarily transmit the force of the cue ball exactly in the way this force was received. In fact, the billiard ball can completely override the intended effect of the cue ball, if, for instance, the student decides to drop out of school.

The phenomenon I have been describing is labelled *mediation* by some researchers (Anderson, 1970; Doyle, 1977; Glick, 1968). In the most general sense, mediation refers to 'certain processes that presumably intervene in the relationships between teacher variables and student learning outcomes' (Doyle, 1977, p. 165). [. . .]

To better understand how mediating variables can deflect (or enhance) the thrust of teacher behavior I will examine briefly two examples. [. . .]

In my own personal experience one of the clearest examples of mediation involves the varying reactions of my two sons to the same elementary teachers. In the case of a strong-willed and highly organized teacher, one son thrived while the other rebelled and literally refused to work. On the other hand, the 'rebellious' son enjoyed the classroom of another teacher who behaviorally was very similar to the first teacher but who was also psychologically sup-portive; the other son found little difference between the experience with the first and second teachers. A third, low-key teacher who paid careful attention to the governing motivations of students became both sons' favorite teacher. In the end I came to believe that it was not so much what the teachers did that influenced how much effort was expended by my sons as it was how the teachers were perceived by my boys. The son who is at times rebellious, including running away from school on more than one occasion, has a strong internal drive for perfection and worries about whether a teacher might yell at him for making errors; he seems to need understanding and support from his teachers before he will risk an activity in which he might fail. The other boy appears to view teachers as people who set goals, often high goals, which he should strive to meet; he too has concern about failure, but this concern causes him to redouble his efforts when he perceives the teacher is dissatisfied with his work.

I can easily envision both of my sons being placed in the high-anxiety cell on an achievement-anxiety dimension in some ATI study. However, though both boys are anxious to succeed, their reactions to an anxiety-related situation may either be essentially the same or quite different, depending on the cues to which each attaches importance and on their personal construc- tions of the situation. Only after probing the perceptions they have of themselves, including their self-confidence, does one start to see the reasons why these two boys, outwardly similar in their desire to achieve and in their concern about failure, can react so differently in one behavioral setting and literally the same in another setting. To the boys, the behavioral settings are not necessarily the same, for it is their personal interpretations of the teacher's behavior to which they respond, not to the teacher behavior itself. While a few researchers, especially those coming out of an ethnographic tradition, are sensitive to the mediating impact of student perceptions, most teacher effectiveness researchers either are indifferent to these perceptions or are interested in them only in so far as they can be manipulated by the teacher (see, for example, Gage, 1978, pp. 69–74).

While the covert nature of student perceptions may account for why they are largely ignored by researchers on teaching, a far more tangible mediating variable, the structure of a subject matter, is equally overlooked by these researchers. It is common for researchers to restrict their research and theorizing to the student and the teacher. Thus the ATI model examines the interaction between student aptitudes and teacher treatments, and the focus of those seeking 'laws' of learning or effective teaching behaviors is obvious. Scholars who believe that the character of a subject matter must be central to any significant inquiry into effective teaching feel it necessary to argue this point (see, for example, Bantock, 1961; Gowin, 1970; Resnick and Ford, 1981, chap. 1; Shulman, 1974). That these arguments are indeed needed is well illustrated by the way researchers frequently portray subject matter as inert material, divisible into small blocks that are movable from one location to another (see, for example, Bloom, 1971, pp. 32–6; Gage, 1974; Gagné and Briggs, 1974; Rosenshine, 1979).

One need not be an advocate of teaching the structures of disciplines to realize that subject matter is something more than a building that can be torn down brick by brick and moved to a new location. While most subject areas do have some relatively discrete bits of information – for instance, historical facts or scientific terms – each field also has complex intellectual operations and conceptual structures that are not necessarily the sum of these bits of information and, indeed, cannot be well taught unless they are intimately understood by the teacher. Research that is insensitive to the intellectual operations and concepts a youngster must master in order to learn the core of a subject matter is not likely to have fruitful outcomes. It may well be no coincidence that whatever success teacher effectiveness researchers have had is largely limited to basic skill instruction, instruction which does not emphasize specialized intellectual perspectives. [. . .]

Recognizing that certain factors – for instance, student perceptions, the nature of subject matters, and student attention to instructional tasks – can mediate the impact of teacher behavior on student learning challenges the validity of the direct-tie assumption underlying the process-product paradigm. Yet the existence of mediating processes can apparently be accounted for by making the process-product paradigm more elaborate. Instead of a two-step paradigm (teacher processes produce student outcomes), Gage expands the paradigm into three steps: teacher processes are seen as influencing student processes (such mediating factors as attending, comprehending, persisting) that in turn influence student outcomes. Gage summarizes this paradigm as follows: '*teaching-process → student-process → student-product*' (1978, p. 71). The revised paradigm, therefore, does include mediating processes, though mediating processes external to the student are omitted, for example, curricular objectives or the characteristics of subject matters.

However, the use of one-way arrows suggests a problem with the revised paradigm. Gage assumes we ought to focus on the flow of influence from teacher to student. While he recognizes that influence on student learning comes 'from sources other than the teacher', he argues that teacher effectiveness researchers need to focus their efforts on teachers, not on those other sources of influence: 'The teacher,' notes Gage, 'is the one primarily responsible for determining what goes on in the classroom and for enhancing its educational value' (1978, p. 72). This claim is a clear statement of the assumed centrality of teacher behavior to student learning.

Though Gage may be technically correct that teachers are 'primarily' responsible for 'what goes on in the classroom', a growing literature suggests that student behavior is the cause, as well as the effect, of teacher behavior (see, for example, Bossert, 1981; Fiedler, 1975; Haller, 1967; S. S. Klein, 1971; Noble and Nolan, 1976). In a particularly fascinating experiment, Gray, Graubard, and Rosenberg (1974) trained seven so-called incorrigible junior high students in behavior modification techniques so that these students could change the hostile attitude that many teachers held toward them. The techniques taught in a special class for the students included such things as smiling, establishing eye contact with teachers, asking for extra help with lessons, sitting up straight, nodding in agreement while teachers spoke. During the five weeks in which the incorrigible students used these techniques to reinforce teacher behaviors desired by the students, the number of positive comments from teachers increased fourfold, and the number of negative comments declined almost to zero. By the end of the experiment the teacher clients were enthusiastic about the project, though most teachers tended to believe that the changes were in the youngsters rather than in themselves. That teachers saw the changes occurring in youngsters may well suggest that teachers do not share the common researcher assumption that influence flows primarily from teacher to student. In an experiment with a similar design, Sherman and Cormier (1974) illustrated that reducing student disruptive behavior led to systematic changes in teacher behavior.

The recognition that student behavior can 'cause' teacher behavior suggests that focusing research exclusively on *teacher* effectiveness is unwise. In reality, it is just as reasonable to call for research on pupil effectiveness to identify ways in which 'students are able to help their teachers improve their teaching behavior' (S. S. Klein, 1971, p. 403). A student effectiveness perspective suggests that differential teacher behavior toward students by sex, by socio-economic status, or by expected level of performance may not result so much from fixed teacher attitudes as it does from the impact of student behaviors on teacher behaviors (Noble and Nolan, 1976). At least some recent research (see, for example Bossert, 1981) does seriously consider how differential teacher behavior toward boys and girls can be in response to variations in the behaviors and interests of the pupils and not simply prompted by their gender. As a result, studying which student behaviors encourage sex equity practices by teachers can be a major contribution to teaching effectiveness research. [. . .]

The logical correlate of making the teacher's behavior central to research on teaching is to assume that the student's learning is an outcome to be maximized. In experimental language, student learning is a dependent variable, thereby suggesting that the student is an object to be acted upon. The student, therefore, becomes 'a passive receptacle whose learning and performance are directly determined by input variables' (Anderson, 1970, p. 349). [. . .]

Interestingly, Dunkin and Biddle claim that 'most teachers' believe that changes in pupil behavior are a function of teacher activity (p. 45). On the contrary, I find most teachers believe students have considerable responsibility for how much learning occurs, both because individual students decide whether to attend to instruction and because successful instruction depends on a variety of factors rooted in the social system of the classroom, for example, the desire of individuals for peer-group acceptance, the dynamics of a particular group, and so forth. If I am correct that teachers assume learning is the responsibility of students as well as teachers, then their assumption is more in line with recent research evidence than is the 'teaching is the fundamental cause of learning' assumption adhered to by many teacher effectiveness researchers.

When we add together the evidence on the billiard ball assumption, including the evidence relevant to the centrality of the teacher and the passivity of the student, I believe it is clear that this cluster of assumptions is seriously flawed. Teacher influence on students is mediated by a variety of factors, and this influence is bidirectional (Glick, 1968). As a result, the process-product paradigm that underlies teacher effectiveness research, and the concept of teacher effectiveness itself, are brought into question.

But the problems with the process-product paradigm and with the concept of teacher effectiveness extend beyond the nature and flow of teacher-student influence. An equally fundamental problem concerns two other assumptions researchers typically make about teaching: that teaching is a natural phenomenon and that teaching is a technical activity in which each teaching problem has a one-best-solution. In the next two sections, the nature, importance, and validity of these two assumptions are examined.

Teaching Phenomena: Natural or Socially Constructed?

No assumption is more important to educational researchers interested in the establishment of stable regularities than the belief that teaching phenomena are natural. This assumption is so fundamental that it is often stated as a primary truth. Dunkin and Biddle, for example, declare that 'the activities of teaching are reasonable, natural, rational events' without feeling the need for extensive defense of this assertion (1974, p. 12). Kerlinger is equally certain that educational researchers must use social scientific methods for 'the controlled pursuit of relations among natural phenomena' (1968, p. 480). Most educational researchers do not even bother to make explicit their assumption that teaching phenomena are natural.

Viewing educational phenomena as natural is a critical assumption because the study of natural phenomena may lead to formulating relations among variables – ideally lawlike relationships – that extend over time and space. The key to this potential generalizability is the stability of natural phenomena. Natural phenomena, basically independent of man, are fundamentally the same from one generation of scholars to another. Whatever change occurs in our knowledge of natural phenomena is largely traceable to researchers – their new questions, new techniques, new instruments – rather than to the evolution of these phenomena. In this way the stability of natural phenomena makes possible the development of cumulative, cross-cultural knowledge (Weisskopf, 1979). [. . .]

Instability occurs not only in curricular and administrative organization but also in the specific content of the instructional program. We may emphasize basic skills and play down the arts, or we may stress some new conception of moral education. We also expect the schools to serve the purposes of social reform when we go to the courts to press for districtwide or interdistrict busing of students. Whether it is because of the impact of social purpose on schools, the honest desire of school leaders to respond to educational 'needs', or outright faddism, the instructional situation is anything but stable (Glass, 1972, p. 15).

The instability of educational phenomena is directly traceable to the man-made nature of these phenomena. Education, to use the words of Ebel is 'a human invention, a construction, a cultural institution designed and built by men' (1967, p. 83). Formal education is a social institution, a means by which a society attempts to perpetuate the knowledge, skills, and attitudes deemed important. Educational phenomena, therefore, will tend to change as a society redefines its central purposes and as educational leaders initiate new programs and new teaching approaches in order to achieve these redefined purposes. In brief, the instability of educational phenomena is a reflection of the instability of the human purposes underlying these phenomena.

The pursuit of laws or generalizations about teaching without regard to underlying human purposes has caused researchers to ask truncated and therefore trivial questions. For example, the moral dimension of teaching in which one person temporarily controls the functioning of another (Hawkins, 1973) becomes reduced to the study of teacher effectiveness, that is, how more content can be taught faster. Similarly, rather than focus on the central curriculum issue – the need to make choices among the vast array of content and to justify these choices (Kliebard, 1977) – researchers on teaching strive to discover instructional theory, which turns out to be nothing more than an attempt to maximize learning without regard to the quality of that learning. However, the maximization perspective, so potent when phenomena are indeed natural, makes little sense if educational phenomena are not so much an instance of fundamental natural regularities as they are the creative attempt of man to determine what succeeding generations are to know and to believe.

The recognition that educational phenomena are man-made rather than natural does not reduce our need to study education (Ebel, 1982). What this acknowledgment does do is to help us realize that we should not be trying to comprehend one of the 'givens in our universe' so much as we should be trying to redesign and reconstruct education to 'serve our human purposes better' (Ebel, 1967, p. 83). Since formal education is a social institution, it can be understood only if its observable features – those focused on by conventional educational research – are directly related to the purposes education is designed to serve. This link between activity and purpose is critical, and it is exactly this link that traditional research on teaching ignores, or perhaps more accurately, that traditional research on teaching attempts to break so that educational phenomena can be studied independent of underlying human purposes [. . .]

Teaching: is There Really a One-best-way?

I have implicitly argued that it is not wise to view teaching as a purely technical activity. That is, teaching has a normative as well as a technical dimension, and inquiry into teaching must attend simultaneously to both of these dimensions. I shall now argue that inquiry into the technical aspect of teaching should not be restricted to the conventional social and behavioral science disciplines because such discipline-based inquiry is grounded on the false assumption that there is a one-best-way to resolve any particular teaching problem. Stated differently, the concept of teaching effectiveness employed by behavioral science researchers is a meaningful concept only if some teaching behaviors or models are consistently more potent than others, either in general or, more likely, in specific situations.

The search for such a hypothesized one-best-way of teaching is the driving force behind teacher effectiveness research. As an introduction to evaluating the reasonableness of this assumption, some exploration of the meaning of the one-best-way assumption is useful. This exploration is done in terms of the aptitude-treatment interaction perspective, though the overall argument applies by analogy to such other approaches as direct instruction, effective teaching behaviors, and so forth.

Applied to the aptitude-treatment interaction orientation, the one-best-way assumption posits that for any particular student in a specified learning situation there is a teaching approach that will maximize his learning. [. . .]

So pervasive is the belief in the existence of best answers to instructional problems that thoughtful researchers often view this belief as self-evidently true: 'It is *inconceivable* [emphasis added] to us,' note Cronbach and Snow, 'that humans, differing in as many ways as they do, do not differ with respect to the educational treatment that fits each one best' (1969, p. 193). This passionate language should neither obscure the weak empirical basis for the one-best-way assumption nor obscure the logical gaps in the reasoning of those who assert that looking for the one-best-way is a reasonable search.

The lack of empirical support – that is, the failure to date of teacher effectiveness research, including ATI – has already been explored, but I want to go further and challenge the logic of those who believe that the search for the one-best-way is a reasonable endeavor. From the perfectly sound premise that students tend to react differently to different kinds of teaching, they move to the conclusion that for each student there is a one-best-teaching-solution to each learning problem. Is it not possible, as Jackson has suggested, to reach a different conclusion:

> Suppose that we begin by imagining two ways of teaching . . . that work equally well in the case of a particular student. . . . Must there always be a discriminable difference in the quality of outcome between alternative methods? . . . Surely skinning cats is not the only activity for which there is more than one equally effective strategy. And once we have conceded that there may be two methods of equivalent 'goodness' why not three, or ten, or seventy-eight, or four thousand and six? That isn't so hard to imagine, is it? (1970, p. 19)

No, it is not difficult to imagine multiple solutions that are of equivalent effectiveness in solving a particular teaching problem. The reason we in education are so fixated on searching for the one-best-solution is partly linguistic, for example, Cronbach and Snow use the word *fit*, which implies degrees of precision. In addition, many researchers are inclined to believe that teaching is directly tied to learning, an overly simplified notion of causality that imples there is a one-best-way of teaching for each type of learning. And we have considerable faith in the power of science to discover fundamental regularities (Popper, 1979), regularities which in our field surely demarcate better, if not best, solutions to teaching problems. In short, many educators are oriented toward searching for the one-best-way not because there is any compelling reason for this search but because of the influence of language and the impact of certain belief systems on our view of the teaching-learning process.

Some may argue, however, that even though 'there is not [now] *necessarily* a best way of proceeding in the individual case surely the *possibility* of there being such a condition is sufficient to justify our continued search for it' (Jackson, 1970, p. 21). This argument does seem plausible, particularly since many scientific discoveries would never have occurred if scientists had failed to pursue possible but not compelling alternatives. However, there is reason to believe that even if a one-best-way were knowable, it would be knowable only after the fact, that is, after one had completed the act of teaching. The critical variables of the teaching-learning process – teaching objectives, subject matter, student aptitudes, and so forth – often are not capable of being specified prior to the teaching act. The teacher may change objectives from month to month or from week to week; unforeseen events – a hot day or one student's open cruelty toward another – may necessitate revising plans; the demands people place on the schools can change from year to year, from community to community; a student's self-confidence may grow or his [or her] regard for his teacher may drop; a district may adopt a new math curriculum or may eliminate the arts in favor of more emphasis on the 'basics'. All of these variables ebb and flow so that the teacher cannot necessarily construct his battle plan in 1984 for 1985, in September for May, on Monday for Friday, or during second hour for third hour. Neither, of course, can we necessarily predict the specific character of mediating processes nor can we anticipate the ways in which these processes will affect the impact of teaching behavior.

Even ATI research, which purportedly is more sensitive to specific situations than are other forms of teacher effectiveness research, is a static approach based on the assumed permanence of objectives, student aptitudes, and teaching conditions. It is through this assumption of permanence that the researcher is able to conduct conventional social science research in education; the researcher needs durable phenomena in order to construct a scientific regularity – that is, before-the-teaching-act knowledge – that becomes needs durable phenomena in order to construct a scientific regularity.

Acknowledging that teaching phenomena do vary over time has at long last forced some educational researchers to postulate that the effective teachers are those teachers whose behavior is 'inherently unstable'. 'Such teachers,' notes

Berliner, 'are expected to change methods, techniques, and styles to suit particular students, curriculum areas, time of day or year, etc.' (1976, p. 374). Hunt believes that 'teachers' adaptation to students is the heart of the teaching-learning process' and that successful adaptation involves 'reading' the student's misunderstanding and 'flexing' or adjusting teacher communication in accordance with what was read (1976, p. 268). In a sense Berliner and Hunt, as well as some other contemporary educational researchers (see, for example, Brophy, 1980, pp. 13, 23–4) have rediscovered the ancient maxim that the effective teacher is flexible, that is, adapts his behavior to the teaching situation.

The plasticity inherent in this flexibility, plus the changeableness of the teaching situation and the unpredictability of mediating processes, suggest that the before-the-act teaching knowledge desired by teacher effectiveness researchers is not likely to be developed. The dynamic nature of teacher adaptability, mediating processes, and the teaching situation itself means that we can recognize teaching effectiveness, if at all, only after the fact. The attempt to find before-the-act teaching knowledge on the best procedures for enhancing learning is also of dubious value because there are neither compelling logical reasons nor empirical evidence for believing that a one-best-solution exists for each teaching problem or even for believing that some solutions are consistently better than others. (For a counterargument on the last point, see Gage, 1980.)

Conclusion

Once teaching phenomena are recognized as being man-made and teaching problems are viewed as having multiple potential solutions whose effectiveness is largely unknown prior to the act of teaching, then the potential of teaching effectiveness knowledge is dramatically reduced. The man-made character of educational phenomena means that any regularities identified through the study of the teaching-learning process are limited in generality and likely to shift over time. Even the search for a regularity of limited generality is likely to be unsuccessful because the typical teaching problem may well have multiple appropriate solutions and because teacher-student influence is both bidirectional and mediated by a variety of factors. Lastly, teaching effectiveness knowledge – should we ever find any – will be inherently trivial, since it is generated by applying a purely technical perspective to phenomena intimately connected to underlying human purposes.

The effective teacher, therefore, is not necessarily the one who has been programmed with research-based prescriptions for various teaching problems. Instead the effective teacher may be the one who is able to conceive of his [or her] teaching in purposeful terms, analyse a particular teaching problem, choose a teaching approach that seems appropriate to the problem, attempt the approach, judge the results in relation to the original purpose, and reconsider either the teaching approach or the original purpose. This and similar conceptions of teacher effectiveness are strongly normative and situational, a feature well captured by Dewey's analysis of the essence of practical activity: 'Judgment and belief regarding actions to be performed can never attain more than a precarious probability. . . . Practical activity deals with individualized and unique situations which are never exactly duplicable and about which, acordingly, no complete assurance is possible' (1929a, p. 6).

Yet it is exactly a striving for certainty that propels those who want to develop general laws of learning and other types of knowledge concerning teaching effectiveness. Researchers on teaching have fixated on certainty, even though teaching-learning phenomena are not capable of being predicted with any degree of assurance. Fortunately, even if teacher effectiveness researchers do not discover significant and enduring regularities, their work may be of use to practitioners. Instead of being a source of rules for guiding practice, research results might serve either as evidence for testing the beliefs of practitioners or as schemata for helping practitioners see classroom events in new ways (Fenstermacher, 1982). A few teacher effectiveness researchers seem interested in having teachers use research findings for evidential purposes (for example, Berliner, 1982; Good and Power, 1976), but few teacher effectiveness researchers envision their work as a source of schemata – one reason, perhaps, why teacher effectiveness inquiry is so conceptually barren.

In focusing on why certainty – or even substantial generalizations – cannot be achieved through the teacher effectiveness model, I have largely ignored an important weakness of this approach. Defining teaching success in terms of raising achievement test scores leads researchers to equate learning with the relatively simplistic content commonly included in these tests. While I believe this overly narrow conception of subject matter to be a disastrous error, I wanted to emphasize the empirical shortcomings of the teacher effectiveness model to illustrate that this model *fails in its own terms*. Research on effective teaching does not enlighten us about the technical secrets of teaching, let alone about which subject matter is worthy of being taught.

References

ANDERSON, R. C. (1970) 'Control of student mediating processes during verbal learning and instruction', *Review of Educational Research*, **40**: 349–69.

BANTOCK, G. H. (1961) 'Educational research: A criticism', *Harvard Educational Review*, **31**: 264–80.

BERLINER, D. C. (1976) 'A status report on the study of teacher effectiveness', *Journal of Research in Science Teaching*, **13**: 369–82.

——— (1980) 'Studying instruction in the elementary classroom', in *The Analysis of Educational Productivity*, ed. R. Dreeban and J. A. Thomas, vol. 1. Cambridge, MA: Ballinger.

BLOOM, B. S. (1971) 'Mastery learning and its implications for curriculum development', In *Confronting Curriculum Reform*, ed. E. W. Eisner. Boston: Little, Brown.

BOSSERT, S. T. (1981) 'Understanding sex differences in children's classroom experiences', *Elementary School Journal*, **81**: 255–66.

BROPHY, J. E. (1979) 'Teacher behavior and its effects', *Journal of Educational Psychology*, **71**: 733–50.

——— (1980) *Recent Research on Teaching* (Occasional Paper No. 40). East Lansing, MI: Institute for Research on Teaching, College of Education, Michigan State University. ED 204 280.

CRONBACH, L. J. (1975) 'Beyond the two disciplines of scientific psychology.' *American Psychologist* **30**: 116–27.

CRONBACH, L. J. and R. E. SNOW (1969) *Individual Differences in Learning Ability as a Function of Instructional Variables*. Stanford, CA: School of Education, Stanford University. ED 029 001.

——— (1977) *Aptitudes and Instructional Methods*. New York: Irvington.

DEWEY J. (1929) *The Quest for Certainty: A Study of the Relation of Knowledge and Action*. New York: Minton, Balch.

DOMINO, G. (1971) 'Interactive effects of achievement orientation and teaching style on academic achievement', *Journal of Educational Psychology* **62**: 427–31.

DOYLE, W. (1977) 'Paradigms for research on teacher effectiveness', in *Review of Research in Education*, ed. L. S. Shulman, vol. 5. Itaska, IL: F. E. Peacock.

DUNKIN, M. J. AND B. J. BIDDLE (1974) *The Study of Teaching*. New York: Holt, Rinehart & Winston.

EBEL, R. L. (1967) 'Some limitations of basic research in education', *Phi Delta Kappan*, **49**: 81–4.

——— (1982) 'The future of educational research', *Educational Researcher* **11**: 18–19.

FENSTERMACHER, G. D. (1982) 'On learning to teach effectively from research on teacher effectiveness', *Journal of Classroom Interaction*, **17**: 7–12. (Reprinted from *Time to Learn*, ed. C. Denham and A. Lieberman, chap. 6.)

FIEDLER, M. L. (1975) 'Bidirectionality of influence in classroom interaction', *Journal of Educational Psychology*, **67**: 735–44.

GAGE, N. L. (1974) 'Evaluating ways to help teachers to behave desirably', in *Competency Assessment, Research, and Evaluation*, ed. W. R. Houston. Multi-State Consortium on Performance-Based Teacher Education.

——— (1978) *The Scientific Basis of the Art of Teaching*. New York: Teachers College Press.

——— (1980) 'New prospects for educational research', *Australian Educational Researcher*, **7**: 7–25.

GAGE, N. L. and R. GIACONIA (1981) 'Teaching practices and student achievement: Causal connections', *New York University Education quarterly*, **12**: 2–9.

GAGNÉ, R. M. and L. J. BRIGGS (1974) *Principles of Instructional Design*. New York: Holt, Rinehart & Winston.

GLASS, G. V. (1972) 'The wisdom of scientific inquiry on education', *Journal of Research in Science Teaching*, **9**: 3–18.

GLICK, O. (1968) 'The educational process in the classroom', *School Review*, **76**: 339–51.

GOOD, T. L. (1979) 'Teacher effectiveness in the elementary school', *Journal of Teacher Education*, **30**: 52–64.

GOOD, T. L. and C. N. POWER (1976) 'Designing successful classroom environments for different types of students', *Journal of Curriculum Studies* **8**: 45–60.

GOWIN, D. B. (1970) 'The structure of knowledge', *Educational Theory*, **20**: 319–28.

GRAY, F., P. S. GRAUBARD and H. ROSENBERG (1974) 'Little brother is changing you', *Psychology Today*, **7**: 42–6.

HALLER, E. J. (1967) 'Pupil influence in teacher socialization: A socio-linguistic study', *Sociology of Education*, **40**: 316–33.

HAWKINS, D. (1973) 'What it means to teach', *Teachers College Record*, **75**: 7–16.

HEATH, R. W. and M. A. NIELSON (1974) 'The research basis for performance-based teacher education', *Review of Educational Research*, **44**: 463–84.

HUNT, D. E. (1976) 'Teachers' adaptation: "Reading" and "flexing" to students', *Journal of Teacher Education*, **27**: 268–75.

JACKSON, P. W. (1970) 'Is there a best way of teaching Harold Bateman?', *Midway*, **10**: 15–28.

KERLINGER, F. N. (1968) 'The doctoral training of research specialists', *Teachers College Record*, **69**: 477–83.

KLEIN, S. S. (1971) 'Student influence on teacher behavior', *American Educational Research Journal*, **8**: 403–21.

KLIEBARD, H. M. (1977) 'Curriculum theory: Give me a "for instance"', *Curriculum Inquiry*, **6**: 257–69.

MEDLEY, D. M. (1973) 'Closing the gap between research in teacher effectiveness and the teacher education curriculum', *Journal of Research and Development in Education*, **7**: 39–46.

NOBLE, C. G. and J. D. NOLAN (1976) 'Effect of student verbal behavior on classroom teacher behavior', *Journal of Educational Psychology*, **68**: 342–6.

PETERSON, P. L. (1979) 'Direct instruction reconsidered", in *Research on Teaching*, ed. P. L. Peterson and H. L. Walberg. Berkeley, CA: McCutchan.

POPPER, K. (1979) 'Creative self-criticism in science and in art', *Encounter*, **53**: 10–14.

RESNICK, L. B. and W. W. FORD (1981) *The Psychology of Mathematics for Instruction.* Hillsdale, NJ: Lawrence Erlbaum.

ROSENSHINE, B. (1979) 'Content, time and direct instruction', in *Research on Teaching*, ed. P. L. Peterson and H. J. Walberg. Berkeley, CA: McCutchan.

ROSENSHINE, B. and N. FURST (1971) 'Research in teacher performance criteria', in *Research in Teacher Education: A Symposium*, ed. B. O. Smith. Englewood Cliffs, NJ: Prentice-Hall.

SHERMAN, T. M. and W. H. CORMIER (1974) 'An investigation of the influence of student behavior on teacher behavior', *Journal of Applied Behavior Analysis*, **7**: 11–21.

SHULMAN, L. S. (1974) 'The psychology of school subjects: A premature obituary', *Journal of Research in Science Teaching*, **11**: 319–39.

SNOW, R. E. (1977) 'Individual differences and instructional theory', *Educational Researcher*, **6**: 11–15.

——— (1980) 'Aptitude, learner control, and adaptive instruction', *Educational Psychologist*, **15**: 151–8.

SOAR, R. S. (1968) 'Optimum teacher-pupil interaction for pupil growth', *Educational Leadership/Research Supplement*, **2**: 275–80.

SOAR, R. S. and R. M. SOAR (1976) 'An attempt to identify measures of teacher effectiveness from four studies', *Journal of Teacher Education*, **27**: 261–7.

TOBIAS, S. (1981) 'Adapting instruction to individual differences among students', *Educational Psychologist*, **16**: 111–20.

——— (1982) 'When do instructional methods make a difference?', *Educational Researcher*, **11**: 4–9.

WEISSKOPF, V. F. (1979) 'Art and science', *American Scholar*, **48**: 473–85.

4

Initial Fronts

Linda Measor and Peter Woods

The initial encounters' phase was marked by teachers and pupils presenting distinctive 'fronts' (Goffman, 1959) towards each other. The teachers carried on the themes of the induction scheme, with its emphasis on discipline, caring, and interest and excitement, while pupils, by and large, conformed to the stereotype of the 'good pupil'. After a short while, however, these fronts began to disintegrate. This phase, therefore, contains two sub-phases: (a) a 'honeymoon' period in which teachers and pupils presented their best 'fronts' towards each other, and (b) 'coming out', in which the seamless fronts began to disintegrate and truer identities emerged. We shall examine each in turn.

The 'Honeymoon' Period

[. . .]

At first, pupils conformed exactly to the formal demands of the school, and tried to show themselves good pupils. The most noticeable thing about the pupils' first week in secondary school was the absolute quiet that prevailed in their lessons, a silence that was quite unnatural to anyone who was familiar with British secondary schools. There was 'no talking' in the lessons, and pupils got on with their work. In maths, when the teacher turned his back on the class to write on the blackboard, pupils did not use the opportunity to talk. When asked to do some work on their own, pupils quietly got their books out and started working immediately, without chatting or asking each other questions. When another teacher entered the room, and distracted their own teacher's attention, pupils carried on working in total silence.

Pupils demonstrated a great commitment to their work. They were rigidly attentive to any instructions or information given to them by a teacher. They rushed to complete their work, displayed a keen competitiveness, and a great interest in doing well. The appearance and presentation of their work also received careful attention. Pupils wrote out titles in blue ink and underlined them in red. They remembered to put in the date. Diagrams were done in pencil, with the labelling in ink. They even wrote neatly in their rough books. Pupils covered their books, or bought plastic folders to keep them in, and generally took care of them.

One of the characteristics of this phase was referred to by more than one teacher as 'the forest of hands' syndrome. Despite pupils' reluctance to ask for help, they were anxious to show their keenness to answer the teacher's questions. When a teacher asked a question, there were numerous pupils almost desperately keen to answer it. Interest and attentiveness to work were simultaneously signalled. Pupils who got the right answer, and a complimentary remark from a teacher, looked pleased and happy. One boy who got an answer right demanded that the boy next to him congratulate him.

All the pupils completed the homework they were set in the first week at school. One teacher did not set homework in a firm way, but requested pupils to do some extra work if they had time. All had finished it by the next day. Pupils even asked if they could take work home with them to spend extra time on it. Sally wanted to do extra work on her design project in her own time. There was a willingness to conform, even when not to conform would not have shown up during the early days. When the maths teacher went out of the room to fetch materials, pupils did not talk. The class had one English lesson in the library. Andy finished his book five minutes before the end of the lesson, and informed the teacher and asked him what to do next. It would have been easy for Andy to do nothing for the remaining time.

Pupils literally rushed to do what they were asked. In science their teacher, who was the headmaster, pointed out the dangers of leaving bags and coats at the sides of work benches. Someone could trip, and if they were carrying acid or a burning taper, the results could be damaging. Before he had finished his sentence, all of the pupils rushed to remove their possessions and place them carefully under the tables and out of the way.

Pupils demonstrated also their deep anxiety about getting anything at all wrong, in a number of other ways which teachers grouped as 'fussing'. Whenever a teacher gave an instruction, a pupil, or several pupils, demanded clarification of its exact details, and were entirely unwilling to take any initiative on their own. Caroline asked her teacher if she were allowed to cover her maths book, to keep it clean and tidy. In a lesson where the work was based on independent learning through worksheets, numerous pupils asked if they were allowed to turn the page and go on to the next page, before they did so. Pupils wanted to know exactly which book they were expected to do which work in, and which side of the page they were supposed to write on, and what titles had to be underlined, and how much space had to be left between work and the next piece of work. This behaviour was markedly different from that which had characterized pupils at middle school, where they had a confident approach, knowing the location of equipment, and the rules and procedures for presenting and ordering their work; it possibly reflects the demise of their co-operative work links, which could be relied upon to provide extra information on teacher instructions.

The 'front' was symbolized by pupils' appearance. It was very noticeable that all boys had just had their hair cut in 'regulation' style. There was not a 'skinhead' among them. Both boys and girls wore neat new uniforms and clean white shirts, and knotted their ties properly. The appearance of their equipment matched their uniforms, with their names on nearly every item. Aprons, books and bags were clean and without the graffiti of youth culture. They carried neat pencil cases, used simple pens and pencils and erasers. The pupil 'front', like the institutional front, was seamless at this point, every element and aspect of it fitting accurately into the image of circumspect pupilhood.

However, both teachers and pupils recognized the phase to be temporary. They knew it was 'a front'. Sally said, 'I think all the [first year] boys and girls are trying to be as good as they can. When they get older, they will answer the teachers back, but now they are as good as gold, pets'. In the same group interview, her friend Amy agreed, 'They want to get a good name from the teachers', and Rebecca chimed in with 'Reputation!' Mark looked back on that stage and recognized the process: 'All the people that were in our class when we first got here were totally different . . . everybody was nervous, so they were different, quiet'.

Mr Ship, an English teacher, identified the first year pupils: 'Temporary personae they have for a couple of days'. Some teachers felt that the length of this particular phase had got less over the years. Mr Ship said, 'Five or six years ago, they were all good and quiet until at least half term, you could rely on it'. Mr Jones agreed that things had changed; now he maintained, 'After a week, they're all behaving as if they owned the place'. This may have something to do with the age of transfer. In the days when the 'honeymoon' period had lasted longer at Old Town, pupils transferred at eleven plus. Ball (1980) observed a similar duration for this phase in his 'eleven plus' school.

Whatever the duration, neither school nor pupils can keep up this front for any length of time, and after about a week, things began to change. The main reason for this was that the pupils' nervousness, was fading. Phillip reported, 'The first day, you know, I wasn't really looking forward to it, but the first day was better than I expected it to be, and it's gone down, the excitement has, but it's just as good as I thought it would be. Pretty good, Yes'. Jenny agreed, 'I was nervous at first, but I think it's better than I thought it would be'. The successful completion of the first week seemed to reassure many of the pupils, and they found the second week somewhat easier.

'Coming Out'

Once this nervous, apprehensive reaction to school had abated, personal concerns became important again. The teachers could not possibly keep up 'the front' either, their own personal differences soon pushing through in places. As the front crumbled, 'real' identities emerged. The main issue was the discipline 'front'. Pupils began to probe for 'living space' for themselves, testing around the edges of the sharply drawn rules, to negotiate the ground rules that actually operated (see also Strauss *et al.*, 1964; Delamont, 1976; Martin, 1976; Woods, 1978; Ball, 1980; Beynon, 1984). Such probing ensured the initial blanket conformity broke down still further as distinctions were discovered. Pupils soon began to discover priorities – important and comparatively unimportant parts of the school day, what they were actually allowed or not allowed to do in lessons, high and low status subject areas of the curriculum, important and less important teachers, and what adjustments to school uniform they could get away with.

Important distinctions among pupils values also began to appear as they reclaimed latent identities, as 'bright' or 'thick', 'good or bad' at a particular subject. Orientations toward school were reaffirmed, as pupils showed themselves conformist or deviant, 'teacher's pet' or 'menace'. Gender identifications were also highly important at this stage of adolescent development, and school was an arena against which they could be highlighted and played out. This phase confirms that pupil adaptations are an active construction on their part, not simply a response to teacher directives. In the rest of this section, we shall document this initial exploratory negotiation.

Appearance

It was the area of appearance, the symbolic manifestations of 'front' that was to change most rapidly; perhaps because first year pupils had older pupils as models. Their appearance made it clear that school uniform could be negotiated; it was more public than what went on in their lessons. The appearance 'front' hardly lasted the first week at school. It was the boys who first began to deviate, particularly those who later in the year were to form an 'oppositional culture' group. Roy and Pete inscribed 'PUNK' on their craft aprons. From such beginnings, deviant strategies grew. By 21 September, Roy was wearing a safety pin in the V-neck of his school jersey, and had a paper clip on the edge of his shirt collar. Pete's group marked the entire surfaces of their personal equipment – aprons, bags and pencil cases – with myriad slogans in rainbow colours. By 26 September, Pete's school books proclaimed uncompromisingly his allegiance to the Sex Pistols, Sid Vicious and Leeds United. Thus the emblems of punk rock began to intrude into the image of circumspection, but only for one group of boys. This group also carried on a consolidated attack against their ties. Keith had his hanging loosely around his neck one day, and he got severely 'told off' in consequence by a senior teacher. 'Why should you go around looking like a rat bag? Dress yourself properly.' Keith's official reaction to this was, 'oh he just tries to scare you. He goes round shouting, just trying to scare people. He don't scare me.' However, Keith did ask his form mistress for help in knotting the offending tie, and asked her anxiously for a mirror to check his appearance. He was making only an exploratory foray into this area of deviance. The rest of the class engaged only partly in this activity. Most boys ceased to wear their ties neatly, and by the fourth week many were wearing them loosely around their necks in their own peculiar styles. Many inscribed the names of football clubs on their own personal equipment, but not on school equipment such as books.

Clearly, pupils were beginning to test for the *real* rules that governed appearance and the uniform of the school.

By the third week the girls had joined in the campaign, following the boys' initial explorations. The girls had less stringent uniform demands than the boys. They did not have to wear ties, were allowed to wear jewellery and nail varnish and any kind of shoes they chose. One group of girls intruded the emblems and interests of youth culture on to the formal equipment of the school. They wrote the names of rock groups on pencil cases. Amy said in a craft class to her friends, 'Everyone writes on my pencil case'. Gradually graffiti spread over their aprons, bags and especially their 'rough books', although it took about another month before all spaces were appropriated. This group of girls wrote the names of popular punk groups on their equipment, but the real significance was attached to the writing of the names of boys in the peer group on books and pencil cases. Such elements from the informal culture split the smooth surface of pupil conformity within a very short time of their joining the school.

Spaces

The institutional framework was also tested out during this period. Pupils quickly found the comparatively 'unimportant' interstices of the school day. For example, the first deviant actions were noted not in a lesson but in registration. Pete answered his name in a silly voice, causing moderate laughter among his colleagues. The boys, generally, began to 'mess around'. Keith said of his form teacher and registration:

> Mrs Conway . . . sometimes we . . . like answer her names to the register funny, sometimes she will laugh too, and other times she will stop the register . . . stand up . . . sit down . . . all this . . . say it properly. It is what we should expect really, because we shouldn't really. But seeing as it is only registration, I don't think it matters. . . . It's not really interesting. If we are doing a lot of interesting things . . . when you're a kid you want to learn, you don't want to sit there answering names and listening to other people.

The curriculum

Pupils' own interests were soon brought to bear on the curriculum itself. As the 'front' crumbled, deviance appeared, but it did not occur evenly through-out all lessons. Some subject areas – notably art and music – attracted deviant strategies earlier than others. For example, on his way to the music lesson, Pete removed his tie and hid it under his jumper. The pupils whispered and giggled as they entered the room, 'messed about' with pens and rulers, and fooled around while the register was called. Keith made a chair 'walk' around the table. When Mrs Skye asked the class what they wanted to do in music, there was a loud and predominantly male chorus of 'nothing'. Pupils talked when they were asked to work. They also chatted while they worked, and when another teacher entered the room there was a loud buzz of talk. At one point, Claire and Valerie began to comb their hair. However, this teacher gave as good as she got and retained control. For example, Keith was being especially noisy and could be heard above the others. Mrs Skye interrupted, and singled him out: 'Look, Sunshine, you had better watch your step in here.' It showed the effect of a particular teacher on events. Mrs Skye was an experienced older teacher. Miss Wright, the other music teacher, was a probationer and, throughout the year, she had extreme problems of control.

Music seemed to have low priority among pupils. Pete said openly 'I don't think music's necessary, it's a waste of time, you're not learning anything from that, nothing at all.' The opposition probably derives from the distinction Vulliamy (1979) has elaborated between 'our music' and 'their music', where adolescent subcultures take musical style as a cardinal point in their definition of an oppositional stance to adult culture. As Roy said, 'We should do things that we want, like punk rock or something.' Furthermore, the pupils identified school music as involved with the world of childhood. It offended against their new sense of adult or adolescent identity. Keith said, 'We're only doing triangles, we were using triangles at first school, we should be getting on to trombones and things.'

The pupils demoted school music in accordance with certain of their own concerns, and therefore their own informal concerns surfaced in it. For some, it tempted deviant activities. Pete, Roy and Keith discovered space for messing around and challenging the teacher and cementing their identities as 'ace deviants'. For others, it offered the space for following up friendship-building activities and the opportunity to get to know other pupils. This was aided by the physical arrangement of the classroom. Pupils were grouped around tables, and this offered more opportunity for informal talking than formal deskbound subjects (Stebbins, 1975; Denscombe, 1980b). The pupils made use of the opportunities. At first their talk was about work matters, then it progressed to more general but important items like 'them dragon flies in the showers' (Uggh!). Finally it moved to the outside school topics of family, pets and TV.

Art and design subjects were also marked down in the same way, and again informal concerns operated more openly. Pupils in Pete's group continued to make exploratory forays to find the discipline limits, consolidating their identities as deviants in the process. Pete forgot his pencil, Keith his art book. Pete, Roy and Keith talked and laughed quite loudly, ignored cues to 'put pencils down' and had to be publicly reprimanded. The rest of the class remained quietly attentive. Pupils were then asked specifically to work individually on a project, without discussion. Pete, Keith and Roy, however, discussed the project loudly and also talked about events they could see out of the windows. Other pupils followed into the territory that Pete, Roy and Keith had opened up. Boys like Phillip and Stewart had shown themselves to have an eager conformist orientation in other subjects. But in art they engaged in 'out of line' activities. Phillip stopped working and started making grimaces at his drawing, and discussed a better way of doing the drawing with Stewart.

Carol and Pat discussed their work together, but both the girls' and Phillip's activity was quiet, and not characterized by the noise and laughter that accompanied Pete and his group.

The front of pupil conformity was also broken by gender differences, especially in the science area of the curriculum. Girls reacted to the physical sciences, boys to the domestic ones. Needlework lessons were a major arena for boys' deviance, their strategies rapidly becoming more and more adventurous. They gave silly answers, they drove wedges of illegitimate activity or talk into lesson turning points, and overplayed the pupil role (Willis, 1977). The teacher managed to retain control with a mixture of firm rebuke, individual treatment (talking to some misbehaving boys quietly about their behaviour) and good humour. Miscreants were labelled 'Menace 1' and 'Menace 2', which made the boys in question smile. Such humorous titles were not altogether uncomplimentary to pupils' desired identities, especially in this curriculum area. However, despite the teacher's competence, the boys never took the domestic sciences seriously. This suggests that perceived value of the subject is basic to pupils' attitudes within lessons.

The girls were much less enthusiastic about the physical sciences than the boys, and these lessons saw their informal concerns surface (for a full analysis, see Measor, 1983). Girls' deviant strategies began to show up in these lessons towards the end of the first month. One group of girls, led by Amy, made their opposition clear. They had been told very firmly, by their science teacher, who happened to be the headmaster, that they must wear glasses. Amy's group made an enormous fuss about wearing the glasses, and introduced silly jokes about them. Amy stated that they didn't suit her, she would look awful in them, she refused absolutely to wear them. Amy, Rosemary and Sally spent a full five minutes 'messing around' with the safety goggles. They tried them on, rapidly pulled them off again, and rearranged their hair, very carefully. These actions were highly significant. The girls were disobeying a strong instruction given to them by their headmaster; in addition, they were putting their eyes at risk from spluttering chemicals. Their behaviour here was very different from the conformity they displayed in other lessons at this point in the year, in this 'initial encounters' phase.

The girls' deviance did not involve a noisy challenge to the order of the classroom. It went unnoticed, therefore, and consequently their work in science fell behind that of the boys, which was not the case in other subjects. After several minutes of 'messing around' the girls turned their attention back to their work, and to the experiments they were supposed to be doing. They argued for a while about them: 'I'm not going first, I don't fancy going first, which one are we making first?' By this time, Phillip and Roland had finished their experiment, most of the class were well into it, but this group of girls had not begun, and they did not finish all the work by the end of the lesson. Personal identity concerns were beginning to surface as the front crumbled.

Among the highly valued subjects were English and maths, mainly because pupils saw them as having vocational relevance. 'You need them for a job, don't you?' was a standard response. It did not mean that informal concerns disappeared entirely, but in these areas pupils' investigation was for the amount of co-operative activity permissible, not for oppositional limits. Pupils remained quiet and fully attentive to their teacher, but after they began working alone, co-operative activity began. Phillip pointed out to Stewart the question he was supposed to be doing. Janet asked the girl next to her, what she was supposed to do next. Normally the questions concerned instructions about work, and represented extremely short bursts of interaction. However, in the case of Carol and Pat, who had been 'best friends' at middle school, there was considerable co-operation also on the answers to the questions. As a result, they infringed the limits of co-operative activity set by this teacher. Carol and Pat argued about how to do a particular question, and their voices rose above the rest of the class. Mr Jones looked up and said loudly 'How's my little chatterbox getting on . . .' he paused while the girls, quietened, blushed and began to work. 'You've got a name to live down now, haven't you?' Carol worked in absolute silence for the remainder of the lesson. She had invoked the tactic that girls fear most – public embarrassment (Woods, 1979).

There were genuine difficulties for pupils, because different teachers had different limits and different styles. Such testing-out, therefore, was essential. The contrast between English and maths was interesting here. Mr Ship made great use of humour to match the particular relaxed atmosphere he cultivated. This presented pupils with more space, and they correspondingly had to push further to discover its limits and proper use. Pupils quickly found they could 'get away with' talking and co-operative activity as they worked, and each day the level of noise as they did so rose. In their second week at school, however, it earned them a rebuke. Mr Ship interrupted as the noise level grew: 'There shouldn't be any need for talking or for asking your neighbour anything'. The limit was set, but he sugared it with his usual humour, 'If you want anything, ask me, that's what I'm here for, that's what I get paid for, so keep me occupied, then I won't feel guilty about all that money I earn'. Thus the pupils found Mr Ship's hidden ground rules. They had in his own words 'realized that I'm not going to kick their teeth down their throats if there's a bit of noise, provided they're working.' From then on, there was always co-operative talk in English lessons.

Pupils had to test for these ground rules separately with each teacher. For example, in science there was much excitement when it came to the pupils' setting up and doing an experiment. The headmaster clearly enjoyed this, unlike the teachers in Denscombe's (1980a) schools, who felt that any kind of noise emanating from a classroom reflected on a teacher's efficiency. The headmaster observed that 'it was work noise after all.' By definition, there is a 'non-working noise', which the finely tuned ear of the experienced teacher could quickly detect, signalling the spilling over of productive co-operative activity into deviance. However, teachers did have different ideas about what was acceptable, and pupils had to negotiate to find out what these were. The teacher's 'front' broke down as a result.

Conformity

At the same time as some pupils were establishing their identities as 'ace deviants', others emerged as adopting an especially conformist line. This differed from the automaton-like conformity of the first two days, and it involved a personal commitment, rather than a strategic response to a situation. The later conformity was a key element in the personal identities of some pupils. Giles was one example. He would enter a class in silence and take out his books, lay out his neatly named pencil and equipment on the desk in front of him and sit waiting, looking attentive. Almost all the other pupils had to be reminded of the need to have their equipment ready.

The conformists attempted to obey teacher's instructions to the letter. Phillip listened with great attentiveness and followed instructions with care. In a science lesson, he was told that the hottest part of the bunsen burner flame was at the top of the dark blue section of the flame. Phillip moved his test tube to different parts of the flame, experimenting carefully and watching patiently to see where results were best. Phillip admitted that he cared about his work and the results he got. 'You know if you've made a good job of it, if it turns out right, you feel alright.' This concern with academic results and with the appearance of one's work is one of the defining characteristics of the conformist pupil.

Sometimes, during the 'coming out' phase, conformist pupils tried to sustain the initial front of conformity of the whole cohort, possibly feeling that the group reflected on their own reputation. Phillip, for example, tried not only to influence the actions of his own group of friends but also, on occasion, the behaviour of the whole class. He insisted that Eric should put on safety glasses before beginning the experiment, while other groups were reprimanded for forgetting to put theirs on. He chose his partners in group work very carefully to ensure a good group performance. Phillip also tried to change the whole class. One rule was that pupils had to stand, when they first entered a classroom, until told to sit by a teacher. In a maths lesson, the class entered and as the teacher was delayed outside, most of the class sat down. Phillip reminded other pupils that they were supposed to stand, which they did. On entering, the teacher smiled and complimented them on remembering his instructions, and asked them to sit down. Phillip thus ensured that the class presented the right image. His behaviour is more significant if his real views on this particular rule are taken into account:

> The teachers have been alright, some of them have been not so good, some of the things that you do, not in lessons, but you know . . . you have to stand up in the class, while they're getting ready. They spend hours, just picking up papers, and moving them from one place to another, and you're standing there like a dummy . . . I can't think why we have to stand up.

Ability

We have argued that one of the underlying issues for pupils undergoing the transfer is that of identity. Pupils move into a new, larger institution, where they are unknown and anonymous. Many seem to have felt the need to re-establish their identity, as conformist or as 'ace deviant' or as the best fighter, or whatever. The irony of the situation is that the pupils came from the middle school in a clearly labelled fashion, where very little room for doubt about pupil identities was, on the part of teachers, possible. This was true of the pupils' academic ability as well as their personal orientation to school. Many of the conformist pupils were anxious to show themselves as bright and academically able, as well as interested and attentive.

The first signals of 'brightness' they gave were through oral questioning, because it was some time before any graded work was returned to the pupils. Teachers spent some time in oral questions, because it helped them to gain a picture of the capabilities of their new pupils. This frequently involved teachers asking a set of graded questions on a subject. Both teachers and pupils noted the hierarchy of 'knowers' that this strategy revealed:

> Sally: And in humanities he [Phillip] can be really good, becuse we were doing . . . oh, all Romans and that, and Mr Jackson asked us what is a C, and he was the only one who knew what number it meant . . . and other questions he was very good at.

More subtle judgements are also involved. 'Brightness' is signalled by getting questions right. Getting them wrong in public can severely diminish status. 'Brightness' also involves making shrewd assessments about which questions *not* to answer. In maths, for example, Phillip never attempted to answer the very difficult questions. He allowed others to fall into that trap. There was also the issue of 'finishing first'. Phillip frequently put up his hand to ask 'What do we do, when we've finished?', or 'What do we do next?', which publicly informed pupils and teachers about his ability. Janet employed the same strategy, and competition between the two of them developed rapidly.

The first piece of graded work returned to the pupils created tremendous excitement. Normal discipline collapsed, as they called out to each other 'What did you get?' or 'How many?' Not until everyone in the class had a sense of how the others had done did they return to their normal reasonable quietness. After a few weeks, a sense of who was who was established for both pupils and teachers. Alan, Bridget and Anna were all established as 'really thick', a verdict that was underlined by the public fact that all did remedial reading. Those at the opposite end of the scale were also identified. Nevertheless there could be shocks, for it became clear that ability in subjects such as technical design or art also had to be taken into account, and skills other than 'academic' abilities counted in the school, as the headmaster had made clear of the induction scheme. An art teacher gave substantial praise to Keith's work, and Stewart looked up from his work sharply and stared in amazement, for such commendation from a teacher went counter to his view of Keith. He commented on the teacher's praise to Phillip. Thus, after about a month in school, a number of pupils had made clear, if introductory, statements about their identity. Teachers as well as other pupils registered these statements and signals, and read them to make a kind of map, whereby they knew their way around the class of people. We have also suggested that teachers revealed their identity during this period, and that pupils found out about their styles, their characteristics, and their demands.

By the end of their first month in the school, most pupils had lost much of their anxiety about the formal institution. They knew their timetables, the routines and procedures of the school, they knew their way around the school and had lost their worries about its size. Most pupils felt settled. Sally said, 'When I got to that open evening, all the school looked strange, now I think "why didn't I know where that is, because now I know where it is"'. Amy agreed, 'It seems not so big. First you think I am going to get lost all the time, but it seems ever so small now'. However, there was interesting evidence about the pupils' feeling of membership of their new school. Carol said, 'You can eat the dinners here, you can't eat the dinners at *our* school, horrible dinners, terrible, all slushy'. Carol still identified the middle school as *our* school. The upper school has its attractions, but as yet cannot claim her total allegiance or give her a sense of full membership.

Some pupils had more difficulties than others. Rosemary said, 'I am getting used to things, but I do prefer my other school.' Years of contact there had built up a credit balance in her account. 'Well, we had lots of good times there, because I have only started here, and I had all them years back there.' The new school still had to prove itself for her, and the 'front' may be important here. Rosemary was not yet prepared to trust what she had seen in her first contacts with the school, and she was reserving her emotional judgement. The importance of teachers in this was clear: 'The teachers there were nice ... I cried me eyes out, when we left.' Another girl, Janet, was in agreement: 'It's all right now', nevertheless, 'I still miss Manor Home [her middle school]. I do more things here, but I still prefer Manor Home.' We need to know more about why some pupils had more difficulties than others, and why some chose to retard their personal transitions in this way. The key factor for these two girls was probably the fact that neither had good peer group contacts in their class from middle school.

References

BALL, S. (1980) 'Initial encounters in the classroom and the process of establishment', in WOODS, P. (ed.) *Pupil Strategies*. London, Croom Helm.

BEYNON, J. (1984) '"Sussing-out" teachers: pupils as data gatherers', in HAMMERSLEY, M. and WOODS, P. (eds) *Life in School: the sociology of pupil culture*. Milton Keynes, Open University Press.

DELAMONT, S. (1976) *Interaction in the Classroom*. London, Methuen.

DENSCOMBE, M. (1980a) '"Keeping 'em quiet", the significance of noise for the practical activity of teaching', in WOODS, P. (ed.) *Teacher Strategies*. London, Croom Helm.

DENSCOMBE, M. (1980b) 'Pupil strategies and the open classroom', in WOODS, P. (ed.) *Pupil Strategies*. London, Croom Helm.

GOFFMAN, E. (1961) *Asylums*. Garden City, Doubleday; also in Harmondsworth, Penguin, 1968.

MARTIN, W. B. W. (1976) *The Negotiated Order of the School*. Toronto, Macmillan.

MEASOR, L. (1983) 'Gender and curriculum choice: a case study', in HAMMERSLEY, M. and HARGREAVES, A. (eds) *Curriculum Practice: some sociological case studies*. Lewes, The Falmer Press.

STEBBINS, R. (1970) 'The meaning of disorderly behaviour: teacher definitions of a classroom situation', *Sociology of Education*, **44**, pp. 217–36.

STRAUSS, A. *et al.* (1964) *Psychiatric Ideologies and Institutions*. London, Collier-Macmillan.

VULLIAMY, G. (1979) 'Culture clash and school music: a sociological analysis', in BARTON, L. and MEIGHAN, R. (eds) *Sociological Interpretations of Schooling and Classrooms*. Driffield, Nafferton Books.

WILLIS, P. (1977) *Learning to Labour*. Farnborough, Saxon House.

WOODS, P. (1978) 'Negotiating the demands of schoolwork', *Journal of Curriculum Studies*, **10** (4), pp. 309–27.

WOODS, P. (1979) *The Divided School*. London, Routledge and Kegan Paul.

5

Science: Group Based Curriculum

John Evans

Teacher Strategies in Group Based Curriculum

Science teachers in their classroom practice (like those in other subjects) focused upon problems of pupil control. Only one of the first year teachers observed in 'initial encounters'[1] with first year pupils did not operate the [Integrated Science][2] course as the policy document recommended. He was a teacher new to the school taking responsibility for a class whose identity as a 'difficult class' had (partly due to staffing inconsistencies) already been established. He noted that

> I can't give these kids the time they need. If I could get around them all it would be OK. But there's always the problem of control. It's always there. If you're around everywhere you can't . . . they've got to be able to focus on you as a teacher . . .

Group work was avoided and class teaching preferred because it structured and limited opportunities for the teacher to establish the kind of positional relationships thought conducive to effective control.[3] The remaining first year teachers, however, endeavoured to introduce the course to pupils in a manner which approximated the intentions of its author. The normal practice was for teachers during week one of a topic to spend part or all of a lesson introducing its content to the pupils and reminding them how the course was to be operated. Groups of pupils, generally allowed to form on the basis of peer friendships, used 'trays' of resources provided to complete the tasks outlined for them in the booklets. 'Booklets' usually took three weeks for a group to work through, during which time the teacher moved around the room from group to group. The main body of topic work thus involved the teacher interacting at an immediate face-to-face level with individual pupils or groups, interspersed with the issuing of public regulative messages.

As in individualized instruction, with the booklet mediating between the teacher and the pupil, the centrality of talk via the teacher of whole class method was restricted. Occasions when it was required occurred during opening introductory lessons or opening phases of other lessons and during the fifth weekly 'test' periods.

A teaching pattern of this nature was, however, a first year, early first term phenomenon, its incidence decreasing as the year progressed. In the second year, the picture was overwhelmingly that of class teaching while in the third year only just over half of the lessons observed were 'group' based.

Mrs Turner and the pupils of Form 1p (the first year case study group) fit this pattern. This process of transition from group based to class instruction was indeed complex and some indication of its dynamics can be discerned from the practices observed. In initial encounters with the pupils of Form 1p, instruction was group based. Pupils had formed themselves into six groups and for the main body of topic work, appeared to progress largely independently of the teacher, using booklets as the primary medium of instruction. There was, at least in early encounters, an absence of public instructional talk. The main body of the lesson proper involved the teacher interacting at an immediate level with groups or individuals interspersed with the issuing of public regulative messages.

While our data is not adequate to provide detailed analyses of the dynamics of small group interaction (cf. Barnes, 1977), it is highly suggestive of certain processes. A characteristic feature was the tendency within small groups for pupils to proceed at a pace defined by the more 'able' pupil. That is to say, the steering group phenomenon characteristic of whole class method was reproduced as an intra-small group phenomenon, but with an important difference. In whole class method the problem lies with the extremes of the ability range. The able pupil is held up while the less able goes unattended. In small group work, however, pacing of this kind does not necessarily signify exclusion from 'learning' for those pupils who fall below the steering group. Consider here the opinions of two pupils, Ryan and Caroline. Each was a low ability child as defined by teacher ratings;[4] both had reading ages (8 years 7 months) well below that required by the booklets to facilitate easy access to its substantive contents. Both portrayed 'interest' behaviours difficult for the teacher, although Ryan was considered the more difficult. Both expressed an emphatic preference for group work as the way of 'doing science'.

> I prefer working in groups 'cos then if you don't understand something you can get help from your friends (Ryan).

and

> I prefer working in groups because if you get stuck, like, if you don't know something, you can ask your friends (Caroline).

Ryan, previously identified as one of the counter-steering group in Maths, worked with Jerry and Rene (also of the counter-steering group) and Peter. The latter, who was more able than all three other pupils (as defined by teacher ratings and NFER tests), had a reading age (above 11) likely to make the mode of transmission more accessible to him than to each of the other pupils, with whom he shared a somewhat detached but definite friendship. Caroline and Odette worked together, neither considered 'able' by the teacher but rather, as in Mathematics, pupils 'typical' of Sageton [the school in which the research was conducted], 'normal' and 'average' in behaviour and ability. (See Table 5.1 for the overall organization of Form 1p Science work-groups.)

Table 5.1   *The work group organization of Form 1p pupils in Science*

Group 1		Group 2	
Mark	B–Br	Jenny	G–Br
Naren	B–As	Lynne	G–Br
Abdul	B–As	Heather	G–Br
Michael	B–WI/Br		
Group 3		Group 4	
John	B–Br	Mary	G–WI
Hugh	B–Eur	Liona	G–WI
Paul	B–Br	Maureen	G–WI
David	B–Br		
Group 5		Group 6	
Jerry	B–WI	Caroline	G–WI
Ryan	L–WI	Odette	G–WI
Rene	B–WI		
Peter	B–WI		

B, boy; G, girl; Br, British; As, Asian; WI, West Indian; Eur, European.

Pupils of group 1 (which corresponded to the fieldworkers' total worker group 1 in Maths) had a stable relationship and displayed all the attributes of 'total' work here as in languages and SMP. All, with the exception of Naren and Abdul whose opportunities to achieve 'able' pupil identity were limited by their absence from many Science lessons due to their need for 'special English', were rated as able and 'well behaved' pupils by the teacher. Jenny, Lynne and Heather were in group 2 and similarly defined, the last two thus achieving an identity comparable to that in Modern Languages. Ability and ethnicity also featured in the grouping of pupils in group 3, John, Hugh, Paul and David. As defined by the teacher's ratings, this was a mixed ability group. John and Hugh were more able pupils with John being the more problematic in terms of behaviour. Paul and David were average and sometimes 'difficult pupils when they got together with John and Hugh'. For pupils of the counter-steering group, located mainly in Science group 5 there was little alteration in their perceived ability or behaviour in the perspective of their

Science teacher. Each received well below average marks for behaviour and attainment in Autumn term ratings. Peter, a 'normal', 'average' pupil in Mrs Turner's perspective (as previously defined in Maths and Languages), retained friendship with the group while maintaining a degree of isolation from their more extreme 'interest' activity. Liona (of the counter-steering group) was similarly defined as very difficult and 'less able'. Though she worked with Mary and Maureen, there was a degree of isolation between these three group members. Both Mary and Maureen achieved successful pupil identities in the perspective of the teacher, though Mary's behaviours were a frequent cause for concern. Maureen thus achieved an identity similar to that in French but significantly better than she managed as a mathematician and considered Science to be a subject in which she 'learns best'. Caroline and Odette achieved identities as 'average pupils', as in Maths.

For those pupils such as Jerry, Ryan, Rene and Liona who lacked the prerequisites necessary to work in Science (ability to handle content and MOT [mode of transmission] independently in the time permitted), group work seemed to provide a limited solution, both to the problem of their progress and to the teacher's contingent managerial demands. As Mrs Turner noted,

Kids can help each other. They often explain difficulties to each other

Less than evident from our observations, however, are the kind of qualitative or co-operative interactions suggested by both teachers and pupils. More characteristic, perhaps, is Peter's retort to one of Ryan's comments:

Yeah ... you just copy off me ... [and] ... you always look at what I've done, you don't do it yourself ...

Nevertheless, we can see in group work what was a form of self-imposed individual piloting. This was a strategy by which pupils who otherwise found difficulty with attaining progress within the limits of time imposed by the scheme, could at least keep pace with the more able peers, but at a cost of understanding what it is they are supposed to be doing. Clearly this was a process which allowed pupils to give only the appearance[5] (and perhaps experience the feeling) of progress. Ultimately, as the process crystallized during test periods, it was an identity which such pupils were unlikely to sustain. Moreover, what was for some pupils an immediate way of coping, was (as we see in the statements above) for others (even close friends) a source of antagonism, frustration and friction. It seemed to infringe a pupils' code of conduct which valued learning as an independent, competitive and isolated experience.[6] Indeed, given the conception of pacing implied in the course (which allows the able to progress alone) and the absence of written material which encouraged co-operative endeavour, it would perhaps be more surprising if pupils expressed attitudes to the contrary.

As the term progressed, teachers (such as Mrs Turner) increasingly confronted problems of pupil control. In group based instruction as in the 'open' classrooms to which Denscombe (1980b, p. 67) refers, the boundaries between proper work and having a chat 'are blurred in a way which could be exploited in the negotiation of work'. Denscombe explains this tendency amongst pupils with reference to a disjuncture between the aspirations of open classroom teachers and the legacy of closed classroom instruction that children bring with them to the open classroom. What he fails to draw attention to, however, is the material (instructional/curricular) base which may underly and interact with a pupil's sociocultural choice not to work. An increase in pupil interaction and opportunity for 'interest' activity cannot help but evoke higher levels of noise and movement than in classes where the teacher is the only person who may legitimately talk. Within the broader framework of senior teacher expectations, increasing noise and movement was particularly problematic. It could, after all, be misrecognized as a lack of control and invite hostility from those who regard it as a threat to the authority of the teacher (cf. Kohl, 1970). The teachers concerned (as in Mathematics) tended to explain their problems of control in terms of pupil ill-preparedness for work with the Science scheme.

> They're very silly and childish . . . waste time . . . they should be more serious (Mrs Turner).

> They started with a serious attitude but now they waste time chatting. S. should take herself more in hand and apply herself (Mrs Cooper).

> It's the attitudes that distinguish them and comprehension; negative attitudes to work, low ability, in reading and writing . . . very bolshy . . . terrible attitude. Mark is low ability but his attitude . . . is, well, so damn good. Chances are he will do well. I can't help them until I've got better control (Mr Pritchard).

Others located a pupil's inability to work appropriately within the course itself:

> I'm not prepared to work from the worksheets as they stand. Things are far too dificult. The pupils have been difficult. Some are quite able, most are not able to concentrate (Mr Lane).

> They need complete overhauling. There's not enough practical work. It's all such boring stuff . . . no diagrams to copy . . . not enough activity . . . it's all theory (Mr Lane).

or in the pupils' home backgrounds:

> Ability wise . . . there's Mark, John, Hugh others, all can think, largely, they have the most articulate parents . . . they're sort of middle class kind of people, Hugh's father has thousands of books at home . . . Hugh can be troublesome though (Mrs Turner).

A failure to display the right attitude (and behaviour) was usually attributed to a combination of factors: for example, the absence of technical abilities (reading and writing) necessary for access to the Science scheme, an unsupportive social class, home background, the course material. All may be interpreted as contingencies producing pupil inability to curb 'concentration from wandering' or the tendency 'to distract others' or 'indulge in silly escapades to relieve the boredom'. They are 'not serious about Science'.

Pupils are distinguished according to their controllability (cf. Jenks, 1972), while the rhetoric of the Science course provides the necessary constructs with which to explain their failure. 'The right attitude is assessed in terms of the fit between the pupils' attitudes and the current ideology' (Bernstein, 1977, p. 109). That is to say, in defining pupils as social types, teachers utilize categories drawn from their construction of what a scientific approach to learning should be within the current, paradigmatic conception of science teaching.

Faced with such problems of increasing pupil involvement in interest activity, there was a concomitant increase in the amount of public regulative teacher talk addressed to a small group of pupils causing most concern. As an immediate strategy for resolving the emergent discipline problems, Mrs Turner (as did many others) often adopted a policy of intervention and isolation, removing the parties concerned from their own to other groups more inclined in the teacher's perspectives towards 'total' work. Rene (one of the counter-steering group) began working with Jerry, Ryan and Peter. Increasingly the teacher was drawn to their activities. Rene, who was found the 'most difficult pupil, defiant, wastes time playing, distracts others. I'll exclude him from experiments if he doesn't change', was removed and placed with a group of workers Mark, Naren and Michael. This strategy however was only partially successful. In the short term it reduced a teacher's managerial problem, reducing levels of noise and movement emanating from group 5. It did not, however, resolve Rene's learning problems. Although placed with a group of workers, he was unable (and made no great attempt to try, possibly because of the subcultural significance of such an act) to penetrate the boundaries of their group solidarity, and commitment to work (see Meyenn, 1980, pp. 108–42). In exasperation, as they continued to ignore his presence he calls out to the teacher 'they keep it all themselves'. His behaviour remained problematic and he was continually drawn towards the interest activity of his previous group of friends.

Within the broader framework of demands for order and control which teachers at Sageton had to work within, they had little opportunity but to invoke more dramatic and attested strategies of control. *They reverted to whole class method*, for example:

I'm not going to let them work in groups again, until they want to learn. I can't allow them to be more independent (Mrs Turner).

The class should be doing work on their own but I daren't risk allowing them to do it (Mrs Cooper).

This reversion to class teaching (evidenced in Table 5.2) was the product of teachers identifying pupils as ill-prepared to work in the pattern required by the scheme. There was a perceived disjuncture between the behaviour of pupils and the conception of learning embodied in the scheme. Table 5.2 outlines how Mrs Turner's talk was differentially distributed amongst the pupils of Form 1p, over 4 × 70 minute lessons.

Despite the opportunities for group work presented in the booklet, in these lessons pupils enjoyed only 17 of a possible 280 minutes of practical activity for which they took responsibility. [. . .] During these lessons John, Mary, Hugh and Heather (group 2) and Jerry, Ryan, Rene and Liona (group 3) received distinctively more public regulative talk than the 'total workers' of group 1, or the pupils of group 4 and also more of the instructional talk with the teacher. When compared with individualized instruction class teaching appeared to offer all groups with the exception of group 3 significantly less opportunity for involvement in instructional talk with the teacher, while at the same time increasing their experience of public regulative messages.

Table 5.2 *Mrs Turner's talk in 4 × 70 minute lessons, excluding beginnings and endings*

Group	Public regulative	Public instructional[a]	Total
(a) as percentage of teacher talk across four groups previously identified in Mathematics			
1 (5 pupils)	10	16	12.3
2 (4 pupils)	18	28	21.5
3 (4 pupils)	53	44	49.2
4 (7 pupils)	19	12	16.9
	100%	100%	99.9
(b) as average per pupil in each group			
1	0.8	0.8	1.6
2	1.8	1.8	3.6
3	5.3	2.8	8.1
4	1.1	0.4	1.5

[a] Refers to instructional talk in interactions between teacher and individual pupils, carried out publicly from the front of the class position.

Despite surface changes in the organization of instruction, science teaching did not give pupils an opportunity to achieve significant alterations in their identity, as social types, as defined in individualized instruction. Only Naren and Abdul experienced any sort of shift in their identity, and were rated as slightly less able than in Maths, due less to their inability to handle content than the difficulties they experienced with the mode of transmission, because of their limited reading abilities. Consequently they were considered 'very enthusiastic, quite able, but they have difficulty with English, writing up experiments. But they're hard working . . . they enjoy science' (Mrs Turner).

The regularities to which Table 5.2 refers are then, we suggest, functional expressions of the situation in which the teacher found herself. On the one hand Mrs Turner controlled the teaching process at classroom level, having to resolve problems of discipline, pacing and content, but she was also 'controlled' or constricted by the interplay of pupil identities, content, time and MOT. Her disciplinary and instructional actions were concretely structured in interaction with specific groups of pupils. As we see in Table 5.2, group 3 pupils (counter-steering group) received significantly more instructional talk than other pupils as the teacher tried to manage their difficult behaviour, but this occurred *pari passu* with the negative identification of their behaviours as pupils.

Class teaching as represented here in the action of Mrs Turner was indeed for the teachers concerned a coping strategy, 'a creative response to problems and constraints that are externally determined' (A. Hargreaves, 1977). It was not a preferred way of teaching but was chosen because of its capacity to effect greater control over pupil behaviour, which itself was generated from a complex interplay of frame factors. As pupils related to content, time and MOT in group based learning, the learning difficulties of certain pupils (particularly the counter-steering group) were increasingly made apparent in interest activity which, given the degree of autonomy and self-direction presupposed and required by the group organization, was increasingly problematic for teachers. Class teaching which resulted was a chosen *second level* coping strategy, in which (cf. A. Hargreaves, 1979, p. 139) 'the moral aspect takes primacy. In this sense, social control becomes inseparable from curriculum planning, preferred styles of teaching and classroom organization'. Group work was returned to only upon the re-establishment of the teacher's authority, once the positional structural relationships of classroom life had been explicitly announced.

> Right I usually do the experiments myself but today . . . we'll have a bash at it. We tried before . . . then it was chaotic. If you get stupid . . . there will be no practical work for you . . . for a long time (Mrs Turner).

Investigatory activity was, then, offered as part of a bargaining process: less boredom, more responsibility, in exchange for pupil conformity.

Class Teaching and the Limits of Control

This strategy of whole class teaching was, however, almost wholly unsuccessful. While it reduced a teacher's problems of transmission of *content*, in the limited time available it neither effectively reduced their problems of pupil control nor resolved pupils' learning difficulties. The reasons are complex and can be considered following some examples of class teaching, observed in years one and two.

Example 1: Mrs Cooper with Form 1s

The lesson proper begins with an eight minute introductory phase. The teacher, positioned at the front of class reads through the investigatory task which all pupils are expected to follow, and this is interspersed with question–answer sessions and the issuing of public regulative messages. A 15-minute writing phase follows: pupils copy out from the booklet the investigatory instruction and content statements. The teacher remains at the front of class, in a supervisory position. There follows a 3 minute organizational activity, pupils are asked to collect materials needed for the class experiment. A further 15 minutes are spent in practical work. In both writing and investigatory phases the teacher's concerns for pacing are manifest, in such statements as 'hurry up and finish. I'm eager to get on'. Ultimately, the problems of completion and 'understanding' seem to be resolved with the teacher spending 20 minutes dictating conclusions, using the blackboard, from which the pupils capture the salient points of the lesson for their exercise books.

Example 2: Mr O'Connor with Form 1q

Following an eight minute settling phase, in which the teacher orders pupils to 'come to the front with your chairs', the teacher systematically works through the content outlined in the booklet, for a period of 28 minutes. The topic is 'Heat' and the investigatory activity to be covered is intended to introduce the notion of 'conduction'. However, it is only via not inconsiderable skill on the behalf of the teacher, the use of a variety of control strategies and a subtle collusion with the pupils, that a semblance of order and productivity can be maintained. The teacher's problem is that of securing levels of attention and co-operation appropriate to class teaching and necessary if some degree of conceptual understanding of the content is to be achieved. This is pursued with the repeated issuing of disciplinary messages which continually breaks the flow of instruction, and the use of carefully directed instructional talk.[7] Using both public regulative messages and instructional questions addressed at 'problem' children, the teacher is able to contain but not suppress/correct pupil 'interest' behaviour. As a result he finally invokes a third strategy, that of indulgence. In this strategy 'Pupils are allowed to go beyond normally accepted bounds of classroom behaviour and teacher's decline to enforce general classroom rules' (Denscombe, 1980b, p. 65; Woods, 1977). Despite growing levels of indifference and interest activity from perhaps two-thirds of the pupils present, this teacher indulges such activity, issuing disciplinary messages only to define an acceptable threshold before proceeding with instruction. For example, after some 12 minutes into the lesson, he asks 'It says the word conduction ... can anyone tell me ... what is conduction?' Faced with a collective silence he again proceeds to read the definition provided in the booklet, a content which he later admits to finding 'far too difficult, that sentence I read, even I didn't understand it'. This is followed by more teacher instruction and a 'clarifying' investigatory task which the teacher completes against a background of indifference from the majority of pupils. At the end of this (28 minute) phase he instructs the pupils to return to their places and 'write up in your books what you think conduction is', a request to which a number of pupils retort 'We don't know do we!' and Mr O'Connor exasperates 'You've just done it!' The problem is resolved with the teacher using the blackboard, providing a series of concluding and descriptive statements for the pupils to copy into their books.

Example 3: Mr Khan with Form 2p

In this example, we find further instances of indulgence, as a teacher atempts to resolve his disciplinary and instructional problems. It takes some 15 minutes of lesson time for Mr Khan to regulate pupil interest behaviour: 'you know how much time you've wasted . . . we'll go on after school . . . I'm going to sit down and wait until you're quieter'. Despite the severity of these statements they are sufficient only to curb the level of pupil interest activity; many continue to ignore the teacher as he begins his class instruction. As the lesson proper progresses, for a period of 45 minutes, its salient feature is the teacher's tendency to direct his class instruction at those pupils positioned towards the front of class and his indulgence of those to the rear who are apparently content to ignore the teacher and class instruction. He intervenes in their activity only when their levels of noise and movement seriously impinge upon his instructional talk, or when they seriously infract the appearance of classroom social order.

Mr Khan	Will you shut up please.
Pupils	[burst out laughing]
Mr Khan	Look you've got to let me finish the lesson.
Pupils	[more laughter] . . . go on then finish the lesson.

Again, only in the closing phases of the lesson proper when the teacher concludes the lesson activity and pupils are required to put 'work in their exercise books' is the attention of all pupils ultimately achieved.

Many more instances of class instruction of this type (adopted by the teacher either because of their control problems or lack of resource) could be provided. However, sufficient has been said to evidence the occurrence of certain processes. The limited conceptual understanding which this approach produced in pupils contravened the intentions of both teachers and the Integrated Science course. We are simply suggesting that the solutions adopted represented a viable pragmatic solution to a teacher's disciplinary, control (or resource) problems. There is little to choose between group work and class teaching as a means of facilitating better conceptual understanding. We have seen that group work contributed to a teacher's disciplinary problems because of the learning problems it presented to children. It too allowed pupils to proceed without necessarily having achieved understanding. The difference between class based or group based teaching can be largely characterized in terms of their generation of collective or individual piloting, respectively. In the lessons described, it could be argued that pupils were merely negotiating forms of behaviour (interest activities and 'escape' from work) possible in group organization (see Denscombe, 1980b). Indulgence was apparent, in combination with the use of concluding statements, as instructional strategies, because they allowed teachers, in a context of constraining and limiting factors, to maintain classroom order and at the same time secure sufficient transmission of content to provide evidence, when required, of teacher competence.

Indulgence, however, also (as evidenced in Example 3) involved a structure of communication which makes explicit the boundaries of a classroom social structure within which the identities of the able and the less able are constructed and repeatedly produced. Figure 5.1 refers to the class teaching in

Figure 5.1 *Form 2p (case study group) seating plan in science*

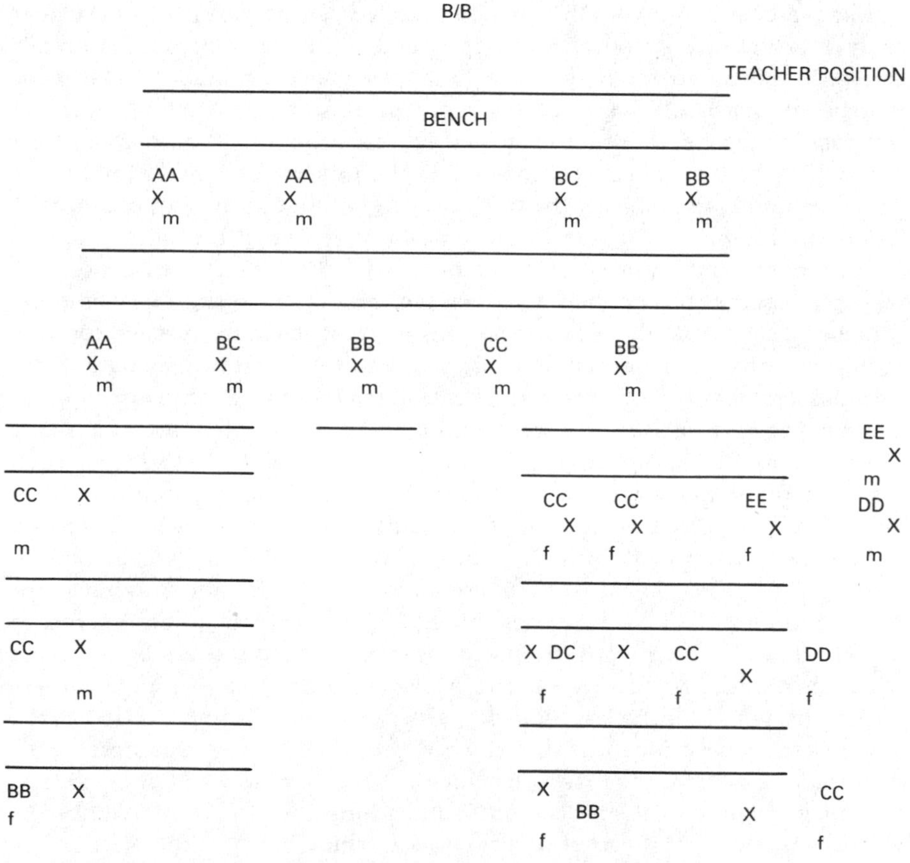

B/B

TEACHER POSITION

BENCH

AA	AA			BC	BB
X	X			X	X
m	m			m	m

AA	BC	BB	CC	BB
X	X	X	X	X
m	m	m	m	m

				EE
				X
				m
CC	X		CC	CC	EE	DD
			X	X	X	X
m			f	f	f	m

| CC | X | | X DC | X | CC | | DD |
| | m | | f | | f | X | f |

BB	X		X		CC
f			BB		X	f
			f			f

X, position; m, male; f, female; A–E, Autumn term teacher ratings: effort and attainment.

Example 3, and the seating position of the pupils involved. Evident in this example is a degree of overlap between the focus of teacher instructional talk (which was directed to the front two benches), levels of pupil interest activity and, with the exception of two girls situated to the rear and rear side of the classroom who score BB on teacher ratings, ability as defined by both teacher ratings and NFER scores. In short, the strategy of indulgence in combination with class teaching, with the added feature of the teacher focusing upon the work progress of these pupils at the front to pace the lesson, celebrated both a steering group phenomenon and differential gender attachment to Science frequently noted elsewhere (Blackstone and Weinreich-Haste, 1980). (This was borne out in pupil questionnaire responses. Only two of 12 boys expressed below average interest in Science, compared with six of the girls for whom we have responses.) In general, a large number of pupils were disallowed entry into the learning process in Mr Khan's classroom.

If you don't want to work he'll just go on with the people that will work (Diane, Form 2p).

Some indication of what this process entailed can be gleaned from further analysis of the interaction of Form 1p (Table 5.2). Such an analysis reveals that girls accounted for only 3% of public regulative talk and 24% of instructional; that is, they appeared to represent less of a problem of control at this stage to teachers, but also received far less individual 'instruction' than boys with whom the teacher interacted in the interest of order. However, it would be invidious to blame the teacher in any obvious sense for causing the failure of the girls by virtue of entrenched stereotyped attitudes. Identity construction is not an inexorable outcome of labelling but a transaction that takes place as the teacher attempts to resolve pressing problems of order, time, content, etc.[8] Certainly expectations may predispose the teacher towards indulgence as s/he prospects the likely action of the pupil displaying difficult or indifferent behaviour. Some teachers, like Mr Khan with Form 2p, did express negative attitudes towards girls in science: 'girls are not really interested in the steam engine ... boys are naturally interested' – such attitudes might well have contributed to the kind of indulgence exemplified above. As Denscombe (1980b, p. 65) suggests 'where they [teachers] come to regard the behaviour as 'normal' for the particular pupil, there is a tendency to indulge the behaviour and cease attempts to remedy the normally unacceptable behaviour'. What we are stressing, however, is that the initial emergence of behaviours subsequently indulged by teachers have their basis in the material conditions of curricular and pedagogical practice to which teachers and pupils, with more or less difficulty, are subject and routinely relate. In the circumstances described it is thus more appropriate to view this stereotyped explanation as a feature of rhetoric which papers over cracks in performance, to explain disjuncture between course intentions and everyday practice. As Woods (1977, p. 288) argues, survival strategies have 'a rhetoric closely attending them', which in the context he describes asserts the peculiar characteristics of these pupils, personal, environmental, mental, which entitles them to special treatment, and the relationships they develop with the teacher concerned, which ensures the success of the survival manoeuvre is presented as evidence of the justification of the rhetoric. Thus the problem is collapsed back in the situation and contained within a solution that masquerades, very powerfully and convincingly, as education.

For those pupils unable to meet the requirements of doing Science, as defined by existing curriculum and pedagogical practice, unable to handle content, MOT (in group work), to work independently in an oblique frame of control within the time made available, Science teaching may represent a frustrating and unrewarding experience and they may by the second year no longer wish to take part in such lessons. In the view of first and second year teachers, such pupils were labelled as 'less able', 'most difficult', 'time wasters', 'not serious', they are 'unable to concentrate', 'don't listen', as 'very silly and childish', and 'immature'. The pupils of the counter-steering group of Form 1p, however, expected their teacher to take a firmer line, to be more strict: 'she doesn't make us work', 'she can't control'. Against the background of a frame of control which their teacher in class teaching subsequently invoked, these statements may appear somewhat contradictory, as the excess of public positional messages which the teacher issued could be seen to accord with pupil expectations and wishes. Yet their behaviour did not improve. There were a number of reasons for this, including the fact that the changing context of control did not alter their pedagogical or curricular opportunities for success at learning. Other reasons can be gleaned from the following statements of pupils of Form 1p.

It's too boring ... nobody likes science ... it's not the teacher, it's just boring, you have to do writing all the time, it's boring (Caroline).

We should do the experiments ... what we are supposed to do ... should learn science not writing and all that (Rene).

If she left us alone to do the experiments we wouldn't be chatting, we wouldn't have time to chat. We would be working. Some of the teachers don't want you to learn. All we do is writing every day. Each time we come to science ... if we do experiments ... you know ... she has to do it first (Peter).

When you do it with the teacher you don't really get the experience. She tells you how it's going to happen (Ryan).

If you don't do it on your own ... if you do it on your own ... you get to learn it for yourself ... yeah ... I understand it better then (Jerry).

Evidently, not only did the less able pupil find difficulty with content, MOT (given reading ability) and the frame of control, but also s/he was subject to a great deal of boredom and frustration. By and large, in the strategy of class teaching adopted by teachers, the pupils' role was relegated to one of passivity and conformity. Pupils placed a high premium on working in groups, on investigatory activity which was associated with doing Science and learning, even if, as we suggested, only of a limited kind. Consequently, while the frame of teacher control over pupil conduct *was* more publicly and rigorously exerted in whole class method, it occurred simultaneously with a reduction in pedagogical practices which, from the pupils' perspective, were regarded as legitimate, proper, science activity. *In effect, an increase in teacher control had a concomitant decreasing legitimacy,*[9] the upshot of which was an increase in pupil frustration, antagonism and alienation, and the placing of teachers in an extremely unenviable position.

[. . .]

Notes

1 Ball (1980), from an interactionist perspective, stresses the significance of initial encounters in the developmental nature of teacher–pupil relationships (following Lacey, 1970).

2 Nuffield Combined Science (1970).

3 D. Hargreaves (1972, p. 204) notes that the most experienced teacher insists that if he [or she] is to survive he [or she] must 'define the situation in his [or her] own terms at once. Basically the initial definition is not so much a statement of the rules that will govern the class but rather a clear indication that a teacher is completely in charge and not to be treated lightly'. We do not think, however, that this analysis pays sufficient attention to the way in which a teacher's opportunities to effect the appearance of authority are structured by course curriculum organization or subject definitions of appropriate method.

4 And as defined by Primary School Test Scores (NFER Verbal Reasoning D.), both are amongst the lowest ability in the class. (We could not administer NFER AH2/3 tests to these pupils.)

5 'Front', as Woods (1980c) argues, which implies a kind of deception (here, self-deception), is an important feature of strategies.

6 Compare with the findings of Galton *et al.* (1980). It is worth mentioning at this point that of the 18 pupils of 1p for whom we have questionnaire responses only four expressed a preference for co-operative group work as a mode of instruction. The majority advocated either 'working by yourself' or 'working by yourself in a group'. In effect this may be little more than confirming preferences/experiences gained at junior school.

7 As Hammersley (1976, p. 108) notes, teachers use questions not to get answers but as a summons and to imply to the pupils that they know when they are not attending them even though 'they might not show it'. Their 'concern with the establishment and maintenance of pupil attention underlies and interpenetrates even those classroom activities that are apparently concerned with the transmission of knowledge'. This strategy explains why the pupils of Group 3 (Table 5.2) experience a higher incidence of instructional talk than all others.

8 See Sharp and Green (1975).

9 Atkinson and Delamont (1976, p. 139) make the point that 'guided discovery is difficult to sustain at the best of times. If the nature of this management is not respected by any of the parties then trouble can ensue'.

Bibliography

ATKINSON, P. and DELAMONT, S. (1977) 'Mock-ups and cock-ups: the stage management of guided discovery instruction', in P. WOODS and M. HAMMERSLEY (eds), 1977, pp. 87–109.

BARNES, D. (1977) *From Communication to Curriculum*. Harmondsworth, Penguin.

BERNSTEIN, B. (1977) *Class Codes and Control, Vol. 3: Towards a Theory of Educational Transmission* (2nd edition). London, Routledge & Kegan Paul.

BLACKSTONE, T. and WEINREICH-HASTE, (1980) 'Why are there so few women scientists and engineers?', *New Society* Feb. 1980, pp. 383–6.

DENSCOMBE, M. (1980b) 'Pupil strategies in the open classroom', in P. WOODS (ed.), 1980b, pp. 50–74.

EGGLESTON, J. (ed.) (1979) *Teacher Decision-making in the Classroom*. London, Routledge & Kegan Paul.

GALTON, M., SIMON, B. and CROLL, P. (1980) *Inside the Primary Classroom*. London, Routledge & Kegan Paul.

HAMMERSLEY, M. (1976) 'The mobilization of pupil attention', in M. HAMMERSLEY and P. WOODS (eds), 1976, pp. 104–15.

HAMMERSLEY, M. and WOODS, P. (eds) (1976). *The Process of Schooling*. London, Routledge & Kegan Paul.

HARGREAVES, A. (1977). 'Progressivism and pupil autonomy'. *Sociological Review* **25** (3), 585–621.

HARGREAVES, A. (1979). 'Strategies, decision and control: interaction in a middle school classroom', in J. EGGLESTON (ed.), 1979, pp. 134–70.

HARGREAVES, D. (1972) *Integrated Relations and Education*. London, Routledge & Kegan Paul.

JENCKS, C. (1972) 'A question of control: A case study of interaction in a junior school' Unpublished MSc (Econ.) thesis. London, Institute of Education.

KOHL, L. (1970) *The Open Classroom*. London, Methuen.

MEYENN, R. J. (1980) 'School girls peer groups', in P. WOODS (ed.), 1980b, pp. 108–43.

SHARP, R. and GREEN, A. (1975) *Education and Social Control*. London, Routledge & Kegan Paul.

WOODS, P. (1977) Teaching for survival, in P. WOODS and M. HAMMERSLEY (eds), 1977, pp. 271–94.

WOODS, P. (ed.) (1980a) *Teacher Strategies: Explorations in the Sociology of the School*. London, Croom Helm.

WOODS, P. (ed.) (1980b) *Pupil Strategies: Explorations in the Sociology of the School*. London, Croom Helm.

WOODS, P. (1980c) 'Strategies in teaching and learning', in P. WOODS (ed.), 1980a, pp. 18–34.

WOODS, P. and HAMMERSLEY, M. (eds) (1977) *School Experience*. London, Croom Helm.

6

How Alice's Chin Really Came to be Pressed Against her Foot: Sexist Processes of Interaction in Mixed-Sex Classrooms

Pat Mahony

There is already a substantial body of literature which demonstrates that females are marginalized from education by its content. For example, I have argued elsewhere (Mahony, 1982) that whether one looks at the history of the official ideology concerning the education of girls, or the differential patterning of career opportunities, or the way in which knowledge is framed (he/man talk), or the content of curriculum subjects, the same picture emerges. This is one in which the content of education is overwhelmingly oriented towards male interests: both in the sense of promoting males' interests in occupying future dominant roles and in concentrating on a stereotyped view of what they are interested in. Put together, these different facets amount to a massive bombardment on girls which functions from their point of view, to channel their development towards the occupation of subservient roles.

But girls' 'below stairs' relationship to education is not brought about solely by the content of the curriculum. There is also a whole set of interactional processes which demonstrably contribute to rendering girls invisible in education. (In reality the content of education and the processes of interaction operate together and cannot be viewed separately except as an aid to academic manageability.)

Some researchers have spent many hours in schools investigating different aspects of these processes in mixed-sex classes (Spender, 1980; Sarah, 1980; Shaw, 1977). Much thought and energy have been expended on the part of some people in trying to change to some extent, those discriminatory aspects of teaching which research has exposed (Griffiths, 1977; Payne and Spender, 1980).

It is the purpose of this paper to first briefly document what we now know about what happens in mixed-sex classes, to further suggest that there is a great deal occurring which is not so widely recognized such as the active harassment of girls by boys and lastly to suggest that sexual harassment is a strategy which boys frequently adopt towards women teachers. The patterning of social relationships in school is much more complicated than we have realized up to now.

As someone engaged in the training of teachers, my relationship to this concern is twofold. First, in making available to mixed-sex groups of students the research evidence on 'sexism in education', I have experienced directly the difficulties involved in being a woman and a feminist teacher. Secondly, I have observed in classrooms young women students, some feminist, encountering similar expressions of male hostility.

Boys' Monopoly of Physical Space

An obvious place to begin a review of the research which has been conducted on mixed-sex situations is with the amount of physical space which boys occupy, relative to girls. Anne-Marie Wolpe (1977) for example, writes:

> What happens in the mixed playground is that boys monopolize almost the total area by playing football, while the girls sit around on benches or wander round the periphery. Some, at great risk, pick their way across the football pitch, but few would dare to do so. There are in fact no chances for girls to participate or to be physically active as all balls are banished from it. . . .
>
> Even though a number of girls during the course of their interviews expressed a desire to join in, when asked why they did not do so they laughed at the stupidity of the question. It simply was not feasible – they would be howled down by the boys.

My own impressions of the situation inside the classroom correspond with Anne-Marie Wolpe's observations. Though I have not checked with a tape measure, it does seem that the space assumed by boys to be theirs, is far greater than that occupied by girls. Boys not only 'spread' into gangways and spaces around their own desks (which are often the ones most central to the teacher), but they also appear not to notice that space is already occupied by girls. It is not uncommon to find a boy leaning across a girl's desk in order to 'flick' another boy, crumpling her work in the process. Neither is it uncommon, when this behaviour is challenged, to encounter a reaction of amazement and incomprehension from the boys. It is apparently usual for them to not notice the physical presence of girls, not to consider it important to do so.

Boys' Monopoly of Linguistic Space

A second area of considerable concern given the importance of talk in learning, is the way in which linguistic space is dominated by boys. Zimmerman and West's research (1975) showed that in male/female conversations nearly all the interruptions (94 per cent), were by men and that females were more silent than males. Dale Spender (1978) found that girls and boys receive different messages about themselves through the processes of linguistic interaction. These are that it is:

normal for the teacher to ignore the girls for long periods of time, but not the boys,
normal for boys to call out, move from their seats, push each other,
normal for girls to be addressed collectively, boys by their individual names,
normal for boys to dominate classroom talk,
normal for boys to talk rough and girls to talk soft.

Jenny Gubb (1980) reveals another factor in her findings, that girls are more likely to offer support in discussion.

In all the tape recordings, videos and personal visits to students in school, I have not been able to find any evidence which contradicts these findings. Neither could I claim any wild success in changing conversation patterns in my own mixed-sex tutor groups from the male standard ('language of authority') to one which is more akin to female speech style ('the language of co-operation') (Spender, 1978). Thus it would appear that a move towards a more progressive, discussion-based approach to teaching favours males rather than females, who simply move from teacher dominated talk to male 'peer' dominated talk. Either way, girls' invisibility is maintained.

Boys' Monopoly of Teacher's Attention

Language is not the only contest in which boys dominate classroom life. Spender and Sarah's book *Learning to Lose* (1980) could be described as a catalogue of the many varied ways in which the majority of a teacher's attention is channelled into the boys. But teachers as a group are not by nature evil or unjust people and any explanation which portrayed them as consciously setting out on a programme of reproducing patriarchy would be idiotic. It would also be inaccurate to assume that all teachers continue to act out of ignorance. Rather, the problem lies in the immense difficulty of achieving in practice, equality of treatment between girls and boys. Vivienne Griffiths (1977) speaks for many of us when she says:

I am fully aware that during my own lessons I frequently treated girls and boys differently: it is remarkably difficult to break through behaviour seen as a norm. For example, when a group of loudly disruptive boys threatened to reduce a whole class to chaos it often seemed simpler and less wearing to focus attention and content on them and try to prevent further disturbance than to stick to principles about not paying more attention to the boys.

Female student teachers find this a particularly acute problem and many have described themselves to be in a 'double bind' situation. If they do not give over-riding attention to the boys then they experience discipline problems. They have little choice but to attend to these, thereby giving boys most of their attention and perhaps even further reinforcing boys' assertiveness and visibility within the lesson.

Teachers' Attitudes

It is of course not the case that all teachers are free of sexist attitudes to the children they teach and in view of what we now understand about the role of teacher expectation in pupils' educational achievement (Rist, 1970; Rosenthal and Jacobson, 1968), teachers' sexist attitudes constitute an area of major concern. It would be a mistake to view teachers' attitudes as homogeneous: they do not fall neatly and tidily into the two categories 'sexist' or 'non-sexist'. There are a variety of subtly different kinds of attitudes and these may affect pupils in different ways and to different degrees.

First there is an attitude, which is expressed by the forerunner – 'I know it's sexist but . . .'. This usually amounts to a recognition that the person to whom the remark is being addressed (usually a woman), is likely to object: a warning is also being issued that the anticipated objection will not be received with warmth and interest.

Alternatively, 'I know it's sexist but . . .' can often be used in the attempt to gain licence for a sexist comment. Some men for example, who consider themselves to have achieved a high degree of consciousness seem to want both to advertise the fact and to continue behaving according to old patterns.

Thirdly, a comment very often made by women teachers is 'I'm not a women's libber but . . .'. This seems to amount to a desire to disclaim the image of 'women's libbers' (whose image?) whilst holding on to the arena in which they can express dissatisfaction, anger, etc. about their treatment as women. Fear of one's own radical ideas and the consequent attempt to disown them must have the effect of rendering those ideas inert and from the point of view of pupils, may even undermine their own critical perspectives. However, given the abuse and harassment which 'women's libbers' experience often before they have even expressed an opinion, this fear is entirely understandable.

Fourthly, there is a whole range of attitudes which are unconsciously sexist. It is in this area, in my view, that initial training courses and in-service work could be most effective, though we need to think very carefully about how these courses might be taught (Mahony, 1982).

Lastly, there are a number of confused and muddled attitudes which emerge when people are beginning to develop understandings about what is entailed by a commitment to anti-sexist practice. For example, a student teaching a drama lesson became concerned when a group of girls refused to work with the boys. This was because the boys it was claimed 'treat us like muck – they're pigs' and they proceeded to describe various incidents which had led up to their refusal. In my view these girls were quite appropriately resisting a situation in which, if past experience was anything to go by, they would be treated with less than respect. Such resistance could have been validated by allowing them to work independently of the boys who for their part, might have benefited from having the situation explained to them. Instead, the student accused the girls of being sexist and insisted that they joined the boys. From the point of view of the girls in this class, there may have been no difference between this student's teaching and that of someone else who would make no claim to an awareness of the situation. [. . .]

The 'Catch 22' situation of girls [is] described by Katherine Clarricoates (1979). She shows in her research that what teachers think (rightly) is that girls at the primary school level 'do consistently better on all subjects than boys'. This achievement however Clarricoates argues, is rationalized in terms of feminine personality traits such as desire to please, passivity, obedience, etc. The net effect on girls she says, is 'the theft' of their intellectual capabilities.

Michele Stanworth (1981) also shows not only how some teachers view pupils, but also that pupils know what their teachers think of them, more worrying still is the suggestion that the teacher's view is internalized by the pupil.

> Female Pupil: 'I think he thinks I'm pretty mediocre. I think I'm pretty mediocre. He never points me out of the group, or talks to me, or looks at me in particular when he's talking about things. I'm just a sort of wallpaper person.'

At this point one may be forgiven for suggesting that a hitherto uncritical belief in the value of mixed-sex grouping, be reconsidered. An argument which has enjoyed wide currency has been that whilst girls appear to perform better academically in single-sex grouping it is nonetheless more normal socially and therefore more desirable, that they be educated with boys. However on closer inspection it appears that what we are being asked to accept as normal is the marginalization of girls from education by the processes of interaction particular to mixed-sex groupings. [. . .]

Boys' Attitudes to Girls

There already exists some documentation concerning boys' attitudes to girls.

Jenny Shaw (1977) has argued that boys in mixed-sex classes may seek to emphasize their masculinity by being as unlike the girls as possible: that is, they use the girls as a negative reference group. Michele Stanworth's (1981) documentation of boys' comments about girls confirms this suggestion. She says:

> In reply to the question, 'Who would you least wish to be like?', all of the boys named the girls (and only girls). It must be emphasized that the characteristic of female pupils most vehemently rejected by boys is the apparent marginality of girls in classroom encounters. The term 'faceless', used time and time again by boys (but by none of the girls) to describe their female classmates, seems to sum up boys' feeling that silence robs the girls of any claim to individual identity and respect.

What the boys in Stanworth's study feel for the girls seems best described as contempt, yet this is outrageous in a context where, as I shall argue, boys themselves make consistent and strenuous efforts to contribute to the marginality they appear to find so objectionable.

Boys' Behaviour to Girls

[. . .] [This is] what student teachers say and my own observations of over 200 lessons.

The social control of girls by boys in the mixed-sex classroom is achieved not only in a variety of ways but also at a variety of levels. One of the most noticeable features of a mixed-sex group as opposed to a class comprised of girls is the huge amount of time and energy which the boys exert in denying the girls' academic ability. They may do this quite overtly as in the case of a lesson in which a student asked a girl to take first turn at reading aloud. A boy said 'Don't ask her she can't read'. The girl was in fact 'the best reader in the class' but on this occasion she went very red and not only refused to read but failed to participate in the rest of the lesson. The boys jeered when girls or other boys made a mistake, using terms like 'stupid', 'dum-dum', 'thick' and 'dimbo', whereas the girls surreptitiously helped each other and some of the boys.

Often, however, boys will be less explicit in 'putting girls down' and will merely express a series of bored sighs and quiet groans. Girls who resist this pressure to be silent run the risk of making public their undoubted intellectual capabilities. One might expect that boys would be forced to acknowledge however grudgingly, the existence of ability in girls but what frequently happens instead is that the question or problem gets redefined as easy, thereby implying that nothing is proved by the girls having been able to answer it. One of the few situations in which boys acknowledge girls' ability is when they ask for help. The surreptitious way in which they do this cannot be solely attributed to the issue in question since any pupil who asks any other for help will be well aware of the possibility of being defined as cheating.

However, what is strikingly different about requests for help between boys is the directness of the approach ('How do you do this one?'). When boys ask girls, it is often under some other pretext ('How much space have you left under the diagram?'), which will be followed by a look at her work. This whole enterprise is often achieved with some difficulty since boys and girls tend not to sit together. I have yet to visit a mixed-sex class in which there is not a striking physical division between boys and girls and where often the girls are seated down the outer edges of the classroom. The movement is therefore by the boys across gangways which perhaps explains in part, boys' monopoly of physical space.

Another powerful strategy used by boys to achieve dominance in the mixed-sex class is to make comments about girls' appearance: they are too fat, too skinny, 'too sexy to have a brain', 'too ugly to have a boyfriend', their hair is too long and too short and their clothes are 'too straight' and 'too flashy'.

A student's notes revealed that at the end of one of his lessons a girl had hit a boy and refused to give any explanation, so she was given detention. In discussion with the student it emerged that some days later he had discovered that when the girl had entered the class the boy had said 'Don't sit over here, you stink' a remark which she had intepreted as part of a whole set of references to the fact that she was known to have begun menstruating. Not only had the student failed to talk the issue through with either of the pupils when he had learned what had caused the upset, but my concern seemed to totally enrage him. His final comment after accusing me of being ridiculous and trivial was 'When's Mr . . . coming in? I want some help with *teaching* not all this rubbish'. I am not of course suggesting that all male teachers are supportive of this kind of male pupil behaviour. However what is at issue is made explicit by this next example. A boy commented after a girl had been congratulated on her written work 'Let's have a look, Monkey Legs'. This name had apparently been assigned to Shirley because of her hairy legs and when I later asked the student what he thought of the comment, he replied 'I agree with him I couldn't fancy it'. I pointed out that I wasn't asking whether he shared the boy's oppressive attitudes to women but rather whether he understood why Shirley would perhaps not be over-inclined to publicly participate in lessons and whether he felt any responsibility to do anything about this. Again what followed initially was a tirade against obsession and bias (mine) and then significantly he said:

> What you're asking me to do is to get through this teaching practice and in the process change the whole way boys operate. I do think what he said was bad, I don't know why I made that flip comment . . . It runs so deep in us.

Where girls do come into their own in the mixed-sex classroom is as wives and mothers. They seem to be regarded by the boys as an infinite source of rubbers, rulers, sharpeners and writing materials. In one lesson a boy left his seat, walked halfway across the classroom to the side to have his bandage fixed by a girl. She was told by the student to hurry up with it and to get on with her work!

Yet there is overt resistance to girls adopting other roles. A Drama student writes:

The problem of finding roles which girls can identify with became an acute one for me on Teaching Practice and when I did manage to do so and cast a girl in an important part which might normally have been given to a boy, I found myself feeling *guilty* because I had denied a boy a plum role. Possibly I was also afraid that my choice might cause disruptive behaviour from the boys. Sometimes the boys challenged me, 'Airline pilot? A girl can't be an airline pilot Miss!' Each time this happened I saw the girl hesitate, waiting for my judgement, waiting to be sent back to her seat. 'Of course she can,' I would retort, thinking at the same time, 'Can she?' Each time I did this particular lesson, three in all, I cast girls as the pilot and navigator and the boys as co-pilot. Each time the girl playing the pilot approached me privately, when the others were busy and whispered was I serious? Could women be pilots? Everytime I reassured the girl that it was perfectly alright and would she please go back to her controls before the plane crashed (Brina, 1981).

Fear of boys' laughter is reported time and time again by students as the reason why girls will not take central roles in class activities, let alone atypical ones.

On the subject of verbal abuse some of which constitutes sexual harassment, some teachers argue that boys' behaviour in this respect is normal ('part of growing up'). This is undoubtedly true. It is also true that lung disease in miners is normal but few would dream of thereby accepting it as desirable. For girls, not only is it degrading and offensive in its own right but it also operates as a pressure to withdraw from public participation of lessons. Often, teachers are not aware of this feature of the interaction between boys and girls in a classroom – they are too busy with keeping the lesson going but what one sees and hears from the relatively free position of a non-teaching role is another story. Sometimes though the extent of the sexual abuse of girls by boys does become visible. Again the Drama student writes:

There is a good deal of abusive language used mainly by boys towards girls in their improvisations. In one day I collected the following insults, used while acting and no doubt considered by the boys who used them as essential to the action. In fact, looking back at the notes which I made at the time, I realize that these insults *were* essential to the action. How else could the boys have conveyed what they felt about women?
'this bird who can't get a boyfriend'
'you dopey cow'
'silly cow' (five times)
'you're a woman ain't ya' (to a cowardly boxer)

'you tart' (the boy was acting beating up the girl prior to raping her)
'she's not even pretty' (one girl to another about a third who was supposed
to be stupid) (Brina, 1981).

The student subsequently documented the activities chosen during one lesson
'in which the brief was to work out a physical trick which depended on careful
timing and group work':

1   woman being 'touched up' at the bus stop and subsequently hitting the
    wrong man
2   a boxing match, in which there being no role for the girl in the group, she
    simpered around playing a hostess
3   *two* women being 'touched up' in the park by the same man
4   a bank robbery which failed because one of the robbers (a girl) broke her
    fingernail and delayed everyone
5   yet another woman being 'touched up', this time on a train (Brina, 1981).
    She comments on this,

> I did not hear any of the girls use any corresponding terms of abuse for a
> boy. But what pejoratives are there which can be used against a male which
> are equivalent of 'cow', 'bitch', 'tart', 'bird' and 'scrubber', all of which I
> heard at some time in my lessons. There is one which the boys assured me
> that girls sometimes used against them and which I know they used against
> each other and that is 'poof'. It is apparently the worst insult to compare a
> boy with someone who is considered feminine (Brina, 1981).

It is reported by some students (mostly women) who have tried to challenge
boys' harassment of girls that one of the chief difficulties lies with male
colleagues' attitudes. In order to show themselves as 'one of the lads' they
actively condone, rather than challenge the boys' behaviour. The bonding
between boys and male teachers becomes even more apparent when women
staff are driven to report incidents of sexual harassment occuring to them,
which they rarely do, due to the likelihood of accusations being made about
their part in 'provoking' such incidents.

The Position of Women Teachers

It would be tedious to document the range of comments which males in school
make about and to female teachers, since in the absence of *detailed* research
(see Whitbread, 1980, for an initial study in this area) this would be either to
merely reiterate the kinds of comments which boys make about girls, or in
more general terms what would begin to emerge would be a very long descriptive account of the many varieties of sexual harassment (verbal and non-
verbal) to which women are subjected in their daily lives. This would be a
complex enterprise and one far beyond the scope of the paper. However there
already exists some work in the area.

Catherine Mckinnon (1979), for example, has devoted her study to the ways 'sexual harassment at work critically undercuts women's potential for work equality as a means to social equality'. In as much as women teachers are employees, it may be the case that much of Mckinnon's analysis applies to them. What has not so far been investigated is the functioning of harassment of female teachers who are structurally in authority, by boys who in the context of the school are structurally subordinate. What is at issue here are two kinds of power: the institutional power which is accorded to people formally designated 'teachers' and male power, maintained in part by such strategies as sexual harassment. Research into this would not only have to provide an analysis to substantiate this claim but also to map the many varieties of its expression in the classroom.

Just as it has been possible to understand the relationship between the racist insult in the classroom and the wider structural position of blacks relative to whites in this society, so we may be able to clarify the link between sexual abuse in the classroom and the wider structural position of women relative to men. It is not beyond the imagination (just), to envisage the day when a Government Report urges us to mount a challenge to such remarks, in the same way as the Rampton Report (1981) suggests that teachers should not tolerate racist comments. [. . .]

I have insisted throughout that we need much more detailed research in order to adequately theorize the extent and implications of the interaction between girls and boys in the mixed-sex classroom. However, even this far understood it seems clear to me that at the moment, mixed-sex classes are a disaster-area for girls. In as much as they have been judged as desirable (Dale, 1969, 1971, 1974) this can only have been from the point of view of those who are either ignorant of the true situation or who are in sympathy with the way in which men treat women in this society. In this case mixed-sex classes provide an excellent training ground for both boys and girls: for boys to practise behaving to women in such a way as to assert their birth-right to dominate; for girls to find unobtrusive strategies of resistance (as in the case of the group of 7-year-old girls who always set out newspaper on the tables for painting, not because they liked to please the teacher but so as to be able to destroy those pin-up images of women which they knew would provoke comments from the boys).

We cannot force those who make decisions in Education to alter their commitment to mixed-sex groupings, but we can at least make clear what is entailed by that commitment. This I have attempted to do.

References

BRINA, MICHELINE (1981) Sexism in Education. Unpublished paper.
CLARRICOATES, KATHERINE (1979) The theft of girls' creativity. Unpublished paper.
DALE, R. R. (1969, also 1971 and 1974) *Mixed or Single-sex schools?* Vols I–III. Routledge & Kegan Paul, London.
GRIFFITHS, VIVIENNE (1977) Sex roles in the secondary school; the problem of im-

plementing change. Paper presented at Conference, 'Teaching Girls to be Women' Essex (April).

MAHONY, PAT (1982) Silence is a woman's glory. *Women' Studies Int. Forum* 5 (5), 463–73.

MCKINNON, CATHERINE (1979) *Sexual Harassment of Working Women.* Yale University Press, London.

PAYNE, IRENE and SPENDER, DALE (1980) 'Feminist practices in the classroom', in SPENDER, DALE and ELIZABETH, SARAH eds, *Learning to Lose: Sexism and Education.* The Women's Press, London.

RAMPTON, ANTHONY (1981) *West Indian Children in our Schools.* HMSO, London.

RIST, RAY (August 1970) Student social class and teacher expectation: the self-fulfilling prophecy in ghetto education. *Harvard Educ. Rev.* **40**.

ROSENTHAL, ROBERT and JACOBSEN, LENORE (1968) *Pygmalion in the Classroom.* Holt, Rinehart & Winston, New York.

SARAH, ELIZABETH (1980) Teachers and students in the clasroom: an examination of classroom interaction. In SPENDER, DALE and ELIZABETH SARAH, eds, *Learning to Lose,* op. cit.

SHAW, JENNY (1977) Sexual divisions in the classroom. Paper presented at Conference. 'Teaching Girls to be Women', Essex (April).

SPENDER, DALE (1978) The facts of life: sex differentiated knowledge in the English classroom and the school. *English in Education* **12** (3).

SPENDER, DALE (1980) 'Disappearing tricks', in SPENDER, DALE and ELIZABETH SARAH, eds, *Learning to Lose,* op. cit.

SPENDER, DALE and SARAH, ELIZABETH, eds. 1980. *Learning to Lose: Sexism and Education.* Women's Press, London.

STANWORTH, MICHELE (1981) *Gender and Schooling: A Study of Sexual Divisions in the Classroom.* WRRC Publications, London.

WHITBREAD, ANNE (1980) 'Female teachers are women first: sexual harassment at work', in SPENDER, DALE and ELIZABETH SARAH, eds, *Learning to Lose,* op. cit.

WOLPE, ANNE-MARIE (1977) *Some Processes in Sexist Education.* WRRC Publications London.,

ZIMMERMAN, DON and WEST, CANDACE (1975) Sex roles. Interruptions and silences in conversations', in THORNE, BARRY and NANCY HENLEY, eds, *Language and Sex: Difference and Dominance.* Newbury House, Rowley, Mass.

7

School Processes: an Ethnographic Study

Cecile Wright

[. . .]

(a) The Study

[. . .] Pupils in the selected year group were examined through the process of classroom observation in two Midlands schools over approximately 900 hours in each school.

Formal and informal interviews were undertaken with individuals and groups of teachers, pupils and other people associated with the schools. Many interviews were tape-recorded, on the understanding that interviews would be confidential and that the identities of individuals would not be disclosed. Access was also provided in each school to confidential school records and reports. [. . .]

(b) Two Midlands Schools: a Description

Schools A and B are mixed comprehensives approximately three miles apart. The ethnic compositions of the two schools vary considerably. The proportion of pupils of Afro-Caribbean and Asian origin in School A is approximately 25% whereas it comprises 60% in School B. Despite the variation in the percentage of pupils of ethnic minority groups in the two schools, the school experiences of the Afro-Caribbean pupils in both schools appears not dissimilar.

(i) School A

Originally a boys' grammar school, this school amalgamated with a boys' secondary modern in September 1975 to form a mixed comprehensive school. Although comprehensive for nine years now there is still a strong grammar school ethos amongst a section of the senior teachers. These teachers exerted considerable influence, holding positions as Heads of Departments or Year

Heads. They saw themselves as wanting to get on with the teaching of their subject, but frustrated by teaching in a comprehensive and not a selective school and further frustrated by what they saw as the poor quality of the pupils. This in turn led to feelings of disillusionment. As a probationary teacher explained when she talked about the general attitude:

> Everybody just seems so disillusioned ... everybody seems fed up ... the staff as a whole, I mean. I came in as a young teacher, enthusiastic, full of new ideas but you soon find that the old attitudes rub off on you, and so you end up thinking, 'Oh, why am I doing this? Do I want to teach after all?' and this is because of what the others say to you, the more experienced teachers. I think instead of encouraging you to try out new ideas they seem to get some kind of kick out of telling you how bad it is ... I don't think it is a bad school.

[. . .]

(ii) School B

School B was originally a girls' grammar school. It became a mixed comprehensive in September 1972 by amalgamating with two single-sex secondary modern schools. Some members of staff at the school felt that it had suffered and was still suffering from the effects of the reorganization. This comment from a Senior teacher expresses a general view held by staff:

> The basic problem for this school, I think you have to go back to the history of it ... When you have a very small, very select, very ladylike grammar school, joined with two rough and ready secondary moderns what basically happened in my view is that when they joined together the grammar school staff, or most of them, couldn't cope with the rough and ready aspect the school then came to have. They were all in positions of Heads of Department, consequently I got the feeling that the secondary modern staff who could cope with it to a certain extent, withdrew labour. I don't mean that they went on strike, it was well, 'let them buggers do it – they're the ones in the position let them do it'. The school has never recovered from this.

[. . .]

Although many of the original grammar school teachers are no longer at the school, there is still a strong academic ethos among some of the senior teachers, though it is sometimes more a sense of nostalgia than something realized in their teaching. There is also an element of nostalgia amongst the original secondary modern teachers, in the sense that, 'the staff knew where they stood within a small school, and with a reliance on a more traditional authority pattern'.

Since the reorganization 12 years ago, the ethnic minority intake has gradually increased to well over half in the first year now. This intake of children from ethnic minority groups has sometimes been associated negatively with what have been perceived as problems within the school – declining standards and discipline problems. This contention is supported by the comment of a teacher who has taught at the school for six years:

> In my opinion there is a great degree of apathy, and fortunately we're just coming out of our apathy, but nevertheless the apathy was there for a long time, and the apathy eventually showed up in the kids, and the kids became apathetic. We often term this as '. . .itis' (name of the school), where you couldn't care less for anything that goes on. You get to a certain position in your job, there are a few promotional prospects, there is little back-up from the top, your job as a teacher is no longer as a teacher, you've got to start policing and so forth.

A Year Head who originally came from the secondary modern school at the time of reorganization had this to say on the status of the school:

> This school is a low ability school because of its catchment area, which consists of a low social class and a high immigrant population. More fundamentally, it is the high proportion of immigrants in this school which is responsible for the lowering standards.

The somewhat disturbing view held by this teacher, is not uncommon among members of staff. [. . .]

For teachers at School A the frustration of having to teach what they considered as 'inferior' pupils is further exacerbated by having as they perceive it, to contend with 'troublesome black pupils'. Similarly, some teachers at School B felt dissatisfied with having to teach predominantly 'immigrant' children, with their 'alien' ways, and having to put up with 'disruptive and troublesome Afro-Caribbean pupils'.

It is difficult to say conclusively that there are obvious differences in the way in which teachers in the classroom interact with Afro-Caribbean pupils and that these differences are influenced by ethnicity. Firstly, there were never more than two or three black pupils in any class, so their presence was not always obvious. Also, what takes place within a classroom context is possibly influenced by factors outside the classroom. However, the following dialogue noted during a classroom observation, demonstrates how a teacher's insensitivity can result in conflict with Afro-Caribbean young people:

> The teacher was talking to the class. Whilst he wrote on the blackboard, a group of four white boys sat talking to each other in an ordinary tone of voice. The teacher, being annoyed by the noise level in the room, threw a piece of chalk at an Afro-Caribbean boy who was not being particularly noisy.

TEACHER: Pay attention! (shouted)
TEACHER: (to an Asian boy) Could you get me that piece of chalk?
PETER: (Afro-Caribbean) Why don't you use black chalk?

TEACHER: (turning to the researcher) Did you hear that? Then I would be accused of being a racist, take this for example, I was down at Lower School, I had a black girl in my class, she did something or another. I said to her, if you're not careful I'll send you back to the chocolate factory. She went home and told her parents, her dad came up to school, and decided to take the matter to the Commission for Racial Equality. It was only said in good fun, nothing malicious.

KEITH: (Afro-Caribbean) (aggressively) How do we know that it's a joke, in my opinion that was a disrespectful thing to say.

TEACHER: (raising his voice and pointing his finger at Keith) If I wanted to say something maliciously racist, I wouldn't have to make a joke about it. I'd say it. I've often had a joke with you, haven't I?

KEITH: (angrily) Those so-called jokes, were no joke, you were being cheeky. I went home and told my mum and she said that if you say it again she would come and sort you out. As for that girl, if it was my father, he wouldn't just take you to the CRE, he would also give you a good thump. My father says that a teacher should set a good example for the children, by respecting each one, whether them black or white. He says that any teacher who makes comments like that in front of a class, shouldn't be in school, that's why he said to us that if a teacher ever speaks to us like that he would come up to school and sort him out.

HARRY: If it was me that you said that to, I wouldn't go home and tell my parents, I would just tell you about your colour.

KEITH: Teachers shouldn't make racist jokes.

One way in which attitudes towards categorization of black pupils was fostered was through 'informal gossip among staff',[1] as Hargreaves describes it. This is an important medium in the school, since a fair proportion of teachers do not actually teach the pupils they hear talked about. Hargreaves explains:

... how in the staffroom in particular, whenever teachers discuss pupils, they import into the discussion their own interpretations and perceptions. This provides the naive teacher, that is one who has no direct contact with the child, with information which categorizes him [or her] in advance of actual interaction and defines the situation in terms of the behaviour the teacher would expect. To the naive teacher, opinions of colleagues will have the effect of acting as a provisional agent of the categorization process. In other words, one of the functions of teachers' gossip about pupils is to add to the preconceptions and expectations by which a pupil is assessed.[2]

Such an explanation is illuminated by a white probationary teacher who expressed how she had misjudged a black pupil:

A lot of teachers jump to conclusions about pupils before they've even come into contact with them and broken through the pupil's resentment. They jump to these conclusions and these conclusions are passed round in the staffroom. You only have to sit in there and you hear the rumours and the gossip that's going around and the thing is, in the staffroom it's always the bad kids that are talked about, never the good ones, which I suppose makes sense in a way, but as a new teacher, you come in, you hear these rumours like, I used to hear rumours about Kevin (an Afro-Caribbean pupil) and I thought, 'Oh, God, I'll have to watch out for Kevin, everybody thinks he's a trouble-maker and that means he's bound to be in my class', but I mean it's not as simple as that, it really isn't ... There are a few white kids that are talked about but I mean that's inevitable. I think to a certain extent the West Indian kids tend to get labelled and these labels they feel they've got to live up to. I mean, you might think 'well, what goes on in the staffroom doesn't get round to the kids' but it does, it does, even if it is just through the teacher's own attitude. They can sense it, they're not stupid.'

This teacher's view that the Afro-Caribbean pupils felt obliged to live up to the labels given them by the school was reiterated by other teachers. A black teacher claimed:

The West Indian pupils, especially the boys are seen as a problem in this school because they are so 'aggressive'. You see, I am using a quote here, they are so openly aggressive and surly ... If it is always assumed that they are intellectually inferior, what else is there for them to do ... every time teachers are constantly amazed by the fact that in the first year they have at the moment – there we have two or three really bright West Indian boys, and it's of constant amazement to people like Mr G ... 'my goodness he's bright where does he get it from'. Pupils here in the 5th year are generally thought to be dross.

How might the behaviour and attitudes of the pupils be affected by the organization of the school and the teachers' attitudes and expectations? Hargreaves suggested that pupils with positive orientations towards school values largely converged on the higher streams, whereas those with negative orientations converged largely on the lower streams. He found that pupils in the lower streams were deprived of status and subsequently developed an anti-school culture which was used to gain status.

From discussions within a racially mixed group of 60 pupils, both from the fourth and fifth year, there seems to have been a consensus of opinion that the streaming system does not truly reflect ability. There was also a consensus that the streaming system works more against black pupils, indicated in the following conversation with four white pupils:

I think that black kids are treated rather badly in this school, for example, there are less black kids in the 'A' band. In my opinion it is not because they are not capable, it's because they are not given the opportunity. Teachers generally hold a low opinion of them, for example, I'm in the 'A' band, I'm doing 'O' level English, I find that some of the 'B' band kids are doing the same syllabus, and in some cases they get the same marks or better marks than us, yet they can't do 'O' level and they're in the 'B' band.

Conversations with two black pupils further revealed dissatisfaction about the school's organization:

We came here because our brother and sister went to this school. They got on badly, they were unhappy with the school, so they didn't try. They were also put in the 'B' band. However, they are now at (another school) in the sixth form. The headmaster would not allow them to go into the sixth form here. Anyway, they're better off there. They are both doing 'O' levels and 'A' levels. Since going there my brother has got 'O' level grade A in maths. He never did any good here.

Further conversations with a group of 16 black pupils reflect the general belief that the school's organization was against them. Consequently, the pupils saw very little point in trying. Further, they interpreted this perception as a *fait accompli*, an inevitable outcome of the school's attitude towards their colour. To black pupils the school seemed to be seen as a 'battle ground', a hostile environment insofar as it rejects their colour and identity. This is clear in the following discussion with a group of eight black boys talking about their feelings when teachers make derogatory comments about their skin colour in front of the class.

MICHAEL: It's like once the man (referring to the teacher) come in the class, and ask me in front of the class, 'Why me coffee coloured', he say, 'How come Wallace dark, and Kennedy black and Kevin a bit browner? How come you that, you a half-breed?' Me say, 'No man, me no look like me half-breed.' Me say, 'just like some a una white like a chalk and another couple a una got blond hair, some have black hair, me no come ask wha that!' . . . That's how he is, he just come around, crack him few sarcastic jokes about black kids.

PAUL: But they're not nice at all. They're not nice. The jokes aren't nice. The jokes are disrespectful.

KEVIN: They're not jokes man.

ERROL: You can't call them jokes. When he cracks a joke or whatever he does in front of the class, he just turn round and laugh. You get him and the class laughing at you.

KEVIN: What he is doing is running you down. He's just bringing you down like dirt. Nobody is bring me down (said with anger). Every time I'm chuck out of (subject) completely man, because every time in (subject) he always keep calling me something about me colour and I answer back.

ERROL: The teachers are forever picking on the black boys.

MICHAEL: Like me now, them no too bother with me because them think, say me a half-breed, you know. Half the teachers in the school think say

96

me a half-breed so they started bothering me. Like the half-caste kids them they used to left me alone.

KEVIN: They don't give half-caste kids no hassle, no hassle whatsoever. However, if the half-caste kids act black, they pick on them hassle man.

The boys were asked how they felt this so-called 'hassle' affected their academic performance. Paul summed up the views of the group:

You're not really given the opportunity to learn. Most of the time we're either sitting outside the Head's office or we are either fighting or we are arguing with them. It's just we got no time, as you sit down to work they pin something on you.

The resentment, bitterness and frustration felt by the Afro-Caribbean boys towards the school – due to the attitudes of certain teachers – is evident in these discussions. All that the boys said emphasized their perceptions of their interactions with teachers as an 'us' and 'them' situation. How then did this estranged relationship between the Afro-Caribbean pupils and their teachers affect the pupils' behaviour? As in the Hargreaves case, these pupils have developed a sub-cultural adolescent group within the school which is not only anti-school, but is also somewhat anti-white. This 'all-black' group is composed of both boys and girls: pupils from the third, fourth and fifth years. The 30 or more pupils move around the school together during the school breaks.

Most teachers were aware of the presence of this group but not of the reason for its development, with the notable exceptions of a teacher from South Africa and the Deputy Headmistress. As the teacher pointed out:

This group is a reaction to the racism in this school, we have what can be described as a very strong 'black mafia' within the school. They feel that they belong together, so they stick together.

Further confirmation came from the Deputy Headmistress:

There is certainly a race problem here at the moment. There is certainly, not so much a race problem between pupils, but there is a great problem here at the moment with the congregation, shall we say, of black pupils. By the time they get to the fourth form there are very few black pupils. There are identifiable groups of black pupils as they move around the school and we have had problems this last year with a particular large group of black pupils who have set out their stalls to appear aggressive.

This group has adopted a typical 'gang behaviour' as described by Goffman[3] in his description of 'Looking Cool' behaviour. The group attempts to assert its presence through both verbal and non-verbal means. As the Headmaster points out:

A number of black children, particularly boys, seem to lose interest in the school's aims (unless they are good at games, then they dissociate that from the rest) in the third year and, from then, become increasingly seen as an anti-culture ... probably the most striking manifestation of West Indian pupils, is just that group of large boys, and the sort of threatening physical presence, which you can see consistently around the school.

This 'gang' behaviour displayed a deliberate assertion of 'blackness' through the use of Patois – used both defensively and offensively by the group. Patois was successfully used to communicate rejection of authority. Although the teachers were aware of this 'weapon' they had great difficulty in finding anything to attack it with. This point was reiterated by the Deputy Headmistress:

We've got a problem at the moment, which is very nasty (I think the Headmaster was hoping to talk to you about it) where we are being faced with a barrage of Patois. It is so worrying because you see when that happens we as teachers have a choice. We either ignore it, but if it's done in public you feel threatened, or you feel that you are showing weakness if you just ignore it. You can either react equally aggressively and verbally back in Spanish, or French, which in fact is what is happening, but that is not helpful, or, as one member of staff said to me today, 'I came very close to clobbering him today.' [...]

As in school A, the nature of the relationship in School B between the Afro-Caribbean pupils and their teachers was frequently one of conflict. In School B the basis of this relationship may lie in the teachers' particular unease with the ethnic composition of the school: an unease at being 'swamped' and having to teach 'these alien pupils'. Many teachers try to obscure the fact that they are teaching in a multiracial school. Little attempt is made to acknowledge the ethnicity of the pupils. However, what is perceived as the belligerent, aggressive, lively, gregarious character of the Afro-Caribbean pupil, cannot be easily ignored by the teachers, and presents a constant reminder of the nature of the school. As one teacher at the school observes:

The pupils in this school come from working class and multicultural backgrounds. It seems to me that very few staff are addressing themselves to the kinds of thing (e.g. resources, teaching style, subject content, and attitudes and the hidden curriculum) that can be used to bring out the best of the pupils' cultures and backgrounds. The attitudes of teachers to West Indian and Asian cultures is at worst negative, and at best condescending and patronising. These cultures are viewed as remote and distant, and few teachers go out into the community to learn or take part in community activities.... Pupils are seen as recipients, with very little to offer to the curriculum. Teachers view themselves as doing a good job by educating 'these immigrants' in the 'best education system in the world' ... For these 'immigrants' to start demanding having a say in the way their pupils are taught and what they are taught is viewed with great disdain.

There is so much that pupils can offer to the school if there can be someone to listen and take notice. The end result is that pupils switch off any interest in the school, and how they manage to go through five years of their school lives still amazes me. They have a negative view of the school; of the West Indies, Africa and Asia and of themselves and their abilities.

Some of these views were also expressed by an Asian pupil in a Social Studies lesson, where the class was looking at the issue of 'Prejudices in Society'. The pupil pointed out to the teacher and the class that she felt that there is pervasive racial prejudice in the school, which the teachers failed to acknowledge. As she says:

We were discussing in form period, Asian languages in this school about people who want to take it, that it would be a chance for people to learn another language, say, if non-Asian children take it they would come to respect it. The form teacher then was on about that the school is for teaching only Western ways of living, and European ways of living. She said that's what you come to school for. That opinion really shocked me, coming from my own teacher. She was trying to tell me that we're nobody. She then said that when there was a lot of Polish people in the school, they never practised any of their culture here, they went away to their own community. She also tried to tell me there wasn't any prejudice in the school. And the worst thing is she was trying to tell a coloured person that there wasn't any prejudice, and that you only come to school to learn about the European way of life. That's the thing that needs bucking up in this school . . .

I said to her, 'I'm not willing to argue with you here because it would get me into trouble but if I ever saw you on the street I would.' Because I made a mistake once when a teacher told me that there wasn't prejudice in this school. I blew up and I tried to tell her, no you're wrong. I got myself into trouble . . . I made a mistake of doing it then in such an organized atmosphere. If I was going to . . . I should have done it out of school because in school everything is organized. The teachers are willing to back each other up. I asked another teacher, 'Well, what do you think?' she said 'You were wrong to shout back at her, full stop! Never mind what you were saying'.

The following comment from a Year Head indicates that the above pupil's perception of some teachers' attitudes towards certain sections of the school population was not wholly unfounded:

I find it difficult to accept the immigrant people and children that I come into contact with. I cannot change my feeling because it is part of my upbringing – I feel that the English culture is being swamped. I do not see how the Asian and West Indian pupils that I am responsible for can take on English behaviour for half a day when they are at school and change to their culture when they are at home.

To what extent then do attitudes of this nature shape the Afro-Caribbean pupil-teacher relationship? Informal discussions with Afro-Caribbean pupils indicated that the pupils felt that certain teachers disrespect them on the basis of their ethnicity and that for these pupils the pupil-teacher relationship was based on conflict, with the pupils then attempting to play the teachers at their own 'game' in order to survive. They saw the school as condoning these teachers' attitudes. A discussion with a group of 20 Afro-Caribbean girls illustrates this:

BARBARA: The teachers here, them annoy you, too much.

RESEARCHER: In what ways do they annoy you?

BARBARA: They irate you in the lesson, so you can't get to work.

SUSAN: For example in Cookery, there were some knives and forks gone missing, right, and Mrs B goes 'Where's the knives and forks?' looking at us lot (the Afro-Caribbean pupils in the class).

VERA: Yeah, all the blacks.

SONIA: Seriously right, in the past most coloured children that has left school they've all said she's prejudiced.

JEAN: She's told some kids to go back to their own country.

SONIA: Seriously right, if you go to another white teacher or somebody, and tell them that they're being prejudiced against you, they'll make out it's not, that it's another reason.

JEAN: When Mrs B told Julie to go back to her own country she went and told Mrs C (the Deputy Headmistress), Mrs C said that Mrs B was depressed because her husband was dying.

SONIA: So why take it out on the black people? ... then she's told black people to do many things, she's even called them monkey.

SANDRA: As for that Mrs C I can't explain my feelings about the woman. Because Mrs B, right she just prejudiced, she comes up to me in the Cookery lesson, tell me to clean out the dustbin, and I was so vexed I started to cry, I was so vexed by it. I didn't come to school for two weeks.

SONIA: You see the thing is, right, they can get away with saying anything to your face, there isn't anything you can do about it.

JEAN: In Geography, this teacher dashed a book at me, and I dashed it back, and I got into trouble for it.

(*group roared with laughter*)

VERA: Most of the things that the teacher says, right, they say things that annoy you they know that you're going to answer them back, so they can get you into trouble. Take Mrs B, she'll walk around with a towel, and if you look at someone and smile and she thinks you're talking, she flash water in your face or she'll slap you over the head, but I've just told her that if she boxed me I'll have to hit her back. Because she's got no right to walk round doing that. If you answer her back in any way, then she'll send you down to Mrs C (Deputy Headmistress) then you're in trouble.

SUSAN: Mrs C is prejudiced herself because, I mean, she said to Karen that she is only getting bad because she hangs around with too many black people. It's not as if (*shouting in anger*) as she says, black people are going to change you to bad.

VERA: Some teachers are alright but others, you can tell that they're prejudiced by the things they do. Every time Mrs B's cooking, even if she's doing say, a boiled egg or something like that, any little simple thing you can think of, coloured people and Asian people have to cook it different . . . Oh, well the coloured people and Asian people always cook their things different . . .

JEAN: (*with disdain*) Is that what she says?

VERA: Yeah, she's really facety you know, that's why I don't get on with her, and when I was telling me mum, me mum was going mad because she must think that we're some aliens, or something . . . If the teachers have no respect for you, there's no way I'm going to respect them.

RESEARCHER: Would you say that the Afro-Caribbean boys have the same experience with the teachers as yourselves?

VERA: The boys I know don't get the same treatment because most of the lads are quicker to box the teachers-dem than the girls, you see.

Assertions from pupils about what teachers call them may not always be believed by sceptical readers. We now quote a Year Head whose reference to the phrase – 'go back to your own country' – supports the girls' assertions – but about a different teacher. His account also demonstrates that staff in positions of authority, if not totally condoning such utterances, do not necessarily rush to condemn them even given the pressure of a parental complaint. The Year Head states:

If I had one parent who sat with me in my office and said 'I have come to see you because that Mr – said to my son "If you don't like it here then go back where you came from and where you belong" and I was so upset at that because my son was born here and I have lived in this country for over 20 years and how *dare* [italics from Year Head's emphasis] he say that, because my son comes from here. I came from Jamaica over 20 years ago and I got married in this country and I have stayed here ever since and although perhaps I might want to go back to Jamaica it's not home to him.'

And that lady was quite genuine. The member of staff when I spoke to him about it afterwards – I did not call him in to speak to him about it immediately because I did not think it was either my place or my duty – I told him that she was very concerned about that being said to her son and quite frankly so was I, and really was that the sort of thing to say and he agreed it wasn't the thing to say but he said 'I was so angry at the time. The pupils had been going on at me about "You're always picking on me"' and then finally the boy said to him that he was picking on him because he was black and he said 'That just triggered it off.' He said 'I just turned to him and said what I said. Yes, I did say that.'

I know he said it in anger but you don't even say things in anger if you don't feel them and that really bothers me a bit. But that's not the only one. I have had others who've actually said 'X doesn't like my child', but then of course X doesn't like any black child. And I think we both know who I'm referring to ... Black children react in a certain way because they feel they are being picked on, and because they react badly then further reaction follows.

Discussions were also held with Afro-Caribbean boys in the school particularly with one group of 15 pupils, who voiced similar complaints to the girls. One of the more vivid examples again illustrates conflict.

RESEARCHER: Do you all go around school together as a group?

ALL: (*defensively*) Yeah, not to cause trouble.

STEPHEN: At break times, we talk and have a laugh, I know she (referring to the Deputy Headmistress) always seem to think there is something going on.

LEE: We normally play football together, we have known each other throughout the years.

GARY: Friends, from long time, isn't it.

STEPHEN: There is a great deal of racial prejudice in the school.

EARL: Although some of the teachers try to hide it, but you can tell by the way they get on with you.

STEPHEN: Really, it's how the teachers treat us. Because I can get on with teachers in this school, it depends on how they treat me. If they treat me friendly I will give them the same respect back. Some teachers, right, think just because they're teachers they're above you and they're something better, and they treat you as if you're nothing, so you think to yourself, 'well who are they to think that' ... so you then treat them without any respect because they don't give you any, so really, it's just a two-way thing, I say.

DAVID: There's a few teachers who have got real interest in, if you say, black children in particular. Like various articles in the papers are saying, that we're supposed to be lacking in education and whatever, we're not exactly tip-top with the Indians and white people, you get the odd person that cares like the Asian teacher, Mr —— but these other teachers don't.

GARY: I can tell that they don't like us because we're black, it's just something about them. It's just certain teachers who are racialist.

LEE: There are certain teachers that's true, like Mrs —— and Mr —— but on the whole most of the teachers are the same.

RESEARCHER: How do the teachers' attitudes you have described make you feel as an individual?

GARY: Resentful.

WINSTON: Hate.

EARL: A bit small.

STEPHEN: When you know that they are sort of negative and they don't really talk to you as a person, you know that they're not really bothered about what happens to you. Whether you pass an exam or not, and you think to yourself, well they're not really bothered about what you do, so that means you don't really think of it in terms of, oh well, he is really taking pride in me or her and really want me to do well, it goes beyond just teaching me, it's not something personal as well.

RESEARCHER: How do the teachers' attitudes affect your behaviour in school?

STEPHEN: I suppose it makes me behave bad, they pick you out, on your colour anyway. They tend to say, oh well, he's black so it's to be expected, they're bound to do that, so when they give you that kind of attitude, you think oh well, blow them, if that's what they think, why not act like that.

DAVID: It's not really as bad for me because they can't really tell that I'm half-caste (this pupil looks more white than Afro-Caribbean) like the rest of them. But I still feel it the same, but not as much as this lot.

LEE: I haven't experienced any problem in classes, but when I'm in the group hanging about the corridors I do, not really in class. Like David. I'm not really full black, I'm half-caste.

Many pupils thus see the conflict as an inevitable response to the teachers' attitudes towards their ethnicity. As one pupil succinctly put it 'you then treat them without any respect because they don't give any, so really it's just a two-way thing'. Nevertheless, the pupils did acknowledge that not all teachers held negative attitudes towards their ethnicity.

A number of senior teachers and other staff were asked whether they acknowledge that something of an estranged relationship existed between the Afro-Caribbean pupils and teachers, and whether they attributed this to negative racial attitudes projected by teachers towards these pupils. The Deputy Headmistress in charge of discipline had this to say about the experience of the Afro-Caribbean pupils:

DEPUTY HEAD: The West Indians are very lively, very gregarious. They like to be together to talk. They do however feel threatened, they do feel people aren't fair to them and sometimes they're quite right.

RESEARCHER: Why do they feel threatened?

DH: If you touch one, the reply is 'don't touch me'. I suppose it's because some people have been given a hard time. I think sometimes people are not fair, and I think they do feel it . . . they sometimes feel picked on and I can see all this when they come in here sometimes. They are very resentful and sulky and always at the back of it is that feeling that they are unfairly treated.

RESEARCHER: Do you think that the pupils may be justified in feeling that they are unfairly treated?

DH: Not within the school no, we bend over backwards to be fair, to get to terms with the pupils, to try to get their confidence. And when you do have to grumble about something, they are always asked 'is this fair', 'did you do this' and only then do you jump. I would never punish any child who didn't agree with me that they had done something ... That's the important thing about discipline, to make them see themselves as they really are, not as they think they are.

A deputy headmaster spoke in defence of teachers:

Because of a few children that we have, many of whom were taken in late in this school, all of which Mr (the headmaster) quite rightly said causes considerable disruption and disturbance within the school, the teachers I think if they're asked, tend to look upon this school ... as a possible source of disturbance to them. I think that they are not comfortable enough in this school, they don't feel secure.

RESEARCHER: Why do the teachers feel insecure?

DEPUTY HEAD: Because we have sufficient children within this school and there are not many, a tiny minority, who have done outrageous things, who've misbehaved outrageously and who've been allowed to persist in their misbehaviour. For example, two children, Simon a white boy, and Jane, a West Indian girl, are two children who have disturbed and disrupted this school ever since they came. Although we have tried hard with Jane, we have not succeeded ... in keeping her calm and amenable and pleasant, as she can be. She is capable of a public display of aggression ... I think that the actions of such children within a class, it can be within a class or publicly in corridors, is sufficient to worry teachers, and disturb them, and make them feel that within the school that is a sufficient threat to affect them psychologically, and I think that this militates against the good work of a school. It prevents teachers collectively and individually from doing their best. Such children because we have failed with them, and it's been apparent that we are not succeeding, despite massive efforts ... Teachers even if they don't teach them know of them, and rumours spread in school – it's not just the ordinary cynicism that you get among staff, rumours spread. I think that's worth a good study, the way in which teachers are affected by rumour.

The two comments do to an extent acknowledge the estranged relationship between teachers and certain groups of pupils. However they see this as being inherent in the pupil with the teacher as the recipient. They suggest also that categorization of pupils' behaviour, and the influence of 'informal gossip' among staff on teachers' judgements is part of the 'hidden curriculum' in this school.

Contrary to the views expressed here by the two deputy heads, conversations with other teachers suggested that the issue of 'race' was frequently the basis of the conflict between some Afro-Caribbean pupils and their teachers. An Asian teacher who had taught at the school for six years stated:

There is a lot of racism in the school and I have often believed that a lot of multicultural talk should start with the staff before it starts with the pupils. There is little racism amongst the children ... I, even as a friend and a colleague of the staff notice it strongly in little points of racism, all the time constantly there, it gets beyond a joke, I've lost friends in the school or I don't associate with certain members of staff purely because of the constant jibbing which eventually gets beyond a joke.

This teacher's annoyance was reiterated by a white teacher who related his experience of the school when he took up his post seven years before:

I had kept fairly quiet while I tried to establish myself and gauge the atmosphere of the school. Even so, I had some fairly sharp differences with several members over their attitude towards the coloured pupils. There were fairly frequent serious and 'humorous' comments made in the staff room and at the dinner table that I sometimes challenged. One or two other teachers were encouraged by my willingness to argue against racial prejudice and became more vocal themselves. On reflection, racialist comments are much less common now, in my presence at least.

A teacher who had been at the school for two years added credence to the points already raised, stating that there is 'racism' amongst staff within the school:

Definitely I have come across incidents where I have actually seen teachers pick on children for no other reasons than the colour of their skin.

RESEARCHER: What evidence have you to support this?

MR M (YEAR HEAD): For example, I had a great verbal battle with him over a West Indian girl called June Green who I teach. She was a bit troublesome and still is to some teachers. She was a bit troublesome to me to begin with but I soon cottoned on to the fact that it wasn't her but the girl she was sitting next to in the class. When I cottoned on to that I started to encourage June, sitting her on her own, it took me a long, long time, she is a very sensitive girl.

Now I can get her to virtually do anything for me. She's great. She is still a bit shy but she's tremendous with me. Mr X wrote me a note 'would I make some notes on her, there is a possibility of her going into the unit' (withdrawal unit for disruptive pupils). I wrote back and said no way did I think that she ought to go into the unit. He came back to me, went on about her being West Indian and all that. I said to him on what grounds did you want to put her in the unit. He said 'she's a trouble-maker'. I said to him you just don't go and put a child in the unit because she is a troublemaker. Of course, she has not been the only case. In each case it has been a West Indian pupil rather than an Asian child.

RESEARCHER: Well, you have only referred to one teacher.

TEACHER: I have not come across such blatant attitudes amongst other members of staff but I would get that feeling, and if I can being white, feel an atmosphere like that, then the children can too, especially if their skins are black.

So far we have reported Afro-Caribbean pupils' perceptions of the attitudes held by certain teachers and how this may influence their behaviour. We need now to assess the extent to which the pupils' experience may affect their educational opportunities.

There is concern within the school about the relative underachievement of pupils – especially among the Afro-Caribbean group. This point is illustrated by the Head of the Sixth form, who describes the composition of the Sixth form:

> This year they're mostly Indians, that is the largest ethnic group of people who stay on to the Sixth form, followed by the white children, then the Pakistani and West Indian in very small numbers.
>
> RESEARCHER: Why is the percentage of Afro-Caribbean pupils staying on in the sixth form so low?
>
> HEAD OF SIXTH: Now I was asked this at my interview and what was I going to do about it. I don't know. I think to try and break down the barriers that some of the West Indian children have against teachers and academic things ... I find them all delightful in the first and second year, something happens between the second year and the fourth year, and in the fourth year they seem to have lost interest in academic things. I don't find them any less delightful, but they don't seem as interested in academic things.

This observation was supported by another teacher's statement:

> There's no specific area that I can lay my finger on to explain why West Indian kids underachieve ... what is inevitable is that a lot of West Indian children particularly the bright ones will do fairly well up to either the beginning or the middle of the fourth year, and for some peculiar reason their progress will fall off towards the end of the fifth year. There's no deterioration in intelligence or anything like that, the intelligence is there. The hard work is missing, the motivation is missing, the need to get on is missing and the exam results inevitably suffer from that.

Conversations with Afro-Caribbean pupils suggest that they, like the Afro-Caribbean pupils at School A, believe that teachers held low expectations of their academic performance. However, unlike the pupils at School A, they saw the organization of the school as having little influence on their educational opportunities, with attitudes of the teachers being paramount, and concluded that the prevailing attitudes held by certain teachers would undermine the organization of any school. As one pupil commented:

> Some coloured children in this school are getting bad because of the way they get treated, and they make out as if we're just doing it because we get low examination grades so we start getting bad with the teachers. They

think it is because we got no sense. We're acting like that because of the way we're treated in the past throughout the school. See if you know that Mrs – and Mrs – can get away with talking about your colour and that knowing there's not a thing you can do about it because they don't believe you.

An Afro-Caribbean boy suggests that pupils can be aware that the acquisition of an adverse label in the school, may influence the teachers' expectations of academic ability:

A teacher called Mrs Z she even said it to us herself that she wants all the black people out of the school. If a black pupil comes to see her a few times she automatically labels them as troublemakers. If anything happens in a crowd their names are always shouted out, so they're labelled in front of all the teachers as a bad person. So then the teachers think if he is like that he's not worth the trouble.

From such observations and discussions in both schools, it appeared that the relationship between Afro-Caribbean pupils and teachers was often one of conflict and that the issue of race was frequently central to this conflict. In School A from about the third form (as the Headmaster pointed out) black pupils became aware of negative attitudes they felt that the school held towards them. Similarly in School B teachers became aware of the barriers between the pupils and the teachers from the second year onwards. The perceived attitudes of teachers seemed to convince them that the school system was 'rigged': some saw very little point in trying.

Many were still frustrated by what they saw as not 'gettting on' academically. From conversations, it appeared that they were not against education *per se*: in fact a number of them had left school to go to further education. However, in school their energy was not always tapped so was sometimes directed towards disrupting the school or, as one pupil said: 'to get our own back on them for the way they have treated us.' [. . .]

Notes

1 Hargreaves D. (1967) *Social Relations in a Secondary School*. Routledge & Kegan Paul, London.
2 Ibid.
3 Goffman, E. (1971) *Relations in Public*. Penguin, Harmondsworth.

Section 2:
The School
Framework

Introduction

The guiding principle for this section of the Reader was that the articles should address 'what new teachers need to know about schools beyond teaching their subject'. It is, of course, impossible to cover that topic comprehensively, but nevertheless it seemed crucial for at least two reasons to try to offer some guidance in a limited range of key areas.

First, new teachers have typically spent a large amount of time discovering how to reveal the mysteries of their subject to their pupils. They do, though, often seem surprised by, and less prepared for, such extra-classroom facets of their work as what the workings of the school as an organization mean for them, or what it means to act in a pastoral role towards a young person, whether formally or informally. They may also, for instance, often take time and effort to find out such things as the legal position regarding children with special educational needs. Even within the classroom, such matters as the standards of work to be expected, and how they are to be assessed often appear to be pressing concerns in the early months of teaching (and often remain problematic, albeit in rather different ways, throughout the teaching career).

The second reason why it seems useful to address these issues is that the experience of schools which we gain as consumers or clients is perhaps less helpful – even misleading – in this area than in others. While it is possible to get some idea of how teaching is done from being on the receiving end, things like the way the school is run, or marks are given, how the whole curriculum is divided into subjects and subjects into lessons, are much more opaque, largely perhaps because they appear to the consumer as 'natural' and effortless, as phenomena that exist rather than policies and practices that have to be brought into being and maintained.

Two papers directly consider the question of how schools organize themselves to achieve what is required of them under the conditions and with the resources they are allocated. Handy and Aitken – respectively a Business School Professor and a retired Director of Education – examine the implications of regarding the school as a complex work organization, while Burgess focuses on the basic division of the school's work into academic and pastoral areas and details some features of its operation in a comprehensive school.

As we mentioned above, we are assuming in a generic reader like this that students' knowledge of subject pedagogy and of the workings of subject departments can be taken largely for granted. A common request, though, is for advice on how to mark work and on just what it is we are doing when we mark work. The complementary pair of articles by Deale and Rowntree addresses these questions. The former is a mainly 'technical' treatise on ways of assessing pupils, while the latter highlights the broader issue of what assessment is and what it means for students.

We looked in the previous Section at how pupils effect the work of schools. In this section we look at two distinct aspects of that issue. First, the papers by Fish and Gavine look at provision for, and how to cater for, pupils with special educational needs. Gavine closely analyses the concept of need, and finds it on the whole unhelpful, suggesting that a firmer guide to practice may come from the use of a 'laddering' technique to transform policy questions into classroom practices. Fish's focus is very firmly on the issues which provision for special educational needs raises for the ordinary school, and on the ordinary school's capacity to recognize and meet a variety of individual special needs.

Among the commonest problems reported by beginning teachers are discipline – which is hardly a surprise to anyone – and their formal and informal pastoral duties – which tend to be rather more of a surprise, especially to the probationer. The papers by Tattum and Pelleschi respectively examine these problems. Tattum discusses a number of key features of what he calls a more constructive approach to discipline. These include developing appropriate rules, employing effective teacher strategies, better teacher-pupil relations, and improving personal and social education. Pelleschi's paper focuses on one of the more acute pastoral problems, that of counselling Asian girls in secondary schools, but in doing so indicates the major dimensions, difficulties and possibilities of this kind of work.

The other aspect of the pupil issue considered is that of how girls may be given greater opportunity to succeed in secondary schools, especially in science. Head discusses the issues of personality characteristics associated with the choice of science, and suggests some ways the curriculum might be organized to accommodate them. Whyte isolates some factors that appear to make science more 'girl friendly' and goes on to discuss how schools might be arranged in a more 'girl friendly' way.

The final reading in this Section consists of a series of short extracts about the state and the nature of a set of school subjects and of the curriculum as a whole. (Though only five subjects are discussed in detail, we trust that the validity of the general point for all subjects is clear.) These accounts were written from different philosophical and educational standpoints, and with different audiences in mind, but they do all serve to show that the very subjects we teach are themselves as 'non-natural' and as much a (permanently changing) social arrangement as any other part of the social organization of the school.

8

Understanding Schools as Organizations

Charles Handy and Robert Aitken

Schools are also organizations. Sometimes the preoccupation with so many children, with the odds and ends of schooling, with the dramas of young people's lives and all their emotions, can blind one to the fact that all the things are happening within an organization tht is itself bound by the laws of other organizations. Box 8.1 shows how it feels, in the words of a primary-school headteacher describing a typical Monday morning in his school.

Box 8.1 Monday morning

I needn't pick up Mrs Churchill this morning. She rang at 7.30 am to say her baby daughter Lisa was ill, and she would have to stay at home to look after her. Funny how calls at 7.30 am at home and 8.30 am at school usually mean some staff emergency!

No work on the stationery requisition today. I will take J2, and the school secretary can rough out stationery requirements after finishing the dinner money. I quite enjoy J2 – a class full of characters, and a challenge. Staff always reckon *I'm happier when I'm teaching*.

Parked at school by 8.10 am. As usual three staff have beaten me to it – deputy, head of infants and nursery teacher. Talked over change of plans with Miss Butler, my deputy. Amended day's information in staff diary before she took it to send round staff prior to start of school. Checked with Mrs Griffin, head of infant department, that all was organized for the hair inspection by the District Nurse at 9.30 am. Half-past eight has passed – no telephone call. No further staff absence today. *We'll manage*.

Children and parents already paying dinner money at secretary's window. Nursery teacher rings on internal line to say she's discovered three broken windows in her activities room. She will find caretaker. Parent arrives with son – she is taking him for a medical but would I arrange to keep a dinner for him? Secretary passes message to cook.

112

Father arrives to ask would I act as a guarantor so that he can buy clothing for children? Agree and sign. What have I let myself in for? Phonecall from professional assistant in Education Department to ask if she could visit school later today to inspect crumbling temporary classroom and state of nursery decoration. Agreed – she knows her way around and staff and children are used to visitors.

Now to J2 ... but no, a knock on the door, NSPCC inspector from Special Unit to discuss report from a neighbour about a possible non-accidental injury to one of our children. It is urgent I talk to him about it because *we are worried about the child too.* Quick message to Miss Butler – take assembly, please. My assembly on 'Treasures' will have to wait. She will use one of her stock for emergencies. Discussing case – panic – who is registering J2? *Panic over.* Miss North, part-time teacher, passes window with J2 on the way to assembly. I eventually get to J2 at 9.40 am.

Monday morning in a primary school!

Box 8.1 captures the atmosphere of school, the pressure of the immediate, the intense involvement with people both inside and outside the school. The emergencies can be of intense personal concern, as with the boy whom the NSPCC inspector wanted to discuss. Always there is the human dimension that is part of the fascination of working in a school; the opportunity to be involved in the daily experiences of people – their frailties and their joys, their values and their growth.

The school in Box 8.1 is one of 20,384 primary schools up and down the country. It has 216 children, aged between 4 and 11. The head has a staff of nine teachers, one of whom is part-time, three nursery assistants, an education assistant to help with the reception and infant classes, a caretaker, five cleaners, a cook and eleven kitchen staff. It is a society in miniature. It is an organization as well as a school.

Any organization needs systems for communicating and arranging things, as well as a structure for dividing up the work and defining the relationship of people to each other. It will require someone to set priorities and define responsibilities and duties. Someone then has to make sure that these responsibilities are carried out and must apportion praise or disapproval when necessary. Without these prior arrangements every problem becomes a crisis, every event something that needs the individual attention of the person at the centre.

The events in Box 8.1 were handled expeditiously and caringly because there was a pre-arranged organization in the school, there were relationships that could be relied upon, and there was support for the school from parents and the wider community. Was this what the head meant when he said, 'We'll manage'? Was he referring to that pre-planned system of organization or did he mean, 'We will cope with these problems. We'll get by'?

Is it only a British habit to use 'manage' in the second, more belittling way, to mean 'coping'? This is to relegate management to a necessary chore, something unnecessary in an ideal world. When the head said, 'I'm happier when I'm teaching', he may also have been reflecting the common feeling among heads that one is a teacher first and always, and a manager by necessity. As we shall see, it is characteristic of professionals to see management as a service function. But professionals do not like to think of themselves as members of an organization, preferring words like 'partnership' or practice' or 'consortium'. The dilemma for schools is that willy-nilly they *are* organizations, not just groupings of teachers, and they have to accept that the management of these organizations is a key activity, not a mere service function. [. . .]

The Primary School

In the opening example the head and his staff were able to deal with the problems that arose because they were able to rely upon:

● the organization of the school;
● the quality of relationships within the school;
● the support of parents and the wider community.

[. . .]

Organization

The first and fundamental step that a head faces (and re-faces each year with changes in children and teachers) is how to *organize* the school. She or he must first decide how to divide the children into learning groups, of what size, age, mix and for what activities, etc.; and then decide how to deploy the skills of the staff to these groups and tasks. The options are many. There is no single answer. In our example the head has chosen to organize his children into seven classes (plus a nursery) of roughly equal size (average twenty-five pupils) according to age; and to allocate each of his full-time teachers to a class, using his part-time teacher and himself to facilitate small-group work or enable teachers to take other classes for special activities. Given the current conventions of British primary education this form of organization is typical. [. . .]

This form of organization makes much sense and has a lot of strengths. It offers security to children and staff alike; they know their place in the order of things. Each class is like a large family with the opportunity during the course of a year to know one another and their teacher well: to know and grow together. The head knows who is responsible for what stage of development. Basic roles are clear. It is an example of a 'job-shop' structure, where each unit has its own independent task to do.

Yet each class is but a mini-society within the larger society of the whole school, and here complications can set in. Each class is likely to develop or exhibit its own character or culture deriving from the make-up and background of the children in the group and in the person of the teacher (who herself or himself has strengths and weaknesses). [. . .]

In practice the situation is more complex than that. Within the setting of a school there are other groupings, each coming from a different position with differing experiences, expectations and values. Children are different from adults; teachers are different (in their professional role) from parents. These form distinct 'peer groups' in the sense that one takes some of one's values and behaviour from people with a similar background. [. . .]

There are of course other groups (including the other adults, the non-teaching staff). The caretaker who lives on site is often an influential figure with a foot in both the local community and the school. From their different vantage-points, or *roles*, these people affect and influence what happens in the classroom.

So a primary-school head has a more complex task than just creating a form of organization. She or he needs to see that the working of that organization is informed by, and recognizes, the influences of other groupings, and to guard against the inadequacies of the organization she or he adopts. This depends a great deal upon the quality of relationships operating within the organization.

Relationships

We have seen that it is one thing for a head to create an organization: yet another to supervise its working. One of the fundamental tasks facing any head is to get the teaching staff to express a collective will. This is necessary because the teacher in her or his own classroom is *the* expression of the school. If discontinuities in the treatment, learning or development of children are to be avoided, then a corporate purpose is needed. Yet teaching is such a personal activity. [. . .] How then does one combine professional autonomy and artistic freedom with a common purpose? This is the challenge that faces all schools and all professional organizations. In the setting of a primary school a head can do this by various means. She or he may choose to lay down the main content of syllabuses and schemes of work and the methods to be used, and leave the interpretation and pace to the professional competence of each teacher. This, however, is unlikely to be sufficient. Content and methods change and need updating. Even reading schemes can become quickly out-dated in a multicultural society. The advent of computers in the clasroom and the need to identify children with special learning needs are other examples of current changes that require response within the organization.

What is important is that the organization knows its way – where it is going – and that those working in the organization know what it stands for and what are the shared set of values to which each is contributing. To achieve this is not easy. The head will be able to use the expertise of her or his staff by allocating leadership roles in areas of the curriculum, such as mathematics. This can be invigorating for the member of staff involved, releasing and enhancing commitment and motivation. But not all staff are equally experienced or capable of such leadership roles. Minor roles can be felt to be insignificant and demanding. The choosing of staff for responsibilities is a tightrope any head or manager has to walk, particularly if promotion remains the main reward for good teaching, for not all good teachers make good leaders of teachers. Schools, like other organizations, have to find ways to reward good performance that do not involve giving the person a different job. [. . .]

The size of a primary school, with 9 or so teachers and 10 or 12 support staff, should mean that the head and staff are able to communicate personally and frequently, unlike in the larger organizations that many secondary schools are. But smaller organizations are not immune from contrary forces. They may become a dictatorship (owing too much for their purpose to one person) or an oligarchy. Anyone who has lived in a small-scale setting (e.g. on a ship) will know that personality conflict can be a real problem and a divisive influence. Primary schools, despite their apparent 'bonus' of relatively small scale, do not escape the need to face and work at the issue of relationships.

The definition of *roles and responsibilities* and the choosing of staff to undertake them is a crucial task for any head, and it can present difficulties. Even the basic task of allocating teachers to classes can be fraught. There are cases where a teacher has taken the same class in the same classroom for ten or more years. It has become her or his class and rightful empire – impregnable to the rest of the school and sometimes a deadweight in the evolving organization. *Territory* is a prized possession in every organization, with its boundaries fiercely defended.

Roles and responsibilities are important both so that tasks can be undertaken and also because they offer security and a place in the organization for the individual. But this of itself is insufficient. A *collective purpose* is still needed. All members of the organization need the motivation to feel they are partners in it and, particularly for teachers, that they are valued as professional people. Their views need to be heard (and if necessary challenged). This process of achieving a collective view is one of the most difficult tasks – if not *the* most difficult – of a head. It cannot be rushed or taken for granted. It is a continuous process and one that cannot be left to casual conversations or a quick discussion in the staff room at playtime – valuable as those can be. A collective purpose can be achieved only if it is truly collective, i.e. representing the considered views of all involved.

Those involved start, obviously, with the staff, but it goes further than that; parents, families and the community have expectations of, and influence on, the organization. Their confidence in the school is an essential ingredient in its successful functioning. They too have to share in the collective purpose if they are to be truly supportive of the organization.

Parents and the wider community
When parents commit their children to attending primary school they do so with a sense of confidence but also with expectations and fears. [. . .] Their

children need to be growing in the company of other children and learning beyond the family under the guidance of specialists. But there can be a sense of loss; the influence of the family can be felt to be waning. Their children will be subjected to other values and knowledge, including those from other children from different backgrounds. This can produce tensions and dependencies and an increasing need for parents to understand the 'influence' of the school system on them and their families. [. . .]

Some parents are over-anxious, and expect more from the school for their child than is realistic. But sadly too many other parents abdicate once their child is at school. Teachers know that the parents whom they really want to see, to know and to help are often the ones who never come to school. [. . .] Whatever the attitudes of parents, this is a critical dimension that the school as an organization has to *manage*, rather than accepting it as part of the scenery. Put in another way, the boundary of the system reaches out beyond the school gates. Organizations are never islands unto themselves. [. . .]

There are strong cultural influences from outside the school that are brought into the classroom daily, but the culture of the school also extends outwards and into the homes of the children.

So not only has the head of any school the problem of securing continuity in the education of pupils through differing teaching styles of her or his staff. She or he also has a need to secure as much common ground as possible between the school and home 'cultures'. She or he needs to work with the staff for a sufficient understanding between home and school so that what is done at school is not undone at home and vice versa. Thus schools and homes are increasingly readily open to parents and teachers respectively, and many schools are developing as community schools with a curriculum expressed in community/family terms.

Although a primary school may seem to be small and intimate it is in fact a complex and relatively large undertaking or *system*. The *average*-sized school will have 30 or so adults and about 200 children *within the organization*. But, as we have seen, the school is inextricably bound up with the culture of the wider community, particularly that of the parents and families.

The primary school is a significant management task, not only for the head but also for each member of staff, because each has to express the purpose of the school in managing her or his own class. Each and every primary teacher therefore has to be a manager. Every teacher has the task of setting goals and targets for a group, for organizing that group and providing the sources for it, for managing the relationships within the group and the relationships between the members of the group and the other groups or families to which they belong. Every teacher has to decide how to excite and stimulate each individual, what style of behaviour to adopt, what methods of persuasion or influence to use, how to reward and punish, how to handle differences and arguments. Knowledge of one's subject counts for little if one can't do these, which are *all* management functions.

The Secondary School

The tasks facing a secondary head teacher are *intrinsically* the same yet even more complex. The functioning of a secondary school similarly depends upon the nature and quality of:

- organization;
- relationships;
- support of the wider community;

and the *inherent* pressures – from both within and without the school – are the same. But *the emphases are different*, and there are additional factors to be accommodated such as:

- size;
- the advancing maturity of the students (including the fact that they have already had seven or so years of schooling);
- the increasing force of peer-group pressures;
- the demands of the examination system;
- employment expectations;
- the approach to adulthood.

Size

There are 4,553 secondary schools in England. They range in size from 45 to 2,001 students. Given a national average pupil-to-teacher staffing ratio of 16.5, this means that the average size of a secondary-school teaching staff is 54. For the larger schools (over 1,200 students) the teaching staff will number more than 80 (including part-timers). There may well be more than 50 other staff.

Secondary schools are therefore large organizations by any standards. In addition to the teaching staff there will be more non-teaching staff, more parents and families and additional outside interests. [. . .]

Organization

The tasks facing a secondary head in creating an organization for her or his school are similar to those of a primary head:

- how to organize the students into learning groups;
- of what size, age mix and for what activities and stages;
- how to deploy the teaching and technical staff to these groups and activities;
- how to relate these to the space and facilities available.

The options are many and the answers are many (i.e. as expressed in the variety of forms of organization being practised). The design (or change) of an organization is a question of values. As for any designer, a decision to emphasize this or that feature determines the place and space left for other features. An order of importance – of what is valued in the organization – is created. And the organization goes on expressing those values. If, for example, specialist subject teaching is the prime basis of a school organization, then, as we shall see, other aspects – such as the provision for pastoral care – may be debilitated. [. . .]

Commonly the five years' schooling between the ages 11 and 16 is seen as two stages: providing in the first two or three years a general course for all students; with more differentiation (options) in the third and fourth years, usually dictated by choice of examinations to be taken. To maintain equality of opportunity and to counter over-early selection or specialization (and therefore narrowing of the curriculum), many schools adopt all-ability groupings in the first year or so.

The basic model relates to a small secondary school with about 90 students (three forms of entry) in the first year divided into classes of about equal size (30). The total number of staff (including part-timers) would be between 25 and 30, and some would be allocated according to their specialisms to teach first-year class/es. Some may teach more than one subject. For larger schools (e.g. eight forms of entry, 240 students per year) the number of classes would of course be greater, as would be the number of staff. The same model would to a greater or lesser extent express the organization also of the second and third years.

There are obvious strengths and weaknesses in this form of organization:

- the classes offer stability and security to the student groupings;
- the roles and responsibilities of staff are clear;

but:

- the differences of style between seven or so staff teaching the same group can lead to differences of response *between subjects*;
- the differences of style between twelve or so staff teaching the same year group can lead to different responses *between classes in the same year group*.

That is not to say that roles are automatically clear or that different styles or responses can or should be avoided. These are potential consequences of the organization adopted and are likely to need other organizational arrangements (e.g. meetings between all first-year staff under a head of year).

The same features and considerations will apply in the second and third years under this form of organization. In larger schools the scale of the task of co-ordination is bigger, with possibly as many as thirty staff teaching first-year classes.

At the fourth- and fifth-year stage the tasks facing the organization become yet more complex. It is necessary to arrange the teaching groups so as to match the examination courses or projects chosen by the students. Teaching groups therefore tend to be formed in relation to subjects (or groups of subjects), examination levels and syllabuses. There are several consequences of this:

- more student groupings;
- less stability and security in the teaching group;
- tendency towards polarization of values (between subjects and levels of course);
- polarization of expectations;
- greater differences in motivation (among students and staff).

The organization has become more fractured, dispersed and unfocused; place and role in the organization are less clear.

[...] The organizational problems of the secondary school intensify in the fourth and fifth year, driven by the demands of academic qualification and subject specialization and the attitudes of students and parents. (The development of Technical and Vocational Education Initiatives, the Certificate of Pre-Vocational Preparation, the new GCSE examination and education for special needs, etc., are adding to these demands.) The school has to work harder to counter the contrary pressures that intensify too. There is a greater need to provide structures within the organization to secure;

- co-ordination;
- continuity;
- commonality of styles and values;
- motivation.

In the language of organization theory, there must be enough *Integrating devices* to match the necessary *differentiation*. These are difficulties that face any organization. The larger and more complex the organization the more difficult these nuts are to crack. And, as we have seen, secondary schools as organizations are both large and complex. They need careful and diligent managing if they are not to disintegrate.

The *differentiation* of secondary schools is forced upon them by the subject syllabus and the examination system. The dangers are that the imperative of academic qualification drives out other values cherished by the school, such as according equal respect and opportunity to all students. The reality is less than the ideology. So, for example, attitudes develop among the people within the organization (staff and students) that some subjects are more important than others, that some courses or classes are more valued than others, some teachers, some activities, some students more than others.

As always, what is important is how the organization is perceived by the individual within it. What is his or her place, role, value? It can happen at this stage that some students feel teachers are competing for their time and minds against other subject teachers. It is unfortunately true that many students, particularly those with low or no academic expectations, feel unvalued at this stage. They are not motivated by the organization (except to fulfil its low expectations of them) and are likely to retreat into the security of their peer group, whose anti-school culture becomes stronger than that of the school. When *motivation* and *identity* are lost within an organization, other motivations and identities replace them.

Such dissonances can occur in any organization. Fortunately it often happens that self-adjusting mechanisms begin to operate within the organization. This is more difficult when the style of operation has become habitually engrained or when the organization is subject to strong conditioning by external influences. Change is then a more difficult process and is slow in coming.

This is the snare that secondary schools are caught in to a considerable extent. Academic values and didactic method are deeply engrained, and these are enshrined in an examination system that is based on subject knowledge. Since the examinations are marked against the average of those being examined, only a minority can ever come out top. And since the examinations are designed for only 60 per cent of the age group, there is a large bottom. These largely external factors contribute powerfully to the problems of internal organization that we have described – particularly to the loss of identity and sense of anomie of many students in an organization where such academic values are over-emphasized and other experiences and achievements are under-expressed.

The possibility that individual students could get lost in a large all-ability setting was recognized by the pioneers of the comprehensive school in the early 1950s. They built into the organization a pastoral or house system whereby, for example, a school of 1,200 students had within it an organization of ten houses each of 120 students. Tutors in the houses had responsibility for the welfare, discipline and pastoral care of their groups, including contact with families, the careers service, the courts, etc.

This system of pastoral care has provided a strong integrating mechanism to counterbalance the disintegrating tendencies in a strongly emphasized academic structure. But the pastoral care organization has been under strain in recent years, especially since the school-leaving age was raised to sixteen in 1973 and in the face of unemployment. In many schools the provision for pastoral care is as yet only 'bolted on' to the academic framework and accorded only one or two tutor-group periods per week.

More recent developments in the pastoral care movement seek a more fundamental synthesis in their approach. They seek to acknowledge and use the resources of the peer group as a positive force in their own education. The main features of this for students are that they:

- work in tutor groups;
- learn by active and experiential methods;
- evaluate their own and the group's performance;
- have more determination of their own development.

This is an example of a self-adjusting mechanism in operation: of positive organic growth within the secondary-school system to cope with a particularly difficult aspect of internal organization. But such changes are not easily achieved. They threaten many established positions and practices. In those schools where this approach is more fully developed, *all* staff have a tutorial role, and learning in academic subjects is based on tutor-group processes. Educational change inevitably involves an organizational shift, which has to be understood, planned for and managed.

Relationships

This example of 'tension' within a school organization – in this case between the academic and pastoral aspects – throws up many issues of *internal relationships*. There is the need to maintain some commonality of will, style and understanding in all the expressions of the organization, as well as continuity in the education and consistency of treatment of students and in the development of staff. The *issues* are intrinsically the same as for primary schools but more complex because of the nature and size of secondary schools. Because of this they are likely to require substructures within the organization and some means of co-ordinating those structures.

Heads know how time-consuming and challenging this task of 'corporate management' – for that is what it is – can be. They have their deputies and heads of faculty to share the responsibility, and the skills and experience of heads of department and pastoral heads. But, even more than in a primary school, factions and differences of values have to be faced. The definition of roles and responsibilities, the choosing of personalities, the vesting of authority and the creation of time and space for the exercise of responsibility are all essential ingredients of this pie.

But, again, that is not all; the senior management is not the whole organization. The contribution and attitude of the 'ordinary' member of staff need to be recognized, especially in a professional organization. The teacher in the classroom is the embodiment of the school. A wise head therefore values and creates space for 'hearing the voice' of ordinary members of staff, whether individually or collectively through trade union representation. Indeed, the trade-union angle is probably one that is under-valued, as a positive force, in school management.

Similarly the *external relationships* are more complex. There is still the need to recognize the 'bond' with the families of the students, including the aspirations of parents as their offspring approach occupational choices. But increasingly the students are reaching out beyond the family and the school and developing their own interests and aspirations. Adolescence can be described as a period of apprenticeship to adulthood. And this is likely to include experimenting with drink, drugs, sex, smoking, fashions and music, some of which may be stimulated by commercial pressures. The 'cultures' of home and school are themselves under pressure from the current youth culture.

There are two more formal external pressures. As the period of compulsory schooling approaches its end, students as individuals have to face the prospect (or lack of it) of employment. What kind of job or career to follow? What are the requirements of employers? What does 'going out to work' mean? What does it mean in terms of a particular occupation? This interfaces with the requirements of examining boards: O levels, CSE, but also City and Guilds, Tec/Bec and RSA.

These are all issues that the secondary school has to address. They are points of contact or external relationships they have to maintain. They are the constituencies of the organization, each one with different expectations of the school. And they need to find expression within the structure of the organization. The boundary of the school never stops at the gate.

Summary

Schools, just like other organizations, need to:

- define their role and their specific contribution;
- deal with individuals and groups;
- run the organization;
- face the future.

9

House Staff and Department Staff

Robert G. Burgess

With the introduction of comprehensive education, questions were raised about methods of organizing a comprehensive school and their influence upon teacher relationships and teacher-pupil relationships. Architects, administrators and teachers considered ways in which large schools could be subdivided into smaller, more manageable units. A survey conducted by Monks (1968) for the National Foundation for Educational Research (NFER) found that the most popular form of internal school organization was the house system. Similarly, Benn and Simon (1972) found that of all the different types of internal organization, it was the house system that was among the most widely discussed forms of vertical unit in the comprehensive school. However, the 'pure' house system was used in only 122 (17 per cent) of the schools they surveyed. This trend was also repeated in the HMI survey of secondary schools as only 59 (15.4 per cent) of the schools studied were organized on a house system (Department of Education and Science, 1979, p. 219) although one-third of the 384 schools in the survey did use houses alongside other forms of internal organization.

A major problem surrounds the term house system as it can involve everything from the purpose-built house to a form of competition used for work or games (Monks, 1968, p. 40). Some schools have adopted the house system to cope with issues that are broadly concerned with 'pastoral care', while academic concerns remain with departments. Boyson (1974, p. 40) drew attention to the difficulties associated with this system when he stated: 'The danger to be averted is that of a permanent alliance forged by the house-masters against the heads of department, each sector believing that its responsibilities are the real ones and that they are undermined by the other group of staff.'

However, on the basis of studying Nailsea School, Richardson (1975) has argued that a house/departmental system can help a school to handle problems associated with size and expansion, but she maintained that it could create structural divisions between pastoral care and the curriculum. In addition, she considered that these divisions might destroy the integrity of the teacher's task and fragment the leadership role of the headteacher and his or her senior colleagues. This chapter will focus on some of these issues at Bishop McGregor school. However, as McGregor was based on the Merston system it is to that which we now turn.

The Internal Organization of Merston Comprehensive Schools

When the Merston authority originally considered the internal organization of comprehensive schools the director of education prepared a background paper in which he summarized the major problems. A key concern was:

> to devise a system whereby the individual pupil is made to feel that he 'belongs' even in a large school of 1500 and in which the careful supervision of progress of the individual is the responsibility of someone who has under his care a manageable number of pupils.

Bridges wanted to: 'take a leaf out of the independent schools' book and to have a house system which was a physical entity'. Indeed, he considered that the authority should not only follow the structural principles of the house system but that it should adopt the principles of staffing used in boarding schools. He proposed that academic and pastoral roles should be linked.

These proposals were considered by an advisory group who appreciated that the advent of comprehensive schooling in Merston would create difficulties for senior staff in secondary modern schools who would find it difficult to obtain posts of similar status in the new schools. Furthermore, they realized that Bridges's proposals would exacerbate the situation as few former secondary modern school teachers would be appointed to a joint position of head of house and head of department. They considered that these difficulties could be overcome if house posts and departmental posts could be separated, since they thought this would give ex-secondary modern school teachers an opportunity to obtain senior posts in the house system. It was this proposal that was accepted by the local authority.

The authority provided detailed guidance on the house system. Charles Bridges summarized the duties of housemasters and housemistresses when he stated:

> We have often used the phrase that the housemaster is guide, philosopher and friend to the members of his house. Another way of describing his relationship is to say he is the personal tutor of his pupils even though he may not himself be appearing as their teacher in their formal time-table at any point.

House staff were therefore to be concerned with the educational progress and moral welfare of the pupils, discipline and overall tone of the school, while departmental staff were to be responsible for the curriculum. Although

Bridges appreciated that this subdivision between teachers was a very delicate aspect of the Merston comprehensive school system, he maintained that it had some potential as 'provided there is no "empire building" on either side any difficulties should be easily resolved'. However, even if these relationships between heads of houses and heads of departments did operate smoothly, the new schools would still present teachers with some problems, as this pattern of school organization had not previously been used in state schools. Teachers taking positions in houses would have to come to terms with different patterns of work. [. . .]

House staff

While all teachers worked in the houses, the term 'house staff' was usually equated with the heads of houses. The importance of house heads in Merston's comprehensive schools was indicated in a letter which one head-master (who chaired the local comprehensive schools' headteachers' commit-tee) sent to his colleagues, when he stated:

> As heads we certainly cannot shoulder all the responsibility [for discipline and good order]: in house heads we have lieutenants whose work can be of crucial importance and help. Clearly, no schemes of curriculum develop-ment, no new teaching methods involving pupil enquiry and movement will stand a chance if our discipline and organization are not strong.

In these terms, house heads were to maintain standards of discipline in order that curriculum development and other departmental activities could take place successfully. They were seen as essential if heads of departments were to work effectively.

At McGregor, the duties of a house head were defined by Mr Goddard (the Headteacher) in the first copy of further particulars for potential staff. He expected them to 'play a very important part in the moral and social education of their house pupils'. Their duties were therefore defined in social terms, which corresponded with the expectations of the authority and other head-teachers in the city. However, in a Catholic school a further dimension was added to the job as house heads were to be responsible for the moral development of their pupils. When the school first opened four house heads were appointed. Each house head had to take responsibility for a subject, because few heads of departments had been appointed and several depart-ments were staffed with probationary teachers.

After five years, Mr Goddard found that he had to appoint a second generation of house heads, as several members of the first group had obtained deputy headships in other schools. When he wrote job descriptions for his second group of house heads he defined their role in greater detail. A set of further particulars for a house head in 1973–4 stated that the job involved:

> responsibility for the pastoral care, social and academic welfare and discipline of each child within the house. He [the head of house] is expected

to be involved in the implementation of agreed school policy and play a major role in helping to plan future school policy.

As far as Goddard was concerned, house heads were responsible for welfare, attendance, discipline, uniform and progress. In short, they were responsible for a range of activities similar to those of a headteacher in a small school. Many of them therefore saw their houses as 'mini-schools' and organized them accordingly – a move which acknowledged structural divisions in the school.

At McGregor, house heads were to interpret and implement school policy. Each head of house was given a degree of autonomy to develop his or her position and house. However, individual house heads defined the school's activities in different ways. When the school opened, house heads had taken the opportunity to establish their own distinctive pattern of work and routine. In letters that were sent to parents, house heads did not merely identify their house colours but indicated differences in their aims, objectives and activities. In Westminster House, the aim was simply to form a link between the home and the school. Meanwhile, in Southwark House, it was emphasized that there would be social, educational and fund-raising activities. In Arundel House and Hexham House, the differences were apparent in terms of the activities which were established. In Arundel there were to be regular house Masses together with a variety of clubs and societies for house pupils. But in Hexham the emphasis was different. Parents were told that the house was named after the Diocese of Hexham and it was intended that direct links should be established with this diocese. Furthermore, there were also house patrons and it was the intention of the house head to involve the pupils in the fund-raising activities of these patrons. Hexham, unlike any other house, also had a house motto which was the word 'endeavour'. [. . .]

Each house therefore developed a distinct set of aims, routines, practices and activities. The result was a group of discrete units which related to the whole school. This was summed up by Gillian Davies who said that her house was 'beginning to develop into a community within the school', a point that was confirmed on ceremonial occasions such as sports days as well as in daily routines. Individual developments in the houses were supported by the headmaster, who stated in a letter to the director of education that 'the strongest form of house system comes when each head of house is set free to create his or her own thing'. In these terms the house system at McGregor was close to the model that had been established in the public schools.

Each house had a different ethos. Maggie Rolls, who was head of Clifton House, followed the 'mini-school' model as she considered that her post was 'the equivalent of a headteacher in a small junior school'. She considered that pastoral work was more important than class teaching and much more interesting than working in a department. She saw her task in social terms: discovering children's backgrounds, visiting pupils' homes, meeting parents, and interviewing pupils who were particular problems to other teachers or in 'trouble' inside or outside the school. She therefore defined 'pastoral work' in terms of administrative tasks: in the sense of gathering information on pupils and their families and maintaining social control.

Many house heads interpreted their task in similar terms – by distinguishing between the pastoral and academic aspects of the school. The head of Hexham House wrote several memoranda to the headmaster in which she stressed the importance of social rather than academic standards in the school. In one memorandum she stated:

> If the pupils are given frequent 'chances' we shall lose our hold over them and the rot will set in. If we are to set any kind of standard for the fifth year now is the time to do it. Academic ability is not really important, it is the willingness to accept that the staff are right to demand certain standards from pupils.

This house head not only emphasized the importance of pastoral work over academic work by means of private communications but also by the way in which she handled day-to-day activities. Her time was devoted to interviewing pupils, issuing orders to staff and pupils and administering punishments. In this respect, her version of pastoral care was defined in terms of social control: routine, discipline, rules, moral standards and achieving compliance from pupils.

Eileen Marsh, who was head of Arundel House, considered it her job to set standards among staff and pupils. On an occasion when a uniform check was taken among all pupils, she did not merely send the headmaster comments about her pupils' style of dress but also commented on the teachers' clothing as she considered that 'McGregor must have the most unprofessionally dressed staff in the city'. But the head did not do anything about her comments or for that matter about the jeans, sweaters and lack of ties about which she had complained. [. . .]

When the heads of houses were criticized by the heads of departments, the criticisms related to the fact that their job did not involve 'real' teaching. David Peel (head of the geography department) summed it up by saying. 'If you're a head of house you just check to see that all your kids are in uniform and that you have enough chairs for dinner sittings and your job's done'. George Jackson considered the job involved 'looking after the children of Mary'. These views were shared by other heads of departments and many subject teachers who thought the house heads were paid large allowances for doing very little. For them, 'real teaching' involved introducing pupils to subjects, getting them to work and obtaining examination successes. In short, the departmental staff considered that the 'real' work of the school was done in subject departments.

Departmental staff

Heads of departments were appointed to develop a curriculum area within the school, to develop the syllabus and teaching methods and to initiate curriculum development. Unlike the heads of houses who had a dozen or so teachers who were not paid special allowances for their duties in the house, each head of department had a team of specialists, many of whom were paid additional allowances for their special duties. The differences between houses and departments and between the departments themselves existed along a number of dimensions. The status of the departments depended on their physical resources, the size of their staff, and the scale posts given to their teachers. In addition, departments were designated *academic* or *non-academic, examination* or *non-examination*, and this influenced the way in which they defined their work. [. . .]

While each of the houses had a base on the ground floor in each of the house blocks, the facilities of the departments varied. The physical resources that were allocated to departments resulted in a hierarchy being established among them. Academic subjects such as English, mathematics, modern languages and the sciences were given suites of rooms. Other academic subjects such as history and geography were given only half of that allocation. Practical subjects such as physical education, home economics and technical activities were given specialist facilities in blocks or parts of blocks. However, the remedial department and the Newsom department were given only one room each. For the remedial department it was their second move in two years. They were established in a redundant house hall with an assortment of furniture that was no longer required by other departments. Even these facilities had been obtained only after members of the department had made numerous requests to the headmaster for improved facilities. The Newsom department was in a similar situation. Its room was fitted out for science and technical activities and housed items of furniture which were surplus to requirements in other parts of the school, resulting in an assortment of desks, tables, chairs and stools.

The differences between departments were also evident in terms of the number of staff allocated to them, and the seniority of their teachers in the school. All the departments except for the Newsom department had at least one teacher who worked in only one department. However, a different number of teachers were allocated to each department. Just as the basic academic departments (English and mathematics) had the largest number of rooms, together with the practical subjects they had the greatest number of full-time staff. The same pattern was true of academic subjects which became optional in the upper school, such as geography, history and music, and those which were only taken in the upper school, e.g. commerce. Finally, some departments, like careers and Newsom, had few teachers who worked within them on a full-time basis.

Each department had a number of teachers with scale posts. The number of scale posts that were held within the departments depended on the number of points (above scale 1) with which they were allocated. The main distinction was between houses and other groups within the school. As a group, the houses were given more points than any department. Among the departments, however, the subjects which commanded most resources held the most points, while those departments which only provided courses in the upper school held the least number of points. The result was that some of the large subject departments had teachers at different stages in their careers. In the English department a scale 2 post was given for responsibility for

1   the departmental library
2   courses for non-academic fifth formers
3   students' teaching practices
4   stock control
5   internal examinations for middle-school forms
6   records of pupils' progress

while a scale 3 post was given for

1   The running of the department in the absence of the head, and
2   first- and second-year English throughout the school.

These middle-range posts in large departments not only provided teachers with higher salaries but also provided experience that would help the individual to gain a higher post in the career structure. In the case of the holders of these posts, Stuart Mills (on scale 2) became the deputy head of an English department in another school, while Jane Adams (on scale 3) became the next head of the English department at McGregor. But departments with few points for scale posts had very few experienced teachers other than the head of the department. This was the case in commerce and music where only the heads of departments had scale posts, while the other teachers were either assistants, or probationers or part-time staff.

Each department (except for the Newsom department) had a head of department who held a scale post. However, different scale posts were held by different heads of departments. The highest posts were held in those departments which represented the basic subjects taken by all pupils throughout the school. Of the subject departments which were responsible for pupils in the whole school, only the head of the mathematics department did not hold a scale 5 post. Current gossip among the staff attributed this to the fact that he was not a Catholic and because the department had some very poor examination results. The criteria that were used by the headmaster to appoint teachers to senior posts of responsibility in departments included: personal academic achievement, and proven teaching ability in a range of schools. [. . .]

Alongside scale post holders and the heads of departments were eleven staff who were in only their second year of teaching, and fifteen probationary teachers who were new to the school and the teaching profession. These teachers were appointed to work within a department, and, like all other departmental staff, were attached to a house, where the vast majority had responsibility for a tutorial group.

Among the departments there were several differences based on resources, number of teaching staff, and posts of responsibility. These structural differences provided a background to the relationships which existed among teachers and between teachers and pupils and influenced the way in which they defined their work.

Relationships Among Teachers

The times when teachers can meet together on a formal and informal basis are defined by the school timetable. At McGregor, teachers came together in house and department meetings, and they also met each other before school, at break time and lunch time, in 'free' lessons and after school. Each of these meetings gave me an opportunity to see the way in which teachers defined their daily activities.

Formal meetings among teachers

At McGregor, there was no single place for teachers and pupils to gather in the early morning. Before the first bell was rung teachers went to the working staff rooms in the house blocks. A quick conversation, a cigarette, and a glance at the morning paper preceded the routine of the day. Once the bell was rung, they reported to their head of house so that the deputy head could be informed of any teachers who were absent and whose lessons needed to be 'subbed' by another teacher.

When the teachers met in house heads' studies, it was a time for gossip to be exchanged about children, about fellow teachers and about the headmaster and his views on school routine. It was also a time when the house heads passed on messages about school activities, duties and changes to the daily programme. The house heads occupied a key role in the communication system, as they transmitted school policy from the headmaster and his senior colleagues to other teachers. They, in turn, were supposed either to relay this information to pupils in their tutorial groups or implement this policy in their daily activities in the house and, to some extent, in the departments in which they worked.

An early morning meeting in a house, therefore, contained several elements which I recorded in my fieldnotes one morning in Westminster House:

About ten minutes before the bell was rung, I went into Ron Ward's study where many of the staff had already gathered.

Ron talked about his study and said how dull he thought it was. Sue and Terry disagreed with him and said that it was much brighter than in the past as the former head of house used to sit in there with the blinds down and the light on. A joke was made by Terry about the sexual significance of drawn blinds. Ron brought some order to the scene and started to make some announcements. He told the staff that the headmaster's advisory committee on social policy had produced a series of plans for activities that could be followed by the fifth year when they finished their examinations. These included: sports, building an adventure playground, social work, camping and teaching English to immigrants. Staff laughed about the last suggestion and Doreen Sharp commented, 'They need someone to teach them English!' Most people laughed and several agreed with this remark. Ron continued to read through the list and suggested that other ideas and observations should be given to Terry Goodwin who was a member of this committee.

Ron then went on to talk about a note that the headmaster had produced on emergencies in relation to dealing with epileptics. He explained that this had been produced because a child had an epileptic fit in a lesson earlier that week. However, he did not agree with the suggestions that were given for dealing with such a situation. Ron asked the members of staff for information about one or two families of pupils in the house. When no information was forthcoming, Ron said that he would go and have a snoop around at the weekend to see where they lived. Ron then continued by reminding us that third-year option forms had to be completed by 1 March. Finally, he told us that as the period after half term would be Lent he had arranged with Eileen Marsh (head of Arundel House) that tutorial groups from Arundel and Westminster would combine on Thursday mornings for a series of Masses. He said that those Catholic teachers who wished to attend the Masses should arrange to have their tutorials covered by other teachers. He then said it was time that the pupils were registered so that tutorials could arrive on time in the hall for assembly.

This illustrates the type of activities that took place in house heads' studies before the teachers met the pupils and will be used to examine the importance of the house system in the school, the position of house head and the teachers' perspectives of the school and its pupils.

All teachers, regardless of their position in the school, had to report to their head of house each day before school started. In this respect, the importance of the house system and the head of house was emphasized to each teacher. House heads were an essential link in the chain of school administration, responsible for passing on messages from the headmaster, reading out notices and keeping registers up to date. They were gatekeepers between the headmaster and other teachers.

House heads were responsible for communicating school policy. In Westminster House (in common with other houses) it was this activity that structured the early morning meeting; a situation where the house head made announcements and the teachers listened, because it was rare for them to discuss formally any points that Ron made. Instead, comments were kept to jokes, gossip, and answers to questions that were directed at individuals by the house head. As Ron communicated messages and school routines to the staff he had an opportunity to define and redefine school policy and promote activities that he considered important for the pupils. In short, house heads were powerful reality definers in the day-to-day activities of teachers and pupils. [. . .]

In common with other early morning meetings with the house head, no teacher disagreed with any of Ron's proposals or suggestions, which indicated that they formally and publicly recognized his position. However, outside these meetings it was usual for some discussion and private dissension to take place among teachers in the working staff room, who would modify Ron's suggestions about routines to be adopted with pupils. In some cases, modifications were involved, while in other situations teachers would claim that they were not going to implement particular aspects of school policy. This occurred at the end of the spring term when Paul Klee announced to several of us that he was no longer going to ask his tutor group to collect or contribute to a charity, because he considered that too many collections had taken place during Lent.

While school routine was the main topic of conversation in these meetings, particular pupils came a close second. On the subject of pupils, teachers contributed freely to the discussions. They taught the children and were, therefore, ready to contribute comments on an individual pupil's ability, behaviour and potential. Often pupils and pupil behaviour were typed by teachers on the basis of slight information. At the beginning of the autumn term, when Terry Goodwin saw the surname McNab in her first-form register she announced to the rest of us, 'Oh my God, we've another McNab!' Other members of the house who also recognized the surname talked about the misbehaviour of several other McNabs who they automatically assumed were older brothers and sisters, and without any evidence imputed similar behaviour to this child before they had seen him. Automatically this gossip established an identity for the pupil that had the potential to structure the early stages of his career in the house and his relationships with teachers.

These regular daily meetings with house heads had no direct equivalent in the departments. While heads of houses met their staff at a set time each day, heads of departments held such meetings on only two or three occasions during each term. Department meetings were opportunities for the staff to discuss departmental policy, teaching methods, curriculum content and the progress of individual children. Unlike house meetings, department meetings usually had a formal agenda which was drawn up by the head of the department. However, within the meetings, discussion took place between all teachers. [. . .]

In the religious education department, Sheila Ryan was in charge of work with pupils in the first three years. While Sheila drew up the agenda for the meeting she did not 'hold the floor'. The meeting was an opportunity for all members of the department, regardless of their seniority, to express their views on the department's work. In this context, the headmaster, heads of houses and assistant teachers who worked in the religious education department were all theoretically 'equal'. However, it was usual for junior staff to look towards the headmaster and the house heads for direction and for points of information concerning resources and school organization. Within this meeting, items of business were devoted to departmental organization and the content of the curriculum which was discussed by all teachers – a distinct contrast to the practice which was followed in the houses.

Another formal occasion when teachers had an opportunity to discuss the curriculum was at open forum meetings held once a month after school. These meetings were designed by the headmaster, not for particular segments of the school, but for all staff. Here, the head wanted to provide a venue in which junior teachers could debate issues that affected the school with senior staff. Despite this attempt to get some dialogue between senior and junior teachers, there were few signs of success. At most meetings the heads of houses were conspicuous by their absence, a situation which thwarted the head's aims. Indeed, Mr Goddard told me that he thought heads of houses would not attend these meetings because they did not want to debate issues concerning school routine with junior teachers. Certainly, of all the senior teachers at McGregor only the house heads were often absent; a situation that emphasized their separation from departmental staff in general and junior teachers in particular.

Nevertheless, at open forum meetings that I attended, the subjects discussed included school organization and the content of the curriculum, as sessions were devoted to the form of the annual prize-giving ceremony and the organization of the sixth-form curriculum. At the meeting when the prize-giving was debated, there were twenty-two teachers; two heads of houses, four heads of departments and sixteen assistant and probationary teachers. The headmaster opened the discussion by explaining that he wanted to see a prize-giving which rewarded academic achievement. But he was quickly reminded by Terry Goodwin that McGregor was a comprehensive school, and that it should be possible to create a new form of prize-giving which rewarded elements of schooling other than just academic work. This point was taken up by other junior teachers who remembered their own school prize-givings as formal speech days when teachers wore gowns, school choirs sang and individuals collected prizes while the vast majority sat bored. The heads of the English and modern languages departments disagreed with these views and recommended that a conventional pattern should be followed. However, by sheer force of numbers the junior staff were able to discuss and design, with the support of each other, a new-style prize-giving with a distribution of prizes, a short period for an address and discussion followed by an evening 'disco'. The headmaster supported the two heads of department who expressed their reservations about this form of prize-giving and who, like the head, were concerned that academic worth should be honoured. Indeed, the headmaster told me afterwards that he had definitely wanted the meeting to recommend a formal prize-giving with gowns and speeches. The recommendation of the majority of staff at the meeting was instead for an informal evening and prize-giving – a recommendation which was later implemented by the headmaster. In this context, junior teachers were able to advance their ideas about school organization which in turn led to a redefinition of the head's view of prize-giving. The structure of some events at Bishop Mc-

Gregor School was therefore not merely based on the ideas of senior staff but involved the participation of everyone. However, junior staff were only able to define school activities in any sense when their numbers at meetings outweighed senior staff, a situation which was rare beyond the open forum.

These formal meetings between teachers highlighted divisions between house staff and departmental staff and between senior staff and junior staff. They were often reinforced by the structure and content of meetings. Firstly, house staff were formally distinguished from departmental staff. The house heads were senior to the departmental staff and they considered it their job to implement some of the headmaster's ideas about school organization. In turn, heads of houses also established their own routines which added to the complexity of school organization and in some cases changed its direction. Secondly, the approach adopted towards the implementation of house and departmental policy was somewhat different. In each house, it was the head of house who defined the situation by advancing his or her point of view, whereas points of practice in departments were worked out by discussion among members of staff. There were also occasions when the heads of houses and heads of departments joined forces against attempts by junior teachers to change school policy. However, the failure of some house heads to attend meetings on school policy where junior staff were present led to situations such as the prize-giving meeting when junior staff could take decisions. Alliances between houses and departments were rare as they were interested in different aspects of education. While the houses focused on social aspects of education, the departments focused on the curriculum. The result was that house heads concentrated on pastoral activities which they interpreted predominantly in terms of administration and social control, while departmental staff were concerned with class teaching. However, as all departmental staff were required to be members of a house and take some part in pastoral work there was an undercurrent of continual conflict between house and departmental duties.

In addition to differences between the formal activities of houses and departments, informal relationships between staff were also influenced by the terms of their appointment.

References

BENN, C. and SIMON B. (1972) *Half Way There: Report on the British Comprehensive School Reform*, 2nd ed., Harmondsworth, Penguin.

BOYSON, K. (1974) *Oversubscribed: The Story of Highbury Grove*, London, Ward Lock.

DEPARTMENT OF EDUCATION AND SCIENCE (1979) *Aspects of Secondary Education in England: A Survey by HM Inspectors of Schools*, London, HMSO.

MONKS, T. G. (1968) *Comprehensive Education in England and Wales*, Windsor, NFER.

RICHARDSON, E. (1975) *Authority and Organization in the Secondary School*, London, Macmillan.

10

Assessment and Testing in the Secondary School

R. N. Deale

School Examinations – Written Papers

Planning an examination

Content validity must still be placed first on our list of requirements and [. . .] an examination specification can be adopted to achieve it.

The problems are similar, though bigger [than those of a short test]: aims and objectives, syllabus content, balance, etc. must be considered not just in relation to a relatively small part of the course but over a whole term or perhaps over a whole year. It must be remembered, though, that not all teaching aims can, or should, be examined; it may be a valid aim of a course, say, in civics, to make better citizens (however this is defined) but it is not going to be possible to say whether this has been achieved until ten or twenty years later, if then. On the other hand, an aim of the English department may be to ensure that no child leaves the school unable to read and write; this can certainly be measured, and should be.

Generally, however, with school examinations, we are likely to be concerned with the more limited and more clearly defined teaching objectives, with skills, abilities and knowledge, and it is in these terms that we should attempt to draw up the specification. But because we will probably have to assess a wider range of skills and cover a broader area of the curriculum than was the case with the classroom test, the specification must also be more elaborate.

To illustrate the way in which a range of techniques can be drawn upon to assess different aspects of the course, we shall take as an example a specification for a fifth-year examination in local studies (see Table 10.1). In this case, the teacher has designed an interdisciplinary course including elements of sociology, urban geography and applied science, focusing on the town in which the school is situated. The course is taken by pupils of a wide

Table 10.1 *Examination specification for a fifth-year local studies course (weightings are given as percentages)*

Ability being assessed	Paper 1(a) (short-answer test)	Paper 1(b) (structured questions)	Paper 2 (essay paper)	Practical test (assignments)	Weighting
Knowledge of facts	15 (30 questions)				15
Interpretation of diagrams, maps, tables, etc.		10			10
Application of knowledge, skills, to simple problems, new situations, etc.		15 (4 questions of 5 parts)	20 (2 questions)		35
Ability to make observations, measurments, etc.				10	10
Ability to record results				10	10
Ability to interpret results			10 (1 question)	10 (oral)	20
Weighting	15	25	30	30	100

range of ability, though mainly intending to leave school at the end of the fifth year, and has a fairly generous allocation of time.

In this course, the simple committing to memory of facts is not considered of major importance and greater emphasis is given to the application of knowledge; only 15 per cent is allowed in the short-answer test for factual recall (short-answer tests [. . .] can be designed to test other abilities besides factual recall, of course) while in Paper 1(b) and in the essay paper it is the ability to interpret data and to apply what has been learned which is important.

The term 'structured questions' means questions set in the form of several sub-questions, all relating to the same topic, and usually forming an incline of difficulty, so that the later parts test higher-level skills than the earlier ones. In the second part of Paper 1, information in the form of tables of statistics, graphs, maps and diagrams is presented on the paper; the use of structured questions allows the teacher to start with some fairly straight-forward sub-questions and to progress to those requiring more sophisticated interpretations and the application to new situations of skills developed during the course – the more difficult parts carrying more marks than the earlier sub-questions.

In the third part, two essay questions are set to give the pupils the op-portunity to develop arguments, to analyse, to discuss and to present points of view. There is a contrast between this part of the examination and the preceding one; here, the pupils have to draw upon their own knowledge in order to support and develop their theses and so the actual importance of factual knowledge is greater than the 15 per cent weighting on the specifica-tion grid would suggest. However, the emphasis here is on the use of facts, and it is the ability to select relevant information to use in the essay which is important.

In the third essay question, the ability to interpret the results of a survey, or other data, is being tested. This overlaps to some extent with Paper 1(b), but here a more complex analysis is being called for and less guidance in the form of the question structure is given; pupils are expected to work out their own interpretation and present reasoned arguments to support it.

The practical test takes the form of an assignment, where the pupil is given a simple investigation to carry out, such as a small-scale traffic survey, a study of some aspect of the welfare services, or the local water supply, etc., which has been a topic during the course. First, pupils have to decide on the method of tackling the problem and this is discussed with the teacher, who can guide the pupils with advice and suggestions where necessary. It is essential to allow for direction at this stage since shortcomings here would affect the subsequent investigations, but because of the difficulty of estimating just how much help has been given, no assessment is made.

The ability to carry out the assignment and to record the results are each the subject of assessments weighted at 10 per cent and the final assessment is an oral discussion (also 10 per cent) of the results with the pupil. An oral assessment is preferable here since it allows greater flexibility to adjust to the actual work done by each pupil.

It should be pointed out that it is not necessary for the practical test to be carried out at the same time as the written examination; indeed, since the assignments arise out of the work done during the course, it is more natural if they are undertaken as the opportunity occurs, though careful planning will have gone into the course beforehand to make sure that suitable occasions do arise.

In this scheme of examination, the teacher has attempted to give opportunities to his [or her] best pupils to use their ability while still offering reasonable chances to the less able. Remembering that the examination is a combination of several discriminating attainment tests, the purpose is to discriminate across the whole of the ability range; thus, Paper 1(a) will probably be most successful at distinguishing between lower levels of ability, while in Paper 2 the high-flyers can show what they can do.

To ensure validity, the teacher has arranged for the different aspects of the course to be reflected in the various components of the whole examination, each part of which is intended to test something different from the others. This is important: examining time is not to be squandered and there is little point in repeatedly testing the same abilities unless the test is so unreliable that repeated measurements are essential. It is also fair to give pupils, whose individual talents may be better suited to one part of the course than another, a chance to show where they can shine.

Finally, we would repeat the warning [. . .] that this is in no sense an ideal specification and that content validity must be judged in relation to each individual teacher's aims and syllabus. Just as each teacher is responsible for choosing a course of instruction which is suited to the needs and abilities of his [or her] own pupils, so is it necessary for each teacher to devise a scheme of assessment to suit that course. [. . .]

Examination techniques – written papers

In the section on planning an examination . . . we looked at the specification for an examination and at the way in which different techniques were used in the various papers; we shall now consider these techniques in more detail.

Essay questions

Essay questions are sometimes referred to as free-response or open-ended questions, which are perhaps more useful terms for our purposes; the word essay carries implications of a formal academic exercise of fairly substantial length, but [. . .] any question which allows an answer of more than a few words is straying over into the essay-type question.

It is more helpful, therefore, to distinguish between controlled response (multiple choice, true/false, etc.), restricted response (short answer, sentence completion) and free response where the pupil has to organize the answer in his [or her] own words. The answers to a free-response-type question may therefore vary in length from a sentence to a paragraph to, at an advanced level, essays of many pages, taking perhaps three hours to write.

The fact that the pupil has to answer the free-response question in his [or her] own words is at once the strength and the weakness of this technique. Strength, because it can allow the pupil to show creativity, a grasp of the wholeness of a topic, the depth and scope of his knowledge and his ability to organize his [or her] thoughts with coherence and relevance. Weakness, because it demands a level of writing skill which may or may not be adequately matched to the pupil's understanding of the subject, because the physical act of writing at any length takes time (thus reducing the number of questions which can be answered, which may affect validity), and because marking the answer is complicated by the mixing of two factors: subject attainment and writing ability.

The free-response question must be used with discretion. It is wasteful to ask pupils to write a half-hour essay which consists of nothing more than connecting facts which could be more efficiently tested by short-answer questions. Yet one analysis of examination papers in science (J. F. Eggleston, *A Critical Review of Assessment Procedures in Secondary School Science*, Leicester University Press, 1965) showed that in many cases, 90 per cent or more of the questions were testing no more than basic knowledge; while no one would deny that a sound basis of factual knowledge is essential in many subjects, not least in the sciences, most teachers would hope to be able to go beyond this level and it is frustrating and unfair for the pupils if the examination tests only the lowest ability.

When we decide to use free-response questions, therefore, we must use them in such a way that we capitalize on their strengths, or, looking at the reverse side of the coin, minimize their weaknesses by restricting their use to situations in which none of the other techniques is appropriate. [. . .]

In most subjects, in fact, there will be some aspect of the course where the ability to give a clear account of an experiment, to write a report or to give instructions in writing will be important; in many occupations after leaving school, such ability will be highly valued and so there is a more general educational justification for including essay-type tests in school examinations. These considerations, however, reinforce the view that the essay should be used with care and essay subjects must be set in such a way that they do, in fact, elicit the abilities which it is desired to test. [. . .]

The use of the quite open essay subject can be questioned. Not only can a subject such as 'Discuss the growth and importance of railways in Britain' present the pupils with considerable problems of selection and organization, but there is the additional risk that advantage may be taken of the open nature of the subject which is to some pupils a positive invitation to bluff and to flannel. This is sometimes done with considerable skill and some pupils can use their sophisticated command of essay-writing techniques to conceal very real shortcomings in knowledge of the subject. Admittedly, this is most likely to occur at fairly advanced levels and the crude attempts made by most school pupils can usually be spotted by the teacher; nevertheless, it would seem desirable to discourage even the attempt.

It may also be felt that the ability to tackle such a vague topic as that given in the example above is one which should be expected only at a very advanced level indeed; the development of the railway system is a topic worth a major historical study. Faced with such a subject to be answered in half an hour or so, the better pupils will be struggling with the problems of what to leave out and the weaker ones will be hard put to it to find something to fill the space. Under these circumstances, the teacher marking the question has only himself [or herself] to blame if he [or she] finds, on the one hand, important points missed out, and on the other, irrelevancies and padding. It is, however, unfair to the children to penalize them for not doing what the examiner wanted, if he [or she] has failed to make this clear – which is another way of saying that the validity of this type of question may be suspect.

This leads, therefore, to the conclusion that matters will generally be improved by using the guided essay question (sometimes referred to as multi-part questions or paragraph questions: also similar in many ways to structured questions – see pp. 42–3) rather than a completely open subject:

> Describe the way in which children were employed in the textile industries in 1800.
> What controls were introduced in the next fifty years by the Factory Acts? How effective were these controls?

This question has two basically descriptive parts and a third element requiring some evaluation; because the different parts of the question are set in fairly specific terms, there is a much clearer directive to the pupils on how to tackle the question and it is also much harder to bluff one's way through. In this respect, the guided question may in fact be harder than the open essay – harder, and at the same time fairer, because it allows the children who really know the answer to demonstrate this.

It will usually be an improvement if the essay subject presents an unfamiliar problem or uses material organized in an unfamiliar way; we need the essay to discover the pupil's ability to use the information he [or she] has acquired, so we must place him in a situation where he [or she] has to do more than just reproduce by rote what has been learned in the classroom or from the textbook.

The following question, for example, tests little more than the ability to memorize:

> Describe in detail how you would determine (*a*) the solubility of sodium chloride in water at room temperature; (*b*) the mass of zinc which would react with 1 dm^3 of molar hydrochloric acid.

(Moreover, although the question is in two parts, there is no real connection between them; they appear to have been put together simply in order to make an answer of equivalent length to that for some other question.)

The ability to communicate is obviously as important for the science pupil as for the child studying any other discipline; the scientist must learn how to use prose accurately and concisely, and, in addition, must be able to illustrate his [or her] answers, where necessary, with diagrams, graphs, etc. The essay subject in the sciences must therefore be set so as to invite the exercise of all the communication skills needed, and, in addition, require the application of these skills to a novel situation, if the mere repetition of previously learned material is to be avoided. [. . .]

141

Structured questions

Structured questions are well suited to meet two of the criteria which we mentioned in the preceding section: they can be arranged to test different levels of ability in the different sub-questions and they can test pupils' ability to cope with unfamiliar material or problems.

If an examination specification has been drawn up, it may be advisable to try to match the sub-questions to the specification of abilities to be tested, though it would be unwise to allow oneself to be too rigidly confined by this and, of course, in some cases it will not be possible. If the questions are structured in this way, they will in effect form an incline of difficulty, so that the pupil is being asked to perform tasks of increasing complexity as he [or she] works through the question. An alternative approach is to aim each sub-question at a different aspect of the problem so that the various factors in it are isolated and dealt with one at a time. Or some combination of these two methods may be appropriate.

However the sub-questions are to be arranged, there are certain points which should be observed:

(i) *If material is provided to form the introductory part of the question, it should be selected with great care.*
The suitability of the introductory material for a structured question is vitally important. Wherever possible, a variety of material – written, maps, diagrams, photographs, etc. – should be used, not only to avoid the risk of boredom for the pupils, but because it is more likely that the various skills and abilities developed in the course will be covered if material of different types is used. It eases the problems of finding suitable material if the habit is developed of keeping an eye open throughout the year so that a stock is gradually accumulated which can be drawn upon at examination time.

(ii) *Introductory material should contain no more than is relevant to the questions to be asked.*
The material should be edited so that superfluous matter is removed. Time is wasted reading through unnecessary words but this point also applies to maps, diagrams, etc. where irrelevant details can confuse the children, distract them from what is being tested and so reduce validity.

(iii) *Sub-questions should be independent, though related to the main theme.*
[...] It can be ... difficult, however, with structured questions, since the subject-matter is common to all the sub-questions; particularly when calculations are involved, it can be extremely difficult to avoid making the more complex operations dependent on the successful solution to the earlier parts. Nevertheless, it is vital that this is done, otherwise one of the main reasons for using structured questions is defeated, and the same effect could be achieved by a single question involving several steps.

An example follows of a structured question in mathematics, which aims to test different levels of interpretation of the graph and the ability to make some calculations from the data given.

Figure 10.1   (Adapted from Examinations Bulletin No. 1, *The Certificate of Secondary Education: Some Suggestions for Teachers and Examiners*, HMSO, 1963, p. 61.)

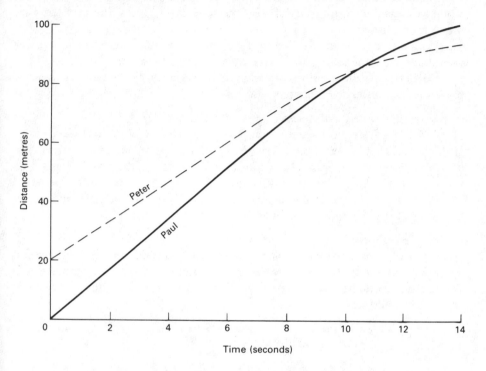

The diagram shows the graphs of two runners Peter and Paul in a 100-metre race.

a   What handicap was Peter allowed?
b   How much further had Paul run than Peter by the time that the race ended?
c   When and where did Paul overtake Peter?
d   What ratio did Peter's average speed bear to Paul's average speed?
e   How far did each runner go before he started to slow down?

It will be seen from these remarks that there is no special mystique about structured questions; basically, the same sort of approach is used as for writing short-answer questions for a classroom test, but with the extra complications of grading the sub-questions and relating them to a single theme. The whole operation is in fact very like setting a short test on a single topic, using questions which may vary from the restricted-response type to something verging on a short essay subject. [...]

143

Marking written papers

Most of the problems of marking the classroom test can be taken care of in the setting of the test, by careful arrangement of the paper, by wording the questions so that the possible range of answers is restricted, and so on. By such means, we can ensure a reasonably objective standard of marking, but when we consider the marking of free-response-type papers, the problems are much more difficult.

It is mainly a question of reliability: we must try to make sure that any paper would get the same mark, no matter when or by whom it was marked.

Considering again the possible sources of variability, we can see that the marking may suffer from unreliability owing to:

(i) *Variations in the judgement of an individual marker*

Nobody is absolutely consistent; standards may change after an interruption, after marking a number of papers; external influences (health, noise, the effect of a meal) may cause an alteration in standards or the marker may be unconsciously affected by untidy writing, by poor spelling, or by personal feelings towards the particular child concerned (or, equally bad, a teacher may be aware of these dangers and over-compensate).

(ii) *Differences between several markers*

Even when steps have been taken to ensure that markers are in general agreement about the qualities which are to be looked for in the answers to the papers, opinions may differ as to the extent to which they are present in an individual script.

It is not possible to eliminate these sources of variability entirely, but we can go a long way towards reducing them.

(i) *Variations in the judgement of an individual marker*

Discussions with colleagues [. . .] are a great help even when one person is responsible for marking all the papers, since it enables one to clarify the mind about the qualities to be looked for. Preparation of model answers is also a useful exercise and certainly a detailed mark scheme should be drawn up; it is in fact usually best if both these are done when the paper is being set, in which case provisional mark allocations can be given on the paper. These serve as a useful guide for the children as to the importance of the various questions.

We must attempt to make the marking as objective as possible and, wherever it is appropriate, the marking should be on a right or wrong basis – this can usually be achieved in a short-answer paper or in certain parts of a structured question. It must be remembered, though, that alterations have to be made to most mark schemes as the papers are worked through, and that in the light of the actual marking, one may find that an unexpected interpretation of the question has led to an answer that had not been anticipated; in such a case, the mark scheme must be amended and previously marked scripts should be checked in case the amendment causes credit to be given to previously rejected answers. Incidentally, it is advisable to try to arrange the mark allocations so that they correspond either exactly or in a simple proportion (half, twice, etc.) to the percentage weighting for the question. It is possible to scale a mark out of 19 to a weighting of 10 per cent but it introduces another source of error and it is better to avoid problems if possible.

In many parts of the paper, of course, a simple marking method will not be applicable and the construction of a mark scheme for essay-type questions is extremely complex. In most subjects, it is advisable to try to assess separately different aspects of the essay, since the essay will probably be used to test several objectives, not just one. Structured questions may often be dealt with in this way; if, for example, the first two or three sub-questions ask for factual information, they might be marked simply on factual accuracy, disregarding the quality of the writing, while in the later parts, requiring perhaps the development of some ideas, the manner in which they were expressed might also be taken into consideration.

In marking complete essays, it will be necessary to consider such matters in the context of the whole, and it may be possible to divide the total mark allocation for the question into various sub-headings, so much for accuracy of facts, so much for development of ideas, so much for quality of writing, etc. A valid division of this nature can only be made if the teacher is absolutely clear about what he [or she] wants to test in the essay and the questions are designed to that end. And even within the categories that have been thus established, there can be room for differing opinions (is 'I walked five mile to school' a grammatical error, a slip of the pen or an example of possibly effective dialect usage?) and for overlap between categories (can you award marks for interpretation of facts, if the facts are incorrect?). In practice, therefore, no analytical mark scheme of this kind is foolproof nor can it be applied absolutely rigidly.

It can be extremely difficult also to reach a judgement on one aspect of an essay without being affected by the others, particularly by the quality of the writing; for this reason some people would prefer to grade essays by the method of total impression, rather than according to an analytical scheme. Impression marking, however, is very liable to suffer from the marker's own variability and it is best to use multiple marking if possible. If this cannot be done, then it is a good idea to choose a number of scripts to use as reference points. The number chosen depends on the mark scale being used but if we assume that the essays are to be marked out of 20, then about five scripts would be enough. After skimming quickly through the pile of papers to get an idea of the general standard, the teacher should choose five that represent a good spread of marks; these are then marked in detail. Supposing that the five scripts are given 17, 14, 11, 8 and 3, they are then retained for reference; the rest of the essays are given marks in relation to these five points, i.e. a little better than 3, but not nearly as good as 8, mark 4.

Depending on what use is to be made of the assessments, it may be found sufficient simply to arrange essays in order of merit, without assigning any marks. The rank ordering alone can provide useful information and, if desired, can later be divided into broad grades. It is essential that some form of grading is adopted if the assessments of the essays are to be combined with another component of the examination which has been given numerical marks; the marks will also produce a rank order which can be graded in similar fashion to the essays and the two sets of grades can be combined. There are difficulties in combining rank orders directly. [. . .]

Even if essays are marked according to an analytical mark scheme or by impression, it is still a useful check if the scripts are physically placed in rank order after the marking is completed. By glancing quickly through the papers in order of merit, it can be seen whether the marking method has been working effectively and whether the 23rd essay is, in fact, better than the 24th.

Whatever method is adopted, it is important to make sure that the whole of the mark (or grade) scale is used. Sometimes one hears the view that a mark of 10 out of 10 should not be awarded because it represents perfection, and some teachers restrict themselves to a maximum of 8 marks out of 10. Of course, 10 out of 10 does not mean that a child knows everything about the subject, any more than 0 means that he [or she] necessarily knows nothing. What it does mean is that he [or she] has achieved the best performance likely on one particular question from one particular group of pupils; and that is precisely what 8 out of 10 means from a teacher who never gives more than this mark. There may be a case for not giving 0 (which is a fairly depressing mark for anyone to get) but it must be remembered that if a teacher never gives less than 3 or more than 8, this is effectively marking out of 6, not 10, and he might as well give marks from 1 to 6. But there is a danger that if the question is weighted at 10 marks, and all those marks are never in fact used, the other parts of the examination where the full mark range is used (the short-answer test, for example) may come to assume much more importance than was originally intended and the balance of the examination will be upset.

If it is possible, it is best to complete the marking of one set of questions in one session, though there comes a time when fatigue exercises an adverse effect and it is necessary to call a halt. When resuming after an interruption for whatever cause, it is wise to spend a little time reading through some previously marked scripts so as to remind oneself of the standard of marking. When the marking is completed, too, it is worth while checking back at random to see if there has been a drift of standards during the course of the whole operation; it is common enough to find that the earlier papers have been marked more severely than the later ones. If numbers are too great for all papers to be marked by a single teacher, a possible compromise is for each teacher to mark all the answers to one question. Some form of standardization is still necessary; otherwise, if marker X is severe and marker Y is lenient, the children who have given good answers to the question marked by Y will score better than those who have answered X's question well.

(ii)   *Differences between several markers* [. . .]

Marking written papers – general points
We would advocate that marked scripts are returned to the pupils after the examination and that in addition to the actual marks there should be written or oral comments from the teacher to indicate where marks have been lost or gained, and how things can be improved next time. Without such feedback an important teaching opportunity is lost and it is hard to see how the children can be expected to do better if it is not explained where they have gone wrong. There is a subsidiary advantage in this procedure in that the pupils will inevitably make a very careful check on the mechanical accuracy of the marking and addition of marks; this is an area where it is easy to make sometimes quite substantial slips and where it is advisable to have some form of checking. Thirty children can check thirty papers much more quickly than a single teacher and at examination time it is good to be relieved of a rather tedious, though necessary, chore.

There is one final matter that we should refer to in connection with marking and that is the insidious 'halo' effect. Halo effect means that one's judgement may be subconsciously affected by some extraneous factor, and because it is subconscious it is difficult to detect. Ways in which halo effect can operate are:

(i)   judgement may be affected unduly by neat presentation, handwriting, etc. which gives an impression of competence which may or may not be reflected in the content (or the reverse – bad writing etc. may create an impression of ignorance);
(ii)   the impression created by the first answer on the paper may carry over and influence the mark given to the next one, which may be much better (or worse);
(iii)   marking may be affected by personal relationships (good or bad) between teacher and pupil.

Unfortunately, it is difficult to know whether one has been influenced in any of these ways or not, so it is best to adopt methods which are less susceptible to halo effect than others. Thus, as far as is possible, scripts should be treated as anonymous, that is, one should avoid looking at the names until marking has been completed (though it may be hard to avoid recognizing the writing). The adoption of a mark scheme as objective as possible should help to eliminate the effect of good or bad presentation and if each question is marked for all pupils (that is, all question 1s marked, then all questions 2s, etc.), not only will it help to maintain standards of marking but it should prevent the carry-over of an impression from one answer to another.

11

The Side-Effects of Assessment

Derek Rowntree

The Competitive Aspects of Assessment

The side-effects of learning for the sake of extrinsic rewards are bad enough. But what when these extrinsic rewards are in short supply? When there are not enough to go round? The side-effects are then worsened by competition. In one sense, of course, there is more than enough knowledge available for everyone to have a sufficiency. As Robert Paul Wolff (1969, p. 66) points out: 'The Pythagorean theorem does not flicker and grow dim as more and more minds embrace it.' Learning is a 'free commodity'. But only so long as we are thinking of knowledge as a source of intrinsic, expressive rewards. Think instead of 'approved' knowledge, legitimated and reified as GCE 'passes', admissions to college, university degrees, and the like. No longer is the supply unlimited. For one person to get more, another must make do with less. A great many assessment systems are competitive in that the extrinsic rewards they offer are in short supply and each student who wants them is asked to demonstrate that he [or she] is more deserving than others, or others less deserving than he [or she] is.

Contesting with others over the extrinsic spoils of learning is one aspect of competitive assessment. Another, upon which it depends and which usually arises early in a child's educational career, before the extrinsic rewards have become so tangible and external, is his [or her] teacher's public comparison of one student with another. A child will not have been in school many days before he [or she] is made aware of individual differences among his [or her] classmates. Roy Nash (1973, p. 17) discovered that pupils as young as eight years were able to say which children in the class were better than them at reading, writing and number; and their self-perceived class rank correlated highly with the rankings made by the teacher at the researcher's request (and therefore not explicitly available hitherto for communication to the children).

Such awareness can encourage learning that is motivated (extrinsically) by what John Holt called 'the ignoble satisfaction of feeling that one is better than someone else'. Jules Henry (1969) describes how a classroom atmosphere of competitive assessment fosters such a tendency. Eleven-year-old Boris is out at the blackboard publicly trying to simplify a fraction while his teacher is being excruciatingly patient and restraining the rest of the class who are bursting to put Boris right. Boris is mentally paralyzed by the situation, however. So teacher finally asks Peggy, who can be relied on to know the correct answer:

> Thus Boris' failure has made it possible for Peggy to succeed; his depression is the price of her exhilaration, his misery is the occasion of her rejoicing. This is the standard condition of the American elementary school. . . . To a Zuni, Hopi, or Dakota Indian, Peggy's performance would seem cruel beyond belief, for competition, the wringing of success from somebody's failure, is a form of torture foreign to those noncompetitive Indians. . . . (p. 83)

But why should it be that Peggy gets a lift from knowing that she has 'beaten' Boris? To say that she has been publicly compared with him and proved superior in fraction-simplification is insufficiently explanatory. No doubt the teacher too is superior but she would hardly be expected to feel joyful on that account. Why, for instance, does Peggy not get satisfaction instead from trying to eradicate the difference between herself and Boris, e.g. by helping him reach the answer himself rather than telling him? And if she has already enjoyed the satisfaction of having climbed to a new standard of proficiency, higher than she has been before, why should she care one way or another to know that others have not yet reached this standard? Perhaps the reason is that she has been persuaded that teacher-approval, and whatever other more tangible extrinsic rewards may follow, are in short supply and to gain what she needs she must not simply (or even necessarily) improve but also get (or merely stay) ahead of others.

Students generally have been led to believe that they cannot all achieve a worthwhile level of learning. They, and for the most part their teachers, often assume that only a few can do very well, the majority doing moderately only, and a few doing poorly or even failing. This expectation is seen institutionalized among teachers who 'grade on the curve'. (The practice is to be found in education everywhere, although the terminology is American – see Terwilliger, 1971, pp. 74–100 for a discussion of this and related techniques.) Such teachers, marking students' work with, say, the grades A, B, C, D, F, will set out with a predetermined grade-distribution in mind. (E is often skipped over because by 'happy' coincidence, the next letter is the initial letter of failure!) Among 100 students, for example, they may expect to award about 10 As, 20 Bs, 40 Cs, 20 Ds and 10 Fs. (Figure 11.1 shows this expected distribution graphically – and also the underlying 'normal distribution curve' from which the method gets its name, and which we'll meet again later.) The teacher who is 'grading on the curve' may, on marking a given set of students, allow himself [or herself] to vary the proportions slightly. But he [or she] would likely feel uneasy if, say, twice as many students as expected appeared to deserve an A or a B. He [or she] might also fear being reproached by colleagues for lowering standards. Some teachers guard against this by making it a principle *never* to award an A. According to a French adage quoted by Remi Clignet (1974, p. 349), the maximum '20 is given only to God, 19 to his saints, 18 to the professor's professor, 17 to the professor himself' – so the student of French composition can't be expected to score more than 16!

Figure 11.1 *Grading on the curve*

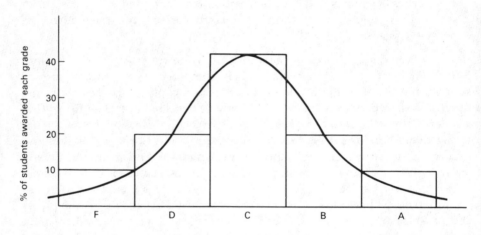

The expectation that students with A or B (or their equivalents in other systems for dispensing approval) will be in the minority has a strong hold in classrooms. Too easily it becomes a self-fulfilling prophecy: 'We can't expect the majority of students to do very well – so don't blame us for the failures.' When year after year the General Nursing Council failed one-third of candidates taking SRN examinations after three years of preparation, few questioned the proportion (*Nursing Times*, 1972). Fear of passing too many students is still preventing the Esperanto Teachers' Association from getting Esperanto examined as a GCE O level subject. They are told the language is 'too easy'. Too many students would get top grades.

The competitive nature of public examinations was brutally brought home to me a few years ago when I was first impressed by the instructional potential of programmed learning. In an excess of enthusiasm I suggested to a GCE examiner that with the help of well-written programmes, we'd soon enable nearly all students to pass O level mathematics. 'Oh no you won't,' he said, 'we'll just raise the standard.' Conversely, the Black Paper pessimist (see Pollard, 1971) can accuse this same self-fulfilling mechanism of disguising the fact that standards are falling as the quality of candidates declines!

Such viewpoints I have since found elaborated in Brereton (1944) who records, almost as an educational 'law', that: 'the standard of an examination adjusts itself to the standard of those taking it' (p. 43). While suggesting the possibility that, as a result of the war, children may become more aware of and more knowledgeable about geography, he considers it obvious that School Certificate examinations should continue to give credit only to about half the candidates. He justifies this implicit raising of the required standard partly in order to encourage pupils to continue caring about geography lessons (as opposed to reading the newspapers) and partly because it would be unfair to give pupils taking geography a better chance of reaching university than pupils taking, say, physics under the war-time difficulties caused by shortage of laboratories and physics teachers.

In such situations – where the best X% of students are to get the As, the next best nX% the Bs, and so on – the grade awarded to a student depends not on the absolute level of performance he [or she] attains but on how he [or she] performs *relative* to other students. That is, he [or she] may improve his [or her] performance by 100%, but if everyone else improves similarly his [or her] grade will be no higher than before. To get a better grade he [or she] must take it from one of the students above him [or her] by out-performing him [or her].

What are the side-effects of an assessment system believed by students (whether rightly or wrongly) to be competitive? For most students they are centred in the need to come to terms with failure. The psychiatrist Ronald Laing suggested once that 'to be a success in our society one has to learn to dream of failure'. And Bergman's film *Wild Strawberries* shows us an elderly professor at the peak of his career, about to receive the highest academic honour in the land, who dreams the night before of failing an examination.

For a few to emerge as outstandingly successful the majority must fail – to varying degrees. The failure may be only partial. Indeed, had the student been in a different (e.g. less selective) school or college, his [or her] performance might well have made him [or her] a success. But, by comparison with those he [or she] has been led to emulate, he [or she] has fallen short. Of course, it should be possible for a student who has 'failed' at one learning task to compensate by his [her] success on another task. Unfortunately, the ethos of competitive assessment often leads the student who has failed on a few tasks (e.g. learned more slowly than other people) to feel that he [she] has failed *as a person*. As a 'failure' himself [herself] he [she] may [...] then become less capable of succeeding in subsequent tasks. His [her] only consolation may be

151

that most of his [her] friends will soon be those who are failing at about the same level as he [she] is. Between them they may be able to construct mutually defensive attitudes to those above them and those (if any) below them in the hierarchy.

These defensive attitudes, based on fear, envy, resentment and self-hatred, may be of various kinds. The least active response is what Philip Jackson (1968, p. 27) describes as 'devaluing the evaluations to the point where they no longer matter very much'. Perhaps this attitude of 'cooling it', 'turning off', 'keeping his [or her] head down', 'disengaging' on the part of the failing student is a special case of what Roy Cox (1967) had in mind when he said: 'it is clear that where students are assessed in a way which is not seen to be relevant to what they are aiming at they will tend to distort and degrade the assessment so that it does not become a source of esteem.'

More actively, students who cannot 'adjust' equably to being labelled 'failures' may seek alternative sources of esteem. Perhaps through their attempts to pull school (or society) apart out of hours. As Dr Samuel Johnson pointed out: 'By exciting emulation and comparisons of superiority, you lay the foundation of lasting mischief; you make brothers and sisters hate each other.' A US Senate subcommittee survey of 1975 reports the case of a seventeen-year-old Detroit schoolgirl who was awarded massive damages after being beaten up and stabbed with pencils by thirty girl classmates who apparently resented that she was more attractive than they and received better grades. This case may be an example, more physical than usual, of what Arnold Wesker calls 'Lilliputianism – the poisonous need to cut other people down to size'. Who knows how much of the physical damage done to property and people arises out of the resentment and frustration smouldering on from school-days? (See Hargreaves, 1967, and Lacey, 1970, for accounts of the 'D-stream sub-culture' in secondary schools.)

Peter Vandome and his colleagues (1972) neatly sum up some of the pernicious side-effects of competitive assessment at college level:

> Students feel they will gain through the poor performance of others and suffer by imparting their own knowledge to fellow students. In this way, a potentially rich source of knowledge – communication of ideas among students – tends to be stifled. To the extent that it does take place, any exchange is biased by the way in which a student's 'self-image' and his image of his fellows is affected by their grades. A 50% student for instance will think twice before putting forward one of his ideas for discussion with a group of 60% students. This is relevant not only to informal interchange between students but also to tutorial discussion. Competitive rather than co-operative behaviour may be manifested in other ways such as the 'illegal borrowing' of library books.

Sadly, teachers too are sometimes caught up in a competitive assessment system – perhaps even as beneficiaries. While the students compete for honours within their class, the teacher may be looking to the class as a whole, competing with other teachers' classes, to bring *him* [her] esteem and promotion. The following quotation from Norman Conway, a grammar school chemistry teacher interviewed by Brian Jackson and Dennis Marsden (1962), shows how the competition for scarce university places (and ultimately for a better job for teacher), especially in the context of bureaucratic mass-assessment [. . .] can allow the instrumental pursuit of extrinsic rewards to drive out the expressive 'educational side':

> I reckon I can do 'A' level chem. in four terms. Four terms flat out mind. We have to go really fast. We have tests twice a week, but we get the results. For instance, last year I got an open at Pembroke, Cambridge, and an exhibition at Trinity Hall, Cambridge, and then I got half-a-dozen places. I've got fourteen places in the last two years and then these opens. I do pretty well; my results are all right. The way we teach, we teach for results. I want the passes, the schols and all those things. Tests all the time, and scrub the teaching methods, forget about the educational side. . . . What I want now is a head of department in a really good school, and then I'd do what our head of department has done. I'd put on the pressure, really hard. Really work those children, tests, tests, tests, and get the results. Get them the results they should have, and that would establish me, wouldn't it? It would give me a reputation. People would know that I could do the job. I might slacken off when I got established – perhaps after ten years or so. I might start looking round and thinking more about the educational side. But you've got to establish yourself first, haven't you? (pp. 36–7)
> [. . .]

The Giving of Grades

Much of the criticism of assessment is aimed at 'the grading system'. Thus we might expect to find that the giving of grades has a crop of side-effects peculiarly its own. This, however, is not the case. The side-effects usually blamed on grades are, in fact, those we have already seen associated with other aspects of assessment systems – emphasis on the easily-measured, unfairness, standardization, competition, extrinsic rewards. The giving of grades no doubt aggravates and facilitates such effects but mostly they could survive in its absence. So are grades an empty symbol, guilty by association but harmless in themselves? Not quite. Their special 'sin' is simply less obvious, being one of omission. (Remember Sherlock Holmes's clue of the dog that *didn't* bark in the night?) Grades are more to be blamed for what they don't do than for what they do do.

And what grades don't do is tell all that is known about the student's performance or abilities. Information is lost. Consider the assessment process. Someone – teacher, examiner, 'assessor' – observes the student at work, or perhaps interacts with him [or her] in some way, or more commonly analyses products of the student's work. The assessor forms impressions of the qualities and attainments discernible in the student's work – his [or her] interests and aversions, hang-ups and hobby-horses, strengths and weaknesses. These impressions he [or she] could perhaps spell out, verbalizing them for the benefit of the student and anyone else who has a legitimate interest in knowing how the student is seen by people close to him [or her]. Sometimes he [she] will do this for an individual assessment event (e.g. in commenting on an essay):

> You have shown a general understanding of the assignment, but could have improved your answers by closer attention to detail. In the first section (music) you failed to answer the part of the question that asked why the particular form used was appropriate, rather than the other forms available. In the second section, although you noted some of the imagery and discussed it intelligently, you often moved too far away from the imagery itself and relied on an 'outside' view of the poem (what you thought it must be about) to interpret it. In the final section you did pay close attention to detail, but it remained only observation of detail. You failed to connect the various elements together or to move *through* the detail to the larger issues of the painting. See the introductory section in the Unit and its explanation of the movement from meaning to form. It is a matter of working-at, responding to the detail, exploring the 'resonances' of the detail and moving from this to a full appreciation of the total effect. (Tutor's comments on an Open University student's assignment, quoted in Kennedy, 1974)

Such comments are more illuminating, particularly for the student, but also for anyone else concerned, than is a mark or grade or percentage label. (That student's essay, by the way, was graded C.) But when the assessor is expected merely to grade the product he [or she] will keep such insights to himself [or herself]. Worse still, he [she] perhaps never articulates them at all unless he [she] expects to have to spell them out. And the tutor's impressions of one student are unlikely to remain vivid after he [she] has looked at the work of a few more students. Thus his [her] students will probably receive from him [her] no feedback of a kind that might help them learn from his [her] response to their work. Donald McIntyre (1970) illustrates what is missing when he suggests that the 'result' of a pupil's mathematics exam, *instead of* 40%, might be recorded as a 'diagnostic profile' thus:

> Has mastered ideas of variable and one-to-one correspondence; not yet clear about functions; gets confused with problems of proportions; still has difficulty in structuring verbal problems (lack of grammatical understanding?); geometry generally competent, but has not learned terminology adequately; considerable skill in analysing visual problems.

Important qualities and features differentiating one student from another are obliterated by the baldness of grades. Thus several students who've all got the same grade may have tackled quite different problems and in quite different ways. As a trivial example, one student may have scored five out of ten on his [her] arithmetic test by answering the five additions correctly and the five subtractions incorrectly while his [her] friend is given the same score for precisely the converse performance! Frances Stevens (1970) in reviewing the marking of examiners in A level English literature, compares the gradings given to two particular scripts and reveals how much information has been lost in labelling the girl C and the boy D:

> Is the more optimistic forecast to be made of the dutiful immature girl who has some mildly appreciative responses, knows her books and has paid careful attention to what she has been told to think, but who has few independent ideas and writes with neither firmness nor joy; or of the mature and independent boy, who may not have studied his notes or perhaps his texts so thoroughly, but who has a sense of relevance, whose judgements are valid, who writes with assurance and betrays in his style ... that he has made a genuine engagement with the literature he has encountered? (p. 130)

Whether or not the assessor's criteria were exactly the same as Frances Stevens's is neither here nor there. They are unlikely to have been less subjective – or contestable. Translating them into a grade is an act of verification, erecting a pseudo-objective façade on what is a very delicate personal judgement. One effect of this façade is to repel debate. The grade seems god-given and immutable whereas the grounds on which it was decided might seem only too human and open to dispute. If an assessor were to respond to the girl mentioned above in the terms of Frances Stevens's assessment, he [or she] might well find her anxious to draw his [or her] attention to other qualities of her work which had been overlooked and which might revise his [or her] overall assessment. Certainly it could lead to a valuable teacher-learner dialogue. In the context of bureaucratic assessment, however, it could only be regarded as 'noise in the system'.

Whether or not we're always aware of the fact, grades act like *averages*. They smooth out and conceal irregularities and variability. One essay may have both first-class and abysmal features and yet be graded neither A nor F; instead it may get a C which fails altogether in letting us know that it differs from another essay graded C which is consistently of that quality in all its parts. Similarly, of two 60% examination scripts, one may contain answers both of failure quality and distinction quality while the other is 60%-ish throughout. And of course, the same variability may lie behind the all-concealing degree class of 'lower second' or a diploma class of 'satisfactory' – for all we know. In short, numbers and labels do not allow us to discriminate even between stable performers and those not infrequently found (see Stevens, 1970, p. 125) 'in whose papers near-brilliance alternates with near-nonsense'.

Grades, percentages and category labels are hopelessly inadequate to convey the load of meaning that we sometimes believe we are putting into them and which other people desperately try to get out from them again. How could a single letter or number possibly tell as much, for example, as is contained in descriptive reports or profiles like those [above]? There is a well-known Peanuts cartoon by Charles Schulz in which a girl is sitting at her school desk querying the C-grade she's been given for her 'sculpture' made from a coat-hanger. She wants to know whether she was judged on the piece of sculpture itself; and if so is it not true that time alone can judge a work of art? Or was she judged on her talent; if so, is it right that she should be judged on a part of life over which she has no control? If she was judged on her effort, then she regards the judgement as unfair since she tried as hard as she could. Was she being judged on what she had learned about the project; and if so, wasn't the teacher being judged on how well he had transmitted knowledge and therefore should he not share the C-grade? And finally, was she perhaps being judged by the inherent quality of the coat-hanger itself out of which her creation was made; and if so why should she be judged by the quality of the coat-hangers on which garments are returned by the laundry her parents patronize – since that's their responsibility shouldn't they share her grade? Her teacher's reply is not recorded.

I cannot applaud the rosy vision of a senior colleague whose spirited defence of grading (and rejection of profiles) climaxed as follows:

> Grading is a method of achieving a shorthand synthesis of every possible quality that one might wish to be included in a profile, consolidated into a symbol which examiners understand pragmatically with reference to a platonic point of reference existing in the minds of a group of examiners who have worked together, while a profile, however detailed, can never be more than an attempt to put down all those qualities.

To which perhaps the only reply is St Augustine's lament:

> For so it is, O Lord my God, I measure it;
> But what it is that I measure I do not know.

References

BRERETON, J. L. (1944) *The Case for Examinations*. Cambridge: Cambridge University Press.

CLIGNET, R. (1974) 'Grades, examinations, and other check-points as mechanisms of social control', Chap. 10 in *Liberty and Equality in the Educational Process*. New York: Wiley (pp. 327–58).

COX, R. (1967) 'Examinations, Identity and Diversity'. Talk given at the symposium on Recent Results of Research in Higher Education, organized jointly by South Birmingham Technical College and the Society for Research into Higher Education, Midlands Branch.

HARGREAVES, D. H. (1967) *Social Relations in a Secondary School*. London: Routledge & Kegan Paul.

HENRY, J. (1969) 'In suburban classrooms' in GROSS, R. and B. (eds) *Radical School Reform*. New York: Simon & Schuster.

JACKSON, B. and MARSDEN, D. (1962) *Education and the Working Class.* London: Routledge & Kegan Paul.

JACKSON, P. W. (1968) *Life in Classrooms.* New York: Holt, Rinehart & Winston.

KENNEDY, D. (1974) 'Preliminary Report on case study project in the Yorkshire Region'. Leeds: Open University (limited internal circulation).

LACEY, C. (1970) *Hightown Grammar: The School as a Social System.* Manchester: Manchester University Press.

MCINTYRE, D. (1970) 'Assessment and teaching' in RUBENSTEIN, D. and STONEMAN, C. (eds) *Education for Democracy* (2nd edn). Harmondsworth: Penguin Books.

NASH, R. (1973) *Classrooms Observed: the teacher's perception and the pupil's performance.* London: Routledge & Kegan Paul.

NURSING TIMES (1972) 'And still they failed', editorial in *Nursing Times,* 27 July 1972.

POLLARD, A. (1970) 'O and A level: Keeping up the standards', pp. 72–9 in COX, C. B. and DYSON, A. E. (eds) (1970) *Black Paper Two.* Critical Quarterly Society.

STEVENS, F. (1970) *English and Examinations.* London: Hutchinson.

TERWILLIGER, J. S. (1971) *Assigning Grades to Students.* Glenview, Ill.: Scott, Foresman.

VANDOME, P. *et al.* (1973) 'Why Assessment?' Paper given limited circulation in the University of Edinburgh.

WOLFF, R. P. (1969) *The Ideal of the University.* Boston: Beacon.

12

Control and Welfare: Towards a Theory of Constructive Discipline in Schools

Delwyn Tattum

Towards a More Constructive Approach to Discipline

[. . .]

Too much of our thinking about discipline has started from the wrong end, that is with questions as to how young offenders might be identified, punished and contained rather than how to create learning environments that might encourage productive pupil behaviour. Too often discipline is considered only in the negative context of punishment and criticism, whilst a more positive approach would emphasize the value of praise and encouragement, incentives and inducements. We aim to deal with the disturbances pupils create more in terms of how to control the child and less in terms of support and help. Children react well to praise; and in a recent document the NAHT (1984) examines 'the positive side of discipline', and gives a comprehensive list of ways schools can use praise and rewards – ranging from a quiet word or public acknowledgement through to 'a letter to parents informing them specifically of some action or achievement deserving praise. (Too often schools write only when something is wrong.)' (p. 3). Furthermore, a positive approach needs an even wider consideration of the school as an institution, and the classroom as a microcosm of school life. The character and ethos of a school is determined by, amongst other things, decisions about the curriculum, the allocation of resources, the grouping of pupils, and the arrangements made for guidance and welfare. The social environment of learning is also about the quality of relationships experienced in the intensity of teacher-pupil interaction. [. . .]

A *crisis-management approach* predominates in many schools, waiting for problems to reveal themselves in personal crises or confrontational outbursts. This also emphasizes an approach to social control, which is school orientated and geared mainly to deal with the indisciplined minority. By contrast a *problem-prevention approach* is person orientated, in the sense that its concern is for the welfare of all pupils. It entails an approach which is both school-wide and anticipatory and designed to support systematically all children in their personal and social development. It recognizes that tension and conflict are an inevitable aspect of teacher-pupil interaction, but also that the negative aspects of such interactions can be reduced by good classroom management and by the establishment of appropriate interpersonal relations. The two models are shown below in table form; and the rest of this paper will be devoted to the five elements identified as problem-prevention approach.

Table 12.1   *Two models of approach to discipline in schools*

Crisis-Management Approach	Problem-Prevention Approach
1 Use of official punishments and sanctions – including special units.	1 Development of school and classroom rules.
2 Use of a school's specialist staff – senior pastoral staff, counsellors.	2 Employing effective teaching techniques and skills.
3 Involvement of external agencies – including special education.	3 Developing positive pupils' self-concepts.
4 Negative involvement of parents.	4 Establishing good teacher-pupil relations.
	5 Teaching of personal and social education.

Whilst conscious that the five aspects of a problem-prevention approach to discipline are not independent but overlap each other, the aim is to focus on features of teacher-pupil interaction which bear on the total learning environment and the messages they convey about the school as a caring community.

1   The Development of Appropriate School and Classroom Rules

In research with disruptive pupils I identified five vocabularies of motives (Tattum, 1982), as the youngsters explained and justified their behaviour in terms of the school's culture, and they tried to give meaning to their learning and behavioural experiences in their day-to-day contacts with teachers and other pupils. The five categories are:

1   It was the teacher's fault.
2   Being treated with disrespect.
3   Inconsistency of rule application.

4 We were only messing – having a laugh.
5 It's the fault of the school system.

The vocabularies of motives range from blaming teacher to blaming the system, but it is not the general attribution of blame that is important but the specific things that they point to that is of value. For whilst these pupils were the extreme exponents of disruptive behaviour they do not stand in isolation from *all* other pupils, but rather at the negative pole on a continuum of indiscipline. Much of what is developed in the following sections arises directly from what they had to say and from my many visits to special units.

The centrality of rules in the above accounts of disruptive pupils is not surprising, and by the same token one would not advocate that teachers deviate from the known practice of applying the rule to the child and not the offence. The problem though, in a large secondary school, is that it is not possible for a teacher to know every pupil, and so the system presents opportunities for injustices and inequalities. When this happens children are frustrated and disgruntled. In fact, a dilemma that teachers face is maintaining good relationships as they vary between domination and coercion and creating a friendly and cooperative atmosphere in their classroom (see, for example, Mrs Chalmers in Best *et al.*, 1983, p. 144). No doubt this is one of the reasons why they are less committed to enforcement of 'around school rules' than they are about classroom conduct (Hargreaves *et al.*, 1975).

Surprisingly, whilst schools can be described as rule-governed, there has been very little research into rules. In an attempt to more clearly understand the extent and complexity of school rules the following five-fold categorization was drawn up (Tattum, 1982).

a *Legal/quasi-legal rules* apply to areas such as attendance, punctuality, corporal punishment, suspensions, and appearance. Appearance and style are important to young people, and many resent a teacher's intrusion into what they regard as personal. But rules are expressions of values and attitudes, and more than neatness, decorum and style are involved for both parties.

b *Organizational rules* are the general rules necessary for a school's smooth-running and good order. They control the movement of large numbers at set times, identify forbidden places and behaviour, and cover such matters as litter, graffiti, etc. Registration, homework, morning assembly and dining room behaviour are regulated, so that rules, ritual and routine pervade school life. But as they move about the school pupils witness and experience differential treatment which makes them aggrieved and disgruntled.

c *Contextual rules* pinpoint the variation experienced by pupils as they move from lesson to lesson as different demands are made covering conduct, task and dress. Different rules appertain to the gymnasium, the laboratory, practical rooms and so on; as in each case the physical setting allied to the nature of the subject determines situational constraints and prohibitions.

Hargreaves *et al.* (1975) identified and elaborated the situational rules around five themes – talk, movement, time teacher-pupil and pupil-pupil relationships. [. . .]

d *Personal rules* provide the greatest 'between-teacher' variance. Pupils are an integral part of classroom interaction, and how they perceive the situation will influence the nature of the ensuing negotiations. Part of such negotiation is 'teacher-testing' as each party tests out the other, the purpose of which is to facilitate present and subsequent encounters. 'First encounters' are a time in any interaction when a great deal of interpretive work goes on, and as the classroom initiative usually rests with teachers it is for them to make explicit the parameters of acceptable behaviour. Assuming pupil knowledge about legal, organizational and contextual rules, it is around the personal and relational rules that most negotiation takes place as each individual teacher faces a partially defined situation which needs to be given substance by the teacher's own *modus operandi*. For the pupils it is an accumulative and comparative exercise, and the knowledge they seek is how strictly a teacher applies contextual rules, and what are that teacher's personal rules (Werthamn, 1963).

e *Relational rules* reflect the highly personal nature of social control in schools. The tone of teacher-pupil interaction is dictated by the teachers. All teachers have to decide on the social distance they will preserve between themselves and the pupils, and experienced teachers advise new entrants to keep initial contacts formal and only gradually narrow the deference gap. Because of the size of secondary schools a great deal of teacher-pupil contact is at the formal or semi-formal level, which is another reason why pupils are differentially treated. Teachers look for clues of a personal nature as they question pupils, assessing appearance and demeanour. Some pupils are more adept at giving acceptable explanations of their behaviour, and at adopting the appropriate posture and tone when challenged. [. . .]

Discipline is a personal matter and it is the area in which teachers are made to feel individually accountable by colleagues. Teaching is also a public activity and so teachers lay great store on 'keeping face'. It is this sense of vulnerability which may explain why the profession devotes so much more time to criticizing bad behaviour than to rewarding good behaviour.

Social control in schools is a complex problem, of which the rule system is only a part; and the ways schools organize themselves influence relationships and the levels of pupil disaffection. As person-changing organizations schools need to examine their person-management methods, and the following recommendations are made regarding rules:

(i) First, both teachers and pupils should become more closely involved in the creation and review of rules. More open discussion will bring better understanding of control methods and their related problems. Teachers work in the isolation of their classroom for much of the time; and rarely does a school give time for teachers and pupils to discuss the rationale and justification of its rule system (HMI, 1982).

(ii)   Second, rules must be communicated to teachers, pupils and parents. Social control is based on the supposition that knowledge of the rules exists among members, and so they must be articulated if uncertainty and inconsistencies are to be reduced.

(iii)   Third, it is important to have as few rules as possible.

(iv)   Fourth, teachers should set themselves as models in their own dress and behaviour, in the way they talk to and treat young people, and by arriving for lessons on time and well-prepared.

It is evident that these recommendations also apply to classrooms, for they relate to the principles that teachers should introduce their pupils to the democratic processes, and that individuals support and implement decisions they have helped to make.

2 Employing Effective Teaching Techniques and Skills

We need to dispense with the commonly held view that teachers are born and not made. People who talk in this vein refer to personality and charisma; and whilst not dismissing the significance of individual characteristics we have to beware of reducing the craft of teaching to intuition. Teaching is a highly skilled activity which should and can be improved through study, experiment and practice.

The importance of effective teaching in preventing unproductive pupil behaviour may be illustrated by Kounin's (1970) research into classroom discipline. He found that the differences between effective teachers and those who had major management problems lay essentially in the successful teacher's ability to prevent discipline problems from arising. Kounin (1970) advises that we attend to what occurs just prior to misbehaviour rather than immediately afterwards. The positive approach is to improve the conditions that gave rise to unwanted behaviour rather than stressing consequences and punishments. The latter may have short-term results but does not address fundamental questions concerning the appropriateness of the teaching, the relevance of the curriculum, or the quality of the relationships (see also Brophy and Everston, 1975).

Successful teachers were found to be better prepared and organized, and moved smoothly from one activity to another. They also maintained pupil involvement in activities by clear instructions and guidance, and not interrupting class instructions to follow other issues. Kounin also noted that the more effective teachers had greater class awareness, as they scanned for potential problems and so dealt with them before they became real difficulties. They also anticipated pupils' needs and minimized restlessness and boredom through work that was interesting and matched the pupils' abilities. Hargreaves *et al.* (1975) examined 'switch-signalling', aimed to cue pupils at the starting or ending of an activity. Secondary teachers who gave clear, unambiguous signals were discovered to have fewer problems than those who gave none or who were imprecise. Other features of good class control highlighted in recent research are the pacing of lessons, the importance of eye contact, and the significance of personal space for teachers and pupils. [. . .]

Teachers tend to exhibit more positive non-verbal behaviour to pupils considered bright than to those considered dull. These behaviours are expressed in tone of voice, body stance, facial expressions, gestures and physical proximity. Teachers also teach more to, spend more time with, and request more from pupils they consider able (Baker and Crist, 1971). Less able pupils are given fewer opportunities to respond, are given less time to answer, and are substantially more likely to be criticized for incorrect responses than their high-achieving classmates. As Brophy and Good (1974) concluded from their extensive research on the communication of expectation, many youngsters are given an impoverished learning experience. Finally, Burns (1982) offers four recommendations on how teachers may counter the negative aspects of the expectancy effect: (i) interact evenly with all pupils; (ii) talk with all pupils; (iii) praise pupils realistically; and (iv) set tasks to suit individuals.

3   Developing Positive Pupils' Self-concepts

The links between this section and the previous one are obvious. From my own research with disruptive pupils it was evident that they often held negative views of themselves as learners; as one boy said, 'School is for learning, but all it learnt me is that I'm no good for anything' (Tattum, 1982, p. 179). A measure of success and achievement is important, otherwise why attend school or pay attention to lessons. Research by Branch *et al.* (1977) reveals a significant relationship between low self-concept as a learner and misbehaviour in the classroom. They evaluated disruptive and non-disruptive middle-school students (eleven to fourteen years) on their professed and inferred academic self-concepts. Those students identified by their behaviour as disruptive had significantly lower self-concepts as learners than did students identified as non-disruptive. The theoretical implication drawn from the study was that students' negative feelings about themselves as learners may be a contributory factor in student disruption, and that self-concept may eventually prove to be a significant mediating variable that will help us understand many types of seemingly unrelated behaviour problems. [. . .]

A practice that contributes to the development of a negative self-concept is that of labelling, and the negative consequences of labelling may outweigh the intended benefits of attempts to meet the needs of pupils who require special help.

> Categories and labels are powerful instruments for social regulation and control, and they often are employed for obscure, covert or hurtful purposes; to degrade people, to deny them access to opportunity, to exclude 'undesirables' whose presence in society in some way offends, disturbs familiar customs, or demands extraordinary efforts (Hobbs, 1975).

Beyond the formal school policies of suspending, ascertainment and transfer, streaming and banding, many pupils complain of being 'treated with disrespect' (Tattum, 1982), as either intentionally or unintentionally, teachers cause them to experience embarrassment, frustration and failure.

> 'Talk to us like a dog. Telling you straight now, they're terrible, can't talk to you nice. And that's what makes me go mad then see. If someone shouts at me I got to shout back at them. If a teacher hits me I got to hit them back,' said thirteen year old Debbie.

Here she expresses one way whereby some youngsters seek to protect their self-images, as they return the verbal, physical and organizational assaults on their perceptions of self with similar abuse. To be passive is a denial of self and a loss of self-respect. Garfinkel (1956) calls such public demeaning acts 'degradation ceremonies', as they devalue the self through subjection to embarrassment, confusion and humiliation. [...]

4 Establishing Good Teacher–Pupil Relations

The school as a caring community only has meaning through the quality of the relationships that exist; and if positive approaches to discipline are to be effective then much depends on how well teachers and pupils relate to each other. Children need to feel that they belong and that adults care about them, and this is as true of school life as it is true of family life. Pupils can be highly critical of teachers whom they perceive as being unconcerned or uninterested in them. 'Some teachers don't want to know and don't care', was the comment of one disruptive girl. Caring personalizes the relationship, and for the pupil it is an opportunity to get behind the formal teacher role into an association that has meaning – the human side of schooling. Wilson (1962) emphasized the importance of affective bonds in a society in which most role relationships are neutral.

The instrumental and affective aspects of teaching are interwoven and both are essential ingredients of an effective learning environment. The therapeutic value inherent in providing individuals with a sense of being cared for and respected is at the heart of the work of Carl Rogers. In describing the ingredients of a relationship which facilitates positive personal growth and learning, he writes,

> There is another attitude which stands out in those who are successful in facilitating learning ... I think of it as prizing the learner, prizing his feelings, his opinions, his person. It is a caring for the learner, but a non-

possessive caring. It is an acceptance of this other individual as a separate person, having worth in his own right (Rogers, 1969).

Research into the 'good teacher' also confirms the importance of both the instrumental and affective areas. Grace (1978) asked head teachers to designate which members of their staff they regarded as 'outstanding' teachers within the context of the inner-city comprehensive school. Poor teachers were seen to be lazy, weak and ineffectual in their classroom organization, and lacked commitment to the welfare of their pupils. By comparison, good teachers were characterized by hard work, a good rapport with pupils, 'and a demonstration of an individualistic welfare commitment to the various distresses of inner-city pupils'. [...]

Turning to the views of the pupils, Weston *et al.* (1978), in a survey of the attitudes towards schooling of thirteen and fourteen year olds, found that regardless of social background or ability, pupils regarded it as a teacher's function to assist them in their personal and social development, and create a happy and supportive ethos within the school. Woods (1979) makes the telling point from his extended conversations with over two hundred fourth and fifth year pupils that for many the intrinsic value of work was alien to their thinking; they were much more interested in the kind of relationships the work situation offered with friends and teachers. If the relationships were tolerable then the work was much less burdensome; in fact, a friendly teacher could make school work pleasant and enjoyable. Wood concludes that 'the simple moral is to make work count, and for teachers to be human'.

Sadly, research by Thompson (1975) into what pupils find particularly lacking in teachers, revealed that these are the very qualities which make them human. In comparison with other adults pupils rated teachers more favourably on their primary role qualities such as interesting, wise, successful – but hard. On qualities such as kindness, fairness and warmth they were less favourably rated. Disruptive pupils openly admitted that their behaviour in the classroom was determined by their attitude towards the teacher, whether he [or she] showed kindness and understanding, and was friendly and helpful. It is suggested that a predominantly utilitarian approach to the teacher's role, focusing on instructional and disciplinary functions, fails to take into account the expectations of pupils and can result in the hostile attitudes found by Corrigan (1979). In response to a statement, 'Teachers don't really care about what happens to me they are just doing a job', of the ninety-three teenage boys involved in his study, sixty-two agreed or strongly agreed with the statement. [...]

5   Teaching of Personal and Social Education

Whilst this section overlaps with the previous one on relationships it is different in that it takes us into the area of the curriculum. [...] Caring for and teaching the child are so much bound together as to be inseparable. But I want

165

to stress the responsibility that schools have for developing a programme for the personal and social education for all pupils. [. . .]

At this point I will only reiterate the view expressed in a recent ILEA report on *Improving Secondary Schools* that:

> social and personal education at its best is an important bridge between the pastoral and academic aspects of the school's work and should serve to integrate a wide range of the school's aims and practices (Committee on the Curriculum and Organisation of Secondary Schools (Hargreaves Report) 1984).

Conclusion

These tentative steps towards a more constructive approach to discipline have concentrated on seeking ways whereby we can create a secure and healthy environment that is conducive to the personal and social development of children. The emphasis has been on teacher initiated behaviour; it involves planning prior to the school year, each day and each lesson. In many respects it requires changes in emphasis to a revision of many entrenched professional attitudes. It also means having regard for youngsters as 'developing centres of consciousness' (Peters, 1966), and respecting them as persons and pupils. It is not claimed that the approach will eliminate indiscipline, but rather that concentration on positive, problem-prevention approaches will reduce it, and in so doing take some of the strain and tension out of teacher-pupil interaction to the welfare of both parties.

Bibliography

ACLAND, H. (1980) 'Research as state management: The case of the Plowden Committee' in BULMER, M. J. A. (ed.) *Social Research and Royal Commissions*, London, George Allen and Unwin.

BAKER, J. and CRIST, B. (1971) 'Teacher expectations' in ETASHOFF, J. and SNOW, R. (eds) *Pygmalion Reconsidered*, Ohio, Charles Jones.

BEST, R., RIBBINS, P., JARVIS, C. and ODDY, D. (1983) *Education and Care*, London, Heinemann.

BRANCH, C., DAMICO, S. and PURKEY, W. (1977) 'A comparison between the self-concepts as learners of disruptive and non-disruptive middle school students' in *The Middle School Journal*, 7, pp. 15–16.

BROPHY, J. and EVERTSON, C. (1976) *Learning from Teaching: A Developmental Perspective*, Boston, Allyn and Bacon.

BROPHY, J. and GOOD, T. (1974) *Teacher Student Relationships: Causes and Consequences*, New York, Holt, Rinehart & Winston.

BURNS, R. (1982) *Self Concept Development and Education*, London, Holt Rinehart & Winston.

COMMITTEE ON THE CURRICULUM AND ORGANIZATION OF SECONDARY SCHOOLS (1984) *Improving Secondary Schools* (Hargreaves Report), London, ILEA.

CORRIGAN, P. (1979) *Schooling the Smash Street Kids*, London, Macmillan.

GRACE, G. (1978) *Teachers, Ideology and Control*, London, Routledge & Kegan Paul.

HARGREAVES, D., HESTER, S. and MELLOR, F. (1975) *Deviance in Classrooms*, London, Routledge & Kegan Paul.

HMI (1982) *Pastoral Care in Comprehensive Schools in Wales*, Cardiff, Welsh Office.

HOBBS, N. (ed.) (1975) *The Futures of Children: Categories, Labels and Their Consequences*, Nashville, Vanderbilt University Press.

KOUNIN, J. (1970) *Discipline and Group Management in Classrooms*, New York, Holt, Rinehart & Winston.

NATIONAL ASSOCIATION FOR HEAD TEACHERS (1984) *Council Memorandum on Discipline in Schools*, Haywards Heath, NAHT.

PETERS. R (1966) *Ethics and Education*, London, Allen and Unwin.

ROGERS, C. (1969) *Freedom to Learn*, Colombus, Merrill.

TATTUM, D. (1982) *Disruptive Pupils in Schools and Units*, Chichester, Wiley.

THOMPSON, B. (1975) 'Secondary school pupils: attitudes to school and teachers' in *Educational Research*, 18, 1 pp. 62–72.

WERTHAMN, C. (1963) 'Delinquents in schools: a test for the legitimacy of authority' in *Berkeley Journal of Sociology*, 8, 1, pp. 39–60.

WESTON, P., TAYLOR, P., and HURMAN, A. (1978) 'Clients' expectations of secondary schooling' in *Educational Review*, 30, 2, pp. 159–66.

WILSON, B. (1962) 'The teacher's role – sociological analysis' in *British Journal of Sociology*, 13, pp. 15–31.

WOODS, P. (1979) *The Divided Schools*, London, Routledge & Kegan Paul!.

13

Pastoral Care and Girls of Asian Parentage

Alun Pelleschi

Introduction

Those of us who work in inner-city schools containing ethnic minority children are caught up in the theory and practice of multiculturalism: a vague, often much-abused term, which one rarely meets in articles on pastoral care and which (quite wrongly) those of us in areas unlike the above assume not to be their province.

Multiculturalism, although being under-theorized, largely depends on the ideal of cultural pluralism as its base. This assumes that society is a 'melting pot' in which different cultures are (or perhaps should be) equal. Much of the recent literature in multicultural education recognizes that there is an imbalance between the 'haves' and 'have-nots' which, in the case of ethnic minority pupils, means that their life-chances are not as great as white pupils' from the same social class. Thus there is a reformist tenor to much of the literature which attempts positive discrimination in favour of ethnic minority pupils: Saunders' (1982) work is a good example of this.

I would imagine that the majority of teachers working in the state sector would agree that equality of educational opportunity is probably the most important guiding principle of comprehensive schooling. However, there is a paradox with regard to such principles when one considers Muslim girls (Harris, 1982). Where equality of opportunity in education refers to access to higher education or employment on the basis of merit, rather than race, class or gender, educationalists find themselves in difficulties when faced with a Muslim community whose elders are determined to preserve the traditional role of women in their culture. What does the pastoral system do when faced with girls who are rebelling against their elders on such issues? Similarly, how does the pastoral system react to or attempt to change what is perhaps the most significant aspect of inequality (certainly in its effects) which manifests itself to them, namely racism. [. . .]

This article seeks to open up the debate surrounding the issues referred to above and hopefully to shed some light on the possible effects of their interrelationship on Asian girls. The original study referred to involved a part ethnographic, part normative study of pupils in the fourth year of a Bradford comprehensive (Pelleschi, 1983).

The School and Pupils' Background

The school in question is an inner-city comprehensive of around 1,300 pupils located in south Bradford. In 1983 over 32% of the pupils were of Asian parentage (since having risen to around 50%). The largest group have parents who come from the Mirpur district of Pakistan, a largely agricultural area. These people are Punjabi-speaking Muslims. Other sizeable groups are Gujarati-speaking Hindus of Indian origin and Sikhs. Over 70% of the pupils were born in this country.

Most of the pupils come from working-class homes and a high proportion of their parents are unemployed. The over-representation of Asian parents amongst the unemployed clearly has repercussions for the school and social services and there are frequently problems of a bureaucratic nature thrown up by this and the implementation of the British Nationality Act 1981 which involve the pastoral system. Much of the debate over the schooling of ethnic minority pupils has centred on the curriculum they should be offered, for example Mother Tongue teaching, the provision of ESL, etc. For pastoral staff the issues facing them are, if anything, far more complex and include such issues as: the counselling of pupils whose parents wish them to become doctors when they are studying for CSEs, maximizing the knowledge gained from a long-term stay in the Asian sub-continent and minimizing the disruption to exam work, attempting to persuade parents to allow their daughters back into the sixth form, what to do with girls who defy cultural norms and disobey their parents' wishes and so on.

It is tempting to think of these pupils as problems, but it is perhaps more relevant to pose the question as to whether these pupils are indeed problematic or whether what we are offering them is appropriate to their education and personal development.

The School Ethos

Although it is doubtful that consensus would ever be reached over the school ethos, there does tend to be a prevailing philosophy which underpins most of the school's work.

Firstly, the school prides itself on its 'multicultural' approach to education. It has been one of the forerunners in Bradford, respecting the wishes of ethnic minority groups and placing a high premium on their cultures. There is no religious assembly although rooms are made available at lunchtime for prayer, there is a multi-faith RE programme, pupils are allowed to wear traditional costume, there are Asian languages on the timetable, different cultural modes find expression in school productions and so on.

Secondly, the school prides itself on its academic achievement with pupils who mostly originate from deprived inner-city areas and over 90% of the intake take public exams.

Thirdly, relationships within the school are personalized rather than institutionalized within the context of cultural pluralism. The 1982 school handbook, for example, has this to say:

> You may know that we have made a number of decisions purposefully to create a responsible and accepting attitude in the school. There is no school uniform and there is no corporal punishment under any circumstances. We are able to concentrate on our main function, meeting the needs of individual children.

The school can thus be seen to have two high-priority commitments: to multicultural education in a spirit of cultural pluralism and to meeting the needs of individual children. There is no doubt that the highly professional input of the staff is directed to these ends but there are a number of important questions that are left begging: does the fostering of minority cultures mean that they have the same cultural level and the same power base as our own (whatever that might be); does such fostering bolster values which are relict in terms of the socio-economic and political systems both here and in their homeland; does the commitment to the needs of individuals cause a conflict with the structured role for the individual within most Asian families. From the point of view of this study, the most important question is what part the school, through the pastoral system, plays in the reproduction of the status and role of women within the Asian community (this obviously might have implications of a much broader nature).

For Asian girls there are three dominant arenas in their lives: home, school and their peer groups. Their interaction with 'western' culture is often restricted to school or to television. Their parents often receive a negative impression of values from the same sources. The following sections take a look at these three areas.

The Home Factor

The family is central in the transmission of cultural values. Khan (1982, p. 197) defines culture as 'the system of shared meanings developed in a social and economic context which has a particular historical and political background'. Two observations spring to mind from this: firstly culture is not static, therefore teacher support for a particular cultural artifact may be condoning retrospection; secondly that the view that children may be 'caught between' two cultures may also be a false premise but that if teachers accept this, it could lead to a feeling of powerlessness in girls seeking support.

Girls' personalities very much depend on the home situation: whether both parents are present, whether they are liberal or traditionalist, the extent of the extended family net, the position of the girl in the family, etc. It can be argued, however, that the overriding factors which affect the girls are firstly the role of women in the family which is the responsibility for domestic labour, and secondly the influence of Islam in which the position of women is decreed.

Pakistani families tend to be of the joint and extended type. They are typically patrilineal, patrilocal and have patriarchal authority with respect related to age as well as sex. Within the family the effects of the kinship net should not be underestimated. The kinship net and the power of gossip become a major force in the preservation of cultural norms and in determining girls' behaviour. As one of the girls put it:

FATIMA: 'I mean, like, if you want to wear some clothing, they sometimes say you shouldn't, you've got relations coming. They talk behind your back and all that.'

A large proportion of the girls' problems would appear to stem from the family and there would seem to be three major sources: families under increasing strain as a result of unemployment, the effects of racism, and worries about the family's future. This rebounds on girls who are expected to uphold the family honour whilst being of modest character. Respect for their parents compounded by Islamic tenets often lead to submissive responses from the girls:

KANEES: 'I put it on (jeela-headscarf) in front of my father and uncle because I respect them.'

Some of the girls do talk to their parents about choice of dress, but in the end usually follow their parents' wishes:

FEEZA: 'I used to wear trousers in my other school, but as you get older your parents say you shouldn't wear them, shows more of your body if you wear them.'

The value systems appertaining to sex, boys and marriage are at the very heart of Pakistani cultural life. The family honour and the girls' modesty discourages them from contact with boys and often from health education. Similarly PE can sometimes be a conflict area between home and school.

Should the girls challenge their parents over these issues, tolerance within the family decreases and gossip becomes a weapon. The consequences of further challenge may be removal from school and/or an early marriage. The girls are often plagued by doubts and fears lest gossip reaches their parents concerning their activities (often innocent) with boys. [. . .]

Tied in with their attitude towards boys is the girls' conceptualization of their role within their culture which they compare with that of boys. The girls appreciate the role of domesticity in which they are usually instructed from an early age. [. . .]

171

The girls virtually all accepted the man's role as being the wage-earner and the woman's as being supportive (secondariness). [. . .]

A major area of dissatisfaction lay in the relative freedom that the males experienced. [. . .]

The girls spent much of their free time either watching television or visiting relatives. This led to a great deal of frustration and boredom:

> FATIMA: 'I haven't got any freedom, I'm not allowed to go out . . . I think most Asian girls, right, their parents are too strict to them. At home they're not allowed out, they're not allowed to do anything, right, and that's why they slam (truant). If the parents gave them a bit more freedom, I don't think they'd slam that much.'

There can therefore be seen to be two conflicting perspectives which help us to understand the development of girls' personalities and which can determine the way the girls operate within the school environment. The first is the demands placed upon the girls by their parents (which have a religious and cultural base) and the second is the girl's reaction to these demands. Few of the girls questioned the role they were expected to play or saw a life for themselves away from the family. Instead girls either totally capitulated to demands by their parents: this caused them a great deal of suffering which was largely internalized and had serious repercussions both for the development of the girls' personalities and their progress in school; or negotiated a settlement with their parents which was not threatening to any home relationships.

The School Factor

School for many Asian girls is an escape from the confinement of family life. It gives them an opportunity to associate with their friends, share experiences, and to identify with aspects of life from which their parents are often far removed. For a few, school represents the opportunity to gain professional status in later life, and in some cases the successful students offset their parents' wishes for an early marriage or containment at home. For the weaker pupil, however, the school curriculum may have little meaning, and in the case of girls who have submitted to their parents' demands over their life-style, this can lead to poor motivation and low spirits.

This article is primarily concerned with the effects of the pastoral system on these girls, and in order to do this one must look at the way that the system is believed to operate by the staff and the way it is seen to operate by the girls.

The school's pastoral system at the time consisted of a year head for boys and one for girls in each year. The system was overlooked by two deputy heads. The year group contained about 360 pupils divided into sixteen tutor groups with a tutor who moved with the group. The Heads of Year were static and did not follow through. There is no job description for tutors hence some operate as administrative functionaries while others are much more involved with the welfare of their charges. The main contact period is for twenty minutes each morning. On one of these sessions each week the fourth year were involved in a tutorial programme of 'active tutorial work'.

The Year Heads have a multi-faceted role and are regarded as the 'specialists' of the pastoral system: they contact the 'care' agencies, parents etc., arrange meetings, are the chief disciplinarians, and are also the people most likely to be involved with the counselling process.

The two year heads for the fourth year and the two deputies were all informally interviewed in order to ascertain the part they felt they played in the pastoral system. What follows relates to these interviews.

The Pastoral Staff

[. . .]

As mentioned previously, the school is committed to the ideal of cultural pluralism. The staff's view in relation to this may either reinforce or negate this ideal. Two quite different perspectives emerged from the two year heads. The year head (boys) said this:

WP: 'I don't, to be honest, think of colour within the groups so much. There is so little time to do the work, that the child who comes to you is just a child.'

The year head (girls) had a different view:

MC: 'I think there is bound to be an inconsistency because of the different cultures and because of different demands put on kids by parents.'

Thus, if you happen to be a boy then you are treated with a certain consistency but the girls are treated differently, according to their ethnic origins. All pastoral staff were aware of the effects of racism experienced by Asian pupils. This was generally held to be due to discrimination by white pupils:

MC: 'I think some of them are treated quite badly by the white population. I'm fed up of having to cut chewing gum out of girls' hair.'

There is a commitment to dealing with racialism, when it flares up, by the pastoral staff, but no overall strategy for dealing with it. In fact the pastoral staff believed that the effects of racialism were lessening: that it was working its way out.

A further issue which proves problematic to the pastoral staff is whether the system is transmissionist or transformationist with respect to Asian culture. One perspective sees this in terms of a culture conflict:

WJ (Deputy Head): 'With the Asian girls it's a different cup of tea altogether because it's asking them to relate to two cultures which is impossible from that point of view I think.'

How, then, may minority cultures be reconciled with the 'culture of dominance'? The suggestion seems to be one of providing equality of educational opportunity subsumed within the present framework of success:

TR (Deputy Head): 'We want our kids to get O levels and A levels and be in just as strong a position as white kids.'

Viewed from a boy/girl framework there tends to be a twofold entrapment of pastoral staff. Incidents where boys and girls are involved tend to be treated as follows: firstly there is a period of counselling which is followed by the parents being brought in, should it fail. The first part of the entrapment involves a misunderstanding of the nature of patriarchy:

WJ: 'They (boys) perhaps take it (counselling) more seriously from a man perhaps because of the respect for the father/man role-dominated society as I see it.'

From this one gains the impression that the liberal notion of equality of cultures is at odds with the equally liberal notion of equality of gender. Taken further, this brings in the second entrapment, namely unqualified support for the parents' wishes:

WJ: 'I think I have to accept the wishes of the Asians in their social setting, and the wishes of Asian parents.'

As can be seen below, this type of cultural relativism illustrates the difficulties of applying fixed ideas of culture to a dynamic situation. This is particularly the case when one considers that intra-cultural differences are as diverse as inter-cultural ones. Once again, though, this kind of relativism is applied differently to boys and girls:

MC: 'Overall, I think, with regard to the Asian girls, we've got to back up the parents ... if the girl is really unhappy, if I think the girl is suffering some form of mental dilemma, then I would pursue it I think. But where it's just the girl kicking against the culture, and in particular moral danger ... then I think you have to come the hard line with them.'

The situation, therefore, would appear to be one in which white girls and boys are allowed to associate freely and in which curbs are only put on them if the parents demand it, whereas the opposite would be true for Asian pupils. [. . .]

Generally, then, staff do seem to follow the principle of cultural pluralism often by supporting the wishes of Asian parents. Such a posture appears to conflict with the principle of equality of opportunity in relation to both class and gender.

The Pupil Perspective

Part of the questionnaire given to all the Asian pupils in the fourth year attempted to identify their attitudes towards school. A high majority of pupils clearly enjoyed school, and when this was compared with absence rates, of those with high absence rate, only 3 pupils out of 46 stated that they did not like school.

There appeared to be three important reasons for girls enjoying school: it gave them an opportunity to be with friends, they mostly enjoyed their lessons, and they saw schooling as a means of delaying an early marriage or being incarcerated at home.

When asked about unofficial absences (slamming), the two groups of girls interviewed had quite different perspectives. One group was totally against 'slamming' which they saw as morally wrong. The other group, however, had members who had 'slammed' in the past and one or two who continued to do so. The reasons for 'slamming' had more to do with the home situation than a reaction to school:

> FARHANA: 'If Asian girls slam, right, probably one reason – they don't get enough freedom at home, and if they want to come to school they say we've got one chance and do it.'

The school played a major part in preventing or reducing 'slamming', mainly due to a quick response involving the parents. This can have traumatic effects on the girls:

> FATIMA: 'I learnt by my mistake . . . she was the one (Head of Year) – I said to her don't. I know that incident depended upon all my life. She wouldn't listen to me. I think she should have given me a chance. I would have stopped.'
>
> [. . .]

When asked to whom they turn for advice on jobs, education or training, only 7% of the girls had sought anybody's advice, and of those whose advice was taken, the year head's was deemed least helpful. Parents appeared to be the people most used, which is not surprising given the need to persuade them to allow further education or training.

A separate question attempted to elucidate whether there was any difference between what the girl wished to do and what their parents wanted. About 20% of the girls indicated that there was a problem and of the rest, agreement had been reached over 'safe' women's careers such as teaching or nursing.

When asked about advice over school matters, whether it be subject choice, homework, racism, etc. a low percentage actually sought help. The tutor was the most frequently quoted source with parents a close second.

Although girls appeared to seek advice about 'personal' problems more often than boys, the pastoral system still proved to be an unpopular source for advice. Parents were again used in most cases, closely followed by friends. This is partly explained by the meaning placed upon 'personal problems' by the girls (most denied they had any), but it is clear that friends were considered both as sounding boards and for support:

> SAMINA: 'You know you have good friends when they try to help you out and get into trouble 'cos of that person who is in trouble.'

Although the tutor stood out as the person in school that the girls would most likely turn to for advice, this very much depends on the way the tutor regards his/her role and the interaction between tutor and pupil. Two particular aspects emerged concerning this relationship:

SHAGUFTA: 'I don't know her well. I don't have lessons with her, she's just my tutor.'

SAMINA: 'What's she going to do about my home problem?'

Thus, often the girls feel they don't know the tutor well enough to seek help, but often the tutor's role is not understood by the girls. The most important factor, though, was whether it was felt that the teachers had empathy for the girls. To them this was reflected by whether the teacher understood their culture, by contact and by discussion. In this context the girls saw the ESL department in a favourable light and would often turn to them for advice:

FATIMA: 'All the ESL teachers, I think, understand Asian children.'

BALQUEES: 'She likes our kind of people – she's alright.'

The person least likely to be approached was the year head. The pupils' responses to a question of how many of them had been seen by the year head over the year indicated that only a very small number had done so, and that most were referred either by a teacher or the year head herself. In most cases the referral was for bad behaviour and only one girl had seen the year head over a personal matter. [. . .]

The final factor I would like to mention in relation to school is the effect racism has on the girls. For them this occurs in their daily contacts with other pupils mainly, but also on occasions with staff. Although not fully understanding the political and socio-economic underpinning of racism, the girls were nevertheless aware of their rights:

RAGI: 'We were born here as well, so we've a right to stay.'

Racialism has a traumatic effect on the girls who are subject to verbal and physical abuse daily:

RAZIA: 'People push us around . . . they pick on us because we're Pakistanis. They say we're black and we come from Pakistan, and go back to Pakiland.'

FATIMA: 'I mean, most English children when we go past them on the corridors, if we dress up in western clothes, right, they say look at them, think they own the place, right. When we dress up in our tradition they make fun of us, right, so what do they expect us to dress up in?'

The girls' response to this kind of treatment was largely to ignore it in fear that if they retaliated they would get much worse. This for them was compounded in that they felt the teachers did not help them in any way, apportioning blame for fights 50–50 as an example.

RAGI: 'You just have to ignore it all. You know you feel really hurt and you just have to cry and that and usually don't tell your parents so I don't tell my mum about this.'

It is noticeable that Asian girls tend to organize themselves into fairly stable friendship groups. This possibly comes about in two ways. Firstly there are the 'push' factors – the school organizing aspects of the curriculum solely for Asian pupils, racism etc. and 'pull' factors' in particular the need for care and emotional support from other girls. The groups which form may be a force for conservation or radicalism in terms of the relationship with school and 'Asian' culture.

The Group Factor

One of the deputies, as mentioned earlier, referred to the girls as being 'caught between' two cultures. If this is the case it could be reflected in low self-esteem or in the girls experiencing an identity conflict.

Considering self-esteem, a self-esteem inventory was administered to the two groups of girls interviewed. The outcome suggests that for the most part, the girls did not experience low self-esteem. Those that could be considered low were in fact those girls most in conflict in their home situations, often having traditionalist parents. There was no indication of low self-esteem being related to a poor image of their cultural background.

Often in the literature one comes across the value of 'modelling' – having ethnic minority teachers in the school. The girls indicated that they saw Asian teachers simply as teachers and thought of them as good or bad in terms of their teaching ability and the relationship between them. As for other teachers they would not turn to them for advice but this was also due to a lack of trust in them.

An individual's search for a credible identity is achieved to a large extent by the interaction between herself and the group to which she belongs. The 'group' can encompass national, ethnic, family or peer boundaries. It was noticeable that the girls felt equally at home in being identified as Pakistani for cultural/ethnic purposes or British for nationality purposes, and there is a great deal of pride in both stances. This helps to explain why the girls seldom made any approaches to white girls for friendship (racism aside) as it can lead to identity conflict and a girl rebelling against her parents:

ZAHEDA: 'She hung around with English girls too much. She didn't take care of herself.' (Concerning a girl recently sent to Pakistan.)

The rising interest in wearing traditional clothes has as much to do with identity as it does with parents' wishes. [. . .]

Significant differences emerged between the two groups interviewed. One group was conformist in school, wore traditional Asian dress and generally had a good relationship with their parents. The second group, however, were non-conformist in school, wore a variety of western and Asian dress and generally had a mixed relationship at home often with the father absent (either dead or in Pakistan).

Both groups were evolving their own style involving particular tastes in music, dress, and the activities in which they were involved. In both cases it can be argued that there was a re-defining of their cultural norms but none of the girls interviewed felt this to be a threat to their being Muslim/Hindu, Pakistani/Indian or to their parents. The more radical group was, however, engaged in activities that could describe them as being almost a counter-cultural group within the school. One thing that did emerge was the shared need to be together:

KANEES: '. . . just good friends you know, they're really kind to you. When you need help they're there and you can trust them as well. If you have family problems or summat, sometimes they can help you and talk about it.'

For both groups there was a clear demarcation line involving right and wrong. Girls that stepped over the line were under a great deal of pressure to conform to the group's standards:

FEEZA: 'When she first started coming round with us we didn't like her, but then when she stuck around with us we started saying things to her: you shouldn't do this, you shouldn't do that.'

The girls' demands are thus relatively simple: to be together, to have fun and to have time away from other pupils and their parents. In the process the girls are subtly transforming their parent culture. What is clearly not happening, however, is for there to be any significant shift away from the traditional roles the girls have to play. The group has a part to play in this as the shared experiences of home life etc. allow the girls support and reduce the possibility of rebellion.

Conclusion

This article has attempted to open up the debate on the effects of the pastoral system of a state school on one group of pupils, namely Asian girls.

In this context it is suggested that the pastoral system has the effect of reinforcing the reproduction of the relations of production, in this case the domesticity of labour of women. This is in spite of obvious attempts to equalize educational opportunity by the school.

This tends to occur for a number of reasons: firstly through the pastoral system being incapable of providing the sort of service which these particular pupils need. This is partly due to the lack of time allocated for pastoral work, partly due to lack of trust, and partly from a misunderstanding by pastoral staff of the girls' needs. The second factor is that of racism. This has the effect of isolating the girls and leaving them to fend for themselves. It is aggravated by lack of support from pastoral staff.

The third factor, partially related to racism, is the need for a group identity involving the sharing of common experiences and the possibility of support. The processes of group identity and membership not only help reinforce ethnicity but normalize the roles played by the girls at home.

If one accepts that the outcome of the girls' educational experience is radically different from the aims and objectives of comprehensive state schooling (at least its stated aims), particularly that of equal opportunities for boys and girls, what can be done to remedy the situation?

It would be naive to believe that changing the pastoral system alone could lead to a structural change involving either the role of women or the class or cultural positions of ethnic minority groups. There are, however, both structural and qualitative changes that may be made in which it would be possible for the individual to renegotiate her position.

The first response would appear to be one in which there is a recognition of the validity of the girls' cultural or subcultural statements rather than a general over-simplification of what is considered to be the norm for a particular ethnic group. Inherent in this is the need to foster biculturalism rather than viewing one cultural attachment as a threat to another.

The second response has to be a commitment to an anti-racist perspective. This in itself is a complex issue, but should include a review of structural racism inside the school, racism awareness courses for staff, direct race relations teaching, and a quick and appropriate response to racialist incidents.

The third possibility is for a restructuring of the pastoral system to allow tutors greater time with their pupils in a co-operative spirit rather than one of formalized bureaucracy. This would be particularly helpful for Asian girls who are rarely involved in anything other than the formal curriculum.

The fourth option relates to the use of counsellors who are acceptable to the pupils. In this particular school Asian counsellors (women) have recently been tried in this context with a great deal of success. Hopefully this will be extended on a permanent basis, although staff selection is problematic. If counsellors are used, they need to be freed from the timetable and from management control (confidentiality). Group counselling using the friendship group is here a useful method of determining the nature of problems and allows for either self-help or follow-up by the counsellor.

The final option is one which involves access to power and decision-making for the girls within the school. There are a number of possibilities here at both pupil level and governor level. Involvement in such processes would hopefully remove feelings of powerlessness and greatly enhance the girls' interaction with the rest of the school.

It is hoped that the findings here will give some scope to thought and discussion about the use of the pastoral system by ethnic minority children and also its effects on them. Clearly there is a great deal of work yet to be done in this area.

Alun Pelleschi

References

HARRIS, J. (1982) 'A Paradox of Multicultural Societies', *Journal of Philosophy of Education* 16 (2), 223–33.

KHAN, V. S. (1982) 'The Role of the Culture of Dominance in Structuring the Experience of Ethnic Minorities' in HUSBAND, C. (ed.) *Race in Britain*. Hutchinson, 197–215.

PELLESCHI, A. J. (1983) *The Part Played by the Pastoral Care System of an Inner City School in Conjunction with Home and Peer-Group Factors in the Reproduction of the Status and Role of Asian Girls in their Social Class and Ethnic Group Locations.* MEd dissertation (unpublished) Sheffield University.

SAUNDERS, M. (1982) *Multicultural Teaching*. McGraw-Hill.

14

Special Education: the Way Ahead

John Fish

The Ordinary School Context

Schools in recent years have been under pressure to improve standards and increase attention to a variety of special needs at a time of falling rolls and reduced resources. As a result of the 1981 Education Act they have also been required to give greater attention to the identification of and provision for special educational needs. It is necessary to look at the issue of improved standards and to relate consideration of special educational needs to other special needs which primary and secondary schools are expected to meet.

In an historic sense it was standards in ordinary schools which determined the need for special education in the case of the largest groups receiving it, namely, those in the categories of educationally subnormal and maladjustment. Although the change to comprehensive education resulted in many more administrators and teachers recognizing the range of abilities and achievements to be expected in a school population, there still remain many politicians and educators who seek a basic standard of performance for the majority. The move from norm referenced attainments to criterion referenced assessment of individual progress is slow and halting. The recognition of individual differences and individual needs, although increasing, is not always very evident in the way schools work in practice. [. . .]

A search for higher standards and more effective schools has considerable implications for special education. These depend on how the search is carried out. On the one hand, it could result in a better matching of tasks, objectives and materials to individuals. On the other, it could result in a narrower common curriculum, a less flexible approach to individual needs and the stigmatization of pupils as not up to standard. The former approach leads to special educational arrangements being seen as a variant of a number of different approaches to learning while the latter may characterize it as charitable provision for failures.

The central point, in discussing the improvement of general standards, is that the ordinary school programme is a potential creator of special educational needs. If the school is sensitive to the problems of less successful learners, if it takes steps within its organization, methodology and curriculum to meet their needs, and if individual progress is emphasized rather than the achievement of norms and examination successes, the number of individuals whose learning difficulties become special educational needs may be minimized. This whole school response to the needs of all pupils who attend it is of crucial importance to the discussion of special educational needs and provision.

The relationship of special educational needs to other special needs in schools is still the subject of some confusion with the terms used interchangeably in many instances. It is perhaps most helpful to see special needs as a general term and special educational needs as a specific example. This is necessary because the latter are now defined in the 1981 Education Act. A number of different groups within primary and secondary schools may have special needs to be taken into account when organizing the work of the school and selecting objectives, methods and materials. These groups may include gifted children, children from ethnic minority groups, traveller's children, socially disadvantaged children and children of service and mobile families. They may need special consideration as individuals and as groups within the school's programme. Special educational needs, on the other hand, are clearly defined as learning difficulties significantly greater than those of the majority of children of the same age. Children with special needs may or may not have special educational needs.

The ordinary school context, its objectives, its priorities and its ethos, has a vital bearing on special education. Although disabilities and significant difficulties can be defined more or less precisely by medical, psychological, social and educational assessment, the need for special educational provision, which may result from them, remains relatively determined, that is, determined by the capacity of the ordinary school to recognize and meet a variety of individual special needs. [. . .]

Major Issues in Special Education

The most significant change which has taken place in the assessment of children with disabilities and significant difficulties is from a system which placed children in categories of handicap to one based on determining individual special educational needs and specifying the means of meeting them. [. . .] There is increasing recognition that recording achievements by norm referenced gradings does not give sufficient information about individual progress. More use is now being made of checklists of individual skills and knowledge, while considerable attention is being focused on individual records of experience and achievement and on pupil profiles in secondary schools and further education.

Individual assessment is becoming more widely recognized as a necessary basis on which to plan teaching objectives. This change in the ordinary school is an important starting point for assessing special educational needs. The better a school's system for assessing and recording the progress of all children, the easier it will be to build on additional procedures for determining the special educational needs of those with significant learning difficulties of all kinds. [. . .]

Building on a school's assessment procedure for all children, the Warnock Report suggested five levels or stages for determining and meeting special educational needs. These have been endorsed in the guidance given in the 1981 Education Act. They are worth restating:

(a) The collection of available information by the class teachers and head teacher, discussion with parents about the learning difficulties experienced and an exploration of the ways in which needs might be met within the school's existing resources and arrangements;

(b) an assessment added to (a) by a special education teacher either on the school staff or from a visiting service, together with a search for possible solutions within the school including help from the special education teacher where appropriate;

(c) an assessment added to (a) or (b) by a visiting specialist available to the school, such as the school doctor, school nurse, educational psychologist, social worker, etc. A decision at this stage would include both seeking solutions within the school, adding special help from the professional concerned or referral for multi-professional assessment;

(d) multi-professional assessment to include as a minimum, medical, psychological and educational components; also to include other relevant professionals, particularly social workers, with a view to deciding whether to make a statement of special educational needs in accordance with the 1981 Education Act or whether to suggest alternative arrangements not requiring a statement;

(e) multi-professional assessment centres to be established to deal with specific, severe and complex problems similar in scope to (d) but more specialized.

Obviously the stages or levels are only differentiated for exposition and are not intended to be gone through slavishly. In practice, (a) and (b) might be telescoped and it might be decided to proceed from (a) to (c) or (d) directly without the intervening stages. The principle, however, is important because it first emphasizes the need to look for solutions within the child's school and only secondly brings in outside expertise and alternatives. It stresses the importance of a school's knowledge and experience of the child, building on that experience and making minimum use of scarce professional expertise in the early stages.

There are a number of important consequences of this approach which have to be recognized. The first is that skills in simple techniques of assessment and programme planning have to be developed in every school. [...] These procedures should not only identify the more common learning difficulties and the means of meeting them in the schools but also reveal more complex problems requiring detailed examination.

It will also be necessary for schools to work out with visiting specialists reasonable criteria for determining the special educational needs which can reasonably be met by the school's own provision. Although the early stages of assessment should reveal special educational needs, they should have another purpose. They should also inform the school about the effectiveness of its general approach to less successful learners. The more special needs that are revealed, the greater is the need for the school to review its ordinary curriculum and methodology for these pupils. It is often the case that special educational needs are actually being created by an inappropriate response to individual differences within the general teaching programme of the school.

A second set of criteria needs to be developed by local education authorities to identify the smaller group of children with special educational needs who may need multi-professional assessment. Schools need guidance, and visiting professionals need to develop a reasonably consistent approach so that relatively simple problems are not referred before school based solutions have been sought and in order that children with serious needs are referred early enough for intervention to be effective. [...]

Thus, the major assessment issues are: how to develop the necessary skills in primary and secondary schools to make the best use of scarce specialist resources; how to develop reasonable criteria for the wider group of special educational needs and for deciding who needs full assessment; and how to ensure that the assessment of these needs is not divorced from a school's assessment procedures for all children. It is also necessary to review the total population revealed by assessment procedures in two contrasting ways. First, it is important to see whether the size of the group could be reduced by appropriate measures to modify the school's general approach to less success-ful learners. Secondly, it is essential as a means of evaluating the appropriate-ness of special educational arrangements in ordinary schools and elsewhere. The important change in emphasis to individual assessment and individually determined special educational provision should not lead to the neglect of the condition which may give rise to special educational needs or of a constant reappraisal of the range of provision to meet them.

Special Education in Ordinary Schools

[...]

Many schools in the past made remedial and other arrangements with two needs in view. Learning difficulties would either be cured or children with them would be taken out of circulation to avoid disrupting ordinary children. These purposes still exist and, because some special needs are transitory, it is not unreasonable to expect cures. Neither is it unrealistic to accept that some children may need a period in a separate group provided the general ethos of the school is an accepting one and social interaction with others is planned and developed. [...] The aim of special educational arrangements in ordinary schools is to maintain in the school as many children as possible with disabilities and significant difficulties by providing various combinations of personal support to individual children and their teachers, special materials and special teaching. The arrangements made to achieve this purpose should be flexible and should include both short- and long-term measures. They should be characterized by close collaboration between ordinary and special educational teachers. The ordinary school can no longer take measures to cure short-term difficulties while expecting long-term ones to be solved elsewhere.

Before turning to a discussion of the kinds of special educational arrangements which can be made by ordinary schools it may be helpful to consider a framework which takes into account the relative nature of special educational needs and the new duties of schools which result from the 1981 Education Act. It is suggested that there are three interrelated aspects of a school's work. These are:

(a) *The whole school approach* Within the planning of the school's programme, its organization, curriculum, methodology and its social objectives, provision will need to be made for less successful learners. The allocation of resources, teachers, materials and facilities to below average achievers is one aspect of the whole school approach. Another is the modifications of the curriculum, including the objectives chosen and the methods used to develop appropriate courses for less successful learners. [...]

(b) *The school's special education response* This aspect of a school's work involves the discovery and assessment of special educational needs and provision for them. A school, with the help of visiting professionals, will need to decide on its own criteria. These will depend on the effectiveness of the whole school approach to less successful learners. [...]

(c) *The local education authority's special educational provision* In order to meet the needs of children who are the subject of statements, or to supplement an ordinary school's resources in other ways, the local education authority may make special educational provision in ordinary schools. Such provision may include special supporting arrangements for individuals in ordinary classes and special classes and units for different combinations of special educational needs. Although this provision will supplement the school's normal resources, it will be important to see that it is also integrated into the school.

The relationship between these three aspects is an important and flexible one. The more effective (a), the less the need for (b), and the more effective (b), the less the need for (c). It is also vital to recognize that assessments made in the context of the school's special educational response should not only lead to provision for individuals but should also be used as an evaluation of one aspect of the whole school response. The more needs that are detected as part of the school's investigation of learning difficulties, the greater the importance of reappraising its ordinary programme for less successful learners.

One important consequence of this framework is that special educational arrangements should be an important item on the agenda of senior management in schools. The arrangements should be an integral part of a school's pattern of organization and not just an added feature when resources allow. [...]

Having made a general statement and outlined a conceptual framework the next question is what constitutes a school's special education response. How is the legal definition of provision additional to, or different from, that available to the majority of children of the same age to be interpreted. It has already been shown that special educational needs are relatively determined and, as a result, they can only be precisely determined in each school. Similarly, although general guidance can be given, only the individual school can decide which forms of provision fit its organization and deployment of resources. [...]

Some arrangements are relatively clear cut. For example, when a special education teacher works with a colleague within the ordinary class or withdraws individuals and small groups for extra help, something additional is being provided. Similarly, a special class set up by the school, taught full- or part-time by a special education teacher, is a clear example of alternative provision. There are, however, more confused situations. For instance, if a special class is taught by a teacher without special educational training or experience, does it provide special education? Where a secondary school streams or groups its pupils and keeps classes or groups for less successful learners as small as possible, and a special education teacher takes such groups, is special education provided or is it part of the school's response to the needs of less successful learners in its ordinary programme? The answers to these questions will be locally determined. The point in raising them is to note that a school's special education response is not always easy to define.

A second difficulty occurs in determining which children are receiving special education as a result of the work of special education peripatetic teachers. Their employment by the local education authority is clearly part of its special educational provision. Some of these teachers, for example those concerned with physical and sensory disabilities, may know of a large number of children with less severe disabilities in ordinary schools. The service they provide may be important in preventing special educational needs arising. Similarly, they may be available to support teachers and make visits to review individual progress. Only some of the children known may receive regular visits, including counselling and instruction and the provision of equipment and materials. Only these could be said to be receiving special education in the strictest sense. [...]

Starting from the least common, but in many ways most promising, provision, namely, additional help in the ordinary classroom, it is possible to identify a number of problem areas. When individual teachers have been used to having a class to themselves it is often difficult for them to accept another teacher in the same room. This may be due to a fear of exposure of their work to another, since teaching has been traditionally a private business conducted by one person behind closed doors. It also stems from the fact that teachers and others judge the progress of children in a class as a measure of teaching skill, and individuals feel a strong sense of responsibility for their own classes. Finally, the introduction of a second teacher may give rise to problems of adult relationships, clashes of personalities, difficulties in sharing relationships with children, and different styles of teaching. [. . .]

Other difficulties on co-teaching include the arrangement of the classroom.[1] Where desks are arranged in serried ranks, co-operative work is more difficult than in less formal arrangements where pupils are grouped. Didactic instruction followed by written work also provides more problems than group teaching and project work. By far the most important factor is how the different teaching functions are shared. This can range between the special education teacher being assigned the role of teaching aide and being accepted as an equal partner in planning and carrying out the class programme. On the one hand, the class teacher may plan all activities, carry out all the teaching and simply expect the special education teacher to help individuals with learning dificulties to master tasks set to the class. Alternatively, both teachers may plan the programme, including tasks for children with learning difficulties, share the teaching of the whole class and each give additional help to children who need it. In practice many co-teaching arrangements fall between the two. [. . .]

There are always likely to be children who need help individually or in small groups outside the classroom. At best this takes place in a suitably equipped resource room and at worst in any available corner in the school. A major and persistent problem is how to co-ordinate this work with the children's classroom programme. Too often work in withdrawal groups will be self-contained, assuming that by overcoming learning difficulties in this context, the child will automatically make progress in the ordinary classroom. At the same time the class teacher is left to provide for the children, often without any detailed information about how to plan tasks for them. Communication is left to staffroom comment on progress, more appropriate for discussing emotions than serious educational problems. The best practice, still relatively rare, demands joint planning by the class and special education teachers to see that special help also includes tackling real problems encountered in the classroom while also developing tasks for children to carry out under supervision in the classroom between special sessions. To achieve this degree of collaboration requires an understanding of its importance, a knowledge of materials and above all the feeling of sharing a significant task.

There are obviously organizational and timetable constraints, so that careful thought and imagination is needed in planning co-operative withdrawal arrangements. These need to be based on an adequate assessment of special educational needs, a knowledge of the range of approaches available and a variety of material and equipment. [. . .]

Special classes and units in the school

These may be set up by the school or by the local education authority. Classes are most commonly provided for learning and behaviour difficulties but units may be designated for any particular disability or combination of disabilities. In the majority of instances it is very clear that the special class or unit teacher has the principal responsibility for the class programme. The main problems to be tackled are curriculum development and integration.

The curriculum issue has two main aspects, its development from a special education point of view and its relationship to the curriculum of the school. It is typical of the English situation that special class teachers are expected to devise their own curriculum, seldom with any help except from infrequent meetings with colleagues with similar classes. Although techniques and methods may be common, the areas of study may or may not be similar. [. . .] By and large special classes of all kinds in ordinary schools are too isolated, teachers do not feel part of a team and the quality of education provided depends on individual initiative. A major concern for the future should be the curriculum in special classes.

The second aspect is equally important, although it will vary according to the nature and degree of disabilities catered for and the extent to which the ordinary curriculum needs to be modified. The curriculum in the host school is significant and should influence the special class programme. The closer the relationship possible, the easier it will be for individuals in the special class to join their contemporaries for some activities and, when appropriate, to move into an ordinary class. Secondly, the individual teacher or small group of special educational teachers will not normally have a complete range of expertise in all areas of the curriculum. It enhances the work of special classes if specialists from the host school can contribute to some areas of the curriculum, just as it enhances the credibility and competence of the special class teacher if they teach some things to ordinary classes. [. . .]

This leads on to a consideration of the process of integration. The location of a class for children requiring special education in an ordinary school does not necessarily imply that integration will take place. The process has to be positively fostered. There needs to be a policy, worked out in the school, which includes both teaching and social situations. Ordinary teachers need to know what to expect and what is expected of them. Special education teachers need to know the school well, know their children, and explore means of supporting them in ordinary classes and around the school. Specific steps may be needed. Peer group tutoring is quite common in the United States as one starting point. For example in a class for very severely disabled children in an elementary school in San Francisco, children in ordinary classes volunteer to spend some time each week, one or two hours, in a one-to-one relationship with the member of the special class, sharing activities, helping their partners and building up relationships. Both partners profit and a basis for ordinary relationships in the school is formed which does not rely solely on incidental contact.

The special class or unit in the ordinary school, even for children with severe disabilities, can provide good quality special education, but above all it can be a starting point for the process of integration. It has the potential to develop good relations between ordinary and special education teachers and between pupils with and without special educational needs. It can become isolated and inward looking and its programme may become unstimulating, but these are problems which need to be tackled. [. . .]

Special education in secondary schools is more difficult to plan for a number of reasons. The larger size of the school and the more complex organization create their own problems. Perhaps most important of all is the general expectation that success in public examinations is the hall-mark of quality, even when this is obtained by blatant distortions of resource allocations to the more able. [. . .] It is, therefore, difficult for special arrangements to receive sufficient resources, to be given enough priority or to be seen as a useful selling point for schools when they are competing for parental choices.

There are, however, other educational problems relating to the management and organization of the school and the responsibility of each faculty and subject department. A combination of social and educational objectives normally determines the organization. The three most common forms of teaching – banding, setting and mixed ability classes – can be found in different combinations. [. . .]

Where classes are banded, the 'bottom' band of lowest achievers is of particular significance. If the variation of the curriculum and the methods used are appropriate, many learning difficulties may not become acute. Special help can be given to the few serious problems on a withdrawal basis, and special education teachers can work closely with subject teachers to develop material and tasks in 'bottom' band classes for those children with persistent learning difficulties.

Where classes are set, the work of teachers taking sets of the lowest achievers overlaps with special education. Again, withdrawal arrangements may be necessary and joint planning by subject and special education teachers of the work of these sets can limit the need for separate provision.

The mixed ability form of organization presents the greatest challenge, particularly to the subject teacher. Before considering special educational needs, considerable effort is needed to plan work and develop materials which challenge and extend the ablest, the average and the least successful learner. The special education teacher can help with the latter, develop co-teaching and withdraw some children for additional help.

But there is another major factor which influences all these forms of organization. This is the extent to which faculties, subject departments and specialist teachers accept responsibility for teaching their subject to all the children in the school including those who have limited literacy skills and those who are slow to learn. Although not expressed so explicitly, there has been a tradition of expecting a level of literacy and competence below which subject teachers do not expect to teach. This was partly due to training, which seldom included provision for the less successful learners, partly due to the status system in the school where high status meant teaching the most able, and partly due to the attitudes of remedial teachers. These attitudes implied that subject teachers did not have sufficient knowledge of learning difficulties and only remedial teachers should be responsible for the curriculum of the slowest learners. There has thus grown up a myth, now being exploded, that children have to be fit for secondary education, and that remedial provision should make them fit or keep them out of the way.

The new approach to special education in the secondary school demands a new relationship between the subject and special education teachers. This can be summarized as follows. Subject departments should be responsible for the teaching of their subject to all children. Their range of expertise is incomplete unless it encompasses not only the ability to teach the able and average, but also the skills necessary to select objectives, materials and methods for teaching their subject to slow learners and semi-literate pupils. The role of the special education teacher is to provide knowledge and experience of the learning dificulties and to use this knowledge to help subject teachers plan their programmes. They should also give special technical help to individuals and small groups who need to develop their learning and behavioural skills. This does not mean that they should not teach ordinary classes and sets as part of their timetable. But it does mean that the responsibility for curriculum objectives and contact should rest on the shoulders of subject teachers. [. . .]

One further point about special education in ordinary schools concerns the importance of developing team work in planning assessment and provision. each school should have a core team to be joined by peripatetic teachers, educational psychologists, advisers, and health and social service personnel as required.

Teams should work at two levels. There is a need to have a significant special education input to senior management decisions. Whatever team is constituted for this purpose it should include a special education coordinator with sufficient experience and status to comment on all aspects of the school's work as it affects special educational provision. At the second level, there will be the need for a group – including house masters [or mistresses] or year group teachers, special education teachers and other relevant visiting specialists – to consider individual problems and manage the first three levels of assessment. Finally, other more *ad hoc* groups should be considered, for example, between subject teachers and special education teachers to plan objectives, methods and materials, and between year group teachers and special education teachers to deal with plans for admission, course choices or the preparation for leaving arrangements.

Note

1   O. Dahlen, paper to OECD-CERI, 1982.

15

Special Educational Needs: Fact or Friction?

David J. Gavine

[. . .]

The publication in 1978 of the Report of the Committee of Enquiry into the Education of Handicapped Children and Young People (the Warnock Report) was greeted with widespread approval. The committee's central proposal was the abolition of the existing 'category system' whereby children were placed in special education on the basis of allocating them to one of the categories of handicap (mental handicap, deafness, maladjustment *etc.*). In its place was recommended a new system based on the concept of 'special educational need'. This system was intended to regulate the discovery, assessment and management of children with special educational needs and, in Scotland, the term 'recording' has come to be used to describe this. This major change required the consent of Parliament and in due time the Education (Scotland) Act 1981 provided the necessary statutory framework. [In all significant respects this Act is identical with the Education Act 1981 in England and Wales except that what is known in Scotland as a 'record' is known in England and Wales as a 'statement' – Eds.] The legislation came into force at the beginning of 1983 and professionals working in the field of special education have now had time to absorb the implications of the legislation and to attempt to use the new concept of special educational need in their decision-making.

Certainly, clear thinking is needed to guide us through the lengthy procedures specified by the 1981 Act and its subsequent regulations. When a child is being considered for recording, multi-disciplinary assessment by an educational psychologist, a medical officer, the child's teachers and any other relevant professionals takes place. Each professional completes an 'assessment form', giving a description of the child, his background and his learning difficulty. The forms also specify the 'needs' established from these descriptions. If the education officer, on behalf of the Education Authority, decides that a record should be opened on the evidence of the forms submitted to him [or her], he [or she] issues a draft 'record of needs' to the parents. This contains summaries of the professional opinions as to the child's impairments, special need and, most importantly, a statement of the provision which the authority intends to make to meet the needs.

It should be clear that the smooth operation of these procedures turns on some assumptions about the concept 'need'.

1 Each professional should recognize 'needs' when he [or she] meets them.
2 The professionals should agree on what constitutes a 'recordable need'.
3 There should be a fairly direct correspondence between needs and provision to meet them.

Experience so far has shown that none of these assumptions hold in practice. The purpose of the present article is to demonstrate that the concept of need, while perhaps useful in day-to-day decision-making, is altogether too vague to sustain the formal procedures described above.

In fact, approval for Warnock's proposals has been far from unanimous. Lewis and Vulliamy criticized the report for failing to take social factors into account and for saying little or nothing about strategies for actually meeting educational needs. They demonstrated how the committee's attempts to abolish categories of handicap were confused and contradictory. Richmond states, 'Continuing use of the word "Special" in the report, because of its traditional associations, has ensured that the very division between handi-capped and non-handicapped, which the committee is determined to elimi-nate, will be encouraged'. The author shares the view of these commentators that the concept of need fails to shift the emphasis sufficiently away from the concept of handicap because it continues to focus on the individual child. In the following analysis, we will try to demonstrate that the use of the concept of special educational need has introduced a significant degree of confusion to the field, with much potential for conflict between professional groups as well as between Educational Authorities, parents and professionals.

Analysis of the Concept of Special Educational Need

In an article on the use of the term 'needs' in education, Dearden analyses the criteria necessary for its use. Firstly, he maintains that there has to be a norm against which to measure the need. For example, a child without artistic flair could not be said to 'need' help to remedy that situation, whereas a child of ten years without any reading ability might be said to have a 'need' in that area. This means that the need is determined normatively by looking not only at the situation as it is but by comparing it with what ought to be. Therefore if there is a norm, and if this norm is not being achieved, then there may be a need: The second important criterion in saying someone is 'in need' is that what is 'needed' is the relevant condition for achieving what the norm prescribes. If I am hungry, then I 'need' food since having food is the condition which enables me to move to the normative state of being not hungry.

Let us see how far these criteria can be applied to the concept of special educational need. Firstly, we have to demonstrate the existence of a norm. Since much educational assessment is based on the idea of a normative distribution then clearly there is always an average level of attainment or adjustment for children of any age. If we take this average as our norm then it follows that half the population have special educational needs and this is obviously absurd. The intention is to record only a fraction of the population and this inevitably introduces an arbitrariness into the procedure. Who is to say what the norm is against which we measure need? [. . .]

A possible way out of this circularity is to use criterion-referenced norms, with children functioning below these criteria being said to have special education needs. However, not only does no consensus exist for the establishment of minimal levels of competence in educational adjustment and attainments, but any such consensus established for the purpose would also be arbitrary. An example of this sort of approach is the establishment of the level of the so-called 'poverty-line'. Here, an attempt could be made to describe monetary criteria for food, shelter, energy, etc. and to use this to calculate a family's financial needs. However, many may say that the level of food, rent, etc. is too low or that a television is a 'need' in present-day society. The level of the 'poverty-line' is arbitrary. Its level is not a question of empirical fact but of values. Similarly in education, it is indeed possible to describe the current situation of an individual child with respect to his disabilities. It is also possible to compare empirically a child's disabilities with an already established norm. What cannot be done empirically is to establish that norm; it is a matter for debate involving the exchange of value judgements.

Dearden further distinguishes between the terms 'lack' and 'need'. We may say that a child lacks the ability to read, without saying that he needs that ability. In order to make the latter statement we must compare the existing situation with what we judge *ought* to be. Therefore any statement of 'need' contains implicit value judgements about what ought to be the case as well as what is actually the case. He concludes by noting the attractiveness of the concept of 'need' in education because it seems to offer an escape from arguments about value judgements by means of a straightforward appeal to the facts empirically determined by experts. However, the great danger in using the concept is that it obscures the values which are being assumed and overlays them with a veneer of facts.

As a prime example of this, it is difficult to imagine how any child could 'need' placement in a special school using the Warnock criteria,[1] since these criteria are about efficient use of resources and about the possible disruption of the education of other children. There is the danger of hypocrisy here if we say a child 'needs' special school because it will be too expensive to educate him [or her] in ordinary school. The education service may be entirely justified in making such a decision but the grounds in this case would be financial, not educational. Difficulties are more likely to arise if these important matters of attitude and belief are glossed-over by the process of attributing special needs to a child.

David J. Gavine

A Ladder of Need

As an aid to considering the assumptions which underpin the apparent special education needs of individual children, the author has found it useful to use the established psychological technique of 'laddering'. In using this technique we simply force ourselves to form general statements about our beliefs by repeatedly asking the question, 'Why?' For example, suppose we started with the following statement made by a head teacher to an educational psychologist: 'This child needs remedial teaching on a daily basis by a visiting remedial teacher'. The answer to the question 'Why?' might be, 'The child needs teaching within a small group'. Again, the question 'Why?' is asked and the answer forthcoming is, 'The child needs more individual attention'. Again, 'Why?' then produces, 'The child needs to make faster progress in learning'. The next 'Why?' leads to, 'The child needs to be literate'. A further attempt at asking 'Why?' produces no elaboration since the final statement is taken as self-evident by the head teacher.

The process above can be represented in diagram form as a 'ladder' with each 'rung' of the ladder being reached by asking the question 'Why?'

Needs to be literate

Why? ↑

Needs to make faster progress

Why? ↑

Needs more individual attention

Why? ↑

Needs teaching within a small group

Why? ↑

Needs remedial teaching on a daily basis

It should be clear that 'needs' can be expressed in a very general way at the top of the ladder or as quite specific statements at the bottom. Note also that we can move 'down' the ladder to even more specific statements of need by asking the question, 'How?' For example, starting at the bottom and asking the question 'How will the remedial teaching be implemented?' may produce the response that the child 'needs phonic drills and arithmetic practice each day'.

This 'need' is now so specific that it would normally be considered within the professional domain of the teacher involved and outside the responsibility of the head teacher, psychologist, parents and others who may be commenting on the child's needs.

Using this framework, the problem of moving from 'need' to 'provision to meet need' is solved by taking one or more steps down the ladder. The need for more individual attention is to be provided for by teaching within a small group. That is, the concept of provision to meet 'need' is itself a 'need' at a more specific level. However, this analysis highlights further problems, three of which invite particular comment.

Firstly, it should be clear that in moving from one level of need to another, assumptions are made which are essentially statements of belief about education, some of which may be backed-up by empirical evidence, whereas others may be common sense and some merely prejudice.

Need   **Assumption**

Needs to be literate

In order to be eventually literate, measurable progress must be noted at this time — lack of such progress is likely to continue indefinitely

Needs to make faster progress

Progress in learning is mainly related to the quantity of teacher time spent with the child

Needs more individual attention

Individual attention can best be provided by placing similar children in a small group

Needs teaching within a small group

Small group teaching is best done by withdrawing children to be taught by a specialist teacher

Needs remedial teaching twice a week by a remedial teacher

The 'needs' at the top of the ladder are bland because the assumptions underlying them are non-controversial. As we move down the ladder the controversy increases. Different people will have different sets of assumptions and therefore construct different ladders for each 'need'.

Secondly, in getting down to making 'statements of need' as required by statute, we have the problem of deciding at what level of need the statement should be made. Since these decisions are to be made by members of a multi-disciplinary team with quite different backgrounds, they are likely to arrive at any case conference with different 'ladders of need'. In order to reach agreement, the statements must be taken from fairly high-up in the ladders where the assumptions are less controversial. But, the statements of need from the top of the ladder are not 'special' at all since they apply to all children. In order to arrive at a 'special' need we must move down the ladder to a need which is so specific that it is not normally able to be provided in an ordinary school. At this level of specificity, genuine agreement is unlikely to be reached.

Thirdly, how is it to be decided which needs should be recorded? Since there is probably no end to the number of features within the educational environment characteristic of schools both ordinary and special, what criteria are to be used for selecting those needs to be recorded once a child has been assessed? If we are being honest I think we subconsciously work backwards from the provision to meet needs which we have already selected. For example, if we state a child's needs as (a) teaching within a small class, (b) curriculum broken down into smaller steps, (c) a peer-group in which the child seems more competent, and (d) a teacher trained to deal with children with needs a, b and c, then that is exactly what is provided in a segregated special school. It would be more honest simply to say that the child 'needs special school' at the outset.

Of course, it is perfectly possible to state some special needs which do not, in fact, form a neat package as in the above example. Take the example of a child who needs a half-hour, twice-a-day session of individual help in preparation of his [or her] work for the rest of the morning/afternoon. In an ordinary school where this need is identified and met as a matter of routine, then by definition, no special need exists. However, in a school where the resources or philosophy do not permit this management, then a special need does seem to exist. In this sort of case, a need is special only when it is unmet. The existence of the special need is not itself a feature of the child but of the educator's willingness or otherwise to deploy resources. To take this a stage further, some special resources, set up to meet special needs, create further special needs of their own. For example, the need to mix with a cross-section of peers from the local community is a general need since this is normally available to children. However, in a segregated special school, this general need is not met so that children in special school have a special need for socialization which would not exist in an ordinary school. Should this need be recorded?

Reasons for the Failure of the Concept

The Warnock proposals and the term 'special educational needs' represented an attempt to escape from the negative consequences of labelling a handicapped population. Although it has been pointed out (e.g. Richmond, 1983) that the concept of handicap is re-introduced as soon as the word 'special' is appended to 'educational need', there is nevertheless a flexibility in the concept which enables it to take more account of individual differences than did the system it replaces. The report recognized that special provision was the key to the problem, by concentrating on what was to be done for a child rather than on his handicap and by describing the conditions under which education might be provided by ordinary schools for all their children. This is at the heart of the problem – what should we do for children who do not respond to the normal curriculum presented in the normal way? Furthermore, how do we judge whether any modifications to the provision result in a more appropriate educational experience for the child? In other words, how do we *assess the ability of the education system* locally to provide for children who do not respond to the 'normal' measures. The old system of ascertainment took exactly the opposite perspective. It was concerned with the *assessment of the ability of the child* to take advantage of what was normally provided. Unfortunately the Warnock proposals effectively re-instated the old system by *defining special educational need as a feature of children who require special educational provision.*[2] The view presented here is that the concept of 'special educational need' was adopted because the committee was unable to cast off entirely a model of learning difficulty which could be termed the 'pathological model'. Both the 'needs model' of Warnock and the 'handicap model' it replaced are expressions of a 'pathological' viewpoint, whereby the source of the learning difficulty is seen to lie within the child. Under the Warnock proposals, needs, like handicap are seen as a relatively static feature of the child, his own private property which he carries around with him regardless of context. The Warnock proposals and subsequent legislation describe an assessment process whereby a 'profile of impairments' gives rise to a 'statement of needs' which, in turn, gives rise to 'proposals to meet needs'. That is, the assessment starts within the child and, mediated by the use of the term 'need', is translated into a statement of what is to be provided for the child.

In opposition to the 'pathological model' we could propose an 'educational model' of learning difficulties, whereby the position is taken that we need only concern ourselves with the range of educational provision in terms of curriculum, teaching skills, resources, *etc.* which could be made available to a child. The educational model accepts that individual differences exist between children but that these differences are only relevant in so far as they impinge on the educational services available. In other words the pathological view sees the educational services as 'given' and the assessment of the child is necessary to see how he [or she] best fits the services, whereas the educational model sees the child as 'given' and assessment of the educational services is necessary to see how they can fit the child. The Warnock proposals demonstrate their pathological basis by recommending an assessment and documentation procedure which focuses entirely upon deficits within the child, deficits within his [or her] home circumstances but never upon any deficits within his [or her] educational environment.[3]

In its definition above, the concept of special educational need has been used in an attempt to reconcile two distinct models of learning difficulty, perhaps in the hope of preserving the best of each of them. However, these two models may be antagonistic and contradictory.

Warnock and the Educational Model

If the foregoing analysis is accepted, the concept of special educational need may represent a transitional phase in a longer term shift in professional opinion from the pathological to the educational models of learning difficulty. In this section we will attempt to describe how professional work in this area has developed since Warnock was published. [. . .]

It follows from the above that categorization, insofar as it is needed at all, should be applied not to the recipients of special educational services but to the services themselves. Warnock gives three broad headings under which the services might be grouped:[4] special means of access to the curriculum; the provision of a modified curriculum; and particular attention to the social structure of the provision. The undoubted vagueness of these headings, which beg more questions than they answer, reflects the traditional lack of explicitness concerning exactly what is special about special education. However, the headings provide starting points for the development of a description of special educational services. For example, how does a particular special educational resource pay 'particular attention to the social structure of the provision'? Does it provide therapeutic activities or a behavioural regime? Assuming it uses a behavioural regime, how does it implement this? Does it use a token-economy, social-skills training, modelling or punishment? Note that we are again using the laddering technique but applying it to educational services rather than to children. As in our previous example, there are underlying assumptions in the answers to the question 'How?' In this example, the assumption is that behavioural methods are more effective. However, by focusing on educational provision rather than children, these assumptions are more explicit and potentially open to evaluation. [. . .]

In any new formulation of assessment, we should not be overly interested in making detailed assessments of individual differences between children. Of course, we must recognize that individual differences exist, but these might be viewed on the basis of how children might respond to the various educational services on offer. The assessment thus takes place within the educational context (e.g. Cornwall, 1981). Educational psychologists in particular have been guilty of conducting over-inclusive assessments in order to justify placement recommendations which may have had unclear benefits for a child. As the description of available special educational services becomes more explicit, the easier it should be to target children who may benefit from available services and the more irrelevant it appears to gather vast amounts of background information on a child.

The role of parents is seen as significant by Warnock:[5] they are to be viewed as partners in the assessment and educative processes. The subsequent legislation appeared to put the politically fashionable cause of parental choice even further to the fore by building a framework with a bewildering complexity of procedures for consultation and appeal. However, one is left pondering Tomlinson's argument that the real message which comes over to parents going through this process is one of compulsion behind a veneer of consultation. If the authorities really wished to put power in the hands of parents, there was no need for the recording procedures at all. Special educational placement could have been made voluntary (e.g. Booth, 1983). Most professionals working in special education can identify provision which parents would voluntarily choose for their children and others which they would wish to avoid. Voluntary special educational placement could be a spur to the development of services which are attractive to parents. There is disquiet in some quarters that the development of genuine parental participation in decision-making may, in fact, be put back by the new procedures (Advisory Centre for Education, 1984).

Conclusion

The confusion presently existing in the field of special education due to the implementation of the 1981 Act has been documented recently by Peters, who discovered that some education authorities are recording as few children as possible whereas other authorities are recording as many as possible. The concept of special educational need has been unable to meet the task of providing a framework for decision-making in special education. At best, the new system may be viewed as an irrelevant piece of bureaucracy consuming large amounts of paper and expensive professional time and running parallel to the professional work of educationists which continues without reference to it. At worst, it seeks to bend professional practice to its own image thus conserving some of the worst aspects of the system it was designed to replace.

Notes Referring to the Warnock Report

1 Report of the Committee of Enquiry into the Education of Handicapped Children and Young People (1978). *Special Educational Needs*. London: HMSO, Paragraph 6.10.
2 Paragraph 3.18.
3 Paragraphs 4.35–4.68.
4 Paragraph 3.19.
5 Chapter 9.

References

ADVISORY CENTRE FOR EDUCATION (1984) 'The 1981 Act – safeguarding your rights', *Where*. March, pp. 32–6.
BOOTH, G. (1983) 'A new, radical deal for handicapped pupils?' *The Scotsman*. 6 September.

David J. Gavine

CORNWALL, K. F., (1981) 'Some trends in pupil evaluation: the growing importance of the teacher's role', *Remedial Education*. vol. 16, no. 4, pp. 156–62.

DEARDEN, R. F. (1972) '"Needs" in education' in DEARDEN *et al.* (eds), *Education and the Development of Reason*. London: Routledge & Kegan Paul.

GIPPS, C. and GOLDSTEIN, H. (1984) 'You can't trust a special', *Times Educational Supplement*, 27 July.

LEWIS, I. and VULLIAMY G. (1979) 'Where Warnock went wrong', *Times Educational Supplement*, 30 November.

PETERS, M. (1984) 'A hard Act to follow', *Times Educational Supplement*, 30 March.

RICHMOND, R. (1983) 'Warnock – found wanting and waiting', *Special Education – Forward Trends*, vol. 6, no. 3, pp. 8–10.

TOMLINSON, S. (1982) *A Sociology of Special Education*. London: Routledge & Kegan Paul, pp. 107–18.

16

A Model to Link Personality Characteristics to a Preference for Science

John Head

[. . .]

Introduction

In recent years there has been a steady accumulation of evidence that personality and allied affective factors play a crucial role in determining subject choice and student success. Unfortunately, this evidence has tended to be fragmentary, a collection of separate, discrete pieces of information lacking a synthesizing theory to provide cohesion and predictive power. The few models which have been developed to date may have been correct as far as they go but are clearly incomplete. For example Roe (1952), Eiduson (1962) and McClelland (1962) suggested that male scientists often experienced a lonely childhood, perhaps suffering social isolation through illness or family circumstances, so that they developed a strong interest in their surrounding material world and a below average interest in other people and relationships. Maslow (1966) and Hudson (1966 and 1968) saw science as providing an emotionally undemanding activity appealing to boys moving from the calm of latency to the turbulence of adolescence. Even if these descriptions are valid they still leave open a number of questions, particularly why the same mechanisms do not operate with girls.

Arising from the evidence in the literature and from our empirical studies at Chelsea College it is now possible to offer a model which is compatible with all the evidence and which also has considerable predictive potential.

What we know about persons choosing science

The evidence for an association between personality characteristics and an interest in science has been more fully reviewed by Head (1979). We need now only take note of the most salient features.

The most obvious one is that of sex differences. The predominance of males, particularly in the physical sciences and engineering, throughout the Western world can no longer be satisfactorily attributed to cognitive differences, which are too small, nor to institutional factors. Equal opportunity in education and employment has not made science any more popular with women.

Furthermore, the characteristics of those students who do opt for science show clear sex differences. Male scientists, both science students and mature, professional scientists, tend to be emotionally reticent, disliking overt emotional expression in others and themselves, and depending upon their partners in personal relationships to take the emotional initiatives. They will also tend to be authoritarian, conservative and controlled in their thinking. These differences can be seen quite early on; we have found boys aged 14 years who were opting for science to be significantly more authoritarian than their peers. Girls choosing science are not particularly emotionally reticent or rigid in their thinking, although they do seem to have low self-esteem in terms of being socially and sexually attractive.

We also know that at about the age of 13 a very high proportion of boys are attracted to science and scientific careers. Thereafter, there is a steady decline of interest in science and this disillusionment extends right through the secondary-school years and into the undergraduate period. In contrast, only a minority of girls express an interest in science at any age but there is no obvious swing from science in the middle and late teens.

Some further evidence has come from our use of sentence completion tests with secondary-school pupils as part of our research programme at Chelsea. Analysis of these responses provides further information on sex differences and between those opting for different subjects.

For example, girls at the age of 12 and 14 years seem to take a more mature attitude to personal relationships, seeing their complexity and reciprocal nature, while boys are more exploitative. In relation to the sentence stem 'A girl and her mother . . .', girls often produce responses like 'often go through a bad patch for a year but once they learn to understand each other, become the best of friends' or 'can help each other with their problems'. Similar questions, when asked of boys, tend to produce banal responses or exploitative ones, for example the parent is seen as the source of money. In contrast, boys seem to have a firmer self-identity and a clearer ambition showing more insight in response to sentence stems such as 'My main problem is . . .' and 'He/she felt proud that . . .'. Such findings give us some clues about the characteristics of boys and girls of these ages.

If we compare boys of 14 years of age who opt for science with other boys, we find that the former have very cut-and-dried views on many issues. For example, they take the view that 'criminals should be severely punished' or that 'anyone who is unpopular deserves his fate'. To the sentence stem 'When a child will not join in group activities . . .', these boys gave responses like 'he is selfish', 'he must be stupid', 'he deserves to be unpopular'. In contrast, other boys and most girls pondered the possible causes and ways of integrating the child into the group. The science boys seemed to possess few doubts or uncertainties, they offered clear-cut answers.

It was this evidence which suggested the possible model for subject choice in terms of ego-identity achievement.

Ego-identity in Adolescence

This model was originally postulated by Erikson (1965) and then developed by Marcia (1966 and 1976).

Erikson suggests that at different phases of life an individual faces a particular psycho-social problem which needs to be resolved before moving on to the next phase. For adolescents the acquisition of a clear ego-identity is the crucial task. At the beginning of adolescence, the individual is a dependent within the family and the school. By the end of adolescence he [or she] needs to make choices about career, life-style, personal relationships and ideologies. The ego-identity of that person is shaped by these choices. Erikson does not suggest that the development of an ego-identity is a once-and-for-all issue. Some problems about identity arise with the young child in the context of home and school, and others occur in later life, for example on retirement. Nevertheless, adolescence is the time when ego-identity development inevitably dominates the personal development of the individual for a while. The adolescent does not, however, need to achieve a clear ego-identity on all topics at one time. He [or she] may have a clear identity in respect to his [or her] career but still be unresolved in regard to personal relationships and ideology. In this article we are concerned with ego-identity achievement in respect to career.

Marcia has put more detail onto the Erikson model and suggests that in going from the initial ego-diffusion condition to that of having achieved ego-identity, two processes are involved: *crisis* and *commitment*. Crisis in this context describes a period of intensive self-examination in which one's beliefs and values are re-examined. Commitment means that the individual has acquired clear and firm beliefs both about himself [or herself] and the world. Figure 16.1 indicates a number of possible routes to ego-identity achievements. A person may undergo crisis and commitment simultaneously and progress by route A. An alternative is to undergo a period of considerable self-doubt and self-examination in which all one's beliefs tend to be very fluid, a period known as moratorium, before acquiring beliefs for oneself and ego-identity is achieved (route B). A further possibility is that the individual may, at least for a time, hold onto beliefs and values taken without question from others, for example parents, teachers, peers. This condition is known as

Figure 16.1 *Possible routes to ego-identity achievement*

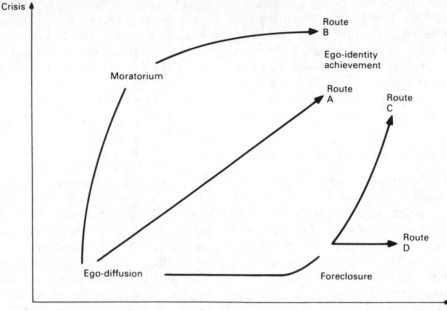

foreclosure. Eventually these persons might have to face up to a period of crisis, of self-examination, and so achieve ego-identity by route C. However, foreclosure does offer an escape route and an individual might postpone indefinitely any real self-examination by clinging rigidly to his [or her] beliefs and values (route D).

Ego-identity and Choosing Science

We can now make the link between this model of adolescent development and subject choice in schools.

For boys at the foreclosure stage, science is likely to be appealing. The physical sciences in particular, offer a conventional career choice which is likely to win approval from parents, teachers and peers. They will tend to regard the overt expression of emotions, including much such expression in the arts, as being soft and feminine. Science, with its masculine image, makes little emotional demand on an individual and seems to offer clear, precise answers to problems. Opting for science will permit and possibly reinforce emotional reticence.

For a girl at the foreclosure stage the situation is very different. There is evidence that girls tend to be socialized into adult roles more through their potential of becoming a mother and housewife than through their career (Douvan and Adelson, 1966). Furthermore, these girls will tend to go into a career with a feminine image, one which already attracts many girls. Consequently, very few girls at the foreclosure stage will enter science unless they receive considerable encouragement and a model to do so from their parents and their school.

Neither boys nor girls at the moratorium stage are likely to be attracted to the science that is usually presented in our schools. They are at a stage when they are likely to be concerned with a variety of complex issues; the meaning of life, the existence of God, ideologies, their emerging sexuality, their future career and life-style – too often science is seen as being purely instrumental with nothing to contribute to these debates. Science, somehow, seems to be scarcely relevant to the most important issues in our life.

A proportion of both boys and girls at ego-identity achievement stage will choose science. In fact, most girls entering science are probably at this stage as they will need some self-examination and sense of commitment to make this unconventional choice. However, only a minority of adolescents will have reached the ego-identity achievement stage at the age when most pupils have to make crucial decisions about subject choice at school.

This model seems to explain our observations. A large number of boys, particularly at the foreclosure stage, are initially attracted to science but there is a drift away throughout later adolescence as they undergo some crisis. The preponderance of boys at the foreclosure stage will yield the rigid, authoritarian attitudes often associated with scientists. The few girls who enter science will not usually show these foreclosure characteristics.

Effects of Curriculum Changes

The real use of this model linking personality development to subject choice is that it allows us to make predictions about how pupils might react to changes in school science curriculum and school organization. We can consider three possible changes:

1 *Delaying subject choice:* Britain is unusual in asking pupils to make crucial choices about subject options in the 13–16 age range. These decisions can only be reversed with great difficulty. What effect would delaying the choice make?

   In the development through the years of adolescence the number of foreclosure pupils will diminish, hence the recruitment of boys into science would be cut. More boys and girls will have reached the ego-identity achievement stage and a proportion of these will go into science. Overall there would be a reduction in the number of students choosing science, but those who *do* so choose will be more likely to stay happily in the subject and to possess more flexible minds. The quantitative loss would be met by a qualitative improvement.

2 *Giving science a more feminine image:* It is sometimes argued that science textbooks are sexist in showing illustrations of boys, rather than girls, doing practical work in the laboratory, and so forth. What effect would a

deliberate attempt to change this image have? It might make it easier for girls at the foreclosure stage to accept science so recruitment might increase. Some of these girls might, however, drift away again when they reach their crisis period. Unless the change in image was immense, boys would probably not be affected, science would still be an obvious, acceptable choice for a boy. Overall there would be some increase in the recruitment of girls, but no qualitative improvement.

3 *Emphasizing the applications and relevance of science:* To obtain a major qualitative improvement to recruitment in science with more girls and with students possessing imaginative, flexible minds it would be necessary to make science appealing to boys and girls at the moratorium stage.

In that event science must be seen to be relevant to the issues which concern them. The probable implication is that science would need to be presented in the context of the needs of society and individuals. Probably a case-study approach involving the application of science, and the interaction with other disciplines, would be needed. Our knowledge about the girls' concern with personal relationships suggests that the introduction of some elements of the social sciences into the case studies might prove attractive.

Is it possible to change school science in this fashion and still preserve the essential character of science itself? Clearly there would need to be some drastic pruning of content. Perhaps science teachers should not attempt to cover their subjects so comprehensively. A history teacher is content to cover the history of one country or continent over a few decades. Perhaps we must make similar choices.

It is interesting to notice that the Association for Science Education (1979) policy statement in Britain and the proposals on school physics coming from the Institute for Science Education (IPN) in Kiel are advocating such changes. The difference is that we are now offering a formal psychological model to suggest that if we want to reduce the current encapsulation of science, if we want to recruit a different sort of student, then certain curriculum changes are needed.

References

ASSOCIATION FOR SCIENCE EDUCATION (ASE) (1979) *Alternatives for Science Education.*
DOUVAN, E. and ADELSON, J. (1966) *The Adolescent Experience* (Wiley: New York).
EIDUSON, B. (1962) *Scientists: Their Psychological World* (Basic Books: New York).
ERIKSON, E. H. (1965) *Childhood and Society* (Hogarth Press: London).
HEAD, J. (1979) 'Personality and the pursuit of science.' *Studies in Science Education,* Vol. 6, pp. 23–34.
HUDSON, L. (1966) *Contrary Imaginations* (Methuen: London).
HUDSON, L. (1968) *Frames of Mind* (Methuen: London).
MARCIA, J. E. (1966) 'Development and validation of ego identity status.' *Journal of Personality and Social Psychology,* Vol. 3, No. 5, pp. 551–8.

MARCIA, J. E. (1976) 'Studies in Ego Identity' (unpublished monograph).
MASLOW, A. H. (1966) *The Psychology of Science* (Harper and Row: New York).
MCCLELLAND, D. C. (1962) 'On the psychodynamics of creative physical scientists.' In *Contemporary Approaches to Creative Thinking* edited by H. E. Gruber, G. Terrell and M. Wertheimer (Atherton Press: New York).
ROE, A. (1952) *The Making of a Scientist* (Dodd Mead: New York).

17

Girl Friendly Science and the Girl Friendly School

Judith Whyte

Approximately three times as many boys as girls take O level physics and approximately four times as many take CSE physics. Over 90 per cent of entries in all technical subjects are from boys. This means that schoolgirls are ineligible for a wide range of courses in further and higher education and for entry to occupations requiring a scientific or technical base. Female exclusion from science and technology, even if it is apparently by girls' own choice, also means that as citizens their ability to understand and control their environment is limited. Nevertheless, most schools consider they are already providing equal opportunities by neutral treatment of the two sexes (Bloomfield, 1984). In effect, ignoring the effects of gender in this way merely reinforces stereotyping because it does nothing to challenge the definition of certain aspects of the curriculum as masculine or feminine.

Girls Into Science and Technology (GIST) was the first major schools-based project addressing problems of sex stereotyping at school, and was an example of 'action research' in education; the project simultaneously took action to improve girls' achievement in science and technology and investigated the reasons for their under-achievement. The project team collaborated with teachers in eight co-educational comprehensive schools in the Greater Manchester area to devise and implement intervention strategies designed to improve girls' attitudes to the physical sciences and technical subjects. Two other schools were involved as controls where attitude testing but no interventions took place.

[. . .]

The approach was collaborative: teachers were invited to work with the team as equal partners in the attempts both to investigate and find solutions to the GIST problem. However, very few of the teachers even recognized the issue as one of professional concern at the start of the project, and most of the first two years was spent in establishing the educational importance of the issue and working towards the development of feasible intervention strategies.

The project and its outcomes have been fully described elsewhere (Smail *et al.*, 1982; Kelly, Whyte and Smail, 1984; Whyte in press). GIST had more success in altering children's attitudes than their subject choices, suggesting that it is easier to change attitudes and beliefs than actual behaviour. Pupils in action schools became markedly less stereotyped than pupils in control schools. They also had slightly more positive attitudes towards science and scientists and were less likely to define them as exclusively masculine. Despite some evidence of change in teachers' attitudes *and* behaviour, they themselves were reluctant to admit that the project had influenced them. According to an evaluation report this may reflect an unwillingness to admit that in the past schools have been sex biased (Payne, Cuff and Hustler, 1984).

The GIST hypothesis was that female under-achievement in science and technology is at least partly socially constructed by the school, an hypothesis based on research evidence as well as critical feminist analysis (see, for example, Kelly, 1981). During the project there was a shift away from locating the issue as one of girls' motivation towards attempts to change the nature of school science. One of the main gains from the GIST project has been the clarification of what is meant by a 'girl friendly', science, that is a science which will appeal equally to the interests and concerns of girls as well as boys. [. . .]

Making Science More Girl Friendly

Several interventions were designed to make science more girl friendly. Schools and teachers tried curriculum development to build on girls' science interests, changing patterns of classroom interaction, single sex groups and classes. The largest scale intervention was the VISTA programme, which consisted of women scientists and technologists visiting schools to talk to children about an aspect of their jobs already being covered in the school science syllabus. VISTA made science more girl friendly in two ways: both boys and girls were offered an attractive image of a competent woman scientist, and talks concentrated on social and industrial applications of science, an element too often missing from science at school. One school was so impressed by the children's positive reactions that they completely revamped the science work in the first two years to include more social and human applications of science.

The survey of children's attitudes helped here: research such as Ormerod's (1971; Ormerod and Duckworth, 1975) had shown that girls were interested in the social implications of science, but did not tell teachers what the desirable teaching approach might be in practice. Would science in the home be a starter? A question from our survey asked children whether they would like to know more about how a vacuum cleaner works; hardly anyone did, and girls were even less curious than boys. This told us that any simplistic assumptions about featuring 'female' domestic interests in science would probably meet with failure. The rest of the questionnaire about science curiosity showed that all the children were enthusiastic about learning science, and that girls were keen to know more about nature, the environment and medical science. Over 50 per cent, and in some cases over 60 per cent said they would like to learn about the human heart, germs and illnesses, how our muscles work, what food is good for you, life in the sea, what makes a rainbow appear and how a record is made. It was helpful that these topics also interested boys. At present the science curriculum is structured around physical science interests, on which boys are keener (how motor cars work, atoms and molecules); we were able to recommend that teaching build on the overlapping interests of the two sexes, because girls as well as boys want to know more about human biology and spectacular features of the environment (animals in the jungle, volcanoes and earthquakes, acids and chemicals). The less immediately attractive parts of science could be approached through these interests, for instance teaching 'forces' by beginning with the action of muscles in the human arm, and 'light' via the dissection of a bull's eye. When women scientists employ such approaches, and describe their own work, as happened during the VISTA programme, girls are receiving double encouragement. These examples indicate some of the features of girl friendly science: it builds on girls' interests, not just boys'; it explicitly encourages girls to see themselves as potential scientists, and it includes some of the social and human implications and applications of science.

Other GIST interventions

All the GIST schools were mixed comprehensives, and at first teachers were most unwilling to separate boys and girls at all, on the grounds that it ran counter to their co-educational comprehensive philosophy. Then certain teachers were particularly struck by the evidence of large differences in the interests and experience children brought with them to school. Girls had far less 'tinkering' experience than boys and the connection with their lesser interest in topics like 'how electricity is produced' seemed obvious. Several special science or craft clubs were organized in the lunch hour for girls only and in two schools teachers planned single-sex teaching. As we shall see, it was in these two schools that the largest measurable changes of attitude and option choice occurred.

For a more girl friendly science, it seems vital that teachers should come to see that when all the masculine packaging, evident in textbooks and resources as well as teachers' and boys' behaviour in the classroom, is removed, girls can be very enthusiastic about science. [. . .]

Alison Kelly sees at least four distinct senses in which it can be argued that science is masculine.[1] First, the pupils, teachers and practitioners of science are overwhelmingly male in terms of numbers; second, school science is packaged and presented to appeal to boys, not girls; third, classroom behaviours and interaction operate to reconstruct science as a male activity, and finally it has been suggested that 'scientific' thinking embodies an intrinsically masculine world view.

The GIST interventions described above relate to three of these: VISTA women, albeit briefly and temporarily, redressed the numerical balance by offering female role models of practising scientists; VISTA and the curriculum development which followed involved a limited 'repackaging' of science to remove its exclusively masculine appeal, and the single-sex classes and classroom observation showed how science comes to be defined as 'masculine' in the mixed school.

The fourth point, the idea that science is intrinsically masculine, can be sustained only by clinging to an irredeemably narrow conception of science and scientific thinking. The industrial and social impact of science on health, on people, on the environment, a focus on the beauty and complexity of the natural world, are notable omissions from the school science syllabus. Girls are not uninterested in science, they are bored by the limited version of it they meet in school.

One of the purposes of an extended period of single-sex science teaching might be to let teachers see how girls approach scientific matters, and to discover, what may well be the case, that girls are just as capable of 'scientific thinking' as boys. Margaret Spear, in a different study from the one reported in this volume, found that for identical work boys were marked higher than girls for supposed understanding of principles, aptitude for science and O level suitability (Spear, 1984).

Outcomes

Children enjoyed the VISTA visits according to the questionnaire returns in the third year; they liked meeting scientists and learning about a range of jobs. Girls were slightly more positive than boys.

Overall, the attitudes of children in the action schools where all the interventions took place became noticeably more liberal, especially on sex role and occupational stereotypes and the 'masculinity' of science. In general, attitudes to science itself became more negative. This is a universal phenomenon (Gardner, 1984). Children begin secondary school with high expectations of science, but become disillusioned and uninterested, especially in physics. However, the decline in science interest was less marked in GIST action than in control schools, indicating a possible causal effect of the VISTA visits and other interventions, and on boys as much as girls.

It appears that if girls' interests are catered for, if teachers become aware of the need for careful classroom management to ensure girls' participation, if the social and human implications of science and technology are stressed, girls will respond positively. There will continue to be problems if science teachers are personally doubtful about girls' ability to do science well; even if their doubts are not voiced (and anecdotal evidence suggests they sometimes are), girls are unlikely to respond unless teachers show they believe that girls have something to offer science as well as the reverse.

The significant difference between action and control schools concerning attitudes was not matched by an action/control difference in option choices. In most schools the percentage of girls choosing physics in the GIST cohort increased in comparison with previous years. However, the increase in control schools was as large as in the action schools!

The girl friendly school

Unfortunately the pattern of option choice and attitude differences is not perfectly matched within each school. That is to say, certain action schools were successful in changing attitudes, while others were successful in shifting option choices. Only one school was successful on both counts. The implication is that pupil attitude change is not sufficient on its own to ensure that pupils will actually make non-traditional option choices. Presumably the major mediating factors are the teachers, and the school, concerned.

Teacher Attitudes

[. . .]

The most interesting aspect of the teachers' response is their unwillingness to admit to any change of attitude or practice as a result of GIST. Yet both the field notes and the evaluation report provide clear evidence that the staff had become much more aware of, and informed about, girls' under-achievement in science and technology and the possible actions which schools could take. Many mentioned the practical steps they had already devised: altering curriculum materials, deliberately avoiding the use of stereotyped language, studying patterns of classroom interaction and thinking of ways to increase girls' participation. The evaluators noted the grudgingness of teachers to admit to changes in their own beliefs or practices and ascribed it to an unwillingness to accept the implied criticism that previous practice had, even unintentionally, discouraged girls.

A national survey of teachers' attitudes to equal opportunities found that men were more likely to be opposed to promoting equal opportunities than women, but that differences in subject taught were more important than the sex of the teacher in determining his or her attitude. Teachers of maths, physical science and crafts were the least in favour of greater equality (Pratt, Bloomfield and Seale, 1984). Spear also found in a study of teachers' attitudes to girls and technology that the most sex-differentiated replies came from science teachers (Spear in this volume). On both counts, of sex and subjects taught, the GIST teachers were the least promising group which could have been chosen to promote sex equality.

Alison Kelly worked with some of her students to carry out a minor evaluation of changes in GIST teachers' attitudes in comparison with a national sample (Kelly *et al.*, 1984). Women again proved to be more emphatic about sex equality than men, and London teachers were more feminist than others. GIST teachers were slightly less traditional and more in favour of equality of the sexes than other teachers. Teachers in GIST schools were also slightly more likely to agree with statements suggesting that girls 'lose out' in classroom interactions and receive less encouragement in science than boys. This is likely to be an effect of the classroom observation work carried out with GIST teachers (for a full account see Whyte, 1984). However, the GIST teachers of physical science were less convinced than their colleagues elsewhere of the importance of finding ways to encourage girls in their subject. It may be that their experience of GIST has given them a better idea of the amount of work and energy involved in trying to change things (Kelly *et al.*, 1984).

School atmosphere
Whatever may be the attitude of any individual teacher, if s/he does not receive adequate support from the school in implementing change, s/he is likely to give up, or decide that the innovation is not worth the extra time and energy required.

[. . .] The extent to which GIST was successful in particular schools appears to have been less dependent on the team's efforts than on the existing school ethos and whether it was consistent with responding to the demand for genuine equality of opportunity. In other words, the project probably did not change schools, but change may have been most likely to occur in schools which were open to the innovation and to the ideas of equality presented by the project.

Closer study of between-school differences (see Kelly *et al.*, 1984; Whyte in press) shows that attitude change was most marked in three action schools. In one, Moss Green, there had also been an increase in the percentage of girls opting for chemistry, physics and technical crafts. In the other two, Edgehill and Meadowvale, there had been an increase in at least two of these.

These schools appeared to have several things in common: first, each could be characterized as an 'innovative' school in some sense. Moss Green was a custom-built community school, with a commitment to multicultural education and a staff who were used to implementing innovations such as open-plan classrooms, and, more recently, an alternative curriculum for fourth and fifth years. At Edgehill, the science department was divided into biological and environmental sciences, instead of the traditional biology, physics and chemistry; the head teacher was a conscious advocate of innovation in comprehensive schooling; in the third school, Meadowvale, the science department had decided to redraft its entire first and second year science curriculum, in part because of the children's response to the VISTA visits organized by GIST.

The least successful schools were those which implemented the minimum programme asked for by GIST: administration of questionnaires to children, allowing women visitors into the school and piloting, more or less reluctantly, teaching materials devised by the team. The successful schools, in contrast, took up more GIST suggestions more enthusiastically, or even developed their own ideas for interventions. For example at Edgehill, a GIST pack for discussion of sex roles – *Gender in Our Lives* – was used in the personal and social education lessons, with teachers talking honestly and openly about their personal experience; as it happened they found themselves in the middle of a discussion about fathers being present at childbirth, and the children were obviously fascinated by this new view of their teachers as emotional beings. [. . .]

Willingness to talk directly to pupils about the aims of GIST was another feature of the more successful schools. Despite requests from the team to discuss the issue with children, few teachers revealed the purpose of the project to their classes. Some teachers told the evaluators that they did not feel justified in talking to pupils about the girls and science problem, and gave the impression that they felt to do so would be tantamount to propaganda.

At Moss Green, GIST was called in to address the second-year class before they made craft mini-options, to stress how important it was for girls to consider getting a grounding in technology. Far greater numbers of girls opted for technical subjects than had ever done so before. The school also ran single-sex clubs.

In comparison, there was no visible explicit discussion of sex roles at either of the two least successful schools. The GIST workpack, *Gender in Our Lives*, was used at another school, but a senior member of management had effectively insisted they use it, and some teachers did so with considerable reservations, afterwards reporting almost complete failure to alter children's prejudices.

We had looked for some impact from the presence of women in senior positions in school, but the highest percentage of women at Scale 4 or above in any school was 35 per cent. In the more successful schools, women held relatively more senior posts in the science department or in the school. In the two least successful schools it is notable that the proportion of senior women was lowest, in one case despite the fact that the head teacher was a woman.

In summary, the most successful schools appeared to have the following characteristics:

- teachers who planned and implemented their own interventions;
- teachers who were prepared to discuss the GIST problem with children, rather than simply accepting VISTA and other interventions and hoping that an implicit message would get through;
- staff, especially at a senior level, who had a positive commitment to the aims of the project;
- a progressive ethos which fitted comfortably with the equal-opportunity aims of GIST;
- a relatively higher proportion of women staff at senior levels.

[. . .]

The third element, the innovative practice advocated, became refined during rather than before the project. The use of questionnaires fed back to teachers revealed the base of interest and enthusiasm for science too often missed by schools concerned to promote a curriculum informally based on male interests. Observation in labs and workshops highlighted the depressing effect on girls' performance of the boys' claim to science as their subject. We are much clearer now than at the beginning about how to approach science in a more girl friendly way (see Smail, 1983, 1984), and the clarity is due in part to the way we have worked with teachers.

The conditions for a girl friendly school may be more difficult to bring about, for it would seem that teachers must be openly and visibly concerned about equality before pupils will change their choices; schools with traditional norms, limited or formal communication channels, and with few women in senior positions will be much slower to adapt to changed female expectations.

Conclusion

[. . .]

Teachers were always busy, and many schools put GIST on a rather lower priority than dealing with the impact of unemployment, school reorganization, discipline or curricular problems. It was often difficult to get schools to provide even basic information such as the breakdown of subject choice by sex, and members of the team frequently had to extract the information themselves from school data. Oddly enough, the control schools, where no interventions took place, were more co-operative and efficient in returning questionnaires than action schools. Similarly, the impact of GIST may have been as great in schools which had no contact with the project at all, because of the changing climate of opinion in which girls' under-achievement in science and technology came to be seen as a serious educational issue.

Acknowledgment

The GIST Project was funded by the EOC/SSRC Joint Panel on Women and Underachievement with additional support from the Department of Industry Education unit, the Schools Council and Shell UK Ltd. I am grateful to these sponsors and to my colleagues on the project, Alison Kelly, Barbara Smail and John Catton. However, they do not necessarily share the views expressed in this chapter.

My thanks also to Sandra Burslem and Sue Thorne who kindly lent me their word processor.

Note

1   See article entitled 'The Construction of Masculine Science' which appeared in *The British Journal of Sociology of Education*, 1985, Vol. 6, No. 2.

References

BLOOMFIELD, J. (1984) 'Option scheme management for equal opportunity', paper presented at Girl Friendly Schooling conference, Manchester Polytechnic, 11–13 Sept.

GARDNER, P. L. (1984) 'Summary and cross evaluation of national reports', presented at IPN/UNESCO International Symposium on Interests in Science and Technology Education, Kiel, W. Germany, 2–6 April.

KELLY, A. (1981) *The Missing Half: Girls and Science Education*, Manchester University Press.

KELLY, A., WHYTE, J., and SMAIL, B. (1984) *Girls Into Science and Technology: Final Report*, GIST, Department of Sociology, University of Manchester.

ORMEROD, M. B. (1971) 'The Social Implications Factor in Attitudes to Science', *British Journal of Educational Psychology* 41 (3), 335–8.

ORMEROD, M. B. and DUCKWORTH, D. (1975) *Pupils' Attitudes to Science: A Review of Research*, NFER, Slough.

PRATT, J., BLOOMFIELD, J. and SEALE, C. (1984) *Option Choice: A Question of Equal Opportunity*, NFER-Nelson, Windsor.

SMAIL, B. (1983) 'Getting Science Right for Girls', paper presented to the Second International Conference on Girls and Science and Technology, Oslo, Norway.

SMAIL, B. (1984) *Girl Friendly Science: Avoiding Sex Bias in the Curriculum*, Longman for the Schools Council, London.

SMAIL, B., WHYTE, J. and KELLY, A. (1982) 'Girls Into Science and Technology: the first two years', *School Science Review*, 63, 620–30; *South Australian Science Teachers Association Journal* (1981), 813, 3–10; EOC Research Bulletin (1982), 6, Spring.

SPEAR, M. (1984) 'Sex bias in science teachers' ratings of work and pupil characteristics', *European Journal of Science Education* 6(4), 369–77.

WHYTE, J. (1984) 'Observing sex stereotypes and interactions in the school lab and workshop', *Educational Review* 36 (1).

WHYTE, J. (in press) *Girls in Science and Technology* (working title), Routledge & Kegan Paul, London.

18

The Social Nature of the Curriculum

(a) Three Curricular Traditions and their Implications, *Ivor Goodson*

Since the nineteenth century 'academic subjects' and written examinations have become closely interconnected. The alliance, whether viewed as divine or malign, was formally enshrined in the School Certificate examination defined in 1917. Since that date certain material implications have followed for those subgroups and school subjects promoting or representing the academic tradition. Questions of theoretical base or methodological perspective have often been subsumed by or channelled into the construction of acceptable written examinations. For the groups and associations promoting themselves as school subjects, and irresistibly drawn to claiming 'academic status', a central criterion has been whether the subjects' content could be tested by written examinations for an 'able' clientele. Acceptance of the criterion of examinability affects both the content and form of the knowledge presented but carries with it the guarantee of high status. The academic tradition is content-focused and typically stresses abstract and theoretical knowledge for examination.

The utilitarian tradition is conversely of low status, dealing with practical knowledge sometimes not amenable to the current A level mode of written examination. Utilitarian knowledge is related to those non-professional vocations in which the majority of people work for most of their adult life. The low status of utilitarian knowledge also applies to the personal, social and commonsense knowledge stressed by those pursuing the pedagogic tradition. Whilst all school knowledge has at least an implicit pedagogy this tradition places the 'way the child learns' as the central concern in devising subject content.

These traditions are viewed as three 'centres of gravity', in the arguments about styles of curriculum. They do not represent a complete list of the 'traditions' in English curricula nor are they timeless entities; they simply represent three clear constellations of curriculum styles which recur in the

217

history of the school subjects under study. In this sense they are perhaps best viewed as strategic clusters employed to help in the scrutiny of curriculum changes and conflicts. [. . .]

The existence of academic, pedagogic and utilitarian traditions in school curricula has its origins in the separate sectors of the educational system which preceded the comprehensive era. The continuance of these traditions and the continuing dominance of the academic tradition bear testimony that the fundamental structures of curriculum have withstood comprehensive reorganization. As in the tripartite system so in the comprehensive system, academic subjects for able pupils are accorded the highest status and resources. The triple alliance between academic subjects, academic examinations and able pupils ensures that comprehensive schools provide similar patterns of curriculum differentiation to previous school systems. For the teachers who have to cater for all kinds of pupils this concentration on a particular kind of pupil and a particular kind of educational success poses the same dilemma voiced by the rural studies teacher in response to the promotion of academic examinations in his subject; 'Once again we can see the unwanted children of lower intelligence being made servants of the juggernaut of documented evidence, the inflated examination.' This conclusion summarizes the continuing choice:

> True education is not for every man the scrap of paper he leaves school with. Dare we as teachers admit this? Dare we risk our existence by forcibly expressing our views on this? While we pause after the first phase of our acceptance are we to rely on exams for all to prove ourselves worthy of the kindly eye of the state?[1]

The deep structures of curriculum differentiation are historically linked to different educational sectors, to different social class clienteles and occupational destinations, to different status hierarchies. Differentiated curricula and the social structure are matched on very firm foundations: by building on these foundations comprehensive reorganization has had to accept the antecedent structures which contradict its stated ideal. [. . .]

The legacy of differentiated status for the academic, utilitarian and pedagogic traditions draws on tripartite patterns of educational organization. In considering curriculum change it is vital to understand that this tripartite hierarchy of status has been reproduced not only in the respective parity of esteem *between* different categories of subject but also to kinds of knowledge *within* subjects. At the later level, scrutiny of 'what counts as education' is necessary. For instance, much of the debate about teaching craft and technology as a way of reinstating practical curricula has missed this point. Given the status patterns discerned one might expect that even if technology were to achieve high status and acceptance the version which would 'count as education' would be academic and theoretical and therefore stand in contradiction to more practical objectives. The differentiated status of academic, utilitarian and pedagogic traditions pervades both the type of subject and the internal form of each subject. Curriculum reform needs to address both of these levels of differentiation.

The differentiated status of the three curriculum traditions discerned and their link with the way finance and resources are allocated and pursued is confirmed by a number of studies already undertaken.

Banks' study of parity and prestige in the English secondary system ends by stressing 'the persistence of the academic tradition' throughout that period of the system's existence.[2] Hanson's study of art education and Dodd's work on technology offer similar evidence.[3] The latter speaking of the Crowther Report noted that they had shown how 'an alternative route to knowledge' lay through practical subjects which did not destroy the intellectual curiosity of the pupil in the way associated with the 'academic' ones. Dodd notes that 'the problems lay in the status of practical subjects by tradition second class. . . . Discussion on its own is insufficient and it requires legitimization by those institutions who hold this facility (universities, examination boards, employers and society at large).'[4]

As we have seen, the legitimizing institutions together with established and indeed aspiring subject groups share the vested interest in the belief that 'a scholarly discipline' is needed if a school subject is to be granted high status. The stranglehold of the academic tradition has seldom been seriously threatened by its overwhelming need to shun 'practical utility'. The theme which Dodd points to was just as common when the 1904 regulations were established. A contemporary noted that the school curriculum was 'subordinated to that literary instruction which makes for academic culture, but is of no practical utility, to the classes for whom the local authorities should principally cater'.[5]

The dominance of the academic tradition is patently supported by the major vested interest groups within education and the broader society. Yet the very need for academic subjects to escape from allegations of 'practical utility' may yet lead to irresistible pressure for change in the period of economic malaise which we currently confront.

Notes

1 P. L. Quant (1967) 'Rural Studies and the Newsom Child', *Hertfordshire Rural Studies Association Journal*.

2 Olive Banks (1955) *Parity and Prestige in English Secondary Education*. London: Routledge and Kegan Paul.

3 D. Hanson (1971) 'The development of a professional Association of Teachers', *Studies in Design Education 3, 2*.

4 T. Dodd (1978) *Design and Technology in the School Curriculum*. London: Hodder and Stoughton.

5 Quoted in Banks, op. cit., p. 41.

(b) The Schooling of Science, *Michael F. D. Young*

Science emerged later as a branch of education and its assimilation into the existing institutions and structures was not achieved without some noticeable exercises of accommodation.[1]

This view of the incorporation of natural science into the school curriculum is taken by David Layton, who offers us a valuable account of this process of 'accommodation' in the late nineteenth century, complementary to his earlier study of the demise of 'the science of common things'.[2] In particular he describes how one conception of 'pure' laboratory science was established which enabled school science to be justified in terms of the prevailing tradition of liberal education and its devotion to 'the discipline of the mind, the attainment of habits of controlled attention and the exercise of reasoning powers and memory'. Thus Chemistry and Physics could comfortably claim a place alongside the Classics and Mathematics. Likewise, the purpose of introducing science into the secondary schools was never in doubt to such leading advocates as H. E. Roscoe, the first President of the Association of Public School Science Masters (the precursor of our Association for Science Education); school science was, for Roscoe, as Layton quotes him, to be 'the means of sifting out from the great mass of the people those golden grains of genius which now are too often lost amongst the sands of mediocrity'.

A consequence of this accommodation was, as Layton puts it, that 'the application of science to everyday life had (by the 1870s) disappeared . . . the learner [of course only those learners who experienced any science teaching at all – M.Y.] was slowly inducted into the ways of the scientist – a particular type of scientist also – the "pure" researcher'. Largely through the method of government recognition and financing of laboratories, the separation of school science into separate 'subjects', physics, chemistry, and biology, became firmly established before the end of the century, as did for quite other reasons the exclusion of geology. Furthermore, the models of 'subject' teaching which dominated (and in many ways still do) experimental work were part of this process. As Layton describes it, school chemistry became the 'easily organized and easily examined exercises in qualitative analysis . . . [in which] packets of powder were sent out [to the schools] and packets of paper were returned when the pupils had completed the routine of taking the solution through the charts'; if anyone asked 'why?', 'training of the faculties of observation and reasoning' would doubtless have been the reply.

Likewise in physics pupils were offered 'a starvation course on the precise measurement of physical quantities . . . [for, as an influential text of the time began] "Physics is essentially the science of measurements"'. Of course, many things have changed, but even in the Nuffield era 'the emphasis has remained on abstract . . . "technically sweet" science, dissociated from its applications and implications'.

Before turning to the attempts to revitalize science teaching which have emerged since the early 1960s, it is important to ask the question 'Why did school science emerge in the way it did?' Is it adequate to see it as an accommodation to existing educational structures, as Layton does? I suggest we need to try and grasp both the innovations Layton describes and the structures they confronted in terms of their wider political and economic significance. Alternative traditions of science education in which scientific knowledge was conceived, among other things 'as an instrument in the pursuit of political independence and social emancipation', had, Layton writes, become 'casualties in a process of natural selection as the educational environment had become progressively more sharply defined'.[3] The problem with this kind of social Darwinist view is that it treats a *social* process, selection, as *natural*, rather than as an outcome of certain activities and interests in particular historical contexts. This is indicated in Layton's references to the views of science on the one hand in terms of 'the disinterested pursuit of truth', and on the other, particularly by those involved in the Great Exhibition, as 'the producer for the industrial market place (so that science was to be studied for the economic benefits it would yield)'. The question of economic benefits of science points to a concern with the character of the economy at the time and to the importance of considering the demise of the attempts to implement a science curriculum 'as practice' and the success of the science curriculum 'as fact'[4] in the context of changes in Victorian capitalism.[5] [. . .]

Science education was envisaged, as David Layton tells us, by some early nineteenth century radicals like Richard Carlile as undermining dogma and leading to social emancipation.[6] The process and practice of the schooling of science, for all its changes, has become almost the opposite – 'necessarily dogmatic' according to Jevons and many others, and producing technological domination rather than emancipation. This paper has largely been limited to the processes within education – the ways they have been part of a wider process of economic and political domination have been little more than hinted at. Inevitably oversimplifying, I would summarize what I have tried to say by suggesting that the schooling of science has produced three kinds of people, whose interrelations have up till now led to opposition to any attempts to realize the emancipatory potential Carlile saw. They are:

(a) 'Pure scientists', whose relations with nature are at best those of abstracted understanding. This is not to deny the discoveries that have been made, but to state that the purposes that have given meaning to the scientists' pursuit of truth have been success in and the sustaining of the scientific establishment.

(b) The 'applied scientist' whose identity is fundamentally pragmatic – given something to be done, he [or she] will work out how to do it. Ends are given, but no one asks by or for whom. Just as the pure scientist, from his [or her] early training, absolves himself [or herself] from the uses to which

221

his [or her] discoveries are put, rather than seeing that the discoveries themselves are inescapably linked to an economy on which he [or she] depends for support, so the applied scientist accepts that others define the goals that he [or she] has to achieve rather than seeing that his [or her] own means or technology itself presupposes a social order, set of priorities or goals.

(c) The identifiable failures of school science – the anti-science anti-technologists who can see science *only* as domination rather than that science as domination is itself a historical product, and the mass of people whose schooling teaches them that science is a specialized activity over which they neither have nor could have any control.

Notes

1   D. Layton (1975) 'Science or Education?', *University of Leeds Review* 18.
2   D. Layton (1973) *Science for the People*. London: Allen and Unwin.
3   D. Layton (1976) 'The Educational Work of the Parliamentary Committee of the British Association for the Advancement of Science', *History of Education* 5, 1.
4   M. F. D. Young (1975) 'Curriculum Change: Limits and Possibilities, *Educational Studies* 1, 2.
5   C. Green (1975) 'Review of Layton (1973)', *Radical Science Journal* No. 2/3.
6   Richard Carlile 'An Address to a Man of Science' referred to by Layton (1976).

(c) The Curriculum and National Identity,
Chris Brown

It is no coincidence that mass schooling was invented at roughly the time when nation states had come into existence and the need arose to instil in their citizens the idea that the new entity had first claim on their loyalties. The more social cohesion was rendered problematic by the existence of cleavages in relation to ethnicity, language etc. the more important was an efficient schooling system. The example of the United States is well known:

> . . . each American school has a national flag flying outside the school and usually a flag in each classroom. Also, the national anthem is regularly used in school assemblies and sporting events: and paintings of George Washington, Abraham Lincoln and other historic American figures are prominent in schools. (Nelson, 1978, pp. 145–6) [. . .]

In Britain it is the curriculum which bears the main burden of transmitting the national idea. History may be cited as an example, not least because in the post-Falklands era several leading figures, including Sir Keith Joseph and Professor Hugh Thomas, have singled it out for special mention in connection with 'understanding the shared values which are a distinctive feature of British Society'. Despite developments such as Schools Council history and a growing interest in African, Caribbean and Indian history, school history is unlikely ever to escape the grip of nationalism. [. . .]

Could one envisage a curriculum without history? Many people would feel that if children grew up to know nothing of their 'heritage' this would be a serious threat to national identity.

People may not remember whatever detailed analysis was developed for them as schoolchildren, but certain models or 'general sketches' ... do remain, and they inform everyday thinking closely, especially as they are exercised over and again by politicians and the media seeking to make public sense of current events. If an example is needed to make this clearer one can be found in the special place occupied by the Second World War in public consciousness in Britain and, more particularly, in Margaret Thatcher's increasingly deliberate manipulation of Churchillian sketches over the period of the Falklands crisis. (Wright, 1984, pp. 49–50)

Unlike history, the 'new' geography would appear to have rid itself of imperialist associations. However, quite apart from the persistence of a great deal of 'geography of the British Isles' syllabuses, the new scientific and conceptual geography has not appeared in schools because of some intrinsic merit. On the contrary, its growth coincided with the collapse of empire. So long as the world was politically, and militarily, if not economically, permeated with British influence, school geography could safely and fruitfully explore even the most unlikely regions. In a world where British influence is conspicuously waning it might not be in the interests of a secure national identity to throw it open for young Britons to gaze on. History, on the other hand, can be continually re-written to buttress the national ideal.

There is little point in reviewing every curriculum subject. Historical and sociological studies of the curriculum have shown us that school subjects are not simply rationally selected for explicit educational aims but are reflections of larger social and political forces. Not all subjects contribute equally to fostering national identity. Nor do they all function in the same way. Science for instance makes its contribution by studiously avoiding social and political comment: it thus misses the way that it is inextricably bound up with dominant values, amongst them attitudes which assume ethnocentric and nationalistic positions. Even modern languages may be detached from their respective cultures and contribute to the unspoken notion that other societies are slightly queer.

The point is that in nation-states, education systems are provided by the state authorities and will thus inevitably have the net effect of focusing positive views of the nation they serve. Britain may not need to flaunt nationalism in the way characteristic of the United States but its education system can no more ignore the task of sustaining the national identity than education systems in any other nation-state.

References

NELSON J. (1978) 'Nationalistic political education: an examination of traditions and potentials', *Cambridge Journal of Education* 8, 2–3.

WRIGHT P. (1984) 'A blue plaque for the labour movement? Some political meanings of the "national past"', in Formations Editorial Collective, *Formations of Nation and People*. Henley: Routledge and Kegan Paul.

(d) Contrasting Models in School Geography,
Rob Gilbert

Differences between explaining physical processes and human action make impossible a unified society-environment study based on a single explanatory paradigm. Explanatory models which serve for one cannot serve for the other. The dominance of the traditions of environmental and economic determinism are a handicap to further profitable application of geographical knowledge to human affairs. As one geographer has pointed out:

> . . . until subject matter theories with different epistemological characteristics have been formulated, the focus of our spatial planning must continue to be on supermarkets, roads and airports, and not on the needs and desires of those individual human beings that the facilities allegedly are constructed to serve.[1]

This tradition and its inherent contradictions have been noted before, as when an historian of the discipline wrote almost twenty years ago:

> Many geographers have never been deeply concerned with ultimate objectives of social character, and some would sincerely regard efforts to provide directives for human action as presumptuous and arrogant. But sooner or later writers ask whether geography really is a human study at all, possibly because some writers on human geography appear to have studied almost everything except the people.[2]

That environmentalism may be superseded in schools, as it appears largely to have been in universities, by the locational analysis school is no guarantee of a more appropriate form of explanation. For, as has been suggested in the texts reviewed, the old paradigms may merely be replaced by a new form of determinism, this time based on space. Here again the results of human activity are explained without recourse to conscious human agents or social contexts. The locational analysis school can be said to have

> reified 'the spatial' as the basis of the subject matter of the discipline. At the same time it diverted attention away from the underlying structural explanations of society and economy, as part of a general process of 'mystification' whereby surface manifestations are confused for root causes.[3]

Thus statements in the text material which attribute spatial differences to 'different kinds of people', or government planning, or factors of location such as the availability and stability of a labour market, have arbitrarily stopped the causal chain at a point which omits social, economic and political considerations. To claim that explanation in geography can go no further is only to say that it is inadequate to its task, and ignores the fact that many geographers are going further:

> Geographical differentiation is a detail – albeit an important detail – and a result of the operation of social systems. It is not a fundamental property of such systems. The space-economy for example is simply the spatial pattern of organization created by the industrial economy; it is not an independent variable. This point has been clearly demonstrated by recent reconsiderations of, for example, the nature of uneven regional development and economic under-development which show that both processes, whilst creating spatial patterns are, more fundamentally, outcomes of the operation of the economy rather than the result of autonomous geographical factors. To concentrate on the latter is not only superficial, it is also incorrect.[4]

The images of human nature and society built into the explanatory paradigms which dominate school curricula and texts are inadequate. They restrict the extent to which human action can be understood, substituting explanations based on a plastic model of the individual and a narrow and amorphous model of social relations and structure. In focusing on concrete outcomes of social activity, and explaining them through natural causal models, geographers have disguised the social origins of these outcomes and the political assumptions and implications of their theories. Olsson, in his analysis of urban geographical theories and their usefulness, concludes that:

> the explanatory power and potential planning applicability of geographic theory does not depend on the employed and usually specified spatial axioms but rather on the unspecified axioms about individual and group behaviour.[5]

Until these underlying images of individual and society are recognized, and their study given the explicit attention it deserves, the significance of geographical knowledge for social practice will not be realized, nor the constraints it currently imposes overcome.

Notes

1 G. Olsson (1972) 'Some notes on geography and social engineering', *Antipode* 4, 1, 1–22.
2 T. Freeman (1961) *A Hundred Years of Geography*. London: Duckworth, p. 182.
3 D. Smith and P. Ogden (1977) 'Reformation and Revolutions in human geography' in R. E. Lee (ed.) *Change and Tradition: Geography's New Frontiers*. Department of Geography, Queen Mary College, University of London, p. 54.
4 R. Lee (1977) 'Anti-space: geography as a study of social process writ large' in R. Lee (ed.) op. cit., p. 72.
5 G. Olsson (1972) op. cit., p. 13.

(e) 'Political' Differences in English Teaching,
Margaret Mathieson

As it has been seen to touch upon every aspect of pupils' lives, most particularly the emotional, English has become increasingly diffuse. Moreover, there are within it, more than most other subjects, marked political differences between the leading figures in the field. As they relate to decision-making about priorities and responsibilities in the classroom, these differences must affect many English teachers' sense of purpose and professional confidence. [...]

Before examining conflicting views about priorities within the four main activities within English – literature, creativity, discrimination, and classroom talk – it is useful to consider the term 'political' in reference to definitions currently being made by leading figures concerned with English in schools. Within the last ten years, during which time interest had shifted to the curriculum of the average and below-average child, widespread dissatisfaction has been expressed with the traditional grammar school education. Its specialist, academic, authoritarian elements have been persistently criticized, partly because they ignored progressives' demands for children's activity, participation and development through discovery, and partly because of the perceived irrelevance of this education to the lives of working-class children, the majority of whom have failed to benefit from it. Progressives, and radicals supporting reorganization of the schools and the introduction of non-streaming, are carrying their attack upon the grammar schools' élitism into the curriculum, dismantling the traditional subjects by rearranging them through interdisciplinary work, projects and themes. As this relates to English, the central concern of which has been the dissemination of liberal culture throughout society, it has undergone considerable revision. Literature, usually the major part of English in the grammar schools, has received the most severe overhauling, but because of the current unacceptability to many educators of a 'middle-class' curriculum for all our pupils, every activity in English has been given a different set of emphases. [...]

Recent anxiety about the grammar schools' perceived responsibility for reinforcing divisions between the middle and working classes, and about the wastage of talent which their continued existence perpetuated, has brought their traditional curriculum under severe attack. In addition, as far as English has been concerned, others besides progressives and radicals have questioned the value of academic approaches for working-class pupils. G. H. Bantock and David Holbrook, who are very concerned about exploitation by commercial culture of working-class pupils, have argued that the watered-down grammar school curriculum has failed to affect the lives of the great majority. Although not wishing to disturb the present social system in any fundamental way, they, like the radical educators, have proposed the revival of popular culture. Instead of set books, periods of literature and preparation for examinations, they propose more mime, dance, poetry reading and writing, an affective education for pupils unreceptive to the academic, and susceptible to the commercial. Thus, both radicals and élitists have severely shaken the early certainty about the worthwhileness of attempts to disseminate liberal culture as widely as teachers' skills and school conditions permitted. And within recent years, the question of which culture is for whom is being raised in connection with every one of their activities. If literature and its related activities are tainted with 'middle-class' exclusiveness and, it appears, that teachers engaging pupils in these are 'imposing' alien values upon working-class pupils, it follows that they must move into the lives of working-class pupils to encourage that culture which, up till now, the largely irrelevant curriculum has 'stifled' [. . .]

After surveying the general scene it is useful to look at existing differences between educators about each of the four main activities.

The teaching of literature has been the activity most profoundly affected by these conflicting views. Pupils of Leavis continue to support his concept of the centrality of the literary experience, denying its identification with middle-class culture and the charge of imposing alien values upon working-class children.

Although G. H. Bantock and David Holbrook attack the 'watered-down' curriculum for secondary modern children, they insist upon the value of literature in the school experience of all pupils. They suggest approaching the average and below-average children through mime, dance and personal composition. Nevertheless, the proposed stimuli are myth and folk song and, hopefully, these are meant to lead on to the poetry of Blake and Shakespeare. Like Arnold and Leavis these writers, concerned above all with what Holbrook calls the children's 'humanity', believe that this can be touched and sensitized by engagement with great works of art. Today, Holbrook and his supporters, opposing the shift of emphasis to 'relevant' social or environmental studies, simply disclaim the accusation of endorsing middle-class values; they insist upon the universality of the literary experience which, if neglected, will mean severe imaginative deprivation for children continually exposed to what, they argue, are the banalities of the mass media. [. . .]

The unwillingness of some English teachers to teach literature stems from their convictions about the neglected richness of working-class culture. While the *Language in Use* team wish to order priorities differently and the Humanities Project's teachers wish to rearrange literature to illustrate relevant social issues, there is an extreme form of resistance to literature on the grounds that it is part of the 'syllabus of established middle-class culture'.[1] In *This New Season*, a book about English teaching in Stepney, Chris Searle expresses his belief in the validity of working-class culture and the English teacher's responsibility to encourage children's pride in their own identity. Literature, apart from a reference to the Liverpool poets, is excluded from his working-class pupils' experience of English in school. Instead, Searle proposes stimulation of pupil's personal writing about their feelings and environment. Having identified the academic curriculum with competitive examinations and the status-seeking of the middle clases, Searle excludes all works of art from the classroom except the pupils' own creations and those which reflect their lives.

Although their reasons differ and their perspectives on literature conflict, the élitists like Bantock and Holbrook and a radical like Searle face English teachers with proposals based on similar assumptions. Arguing that the curriculum of the working-class pupils should be specially chosen to suit their environment, experiences and abilities, they indicate their lack of interest in the question of academic achievement with its possibility of pupils' upward social mobility. Bantock and Holbrook seek no reorganization of the social structure, investing their hopes for greater happiness in the power of creativity and great art to bring self-awareness and fulfilment. Searle, and teachers with his views, reject the present social system, recommending that ways be found to give working-class pupils confidence and pride in their cultural identity. They do not propose to enter into work in school which makes achievement in competitive examinations possible, having judged this to be highly undesirable.

Turning to the field of children's creativity we find that the area of agreement is far larger than that about literature. So strong have been the influences here – of progressivism with its romantic view of childhood's vision, of anti-industrialism, of egalitarianism which has democratized art in every form, of therapy – that the great majority of educators wish to encourage pupils' growth through creativity. Disagreement is mainly about whether great literature or the children's own environment and experiences should provide the stimuli for this work. It is a debate which reflects the overall political dispute about the role of high art in the classroom. While Bantock, Holbrook, Inglis and those English teachers who support the 'élitists', recommend the employment of stimuli drawn exclusively from the music, painting and literature of high art, and make it clear that they view creativity partly as a way back into appreciation, a radical teacher like Searle rejects this culture completely. Unlike the élitists, many of whom wish to compensate for working-class children's loss of traditional agricultural satisfactions through a mainly affective curriculum, Searle recommends creativity to strengthen working-class children's confidence and pride in their own identity.

The severest critics of exclusively personal, creative writing are the *Language in Use* team, who argue that such work does not help pupils achieve social competence. [. . .]. The charge is that exclusive concentration upon the personal can, in its effects, be socially divisive. Unless working-class children are given linguistic means of control over the disciplines of the curriculum, and situations in the outside world, they are unlikely to stand much chance of being upwardly mobile. What this criticism draws attention to is the bitter truth about teachers' exclusive concentration upon creativity with working-class pupils. Whether this is stimulated by the myths and ballads proposed by David Holbrook, or is a reflection upon the living conditions of society's victims suggested by Searle, teachers' limitation of the pupils' work in English to 'personal' writing can be interpreted as giving their support to the *status quo* of the social system. Since this decision relates, in English, to what has come to be accepted as a key element in children's potential to achieve at school, that is their linguistic competence, the English teacher has a heavier responsibility when he [or she] attempts to resolve it than staff concerned with other parts of the curriculum. He [or she] has to decide whether it is more in his pupils' interests for him to accept the existence of the present social structure and to give them help to advance within it, or for him to have rejected it, on their behalf, as stifling, competitive and exploitative and to encourage them to find fulfilment within themselves and their environment. It will be appreciated that these decisions within English teaching, as they are seen as likely to affect pupils' future working and leisure conditions, might be poignantly uncomfortable to resolve for working-class teachers. Having achieved professional status by means of success in competitive examinations, they are likely to feel a sense of obligation to working-class pupils to equip them in a similar way. It is unlikely to be easy for them to decide, on their working-class pupils' behalf, that personal fulfilment derives solely from their inner selves and their environment, unrelated to questions of higher social status and improved working and leisure conditions. What is certain, however, is that currently English teachers are being urged by the majority of voices in their midst to concentrate upon encouragement of their pupils' creativity.

And as discussion moves on to include the other major activities within English – critical discrimination and classroom talk – it becomes clear that the central difficulties remain. [. . .] There are firmly held opposite views on where the main emphases should be placed. The crucial question of 'standards', of teachers' commitment to what have traditionally been accepted as cultivated or educated taste and speech, recurs in connection with both these activities with disturbing persistence.

Note

1 C. Searle (1973) *This New Season.* London: Calder and Boyars, p. 15.

(f) Changes in School Mathematics, *Barry Cooper*

[. . .] In the 1950s, secondary school mathematics was clearly differentiated by 'ability' and, to a lesser extent, by sex. The main boundary was between what I have termed selective and non-selective school mathematics but there was also differentiation within these, especially the latter. There was not, however, a one-to-one correspondence between these two subject subcultures and the selective and non-selective school sectors. As the 1950s passed, more and more pupils were being entered by the secondary modern schools for the GCE and, as a consequence, the most 'able' pupils within these schools were being brought into contact with the selective mathematics tradition. Broadly speaking then, at this time, two versions of mathematics were being taught to two different categories of pupil, largely in different types of school, by teachers who, again broadly speaking, had been educated in two different types of post-school institution: the university and the teacher training college. The latter teachers were more likely to be non-specialists.

On this basis, it can be suggested that the two mathematical educational subcultures existed both at the level of ideas and at the level of social relations. The first, the selective, was a part of [the] 'public school tradition'; the second, the non-selective, of [the] 'elementary tradition'. It was also shown that the pedagogical perspectives held by mainstream mathematical educators, broadly 'psychometric', were such as to legitimate the broad outlines of a curriculum differentiated by 'ability' (but not so clearly its differentiation by sex).

A discontinuity of both content and approach existed between selective school mathematics and some currents within university mathematics, especially pure mathematics. [. . .]

In the case of the Mathematical Association, many of the older school-based members will have constructed their careers in terms of existing definitions of school mathematics and [. . .] will have had an interest, all other things being equal, in resisting changes which might be seen as leading to the relative devaluation of their 'knowledge'. Some university mathematicians, on the other hand, especially those pure mathematicians teaching the post-1800 algebras, were beginning to express some concern over the nature of school mathematics. [. . .] This might be seen as an expression of concern by university mathematicians about the subject socialization of their potential students. For several reasons, it might also have been expected, and will be seen later to have been the case, that some of the younger teachers in the higher status selective schools might become allies of those in the universities beginning to press for change. This would be expected because, first, they would have been socialized into a version of mathematics nearer to that of the university 'modern' pure mathematicians than that of their elders and because, secondly, they would have had a potential interest in changes that could, within schools, challenge the seniority of their elder colleagues or, at least, they would have had less of a vested interest in current practice. [. . .] By mid-1959, other pressure groups external to the schools, in the form of an alliance of university mathematicians, representing mainly the applied segment of the subject, and employers of graduate labour had also invested some of their considerable resources of time, money and status into conveying to teachers from the selective sector (who prepared their students and employees) their 'requirements' of the school curriculum. They legitimized these by reference to the nation's 'needs' for scientific and technological manpower. [. . .]

More generally, it is important to stress that the active interest developed by major companies in the 1950s in mathematical and scientific education [. . .] represented a major shift in the resources potentially available to those promoting various missions within mathematics. Not only was money now possibly available, but, as a result of the conferences, 'authoritative' statements supporting curriculum reform had become available from an influential source. [. . .]

During the same period, however, a group within the leadership of the ATAM was beginning, partly under the influence of the ICSITM, and using resources generated by developing the Association's membership in arenas relatively untapped by the Mathematical Association, to argue for the introduction of post-1800 algebraic ideas [. . .] into school syllabuses. The leadership also continued to campaign for pedagogic changes, partially legitimizing both elements of its mission in terms of improving the child's 'understanding' of mathematics. [. . .]

By mid-1959, therefore, there existed, scattered throughout the selective schools, [. . .] a number of teachers, partly in contact with one another through the associations and conferences, interested in the possibility of changing the nature of school mathematics and aware of possible sources of support for this mission. Others, less directly committed to change or worried as to how their institutions would cope with its demands, would, nevertheless, have been finding it increasingly difficult to regard school mathematics as fixed and unchangeable. [. . .]

While there clearly was an 'objective' discontinuity of subject perspective between selective school mathematics and the practice of some segments, increasingly dominant within some countries, of university mathematics, and had been for some years, it again required interested actors, utilizing the climate of 'crisis' resulting from the campaign on teacher supply as a major resource, to enter various arenas in order to persuade others of the 'need' for change.

Such actors, especially the university pure mathematicians, with their followers in the ATAM, and the applied mathematicians, with their industrial allies, did have considerable success in convincing school teachers of the 'need' for change in school practice, while fending off attacks 'from below' on their own curricular practices. In both cases the success of the university sub-disciplinary segments can be seen as having partly resulted from their having found allies outside of their own organizations. The supporters of modern algebra within the ATAM, who had come into contact with the pure mathematicians in various European-wide meetings, such as Royaumont and the ICSITM conferences, gradually made 'modern mathematics' more acceptable to many school teachers by combining it with those elements of their original mission concerned with Piagetian ideas, and proposing 'intuitive' and 'experiental' approaches to its study. The applied mathematicians found themselves able to claim that 'industry' also approved of 'modelling', numerical methods and so on, as well as being able to derive resources of personnel and money from companies with which to further the promotion of their version of 'mathematics'. [. . .]

By late 1961, therefore, the 'need' to reform school mathematics was seen as legitimate by actors in a number of arenas, including the industrial and political. In this climate, various groups of individuals who had been involved in the conferences and activities of the preceding few years were to move into the drawing up of detailed proposals for curriculum development and the search for funds with which to implement these. [. . .]

Both SMP [originating in the boys' public schools] and MME [originating in state secondary schools] produced proposals for the redefinition of school mathematics that were clearly orientated to the demands of various powerful, i.e. resource-controlling, extra-school groups. Hence, they might both have expected to receive considerable support from such sources. In fact, initially, SMP received major, and MME only minor, financial backing. Accounts of SMP's 'success' from within the subject have tended to underplay this difference, stressing instead individual and organizational factors. [. . .]

SMP's 'success' relative to such projects as MME must be understood, at least partially, in terms of the differential availability of such resources as status, academic legitimacy and finance, and not merely in terms of such factors as 'flair', something SMP members themselves seem to have well understood. [. . .]

The very success of SMP, in ensuring its diffusion 'downwards', brought a curricular selection originally developed within the prestigious independent sector of the selective subculture, and only modified by teacher-writers experienced with 'less able' children, into contact with many teachers whose subject and pedagogical perspectives derived from within the non-selective subculture in which criteria for selecting mathematical content differed considerably. This, together with the dissatisfaction of members of various university disciplines and sub-disciplines ensured that SMP would be continuously subject to criticism.

Glossary of terms
ATAM   Association for Teaching Aids in Mathematics
ICSITM International Commission for the Study and Improvement of Teaching Mathematics
SMP   School Mathematics Project
MME   Midlands Mathematical Experiment

(g) Patriarchy in School Textbooks, *Marion Scott*

I examined numerous texts (English, social studies, history, geography, maths and science) which were used mostly with the fourteen plus age group to locate some of the sexist trends in curriculum materials.[1] [. . .]

Social studies teachers and departments have been placed in the vanguard of progressive teaching, ostensibly because social studies is seen as a context in which individuals can develop their consciousness and understanding of society. Their curriculum materials, however, stand in sharp contrast to this rationale, and their texts are no less open to criticism than those of other subjects. There are some issues within social studies itself which are interesting. There is a continual debate as to whether the role of the social studies curriculum is to *describe* things as they are (in this case, to show a sexist world without necessarily singling out that sexism for comment or criticism) or whether it should adopt a critical perspective. To my mind the answer is simple: when a critical approach is accepted as a legitimate element of social studies teaching (and surely a critical approach is not one which is to be avoided) then textbooks will be obliged to present *alternatives*, rather than just describing the sexist norm and failing to evaluate it. Social studies texts (or sections of them) fall into three categories which are crudely sexist.

1 *The derogation of women*
   In these texts women are relegated to a subordinate role or else portrayed through grotesque cartoons. They also present women serving primarily a 'decorative' function.
2 *The invisible woman*
   These books do not focus on women at all.
3 *The insignificance of women*
   These books treat women inadequately and are the most common genre.

It should be stressed that since the subject of social studies is society, and particularly individuals and social groups within society, it is difficult to accept that women as a group can be of little concern to its practitioners. Surprisingly perhaps, while blatantly sexist material in the form of caricatures is not common, and usually used with critical intention, it is fair to say that many social studies texts produced for examination classes frequently neglected women, though there were some exceptions. (There are, it must be said, changes taking place at the level of examination syllabuses and question papers where the role of women appears with increasing frequency.)

In both general texts and volumes dealing with special topics, I found that women were often invisible. Books about leisure, crime, courtship, education, advertising, general introductions to social studies and sociology, all showed weaknesses here. [. . .] Where books were inadequate it was usually a result of their sketchy approach to a subject. Many books deal with women at work, perhaps focusing briefly on their dual role at work and home, or looking at housework, but not exploring *the extent* to which women work and contribute to the work process. I am not arguing that the lack of feminist analysis makes the accounts unsatisfactory, but rather that indisputable facts are actually *withheld* and half of society is virtually ignored.

I need to emphasize two points here: firstly, most textbooks represent a misleading view of reality in which women are neglected or treated in a cursory manner and this is their ideological function. Secondly (and this is a more subtle and complex point), I would suggest that while some writers may believe that they are presenting reality, they are, in effect, reinforcing stereotypes and patriarchal relations. While we know that more men at present work in certain jobs, as engineers, in factories and so on, we still need to see and read that *women can also do these jobs*. As with so many books, social studies texts are often more reactionary and stereotyped than life itself. [. . .] So much of the curriculum is weighted in favour of males, and if such inequality is to be redressed, then curriculum materials must move towards 'positive discrimination' in favour of women.

Geography, as a subject, tends to concern itself with what is done, in what manner and where, especially when it looks at industry and resources. Its focus is not so much on the individuals who work and produce as on the production process, and this rather impersonal and abstract approach makes it difficult or even unnecessary to look for any exclusion of women, although this occurs. For example, a text which adopts a general, objective style can often create the wrong impression through its use of the pseudo-generic 'man'. Although the written text may be very general and refrain from referring either to men or women, the illustrations make a definite point for the majority contain male figures. Where women are illustrated the results are often less than desirable for they frequently seem to be included for their decorative or 'selling' power.

Among the geography texts I examined there were two particular sexist tendencies. The first was in terms of the invisibility of women who were ignored, or under-represented. For example, in Third World countries women play a crucial role in farming but this was certainly not the impression which would be gained from the books. The second tendency is the desire to simplify (or avoid) any analysis (a rather ironical position) which of course makes distortion almost unavoidable. Examples of this were discussions of population growth which made no mention of birth control and figures on the distribution of the sexes through occupations which were offered without explanation or analysis. [. . .]

History textbooks also provide interesting documentation for even among highly qualified history scholars the centrality of women in history is not yet accepted. Since school texts so frequently seem to depend upon the received knowledge of at least one intellectual generation before them, children will be condemned for some time to reading about the exploits of men. History as an intellectual discipline now includes social history which looks at how people actually lived within the limitations of the economic and political events. Labour history too has developed into a recognizable historical research area and women's history is following suit. These approaches have a preoccupation with the activities of ordinary people rather than with important figures and are concerned with providing an alternative perspective on our past. Women's history has yet to take root within our universities and so must wait even longer before it makes an impact in the classroom despite the availability of many histories of women produced in the last decade or so, which could provide starting points for a better balanced approach to history.

More social history is being taught but examination syllabuses still focus on political and economic history which conventionally excludes women. I looked at several texts directed at the upper half of secondary schools and roughly the same categories emerged as for social studies. Typical was a view of the past which left women invisible. A book on the First World War made no mention of women's contribution to the war effort at home or abroad. A book on Britain since 1700 ignored the nineteenth-century feminists and the birth control movement; books on political and economic history were almost exclusively about men. There was even a chapter in one book entitled 'The Home' in which the focus was on the man, portrayed relaxing after some 'Do-it-Yourself' work. There are modern history books which ostensibly focus on periods of great social change but the reader could be forgiven for reaching the conclusion that there have been no social changes which have involved/affected women.

There are, of course, history books, or rather sections and chapters in books, which do focus on women. Generally these are inadequate, non-analytical and sometimes almost caricatured. Historians' treatments of the suffrage movement are a case in point: the coverage is frequently brief and uninformative. Sometimes discussion which starts well descends into trivia, such as a discussion of women's part in the labour market in the twentieth century which ends in an uninspired discussion of fashion. I also noticed a tendency to assume that by the twentieth century women had overcome most of the problems of inequality. Mention is made of the Equal Pay and Sex Discrimination Acts but there is no attempt to question their ultimate effectiveness. One book included a comment that Hitler had a 'mystical appeal' to women, but fails to discuss why or how, and suggests that Hitler's views on the home as women's place seem old-fashioned to us today, something unfortunately far from the case. Another book claimed that by the end of the First World War much of the old prejudice against women having an equal place with men in society had gone. I found, too, an assertion that fashion today is a sign that women's emancipation is well underway – a claim that cannot go unchallenged. The lack of feminist perspective is emphasized by statements such as: 'There can be no doubt that women and girls have failed to make full use of the opportunity now open to them', which implies an ideologically and materially unfettered equality of opportunity. Another historian notes that women have not come to rival men, despite the equality established through legislation (!), but needs to add a critique of such legislation and society if he is to understand its failures.

What is required in history, if girls are to have equal opportunity with boys in school, is both a full investigation and exposure of women's past – recorded and documented in special women's history books – *plus* an integration of women and their contribution to history within existing accounts. This means studying the women who were great and important ('heroine history') as well as the ordinary women. The two sexes are not experiencing equal educational opportunity while the only version of the past they are presented with looks almost exclusively at males and has been recorded almost exclusively by males.

Science and mathematics, because of their subject matter, necessitate the adoption of a different approach. This is not the place to explore arguments which characterize the scientific mode of thought as in some sense masculine (though this may have a vital role to play in our understanding of the science of our culture if it is so: see Kelly *et al.*, 1979). I intend to analyse the sexism in such texts on a more immediate, if mundane, level. Questions which can be posed include: what impression do we get of the 'mathematical world' and way of thinking; what does maths connect with; who might it concern; who are these books directed at? (The same questions could also apply to chemistry and physics.) Sensible of the fact that maths is not a popular subject among children in general there is often an attempt to show how the 'everyday' can be viewed mathematically. However, the 'everyday', according to these texts, is a world of football, cricket, men driving cars and traditional boys' hobbies whether the topic is statistics, measurement or velocity. The world of maths is male and this is reinforced in several books by the number of questions which revolve around men and boys doing things susceptible to mathematical calculation. Occasional gestures towards the girls being included in maths are made, typically, via a girl sipping tea or standing decoratively posed in a mini skirt in a phone booth. The School Mathematics Project books are more abstract than many, depending less on pictures. But even in these boys feature more through their visibility in the questions and examples. A supreme example of sexist attitude can be found in the early pages of one SMP volume demonstrating the use of flow diagrams (Book F; 4-5). A flow diagram discriminates between girls and boys, directing the girls to consider a flow chart dealing with a knitting process, while the boys are to examine a flow chart of a cement mixing operation. The two sexes are told exactly what they should be interested in, and all in the name of mathematics. It would be a short sighted solution to try to remedy this bias by showing mathematics operating in the domestic realm to the same extent as it operates outside it, just to draw girls' interest. The main point is that even when examples could be *non-sex specific*, these books make them *sex specific*. No attempt is made in any of the books I looked at to integrate girls into the world of engineering or technology.

Chemistry and physics books revealed the same patterns. The male predominates in the pictures, examples and the questions. One very lively looking book provides typical examples of the features I would criticize: a focus on the history of the science dealing with the main discoverers who all seem to be men; a use of the pseudo-generic 'man' and 'he' when the reference is to men and women; more pictures of men than women; a series of cartoons in the margins which portray boys more frequently than girls to illustrate some concept or show active participation in scientific experiment. But we should note that the process of deterring girls from science begins well before they enter secondary school. It takes the form partly of encouraging them to relate to the personal and subjective while boys begin to grapple with the impersonal and objective.

Our school textbooks present a biased, distorted and sometimes explicitly sexist view of the world and there is no doubt that they could be improved.

Note

1   For reasons of space, all detailed references to texts have been omitted.

Section 3: The Social Framework

Introduction

As the last extracts indicate, schools and teaching exist in a social framework. That framework shapes the broad conditions in which they operate and more specifically lays down both what is expected of them and under what circumstances and with what resources they go about achieving those goals.

Those are the kinds of broader social issues raised in the articles in this Section of the Reader. A good example of the changing social framework within which schools exist, and, equally important, an exposition of the background to one of the key contemporary issues, is Ali Rattansi's 'Race, Education and British Society'. This traces the black presence in Britain and its historical and present outcomes, with special attention to current debates on so-called 'black underachievement'.

The broad social framework underlies the specific problems which education policy attempts to tackle. While specific expectations of education vary, they tend to do so around three key expectations, that the education service will support the national economy, make good citizens and enable young people to make the most of their various talents. A moment's thought, however, demonstrates that these three main aims are not necessarily mutually complementary; they could even be mutually contradictory. At any rate, it seems difficult for them all to be given equal emphasis all the time. In recent years we have been witnessing an attempt to place more emphasis on the first two purposes of education to redress what is considered an imbalance in favour of the third in the three decades following the 1944 Education Act. Now the explicit policy aim for schools is much more a directly vocational one, and the article by Moore traces out some of the connections between education, qualifications and the labour markets young people are seeking to enter. Not all of his conclusions are what might be expected given the current stress on the importance of vocational education and training.

Another contemporary issue, though in this case an old one taking on a new form, is the provision of more equal educational opportunities for girls, and for young people from ethnic minorities. We have already alluded to this problem in the General Introduction, and the paper by Williams amplifies and develops the issue. She looks at national and local policies for mitigating the educational effects of gender and ethnic differences. She shows that these are very distinct sets of problems, which have received very distinct sets of answers, with rather different implications for teachers.

Moving from what is expected of the education system, the next three articles look at aspects of the circumstances in which schools attempt to meet these aims. The paper by Fitz, Edwards and Whitty examines the philosophy and operation of the Assisted Places Scheme. This not only reminds us of the existence of a non-state section of education (which as we write in mid-1987 seems set only to increase in size), but also in drawing attention to the relations between the state and non-state sectors, points out features of the conditions under which the former operates that are frequently taken for granted. One aspect of this operation over which state schools, at any rate, have minimal control is the pupils who come to them. These pupils are shaped by many other factors than their schooling, and the extract from Coleman's *The Nature of Adolescence* considers some of the main features influencing adolescent development and their relation to school. Another factor affecting the way schools work is the way they have always worked. There are certain fundamental, seemingly inevitable, features of schooling in this society which persist, irrespective of changing aims and resources for education. Features like these are best located through comparative or historical analysis and Brian Simon's 'Why No Pedagogy in England?' provides both. It also provides valuable substance on the nature of teaching methods and their relationship to psychological theory as well as to the overall aims for education.

One of the most dramatically changing aspects of the context and content of education recently has been the expectations and especially the control of teacher's work. This appears very likely to culminate in some form of official appraisal of their work. The process leading up to this and its likely consequences for teaching are discussed in detail in the article by Walsh.

A central question addressed in this section is 'what is schooling for?' We have already considered the varying aims for schooling, and the circumstances under which it is carried out. One major aspect of the question which often gets overlooked, however, is not so much the outcomes of schooling for young people in terms of qualifications, etc., but what part it plays in their overall development into adulthood. Much of what is written about education seems to assume, with the best possible motives, that only what they get from their schooling, influences, or can 'make' or 'save', young people. The extract from Clarke and Willis takes a different view, arguing for multiple transitions from youth to adulthood, and examining the place of schooling in that process, especially for working-class young people.

Finally, we have thought it worthwhile to reprint, yet again, Basil Bernstein's classic, 'Education Cannot Compensate for Society'. Although not far short of 30 years old, written in social and educational circumstances far different from those that prevail now, and in response to specific problems that no longer have a major place on the agenda for schooling, its basic message remains inspirational.

19

'Race', Education and British Society

Ali Rattansi

The purpose of this chapter is to provide some part of the conceptual clarification and social and historical background that is essential to an analysis of the nature of 'race' as an element in British education and society.[1] Teachers and other educationalists cannot be expected to come to an adequate understanding of recent trends in multicultural and anti-racist education, nor can they develop an independent critical judgement on recent controversies in this area, without some grasp of the deeper structural and ideological issues that underly the racial dimension in education, politics and the economy.

Cultural Diversity in Society and Education

The immediate context for the discussion of 'race' in British education is provided by the development of the multicultural and anti-racist educational movement in recent years.[2] However, although 'multiculturalism' as an educational movement dates from the 1970s and is primarily a response to the post-Second World War migration of black communities to Britain, it is important to recognize that multiculturalism is a perennial *social* issue, for all but the simplest of societies are characterized by cultural diversity. It could be argued, therefore, that good education ought always to be based on multi-cultural principles.

Cultural diversity is a central feature of modern British society. It has long been recognized that a variety of structural divisions have generated more or less distinct cultures and sub-cultures, whether based on class divisions, age, gender or religion. Moreover, British society has been characterized by significant 'sub-national' cultures – Scottish, Welsh, Irish – which are interwoven with linguistic and religious differences. Taken together, these forms of differentiation have produced a highly complex pattern of cultural diversity, although the existence of this cultural pluralism must not be taken to imply a basic equality of power and influence between the various groups. On the contrary, many of the cultures and their interrelationships are deeply marked by relations of discrimination and subordination stemming from structural inequalities. This is most obvious in the case of social class-based cultures, but the more recent resurgence of Scottish and Welsh nationalism and the 'troubles' in Northern Ireland have underlined that the dynamics of regional and 'sub-national' cultures in Britain also need to be understood in the context of material inequalities and patterns of cultural domination, subordination and conflict. This is a point that becomes even more acutely relevant when considering the relation between black and white cultures in modern Britain.

The cultural diversity of British society has, of course, been much enriched by successive waves of migration into the country. Earlier British history is characterized by settlement and conquest by a wide variety of foreign groups, including the Romans, Vikings and Normans. In the Middle Ages Jews, Flemings and Italians were prominent in the economic life of the country. The nineteenth and early twentieth centuries saw the arrival, of amongst others, the Irish, especially in the 1840s during the great famine (Walvin, 1984, pp. 48–60; Miles, 1982, pp. 120–50) and Eastern European Jews, fleeing from racist persecution in the period from 1880s to the First World War (Walvin, 1984, pp. 61–677).

The Origins and Early Development of the Black Presence in Britain

Many of the features which characterize the formation of the British nation are generally known, although until recently there has been a widespread failure to draw the necessary conclusions about the heterogeneity of cultures in British society and the real complexity of British 'national identity'. There is, however, considerable ignorance about the deep historical roots of the black presence in Britain, using the term black here to refer to African, Afro-Caribbean and South Asian communities.[3] Although references to the presence of black people are available from the Roman period onward, especially in the early sixteenth century, the most famous of the early documented references is the arrival in 1555 of a group of five Africans, brought here by a merchant to be taught English so that they could return to Africa to act as interpreters for British traders. The significance of the date is well underlined by Fryer in his magnificent history of black people in Britain: 'It was the summer of 1555 – before we had potatoes, or tobacco, or tea, and nine years before Shakespeare was born' (1984, p. 5).

It was in the second half of the eighteenth century that the presence of black people in Britain began to give rise to recognizable black communities, with a total black population of probably around 10,000, although some historians have produced even higher estimates. The black people of London were particularly well-organized, meeting together regularly at clubs for musical events and celebrating christenings and weddings.

Scores of black people played a prominent part in British public life in the nineteenth century, often as members of radical organizations and participants in some of the major political events of the times. One of the better known is William Cufay, an important figure in the Chartist movement who was exiled to Tasmania in 1849. Another is Mary Seacole, the Jamaican-born nurse whose extraordinary abilities and dedication in caring for the wounded and sick during the Crimean war won her a reputation, at the time, equal to that of Florence Nightingale but who was soon forgotten, until the more recent attempts at reconstructing the history of the black presence in Britain. The nineteenth century witnessed too a growing Asian presence in Britain, developing from earlier groups of servants, sailors and traders, and several Asians were also prominent in British politics, the most famous being Bombay-born Dadabhai Naoroji who, apart from championing the Indian cause in London, also entered the House of Commons after winning Finsbury Central for the Liberals in 1892 and supported women's suffrage, trade union rights and Home Rule for Ireland (Visram, 1986, pp. 78–92).

Racism, Slavery and Imperial Domination

Black people found themselves on the receiving end of racism in all manner of forms from the beginning of their arrival in Britain. Queen Elizabeth I, her penchant for black servants and entertainers notwithstanding, took the opportunity to 'scapegoat' the black communities, and attempted to expel them without compunction when there appeared to be political advantage in doing so for managing her economic difficulties. Even at this early stage of contact between white and black in Britain, it is clear that she would have been building on already existing racial caricature and prejudice rather than creating an artificial tide of hostility against black people. For one thing, the negative associations of blackness with impurity, evil, misery and dirt had already become established in the English language, partly through the colour symbolism of Christian doctrine (James, 1981; Dabydeen, 1985a). Travellers' tales, especially from traders, had in addition begun to circulate fictitious images of African peoples with bizarre physical features (no mouths or noses!); accounts of the supposed promiscuity and general beastly immorality of African societies mingled with more accurate descriptions of the wealth and refinement to be found on the continent (Walvin, 1973; Jordan, 1974; Husband, 1982).

Britain's growing involvement in the highly profitable slave trade from the middle of the seventeenth century gave further impetus to the spread of racist caricatures and subsequently to the developments of the more systematic racial classifications and doctrines of the eighteenth and nineteenth centuries, which added a pseudo-scientific legitimation to earlier myths (Banton and Harwood, 1975). The significance of these beliefs in creating a commonsense culture of taken-for-granted racism in Britain is difficult to underestimate, although widespread illiteracy may well have protected the subordinate classes from the level of immersion in racism experienced by the upper classes who were fed a growing diet of racist mythology in fiction, newspapers and missionary tracts (Lorimer, 1978; Miles, 1982, pp. 118–19).

However, the significance of the slave trade, and subsequently the establishment of British colonies in the Caribbean and the imperial domination of India, lay not merely in their ideological impact on the growth of racism at home, but also, and some would argue more importantly, in their economic impact on Africa, the Caribbean, India and Britain. Slavery and imperial domination have been crucial social forces in the emergence of a modern world order, characterized by the striking inequalities which provide the essential backdrop to an understanding of the post-Second World War migrations of black communities to Britain, and which continue to generate migratory pressures on peoples from the Third World. To put it slightly differently, it is important to understand that the poverty of the Third World and the wealth of the West are the outcome of an interlinked process in which the rapid and massive growth in Western prosperity has occurred and continues to do so at the expense and underdevelopment of the Third World.

Consider, first, the impact of slavery on Africa. It has to be remembered that prior to the arrival of European traders of any kind the African continent had a large number of flourishing economies and civilizations which had food surpluses, extensive trade networks, cities, complex technologies and craft products, and elaborate political systems (Davidson, 1974, pp. 67–174). Over a period of some three centuries, the European slave trade deprived these societies of anywhere between 15 and 60 million people – exact figures are inevitably difficult to calculate. Some of these died in captivity while being brought to the coast from the African homeland, and even more lost their lives in the brutal conditions on board the slave ships during the notorious Atlantic crossing or 'Middle Passage'. One recent estimate suggests that of the scores of millions that Africa lost, some ten million survived to undertake forced labour and to endure dehumanizing captivity in the Caribbean and African plantations (Curtin, 1969). For some of the societies of West and Central Africa the loss of such large numbers of able-bodied young men and women was catastrophic in several respects. First, there was the simple fact of depopulation which diminished the general size of the market and the level of demand for indigenous manufactures, and no doubt thereby arrested the economic development of the whole region; second, the depopulation affected agriculture, reducing some previous food exporting regions to starvation levels by the nineteenth century; third, African production of cloth, metal-ware and other handicrafts was severely affected, not only by the loss of so many of its producers, but also by the fact that in return the slave traders penetrated the markets of the coast and hinterland with European cotton and manufactured goods; and fourth, as the demand for slaves multiplied and as many African kings and merchants became even more dependent on European trade, war raids for the capture of potential slaves from neighbouring societies became even more frequent, injecting political instability, consuming precious economic resources, and creating a vicious spiral in which rival kingdoms became ever more dependent on the slave trade to acquire the fire arms necessary for capturing more slaves and in turn defending their slaves against slave-hunting raids from neighbouring kingdoms (Rodney, 1972, pp. 104–23; Davidson, 1974, pp. 206–10; Inikoria, 1982).

The ties of dependence that originated during the period of slavery became even more extensive in the period of the formal colonization of Africa, and after dependence too, creating economies substantially dependent on a limited range of cash crops and raw materials required by the metropolitan economies which retained control over major sectors of production, pricing and the flow of profits (Brett, 1973; Leys, 1975; Howard, 1978; Rodney, 1972; Davidson, 1974).

A major destination for African slaves was the Caribbean islands where British settlers had begun to generate a huge demand for forced labour on sugar, cotton, coffee and tobacco plantations. The form of slave production and exploitation and subsequent colonial development of the West Indies has also ensured for most of the islands a fate similar to that of many modern African states: a form of 'peripheral' development in which individual economies are dominated by a very small number of cash crops, often the same as those cultivated under the original system of slavery, the income from which is dependent on world commodity prices subject to considerable fluctuation and open to manipulation by metropolitan powers (Beckford, 1972).

A fuller understanding of the international economic order and modern migratory pressures also requires an analysis, inevitably a very brief one in the present context, of the British impact on the Indian states that came to form one of the centrepieces of the British Empire and the so-called 'jewel in the crown'. British colonial policies offered both food and industrial production. A rapacious British land taxation policy was partly responsible for a series of famines in Bengal in the second half of the eighteenth century, while elsewhere in India the staple foods of the poor such as millet and pulses were displaced by the production for export of grains and commercial crops (Bagchi, 1982, pp. 79, 84, 86). The process of de-industrialization in India under colonial rule began with the deliberate destruction of the cotton manufacturing industry and the opening up of Indian markets to British cotton manufacturers; from a net exporter, India was reduced to a major importer of cotton manufactures, most of these from Britain, and indeed India was forced to become the single largest importer of British cotton manufactures, sometimes taking as much as 40 per cent of British exports. A variety of other industries were also ruined by British policy: silk goods manufacturers, for example, were compelled to restrict themselves to the production of raw silk, while gun making was seriously affected by a restrictive licensing policy and other means (Bagchi, 1982, p. 82). Economic development in India was also thwarted, as in other colonies, by forms of racist discrimination which excluded locals from engaging in entrepreneurial activity. Even the railway system constructed under British rule can now be seen to have had an ambiguous role in relation to the Indian economy, for its benefits have to be set against its encouragement of export-based production and its role in opening up India to the inflow of manufactures, mainly from Britain (Bagchi, 1982, pp. 85–6).

However, while slavery and colonialism contributed to the 'underdevelopment' of Africa, the Caribbean and India – and similar processes were at work in other colonies, often under other colonial powers, although not in the white Dominions of Australia, New Zealand and Canada – Britain obtained significant economic benefits from its imperial domination. To continue with the example of India, it is well documented that there was a massive economic 'drain' which transferred substantial export surpluses of goods and bullion to Britain. For the period 1757–1822 it has been calculated that the aggregate drain was approximately £250 million, while it has been pointed out that for the period from the 1850s to the First World War surpluses from the Indian economy were crucial in allowing Britain to balance its deficits with Europe and the USA (Bagchi, 1982, pp. 81, 88). The Indian economy was made to contribute heavily during the First World War, including a gift payment of £100 million.

The fortunes made out of slavery and the allied triangular trade in sugar, tobacco, cotton and other commodities produced in the Caribbean islands and America also played an important part in British economic development. The enormous growth and prosperity of both Bristol and Liverpool in the eighteenth and nineteenth centuries were almost wholly due to the slave trade. Some indication of the fortunes made out of slaves, sugar and cotton can be obtained from the size of estates of the traders in Bristol and Liverpool and London. In the eighteenth and nineteenth centuries those who had climbed to prosperity on the back of the slave trade were regularly leaving property and assets worth anything between £16,000 and £1 million. They began to acquire for themselves important political positions, especially in Parliament, and the 'West India lobby' became a powerful political force (Fryer, 1984, pp. 40–50). Of course, the fortunes were not spent or invested in the Caribbean. Instead they funded the rapid development of Britain into a major industrial economy and formidable international power. A substantial portion of the surpluses generated out of slave labour and the trade in cotton, sugar and tobacco was channelled into banking operations and undoubtedly provided one important element in the emergence of Britain's banking system, with most of the major banking corporations of today tracing some part of their profits to earlier banks set up with funds derived from the triangular trade (Fryer, 1984, pp. 40ff).

The exact significance for Britain's economic development of the surpluses generated out of the triangular trade and Britain's imperial domination of India and Africa will no doubt continue to be debated. However, although it is very likely that the British industrial revolution would have occurred without these funds, it is difficult to imagine that Britain would have achieved the kind of scale and pace of industrial development that it did without access to these funds and to the markets provided by the colonies. In turn, as pointed out earlier, British domination contributed to the underdevelopment of the colonies by the drain of surpluses, destruction of indigenous industries, and other means. Again, the precise effects of British imperial domination are inevitably matters of dispute (Kumar and Desai, 1983) and it is important to emphasize that the claim here is *not* that the level of present development of the regions of the Third World in question is simply the outcome of their colonial experience, but that it is difficult to understand the nature of this underdevelopment and the continuing exploitation of these countries within the international economic order without a grasp of the imperial impact. In other words, without it one cannot explain why at the present time there is a maldistribution of world wealth and income such that the countries of the Northern hemisphere contain only 25 per cent of the world's population but obtain 80 per cent of the world's income, while the countries of the South contain 75 per cent of the world's population but obtain only 20 per cent of the world's income.

This profound asymmetry in the structure and evolution of the world economic system provides the essential background to the more recent migrations of black communities to Britain in the post-Second World War period, for one of its main effects has been the creation of pools of under- and unemployed workers in circumstances of poverty and restricted opportunity in the Third World, who find themselves having to undergo the painful dislocation entailed by migration and travel thousands of miles in search of work.

The Post-War Migrations to Britain

Poverty and restricted opportunities for employment as a result of under-development are usually regarded as so-called 'push' factors in the explanation of patterns of emigration from less developed countries, and in the case of the Indian sub-continent and the Caribbean Islands have operated powerfully throughout the nineteenth and twentieth centuries in compelling sections of their populations to find work abroad, very often servicing the economic and military needs of the British Empire. The Indian presence in far flung outposts of the Empire, for example, from Malaysia to East Africa, can only be understood in this context, and it is important to note that a tradition of emigration from Jamaica had already developed in the nineteenth century, with 2,000 Jamaicans migrating to build railways in Panama, followed by well over 80,000 who went to work on the first attempt at constructing the Panama Canal in the 1880s.

As the above examples illustrate, migration depends not merely on 'push' factors such as poverty and unemployment, but also the 'pull' factors of employment opportunities in other regions or countries, coupled with favourable political climates and legal frameworks which enable and encourage movement. These 'pull' factors operated with particular force in the post-Second World War period as many of the European countries began to reconstruct and expand their economies at a rapid rate and found themselves suffering acute labour shortages which could only be relieved by the employment of foreign workers.

Labour shortages, especially in iron foundries, textiles, vehicle production, construction and food processing; in service industries, such as transport, catering and hotels; and in the state sector, in the growing National Health Service, provide the essential backdrop to the increase in black immigration to Britain in the post-war period. Moreover, in all these sectors, shortages were particularly experienced in jobs involving unskilled and semi-skilled work, low pay, shift working, unsocial hours and unpleasant working conditions (Smith, 1977, pp. 64–81).

Initially, an attempt was made to fill the labour shortages by allowing over 100,000 Poles to stay on in Britain and by encouraging immigration from other European countries, but soon it was felt necessary to look to other sources of cheap labour, and immigration from the Caribbean and the Indian sub-continent was encouraged. Indeed, organizations such as London Transport, the British Hotel and Restaurants Association and the National Health Service directly recruited workers in the Caribbean, although most black immigration to Britain during this period was not planned and regulated in this manner. Nevertheless, there was a very close relationship between employment opportunities and trends of immigration, especially from the Caribbean; Ceri Peach's research demonstrates that throughout the 1950s periods of economic expansion led to a rise in immigration while periods of recession led to a decline (Peach, 1968).

Immigration to Britain from India and Pakistan has followed a slightly different pattern, with the real increase coming in the early 1960s, and later in response to the threat of the immigration controls that were eventually enshrined in a series of Immigration Acts, beginning with the 1962 Act (Robinson, 1986). Immigration patterns have been substantially affected by the Acts. While before 1962 most immigration into Britain consisted of men, temporarily migrant and unaccompanied by families, the post-1962 period has been one of permanent settlement with workers and their families (Braham, 1985, p. 112). The irony has often been noted that the imposition of legislature controls actually resulted in a dramatic increase in immigration from the Caribbean and the Indian sub-continent, as people attempted to beat the ban, this severed the previously close connections between employment opportunities and migration to Britain.

Black immigration into Britain in the post-war period should be seen in the context of overall patterns of migration in relation to the United Kingdom. That is, it is important to remember that for every year from 1966 to 1983, only two years, 1979 and 1983, were characterized by *net* immigration; in all other years more people left Britain than entered (Gordon and Klug, 1985, p. 22). As a result of the various Immigration Acts there is now virtually no 'primary' immigration from the New Commonwealth; most settlement comes from the close relations and dependents of those already resident in Britain (ibid.).

There are now about 2.4 million black people in the UK, comprising 4.3 per cent of the total population. Over 40 per cent of these are born in the UK (Gordon and Newnham, 1986, p. 6) and a very substantial proportion of Asian and Afro-Caribbean children in British schools are now British born. Thus it makes little sense to refer to 'immigrant' communities; what we now have are minority black British communities, that have already made a very substantial contribution to the growth and prosperity of the British economy.

The Post-War Economic Boom: the Contribution of Migrant Labour

It cannot be doubted that the post-war black migrations have been of considerable economic benefit to Britain, just as the migrations from North Africa, Turkey, Greece and Italy have boosted the economies of Western Europe. Several economic advantages can be identified. First, black workers were recruited for precisely those jobs, usually poorly paid and involving unpleasant working conditions, which the indigenous white working class was able to reject at the time of economic expansion, thus preventing the development of bottlenecks in production and permitting higher levels of capital accumulation. Second, several surveys have concluded that the importation of foreign labour was an important factor in constraining wages and controlling inflation (Castles, Booth and Wallace, 1984, pp. 27–8). Other economic benefits of migrant labour include the recruitment of migrants to particular jobs at lower wages than indigenous workers, partly because job titles and grades could be invented to cover up the fact that job content remained the same, and also because of the threat of repatriation and other forms of intimidation; the enhanced possibilities for the introduction of shiftwork and piece-work, deskilling, and the slower introduction of safety measures; the avoidance of national insurance payments by the recruitment of illegal migrants; and the ability to shed and recruit with relative ease, thus avoiding the costs of labour hoarding (Paine, 1977; Fevre, 1983).

The recruitment of migrant labour has also had what one might refer to as a series of indirect benefits, especially in the earlier phase of immigration, because Britain and the other importing countries were able to avoid the costs involved in actually producing the immigrant labour power, from the birth to the maturation of the workers concerned, and because of the lower demands on the welfare state of economically active, healthy, single, young men and women who nevertheless paid the same rate of taxation as other workers (Gorz, 1970).

Racism, Power and Inequality

The previous discussion has emphasized that black workers were recruited for particular types of jobs in specific sectors of the British economy. This has also produced very distinctive geographical concentrations of black communities in Britain as well as specific locations within the urban conurbations where they have settled. And it is crucial to recognize that widespread racial discrimination has been an important factor in reproducing these patterns of employment and settlement and, as we shall see, also has a significant role in explanations of levels of achievement by black pupils in British schools.

High levels of direct racial discrimination in employment have been repeatedly demonstrated by national and local studies, both at the level of initial recruitment and in relation to promotion. The most recent studies suggest that more than a third of employers discriminate against black applicants for jobs, and that levels of discrimination are the same for Asian and Afro-Caribbean applicants, for men and women, and vary little between job categories, although previous studies have documented higher levels of racial discrimination in relation to unskilled manual jobs (Brown and Gay, 1985; Smith, 1977). The latest report on the employment of black graduates also concludes that they experience greater difficulties than white graduates in obtaining employment; in addition, the jobs obtained appear to be inferior to those gained by white graduates (CRE, 1987).

Given the original form of recruitment of black workers and the operation of racial discrimination it is not surprising that a much larger proportion of black employees are manual workers than the white population in Britain. A recent Policy Studies Institute investigation reveals that while 83 per cent of Afro-Caribbean men and 73 per cent of Asian men are manual workers, the proportion of white male manual workers is 58 per cent. Also, larger proportions of Afro-Caribbean and Asian manual workers are in unskilled and semi-skilled work, and larger proportions than white manual workers engage in shift work. Moreover, while 5 per cent of Afro-Caribbean men and 13 per cent of Asian men are in professional and managerial occupations, 19 per cent of white males are in such jobs; but it is important to note that the 'Asian' category conceals significant material differences, with 25 per cent of African Asians being in the professions and managerial employment, and nearly 70 per cent of Bangladeshi workers occupying semi-skilled or unskilled jobs (Brown, 1984).

For women workers there is a different pattern: 47 per cent of Afro-Caribbean women and 52 per cent of Asian women are manual workers, while 37 per cent of white women are manual workers; and 1 per cent of Afro-Caribbean women as compared to 6 per cent Asian and 7 per cent of white women are in professional and managerial occupations. The largest proportions of all women are either in low-level non-manual work or in semi-skilled manual work (Brown, 1984).

Moreover, as Gordon and Newnham (1986) recently emphasized, 'Black people who do find jobs consistently earn less than white people and are in lower level jobs, even when differences in qualifications, work experience and language difficulties are taken into account. These differences can therefore only be explained by racial discrimination' (p. 16).

Black youth has also experienced high levels of racial discrimination when applying for work or training (Troyna and Smith, 1983). An investigation into the Youth Training Scheme, for example, points out that a much smaller proportion of young black people were obtaining places on the Mode A schemes, which offered better chances of permanent employment, and in larger proportions found themselves placed in Mode B schemes, with worse prospects (CRE, 1984).

Given the well-documented existence of widespread discrimination against black job-seekers it is hardly surprising that levels of unemployment within the black communities are substantially higher than those for white people. In 1984 the unemployment rate for the latter was 10.6 per cent, but it was 23 per cent for Afro-Caribbeans, 34.6 per cent for people of Pakistani and Bangladeshi origin, and 15.2 per cent for those of Indian origin. Black youth suffers particularly high levels of unemployment: in 1983, for example, when unemployment rates for white young people were 30 per cent for men and 23 per cent for women, the levels were 46 per cent and 50 per cent respectively for Afro-Caribbeans and 35 per cent and 47 per cent respectively for Asians. As many as 65 per cent of Afro-Caribbean youth in Handsworth, Birmingham, were unemployed in 1985 (Newnham, 1986).

Although much of the racism that black job-seekers experience is of a direct and overt kind, it is important to recognize that a variety of indirect forms of discrimination also operates against black people in the search for employment, ranging from common employers' practices like recruiting relatives and children of existing workers to the operation of particular conceptions of the 'good' worker which militate against the employment of workers thought to be different in manner or appearance (Lee and Wrench, 1983; Blackburn and Mann, 1979; Jenkins, 1986). Moreover, research in this context has demonstrated the existence of misleading stereotypes of the abilities of black workers, with images that are often contradictory as between employers, and which reflect a willingness to generalize about ethnic characteristic on the basis of very limited experience (Lee and Wrench, 1983; Jenkins, 1986).

The racism which manifests itself in employment is only one, albeit crucial, part of the general experience of discrimination and subordination that black people have had to confront in Britain. In an introductory discussion of the kind undertaken in this chapter it is simply not possible to discuss comprehensively the various forms, spheres and agencies of racism that operate in British society, for example, those deriving from the state's implementation of increasingly tighter immigration controls as well as nationality legislation, or the activities of some sections of the police (Dummett, 1982; Gordon and Klug, 1985; Benyon, 1986). Moreover, there is the extremely serious issue of harrassment and physical violence directed against black communities which in some urban areas takes places on a routine basis with highly distressing and in some cases fatal consequences (CRE, 1979; Home Office, 1981; CRE, 1981; Klug, 1982).

However, the question of housing does require more extended treatment, both for its centrality as a material resource in the pattern of life chances of black people and for its possible role in understanding black pupils' achievements in British schools. Widespread racial discrimination against black people in the availability and allocation of housing has been extensively discussed in a range of surveys and investigations. In the private sector a large number of estate agents, landlords, accommodation agencies and building societies have been found to operate discriminatory registers, refusing to let or sell or lend to black individuals and families, while direct and indirect discrimination in many local authority housing departments has led to black tenants being allocated inferior council housing (Gordon and Newnham, 1986). For all forms of tenure, black families are more likely to be in property that is older, more crowded and in areas that are likely to suffer from a variety of disadvantages in relation to environmental and other conditions (Brown, 1984, pp. 66–127). There is evidence that the high incidence of unemployment amongst black people will make housing conditions, especially overcrowding, worse as young unemployed people are finding it difficult to move out after marriage and set up their own homes (Brah, 1986).

Sociologists have often pointed out that the various processes and outcomes of racial discrimination referred to above have produced a very distinctive location for black people in the British class structure. Rex, for instance, has argued that most black people form an underclass in British society, occupying the most disadvantaged positions in employment, housing and other areas relative even to the white working class (Rex and Tomlinson, 1979), while Miles refers to the formation of a distinct black 'fraction' of the working class (Miles, 1982).

Moreover, this distinctive structural location has been remarkably resilient to change and it is commonly argued that schooling plays a big part in the reproduction over time of the position of black people in British society. More specifically, it has been suggested that the 'underachievement' of black pupils in schools has played a significant part in ensuring that second and third generation young British black people continue to find themselves suffering the 'disadvantages' encountered by their parents and grandparents. However, as we shall see, the issue of black 'underachievement' in schools is rather more complex than might first appear to be the case.

Black 'Underachievement' in British Schools: Some Critical Questions

There has been widespread concern in the last 20 years that children from Afro-Caribbean and Asian communities are underachieving in British schools and, therefore, are at a disadvantage in entering further and higher education, acquiring professional and technical qualifications and in finding employment. Investigations carried out by ILEA in the 1960s tended to bear out this anxiety (Little, 1975), as did a variety of other surveys (for a useful review see Tomlinson, 1983, pp. 27–59). Much of the concern came from the black communities: in 1971 Bernard Coard, a black teacher, published an influential document entitled *How the West Indian Child is made Educationally Sub-Normal in the British School,* while Afro-Caribbean parents and local teachers in Redbridge, frustrated by the relative lack of research and support, conducted their own investigation and in 1978 published disturbing evidence on the school performance of black children. A national inquiry was eventually established, initially under Anthony Rampton and then Lord Swann.

Both the Rampton Report, *West Indian Children in Our Schools* (1981) and the Swann Report, *Education for All* (1985) appeared to confirm earlier anxieties. A survey of six LEAs conducted for Rampton revealed that only 3 per cent of Afro-Caribbean school leavers gained five or more O level passes or CSE grade ones in 1978–79, compared with 18 per cent of Asian pupils, 16 per cent of other school leavers in these LEAs and 21 per cent of all school leavers from state schools. Furthermore, at A level, only 2 per cent of Afro-Caribbean students obtained one or more passes, compared with 13 per cent of Asians, 12 per cent of other school leavers in these LEAs and 13 per cent of all leavers from state schools.

However, the evidence on 'underachievement' that is now available from this and other investigations should be treated with considerable caution. One important issue here concerns the comparability as well as the validity of measures of achievement. For example, although Rampton and Swann rely on public examinations, other studies have based their conclusions on a variety of other measures, including teacher assessments of reading or mathematics; moreover, many of these tests are likely to contain cultural bias or be affected by the fact that they were administered by white teachers or researchers (Hegarty and Lucas, 1979; Bagley, 1975).

It is also questionable whether research undertaken in the 1960s and 1970s is relevant today, for the achievements of Afro-Caribbean and Asian pupils are constantly improving. When the six LEAs in the Rampton survey were studied again for the Swann Report, a larger proportion of Afro-Caribbean pupils were obtaining academic qualifications: the percentage of such pupils obtaining five or more higher grades at O level and CSE and those obtaining one or more passes at A level had doubled in the period from 1979 to 1982.

Most studies focus on school achievement, but this may be misleading because there is evidence to suggest that Afro-Caribbean and Asian students are more likely than white students to stay on in further education and some do manage to obtain academic qualifications that had eluded them at school (Craft and Craft, 1983), while one investigation suggests that young black people in inner city areas had gained better academic qualifications than white youth in the same areas (Roberts, Duggan and Noble, 1983), a finding borne out more generally by some other studies (Brown, 1984).

Blanket comparisons between white, Afro-Caribbean and Asian pupils of the kind prevalent in most investigations can be highly misleading. For example, although Rampton-type surveys suggest that Asian pupils are performing as well as white pupils, there is growing evidence of wide variations in school achievement within the Asian communities: in particular, children of Bangladeshi origin appear to be achieving at much lower levels than other Asian groups (House of Commons Home Affairs Committee, 1986).

Undifferentiated comparisons which ignore parental occupations and educational backgrounds and environmental conditions like housing are also of very limited value. In other words the dimension of *social class* needs to be considered. However, few studies of relative achievement have taken social class into account and this is very unfortunate as there is now overwhelming evidence of a strong relationship between social class and educational achievement (for a recent overview see Mortimore and Blackstone, 1982). It is hardly surprising that the studies that have taken account of the social class background of white and black pupils tend to reveal that the dramatic differences produced by simple comparisons tend to diminish, often considerably (Bagley *et al.*, 1979). Thus, the achievements of white working class pupils – children whose parents are manual workers – are much closer to those of Afro-Caribbean pupils, and it is arguable that the findings of Rampton, Swann and similar investigations can be explained by the fact that a larger proportion of Afro-Caribbeans than whites are working class, and are likely to be earning less and living in worse housing than whites, as documented earlier in this chapter (Brown, 1984; Reeves and Chevannes, 1981). Similarly, the poorer progress of Bangladeshi children could in part be accounted for by the fact that Bangladeshi communities suffer from the effects of poor housing, poverty and high rates of unemployment (House of Commons Home Affairs Committee, 1986). Indeed the continuing higher levels of poverty and unemployment amongst all the black communities are likely to further affect the educational chances of black children, not least because of the implications of material deprivation and unemployment for the physical and mental health of both adults and children (Arnot, 1987; Taylor, 1987; Townsend, 1987; Brah, 1986).

It is also important to differentiate between boys and girls. Some of the few studies that have taken account of gender suggest that Afro-Caribbean girls are achieving higher levels than boys at school level, partly because they are pursuing different strategies, which are necessary in order to survive in the context of high unemployment and low wages for black male workers (Fuller, 1983; see also Riley, 1986; Driver, 1977). Little systematic evidence on Asian girls is available at present, but it is emerging that their educational achievements are continually improving and it is clear that the common image of the docile Asian girl uninterested in education and 'torn' between western and

Asian cultures is a gross stereotype (Brah and Minhas, 1986). In addition, it is likely that unlike other girls they have a more positive attitude towards the sciences (Amos and Parmar, 1981; Fuller, 1983).

Much previous research, in ignoring the social structural features of class and gender, has tended instead to focus on a variety of other factors in explaining supposed patterns of 'underachievement', most of which are now regarded as highly dubious. The five most common explanations have been: Afro-Caribbean family structure; lack of parental interest and support for black pupils; low self-esteem; differences in IQ; and language difficulties. With regard to the first, it was often argued that Afro-Caribbean family and child-rearing patterns harmed the intellectual and educational development of black children, but the misleading assumptions about these patterns and consequences have now been effectively contested (Cross, 1978; Reeves and Chevannes, 1983). Moreover, all recent evidence suggests a high level of interest among both Afro-Caribbean and Asian parents in their children's schooling and records high aspirations for their children's performance (Tomlinson, 1984). The third common explanation suggested that growing up in a white racist society and with few positive black public images created low self-esteem and self-concept in black children which in turn led to poor performance in schools. However, the evidence on this has been vigorously contested, especially by Maureen Stone, who argues that 'no body of research has ever demonstrated unequivocally that the children of the working-class as a whole, poor children or black children in particular, suffer from poor self-image or self-esteem' (Stone, 1981, p. 8), while Milner concludes that there are now higher measures on tests of black self-esteem than in earlier studies because of the rise of black political movements in both the USA and Britain which has fostered positive black self-images and consciousness (Milner, 1983).

The idea that the educational achievements of black students can be explained by genetically inherited lower intellectual ability relative to whites, as measured by IQ tests, has been even more vigorously challenged, with Kamin providing one of the most effective critiques (Kamin, 1977). A recent review of the IQ debate, commissioned by the Swann inquiry, concluded that the largest variation in IQ scores was caused by the social and economic conditions under which children grew up and pointed out, 'If, therefore, we wish to affect the IQ scores of children from ethnic minorities, or indeed their school performance, we might make a start by improving the social and economic circumstances of their families' (Mackintosh and Mascie-Taylor, 1985, p. 148). Finally, with respect to language issues, a variety of debates are still in progress and it is premature to draw firm conclusions; however, there is some evidence to suggest that bilingualism may actually enhance educational performance (Houlton, 1986), that in the case of Afro-Caribbean pupils there may well be 'dialect interference', although it is clear too that some of the problems here may derive from the negative attitudes of teachers towards Creole (Edwards, 1979), and that in the case of some Bangladeshi pupils lack of familiarity with English may be an obstacle to academic achievement (House of Commons Home Affairs Committee, 1986).

Racism, Teacher Expectations and 'Underachievement'

The Rampton Report, in particular, emphasized the role of both intentional and unintentional racism in the school context in depressing the performance of black pupils. The committee of inquiry found that many of the teachers they met held the view that Afro-Caribbean pupils 'inevitably caused difficulties' and were unlikely to achieve in academic terms, although they had high expectations of their potential in sport and the expressive arts (Rampton, 1981, p. 13). Other studies have also shown that many teachers express stereotyped and often contradictory generalizations about black pupils, with some teachers tending to regard Afro-Caribbean pupils as lazy and withdrawn while others thought them to be aggressive and disruptive; a common stereotype of Asian pupils among teachers is that they are passive and industrious but they and their parents are over-ambitious (Brittan, 1976; Giles, 1977; Verma, 1982; Lee and Wrench, 1983; Swann, 1985; Eggleston *et al.*, 1986).

Although research in this area is limited, what there is indicates that teachers' negative conceptions of their black pupils often translate themselves into discriminatory practices in a variety of school contexts. For instance, it is difficult not to see a connection between the prejudiced views of heads and teachers involved in ESN-M referral processes and the overrepresentation of Afro-Caribbean children in special schools (Tomlinson, 1981). Green's research reported in Swann (1985) demonstrated that intolerant teachers gave least time and attention to Afro-Caribbean boys and Asian girls, while a major investigation, *Education for Some*, documented that academically able Afro-Caribbean pupils were finding themselves relegated to lower bands and were being entered for examinations below their abilities, with teachers perceptions playing an important part in the discriminatory misallocation (Eggleston *et al.*, 1986). An inquiry into the referral and suspension of Afro-Caribbean pupils from Birmingham schools recorded that they were almost four times more likely to be suspended from secondary schools as white pupils; even when the main reason for expulsion was common to both white and black pupils, the latter were more likely to be suspended and the inquiry alluded to a considerable level of hostility, mistrust and 'cultural misunderstanding' as between black pupils and white teachers (CRE, 1985; see also Driver, 1979).

Afro-Caribbean and Asian children are indeed painfully aware that many teachers view them negatively and some studies have documented reports of routine racist remarks by teachers (see for example Wright in this volume). It is arguable that teacher expectations and behaviour could be creating an interactive process of low expectations, low achievements and black pupil resistance, although it is important to recognize that teacher expectations do not automatically translate themselves into self-fulfilling prophecies (Short, 1985).

Equally important may be the 'institutional racism' embedded in various taken-for-granted features of the school. For example, the curriculum may ignore or devalue black cultures and achievements and may also ignore racism as a structural phenomenon and as part of the daily experience of black pupils. Assemblies, dress requirements, school meals provision and links with parents may be insensitive to different cultural backgrounds and linguistic diversity. There may be few black teachers in the school and fewer in senior positions. This is why the emphasis in multicultural and anti-racist education is now towards 'whole school policies', involving a fundamental reappraisal of the assumptions, practices and outcomes, intentional and unintentional, of school life (Straker-Welds, 1984; Arora and Duncan, 1986).

Thus, on closer inspection, the issue of the 'underachievement' of black pupils in British schools turns out to be rather complex. Given the inconclusive nature of the evidence on patterns of performance and the negative connotations of 'underachievement' it is time to drop the term and refer instead to relative levels of *achievement*. It should also be clear that future investigations and policies must take account of class and gender and be sensitive to possible differences between minority black communities.

Conclusion

Indeed one of the major conclusions to be drawn from the historical and sociological discussion in this chapter is that a proper analysis of the operation of 'race' as an element in British society and education requires an understanding of its interrelationship with the structured and cultural divisions which derive from class and gender relations, in the context of an understanding of Britain's past imperial domination and its continuing legacies.

However, it is also important to appreciate that the dynamics of 'race' and racism as dimensions of British society and education are now significantly affected by the 'racialization' of British politics and the accelerated decline of the British economy in the context of recession and very specific state policies, some of which bear down particularly hard on black youth. The 'racialization' of British politics throughout the last 20 years has ensured that most areas of public debate – law and order, the welfare state, unemployment, youth, education, the inner cities, the family – now have a racial dimension and often one in which black communities, but especially black youth, appear as threats in a wider demonology of scroungers, shirkers, muggers, drug pushers, school failures and inadequate parents (Hall *et al.*, 1978; CCCS, 1982). The decline of British manufacturing industry has had a devastating impact on the inner cities where such a large proportion of the black population live and this has been exacerbated by racial discrimination by employers to yield high levels of black youth unemployment (Martin and Rowthorn, 1986; Newnham, 1986). Insensitive and often racist policing have fused with inner urban decay to create a climate of both despair and rebellion in which black (and white) youth's sense of injustice has on several occasions provoked urban revolt (Benyon, 1984; West Midlands County Council, 1986; Gifford, 1986).

Schools may feel powerless to alter a situation in which wider economic and political forces have such a crucial influence. But to ignore these issues would be a serious abnegation of their responsibility in combating racism and giving black communities a fair opportunity to make their rightful contribution and participate on equal democratic terms as citizens. Some schools and LEAs have already begun to construct multicultural and anti-racist policies; it is up to the majority of institutions that appear not to have grasped the urgency of the issues to follow their lead.

Notes

1 The term 'race' is set in quotation marks throughout this chapter to denote and emphasize the fact that, scientifically speaking, separate 'races' cannot be said to exist. See the review of recent scientific thinking on this subject in Banton and Harwood (1975).
2 It must be remembered, however, that the Afro-Caribbean and Asian communities have been attempting to bring many of these issues to public notice for much longer.
3 The term 'black' is used not to dissolve the real cultural differences between these groups but in line with common usage to emphasize their common experience of racism in British society.

References

AMOS, V. and PARMAR, P. (1981) 'Resistances and Responses: The Experiences of Black Girls in Britain', in McROBBIE, A. and McCABE, T. (eds) *Feminism For Girls*, Hutchinson, London.

ARNOTT, H. (1987) 'Second-Class Citizens', in WALKER, A. and WALKER, C. (eds) *The Growing Divide: A Social Audit 1979–1987*, Child Poverty Action Group, London.

ARORA, R. and DUNCAN, C. (eds) (1986) *Multicultural Education: Towards Good Practice*, Routledge and Kegan Paul, London.

BAGCHI, A. K. (1982) *The Political Economy of Underdevelopment*, Cambridge University Press, Cambridge.

BAGLEY, C. (1975) 'On the Intellectual Equality of Races', in VERMA, G. and BAGLEY, C. (eds) *Race and Education Across Cultures*, Heinemann, London.

BAGLEY, C., BART, M., and WONG, J. (1979) 'Antecedents of Scholastic Success in West Indian Ten Year Olds in London', in VERMA, G. and BAGLEY, C. (eds) *Race, Education and Identity*, Macmillan, London.

BECKFORD, G. (1972) *Persistent Poverty: Underdevelopment in Plantation Economies in the Third World*, Oxford University Press, Oxford.

BANTON, M. and HARWOOD, J. (1975) *The Race Concept*, David and Charles, Newton Abbot.

BENYON, J. (ed.) (1984) *Scarman and After*, Pergamon, Oxford.

BENYON, J. (1986) *Race and Policing: A Tale of Failure*, Centre for Research in Ethnic Relations, University of Warwick.

BLACKBURN, R. and MANN, M. (1979) *The Working Class in the Labour Market*, Macmillan, London.

BRAH, A. (1986) 'Unemployment and Racism: Asian Youth on the Dole', in ALLEN, S. *et al.* (eds) *The Experience of Unemployment*, Macmillan, London.

BRAH, A. and MINHAS, R. (1986) 'Structural Racism or Cultural Difference: Schooling For Asian Girls', in WEINER, G. (ed.) *Just a Bunch of Girls*, Open University Press, Milton Keynes.

BRAHAM, P. (1985) 'Migration and Settlement in Britain', Unit 2 in *Migration and Settlement*, Open University Press, Milton Keynes.

BRETT, E. A. (1973) *Colonialism and Underdevelopment in East Africa*, Heinemann, London.

BRITTAN, E. (1976) 'Multiracial Education 2. Teacher Opinion on Aspects of School Life', *Educational Research*, Vol. 18, Nos 2, 3, pp. 96–107, 182–92.

BROWN, C. (1984) *Black and White Britain*, Heinemann, London.

BROWN, C. and GAY, P. (1985) *Racial Discrimination: 17 Years after the Act*, Policy Studies Institute, London.

CCCS (CENTRE FOR CONTEMPORARY CULTURAL STUDIES) (1982) *The Empire Strikes Back. Race and Racism in 70s Britain*, Hutchinson, London.

CASTLES, F., BOOTH, H. and WALLACE, T. (1984) *Here for Good: Western Europe's New Ethnic Minorities*, Pluto Press, London.

CRAFT, M. and CRAFT, A. (1983) 'The Participation of Ethnic Minority Pupils in Further and Higher Education', *Educational Research*, Vol. 25, No. 1, pp. 10–19.

CRE (COMMISSION FOR RACIAL EQUALITY) (1979) *Brick Lane and Beyond: Racial Strife and Violence in Tower Hamlets*, Commission for Racial Equality, London.

CRE (1981) *Racial Harassment on Local Authority Housing Estates*, Commission for Racial Equality, London.

CRE (1984) *Racial Equality and the Youth Training Scheme*, Commission for Racial Equality, London.

CRE (1981) *Birmingham Local Education Authority and Schools. Referral and Suspension of Pupils*, Commission for Racial Equality, London.

CRE (1987) *Employment of Graduates from Ethnic Minorities*, Commission for Racial Equality, London.

CROSS, M. (1978) 'West Indians and the Problem of Metropolitan Majority', in DAY, M. and MARSLAND, D. (eds) *Black Kids, White Kids, What Hope?*, National Youth Bureau, Leicester.

CURTIN, P. D. (1986) *The Atlantic Slave Trade*, University of Wisconsin Press, Madison.

DABYDEEN, D. (ed.) (1985a) *The Black Presence in English Literature*, Manchester University Press, Manchester.

DABYDEEN, D. (1985b) *Hogarth's Blacks: Images of Blacks in Eighteenth Century English Art*, Dangaroo Press, Mundelstrup.

DAVIDSON, B. (1974) *Africa in History*, Paladin Books, London.

DRIVER, G. (1977) *Beyond Underachievement*, Commission for Racial Equality, London.

DRIVER, G. (1979) 'Classroom Stress and School Achievement: West Indian Adolescents and their Teachers', in KHAN V. S. (ed.) *Minority Families in Britain*, Macmillan, London.

DUMMETT, A. (1982) 'The Role of Government in Britain's Racial Crisis', in HUSBAND, C. (ed. 'Race' in Britain, Hutchinson, London.

EDWARDS, V. (1979) The West Indian Language Issue in Schools, Routledge and Kegan Paul, London.

EGGLESTON, J., DUNN, D., ANJAW, M. and WRIGHT, C. (1986) Education for Some. The Educational and Vocational Experiences of 15–18 year-old Members of Minority Ethnic Groups, Trentham Books, Trentham.

FEVRE, R. (1983) Cheap Labour and Racial Discrimination, Gower, Aldershot.

FRYER, P. (1984) Staying Power: The History of Black People in Britain, Pluto Press, London.

FULLER, M. (1983) 'Qualified Criticism, Critical Qualifications', in BARTON, L. and WALKER, S. (eds) Race, Class and Education, Croom Helm, London.

GIFFORD, LORD (1986) The Broadwater Farm Inquiry, London.

GILES, R. (1977) The West Indian Experience in British Schools, Heinemann, London.

GLC (GREATER LONDON COUNCIL) (1986) A History of the Black Presence in London, GLC, London.

GORDON, P. and KLUG, F. (1985) British Immigration Control, Runnymede Trust, London.

GORDON, P. and NEWNHAM, F. (1986) Different Worlds: Racism and Discrimination in Britain, Runnymede Trust, London.

GORZ, A. (1970) 'The Role of Immigrant Labour', New Left Review, 61.

HALL, S., CRITCHER, C., JEFFERSON, T., CLARKE, J. and ROBERTS, B. (1978) Policing the Crisis, Macmillan, London.

HEGARTY, S. and LUCAS, F. (1979) Able to Learn: The Pursuit of Culture – Fair Assessment, NFER, Slough.

HOME OFFICE (1981) Racial Attacks: Report of a Home Office Study, HMSO, London.

HOULTON, D. (1986) Cultural Diversity and the Primary School, Batsford, London.

HOUSE OF COMMONS HOME AFFAIRS COMMITTEE (1986) Bangladeshis in Britain 3 vols, HMSO, London.

HOWARD, R. (1978) Colonialism and Underdevelopment in Ghana, Croom Helm, London.

HUSBAND, C. (ed.) (1982) 'Race' in Britain: Continuity and Change, Hutchinson, London.

INIKORIA, J. E. (ed.) (1984) Forced Migration, Hutchinson, London.

JAMES, A. (1981) '"Black": an inquiry into the pejorative associations of an English word', New Community Vol. 9, No. 1, pp. 19–30.

JENKINS, R. (1986) Racism and Recruitment, Cambridge University Press, Cambridge.

JORDAN, W. D. (1974) The White Man's Burden, Oxford University Press, Oxford.

KAMIN, L. J. (1977) The Science and Politics of IQ, Penguin Books, Harmondsworth.

KLUG, F. (1982) Racist Attacks, Runnymede Trust, London.

KUMAR, D. and DESAI, M. (eds) (1983) The Cambridge Economic History of India, Vol. 2 1750–1970, Cambridge University Press, Cambridge.

LEE, G. and WRENCH, J. (1983) Skill Seekers: Black Youth, Apprenticeships and Disadvantage, National Youth Bureau, Leicester.

LEYS, C. (1975) Underdevelopment in Kenya, Heinemann, London.

LITTLE, A. (1975) 'The Educational Achievement of Ethnic Minority Children in London Schools', in VERMA, G. K. and BAGLEY, C. (eds) Race and Education Across Cultures, Heinemann, London.

261

LORIMER, D. A. (1978) *Colour, Class and the Victorians*, Leicester University Press, Leicester.

MACKINTOSH, N. J. and MASCIR-TAYLOR, C. G. (1985) 'The IQ Question', in Swann, *Education for All*, pp. 126–63.

MARTIN, R. and ROWTHORN, B. (eds) (1986) *The Geography of De-Industrialisation*, Macmillan, London.

MILES, R. (1982) *Racism and Migrant Labour*, Routledge and Kegan Paul, London.

MILNER, D. (1983) *Children and Race: Ten Years On*, Ward Lock, London.

MORTIMORE, J. AND BLACKSTONE, T. (1982) *Disadvantage and Education*, Heinemann, London

NEWNHAM, A. (1986) *Employment, Unemployment and Black People*, Runnymede Trust, London.

PAINE, S. (1977) 'The Changing Role of Migrant Workers in the Advanced Capitalist Economies of Western Europe', in GRIFFITHS, R. (ed.), *Government, Business and Labour in European Capitalism*, Europotentials Press, London.

PEACH, C. (1968) *West Indian Migration to Britain*, Oxford University Press, Oxford.

THE RAMPTON REPORT (1981) *West Indian Children in Our Schools*, HMSO, London.

REEVES, F. and CHEVANNES, M. (1981) 'The Underachievement of Rampton', *Multi-Racial Education*, Vol. 10, No. 1, pp. 35–42.

REEVES, F. and CHEVANNES, M. (1983) 'The Ideological Construction of Black Under-achievement', *Multiracial Education*, Vol. 12, No. 1, pp. 22–41.

REX, J. and TOMLINSON, S. (1979) *Colonial Immigrants in British Society*, Routledge and Kegan Paul, London.

RILEY, K. (1985) 'Black Girls Speak for Themselves', in WEINER, G. (ed.) *Just a Bunch of Girls*, Open University Press, Milton Keynes.

ROBERTS, K., DUGGAN, J., and NOBLE, M. (1983) 'Racial Disadvantage in Youth Labour Markets' in L. BARTON and S. WALKER (eds) *Race, Class and Education*, Croom Helm, London.

ROBINSON, V. (1986) *Transients, Settlers and Refugees: Asians in Britain*, Oxford University Press, Oxford.

RODNEY, W. (1972) *How Europe Underdeveloped Africa*, Bogle–L'Overture Publications, London.

SHORT, G. (1985) 'Teacher Expectation and West Indian Underachievement', *Educational Research*, Vol. 27, No. 2, pp. 95–101.

SMITH, D. (1976) *Racial Disadvantage in Britain*, Penguin Books, Harmondsworth.

STONE, M. (1981) *The Education of the Black Child in Britain*, Fontana, London.

STRAKER-WELDS, M. (ed.) (1984) *Education for a Multicultural Society. Case Studies in ILEA Schools*, Bell and Hyman, London.

THE SWANN REPORT (1985) *Education for All*, HMSO, London.

TAYLOR, D. (1987) 'Living with Unemployment', in WALKER, A., and WALKER, C. (eds) *The Growing Divide: A Social Audit 1979–1987*, Child Poverty Action Group, London.

TOMLINSON, S. (1981) *Educational Subnormality: A Study in Decision Making*, Routledge and Kegan Paul, London.

TOMLINSON, S. (1983) *Ethnic Minorities in British Schools*, Heinemann, London.

TOWNSEND, P. (1987) 'Poor Health', in WALKER, A. and WALKER, C. (eds) *The Growing Divide: A Social Audit 1979–1987*, Child Poverty Action Group, London.

VERMA, G. (1982) 'The Problems of Vocational Adaptation of "Asian" Adolescents in Britain: Some Theoretical and Methodological Issues', in VERMA, G. and BAGLY, C.

(eds) *Self Concept, Achievement and Multicultural Education*, Macmillan, London.

VISRAM, R. (1986) *Ayahs, Lascars and Princes: The Story of Indians in Britain 1700–1947*, Pluto Press, London.

WALVIN, J. (1973) *Black and White: The Negro and English Society 1555–1945*, Allen Lane, London.

WALVIN, J. (1984) *Passage to Britain*, Penguin Books, Harmondsworth.

WEST MIDLANDS COUNTY COUNCIL (1986) *A Different Reality*.

20

Education, Employment and Recruitment

Robert Moore

This chapter will consider the way in which educational qualifications are *actually* used in the labour market in the recruitment of young workers. In general, recent studies have found that the use of qualifications varies significantly between different sectors of the labour market and is subject to considerable regional variation. Non-educational criteria almost invariably have priority in recruitment over educational ones and employers tend to have only the vaguest notions as to what particular qualifications entail or imply.

These factors are differentiated by sex and race and also work to reproduce gender and racial differentiation in employment (and unemployment). The findings to be considered here (and the broader body of research of which they are typical) suggest that the link between education and occupation is much more tenuous than is often supposed and call into question many of the assumptions currently held about employers' attitudes to young workers and to educational standards. This is particularly significant given the place of these assumptions within the occupationalist rhetoric of the present assault upon education and liberal education in particular.

Qualifications and Recruitment

A number of illuminating pieces of research have been published recently which look in detail at the way in which qualifications are used by employers in the process of the recruitment of young workers. Cumin, for instance, traces a group of school leavers from school, through the labour market and into employment. He notes a sharp contrast between the expectations of pupils, parents and teachers about the importance of qualifications and their real significance (Cumin, 1983). A study by Jones (Jones, 1983) provides detailed evidence on the almost complete lack of communication between examination boards and employers and on the uninformed and arbitrary way in which employers use qualifications. Ashton *et al.* (1982, 1986), in an extremely thorough investigation of the relative positions of young workers in contrasting local labour markets, define a number of different recruitment strategies in which qualifications vary in significance, are used in different ways and are almost invariably of secondary importance relative to other factors. It is precisely the subordinate role of qualifications which is the striking feature of this type of detailed work.

(a) Expectations and practice

The study by Cumin follows a group of school leavers from their college in Leicestershire out into 'the world of work'. The purpose was to discover precisely how important qualifications were in determining their occupational chances. The study begins by noting the high expectations that the pupils, their parents and their teachers had in this regard. Fifty-seven per cent of pupils and 62 per cent of parents thought that qualifications would be *very important*, and 98 per cent and 96 per cent respectively thought they would be either *very* or *fairly* important. After examining what happened in practice, Cumin concludes that these expectations were not 'based upon actuality' (p. 58).

The study found that 56 per cent of the jobs taken by the young people in fact had no formal educational requirements attached to them. In the end, only 15 per cent of the school leavers considered that their qualifications had been essential to their getting jobs. Cumin makes the significant point that employers appoint school leavers to posts *before* examination results are known in any case. It is very rare for young people recruited on that basis to be sacked if they subsequently fail to pass the exam or gain a certain grade. Obviously the simple non-availability of the result must severely limit the significance that employers can place on exam-passing *per se*.

However, the limitations upon examinations in shaping recruitment practices are not restricted to the effects of this particular practical exigency. Employers in the main seem to see little direct relevance of education to specific job requirements. This would seem to be the general conclusion of research in this area, and Cumin's conclusion that:

> In terms of the overall needs employers had of young people, it was clear that non-academic criteria, attitudes to work and personal characteristics, and basic skills, essentially those of reading, writing and arithmetic, were far more important to employers than academic qualifications. (ibid, p. 57)

is one widely echoed elsewhere.

(b) Employers and qualifications

The study by Jones (op. cit.) provides information on the use of qualifications by employers in three English regions (London and the South East, the West Midlands, and Yorkshire and Humberside) and also includes some comparisons with other European countries. Fifteen hundred establishments were surveyed, ranging in size from employing less than 25 to more than 500, and spanning 10 sectors of the Revised Standard Classification of Industry. Five categories of workers were defined: *professional and managerial, technician, clerical and sales, skilled manual* and *operatives*. These categories were represented to varying degrees in the various sectors. Employers were found to use five main selection devices: *application forms, academic qualifications, school references, performance in aptitude tests,* and *interviews*.

The relative importance of academic qualifications varied between categories, being more significant for non-manual than for manual workers. In all cases the interview was the most important device with qualifications coming second for non-manuals. The level of qualifications varied according to the level of employment. There was particular emphasis upon English and Maths. Jones concludes her detailed investigation by saying that:

> These figures suggest that employers, at least with the present education system, largely feel that basic knowledge in a few subjects is all that they find useful for their purpose. Case study experience further suggests that even this use is questionable. Observation ... suggest(s) that employers' expectations of the subject content and skills are often very wide of the mark. This appears especially true of Maths. Physics and English, the most frequently required subjects. (ibid, p. 22)

The report shows that employers tend to have only extremely vague notions as to what examinations in particular subjects actually involve. There was virtually *no* direct communication between employers and examination boards. Out of 22 GCE and CSE examination boards, only 8 (all CSE) gave out information specific to employers and only 9 (8 CSE and 1 GCE) actively disseminated information to employers. At the same time, only 11 boards (8 CSE and 3 GCE) reported ever having received requests for information *from* employers. Only 3 boards (1 CSE and 2 GCE) had an interest in researching employers' views.

Given this, it is probably not surprising that even where qualifications were stipulated, the requirement was not rigidly enforced. Jones found that although a reasonably high number of employers thought that qualifications were desirable, less than half thought them to be essential. Even where they did, there was a fair degree of flexibility. Interestingly, *'very few'* employers saw examinations as essential for *specific jobs* (ibid., p. 23). Rather, they were demanded most rigorously where *further training* involved FE or professional courses where the educational qualification was an *entry requirement*. In other words, the educational qualification was related to further *educational* needs, not to the needs of jobs as such. Jones concludes that 'These results support the ... assertion that desirability of certain qualifications is not closely related to actual job performance.' (loc. cit.)

(c) Recruitment strategies

The findings of Jones's work are very much in line with those of Ashton *et al.* (1983). Only half of the employers interviewed in Leicester, Sunderland and St Albans thought that qualifications were useful as *'yardsticks of a candidate's ability'* (ibid., p. 55). Twenty-three per cent of them thought that *'they could possibly be of some use with certain reservations'* and 27 per cent of them considered them to be of no use at all. Forty-five per cent of the first group (i.e. 45 per cent of 50 per cent) thought them to be a true measure of ability and a third saw them as useful indicators of attitude. In the second group, 69 per cent thought that other factors were more important than qualifications, and in the third, 75 per cent ignored them altogether or considered them meaningless.

Ashton *et al.* found that employers adopt a range of *recruitment strategies* in which educational qualifications are combined with other attributes to varying degrees. The most common approach was that where *'the balance between academic and non-academic criteria shifts in favour of the non-academic'* (ibid., p. 52). It is important to note that the educational qualifications are not being treated as an *index* of non-educational attributes (e.g. docility). The other factors which employers take into account (*self-presentation, attitude to work, interest in the job, family background*) are seen as *independent* from education.

The authors define *five* recruitment strategies which can be summarized as follows:

1 educational qualifications perform a *determinative* function. Here the qualification is the most important criterion in recruitment although other factors might be considered in the interview stage, though in a subordinate role;

2 educational qualifications perform a *screening* function. Qualifications are used to pre-select the sample of candidates. A minimum level is set and those at or above that level are then selected by *non-academic* criteria. Qualifications above the minimum bestow no advantage;

3 educational qualifications perform a *focusing* function. They will be waived if a candidate possesses the appropriate non-academic criteria. This is the point at which non-academic come to take precedence over academic criteria.

4 educational qualifications are *functionless*. Recruitment is based on personality or physical attributes which are seen as having *nothing* to do with education;

5 educational qualifications have a *negative* function. Qualifications *disqualify* the person from being considered (e.g. on the grounds that they will become easily bored or might become a trouble maker). It is, of course, being assumed here that there is some kind of relationship between the qualification level and the nature of the work.

In this study it was the *third strategy* which was most commonly used (53 per cent) followed by the fourth (39 per cent). Hence non-academic criteria have a clear priority over the academic.

The use of strategies varied according to the occupational category:
at the *professional and managerial* level, 82 per cent of employers used strategy 2, and at the *technician* level it was used by 74 per cent. Strategy 3 was that

267

most used for *clerical and sales* (57 per cent) and for *skilled manual* (60 per cent). At the *operative* level, strategy four is most common (see ibid., Table 49).

The use of different strategies relates to the size of the firm. In general, larger firms tended to make more use of qualifications (possibly reflecting the existence of a trained personnel staff who themselves owe their position to qualifications). More reliance was placed upon O than A levels. The study found that 72 per cent of employers in the top size band saw qualifications as useful as against only 30 per cent in the smallest, where 49 per cent saw them as not useful compared with only 12 per cent in the largest (see ibid., Tables 46, 48 and 50).

The size of the establishment could reasonably be expected to affect the number of young people being exposed to the different recruitment strategies (although the relative numbers of small employers would also have to be borne in mind). However, it was found that many large companies took on very few young people (20 per cent of those employing above 1,000 recruited fewer than ten per year (ibid., p. 47)). Hence, 'the relationship between the size of the employing unit and the number of young people recruited each year was not as close as might have been expected' (ibid., p. 47).

Ashton *et al.*'s extremely detailed studies indicate the dangers of generalizing about the education/production relationship. Their more recent work emphasizes the very considerable regional variations which reflect relative unemployment rates. The complex variations and interactions between factors such as recruitment strategies, size of firm, sector, area and local industry mix introduce a wide range of contingencies into the situation which are further complicated by gender and race.

Employers, Educational Standards and Young Workers

A central plank of the current attack upon education and the teaching profession (and one which has grown since Callaghan's Great Debate speech) is that of employers' dissatisfaction with educational standards and with the quality of young workers. This alleged 'failure' on the part of teachers is a main feature of the rhetoric which legitimates the changes which are being imposed. Consequently it is important to critically examine its basis in reality.

The type of detailed empirical research reviewed above suggests that scepticism is to be strongly recommended. Employers, in fact, appear to be not only ill-informed about education but relatively arbitrary in the uses to which they put it. Given the crucial role that the Manpower Services Commission has played in the undermining of education and the construction of its current occupationalist surrogate, its contribution to this debate deserves close scrutiny. It is ironic that the (MSC's) Holland Report was published in the same year (1977) as the Shirley Williams' Green Paper on

Table 20.1 *Employers' evaluations of young workers on 'essential attributes' compared to adults (Holland report)*

| Attribute | % of employers agreeing 'essential' | No | % of employers saying that young people are: | | | Rating (B–W) |
			Different Yes	Better	Worse	
1 willingness/ attitude to work	81	46	54	11	43	−32
2 good level of general fitness	47	70	30	24	6	+18
3 appearance/ tidiness	39	60	40	6	34	−28
4 specific physical attributes	36	72	28	22	6	+16
5 basic 3Rs	21	46	54	10	44	−34
6 mature/stable	20	40	60	5	55	−50
7 ability to communicate	18	53	47	11	36	−25
8 willingness to join union	16	89	11	8	3	+5
9 good level of numeracy	13	50	50	8	42	−34
10 past experience	7	39	61	2	59	−57
11 good written English/literate	6	40	60	9	51	−42
12 existing union membership	4	85	15	4	11	−7
13 specific educational qualifications	2	49	51	28	23	+5

education which followed on from 'The Great Debate'. The Holland Report looked explicitly at the issue of employers' dissatisfaction with young workers and presented its information in such a way as to support the idea of education's failure in this area. I have suggested elsewhere[1] that their presentation of their evidence benefits from closer examination.

The Report discusses employers' evaluations of young workers relative to older ones in terms of thirteen 'essential attributes'. In the case of unskilled/ semi-skilled young workers (i.e. the YOP/YTS target group), 81 per cent of the employers listed *'willingness/attitude to work'* as the most important attribute. The second most popular one was *'good level of general fitness'*, mentioned by 47 per cent, followed by *'appearance/tidiness'* (39 per cent) and *'specific physical attributes'* (36 per cent). *The first specifically educational attribute ('basic 3Rs')* appears fifth, being mentioned by only 21 per cent of employers. The rest of the thirteen essential attributes range between a mention by 20 per cent for *'mature/stable'* down to a mere 2 per cent for *'specific educational qualifications'*(!)

The discussion which follows in the Report for young people *in general* is based mainly on a *rating* which is established by subtracting the number of employers who think that young people are *worse* than older workers from those who think that they are *better* on each of these attributes. On this basis they come out very badly with *negative* marks on nine out of the thirteen attributes. However, inspection shows that there are in fact three employer positions: *(1) young people are no different/noncomparable*, or, if they are different, are *(2) better* or *(3) worse*. The *rating* on which young people do so badly is derived *only from that fraction of employers who say they are different.*

It is a simple arithmetical exercise to reconstitute the original figures. When this is done, a rather different picture emerges. In fact, young people come out worse *overall* on only *three* out of the thirteen attributes relative to older workers. Two of these are directly *age related* – 'past experience' (*worse: 59 per cent*), and 'mature/stable' (*worse: 55 per cent*). The third is 'good written English/literate' (*worse: 51 per cent*).

Ironically, the attribute on which young people do best relative to older workers is *specific educational qualifications* which actually comes *bottom* of the employers' list of essential attributes, being mentioned by only 2 per cent of employers! In fact, employers give *all* the educational attributes a low priority.

Table 20.2 *Position of educational 'essential attributes'*

Attribute	Position out of 13	Essential %	Worse %
basic 3Rs	5	21	24
good level of numeracy	9	13	21
good written English/literate	11	6	51
specific educational qualification	13	2	12

(constructed from *The Holland Report*, Tables 7:1 and 7:2)

The data corresponds precisely to the situation described by Ashton *et al*'s recruitment strategies with *non-educational* criteria taking priority over educational ones. The top four attributes are each of this type. If we take the attribute which employers most often saw as 'essential', *willingness/attitude to work* (mentioned by 81 per cent), we see that the MSC's poor rating of -32 in fact reflects a negative judgement by less than half of employers (53 per cent said that young workers are *different* in this respect and 43 per cent of those said they were *worse*). In fact, this represents the precise *opposite* of the MSC position – *the majority of employers think that young workers are either no different or better!* Interestingly this figure is consistent with that most often encountered in the literature in this area where usually between 70 per cent to 80 per cent of employers are favourable to young workers. Ashton *et al.*, for instance, say that:

> Despite the many grumbles and adverse comments, 70 per cent of all employers interviewed claimed to have been satisfied with the standard of work of young people taken on by them in the previous two years, and only 14 per cent expressed dissatisfaction. Indeed, of the respondents in the 60 establishments employing over 5,000 workers, all but one expressed satisfaction. (Ashton *et al.*, 1983, p. 56)

The probable significance of all this is that it is mistaken to attempt to *generalize* about employers' attitudes to young workers. Clearly many *are* dissatisfied and feel that they *can* point to declining standards (e.g. in the numeracy of engineering apprentices), but this situation is more likely to reflect changing social patterns of recruitment rather than a real decline in 'educational standards'. Paradoxically it could result from an actual general *improvement* in standards combined with expanding opportunities in further and higher education. The 'type of lad' who once became an apprentice now goes on to take an engineering degree and is replaced at that qualification level by a different category of young person. In earlier times the former had been *underachieving* educationally whereas the latter are now near the *peak* of their attainment level. If these complex changes over time in the relationship between general improvements in attainment, social bases of recruitment and expanded further educational opportunities are not taken into account, the general improvement can appear from the *fixed position* of an employer as a *decline* in standards.

Work experience

As the examination of the Holland Report data indicates, the problem which young people have in the labour market reflects the age-related issue of *lack of experience*. It is this rather than defective education that disadvantages them. An examination by Richards (1982) of the factors employed in the recruitment of apprentices in the East Midlands illustrates some of the problems in this area, especially in relation to the current occupationalist assertion that young people will benefit from a more 'vocational' education in order to counteract their lack of experience.

Richards asked employers about the factors they took into account when recruiting apprentices. The percentages of employers mentioning the following were: *evening classes* (92 per cent), *holiday jobs* (85 per cent), *Saturday jobs* (84 per cent), *hobbies and interests* (77 per cent), *paper rounds* (73 per cent), *membership of clubs and social societies* (68 per cent), *school work experience schemes* (52 per cent) (Richards, 1982, Table B, p. 7).

The poor showing of school work experience is striking. The reasons for this are illuminating. The contrast between work experience schemes and *informal* work experience lies in the fact that the latter is taken by employers as evidence of *initiative, an interest in earning money* and *the ability to sustain regular work discipline (getting up early, etc.)*. Paper rounds in particular were seen as significant in these respects. Work experience, on the other hand, was seen by employers as part of *the school's* discipline and as giving little information about the pupil as an individual. Richards says that:

> The features that impressed these employers about the spare/part-time jobs of young people applying for apprenticeships in their firms were mainly elements which were absent in WE schemes. WE schemes did not involve the 'initiative' involved in going out and finding your own part-time job. This was all done by the school following DES and LEA guidelines. The element of 'reliability' (getting up early consistently for a substantial period of time etc.) was also absent. (ibid., p. 9)

Where employers *did* see value in work experience schemes, it had to do with information about *career choices*. They felt that such schemes allowed young people to have direct experience of engineering rather than relying purely upon second-hand information (from teachers or the media). If they then still chose to seek engineering jobs, this could be seen as evidence of *commitment*. This is a central feature of the employers' view.

Richards found a preoccupation amongst employers with the *image* of engineering. They were very concerned that pupils, and the 'bright' ones in particular, should be given a *positive* view of the industry and be attracted to it. This was the main value they attributed to school work experience rather than seeing it in any direct sense as *preparation* for engineering work. Richards's conclusion is that:

> According to these employers it was teachers who needed WE more than pupils, so that they could get a picture of what engineering was really like (as opposed to media misrepresentations – strikes, redundancies, etc.) and so put across a 'good image' of engineering, hopefully attracting the 'brighter pupils' into the industry. (ibid., p. 11)

As far as the actual *content* of the education was concerned, the employers wanted no more than a solid, old fashioned grounding in 'the basics' and that 'bright pupils' should be positively encouraged to seek jobs in the industrial sector rather than in the academic world or public services. The major problem was seen to be the *hostility of teachers* towards industrial and commercial values and the way in which this deflected 'bright', *traditionally educated* pupils away from industry. It was not *direct preparation* for production that the schools should be providing but *image building*. Furthermore, this exercise should be aimed at the 'bright' pupils. Richards says that:

> Some writers went on to argue that attracting high ability youngsters into manufacturing industry was one of the conditions for a regeneration of the British economy. Employers making these connections between the 'ignor-

ance' of 'our brightest children', WE, the entry of these youngsters into manufacturing industry and the rejuvenation of British capitalism were clearly *not interested in the notion that WE was essentially concerned with ROSLA or the 'average and below average ability ranges'* (ibid., p. 16, my emphasis).

We can say that the problem being defined here is not so much that the pupils are getting *the wrong education* (though they might be getting the wrong teachers) as that industry is getting the *wrong pupils!* The 'high fliers' go elsewhere. This reflects the antipathy towards industry and commerce from traditionally educated, liberal-humanist teachers. It is *they* who need to be changed.

Richards argues that employers' attitudes imply a *dual system* of work experience – *image building* for the high-fliers and *realism* for the rest. In the case of the former, it is a *traditional* rather than a vocational education which is required, and as to the latter, the evidence suggests that employers are really indifferent to *their* education.

Given that so much of the occupationalist initiative in education and outside (YTS, etc.) is aimed at the lower academic ability bands, it is useful to emphasize certain points:

1   the evidence strongly indicates that employers are not especially concerned with the educational attainment of young workers in those sectors of the labour market in which such individuals tend to seek employment. Non-educational criteria have a clear priority in recruitment strategies;
2   in part this reflects the fact that occupational skill levels are of such a low order that they present no real requirement for educational preparation. Indeed, even *training* is problematical – as the Further Education Unit, for instance, has conceded.[2] Where extended education or training is provided (e.g. in response to youth unemployment) it tends, consequently, to stress so-called *social and life skills* or *personal effectiveness* rather than technical skills. This has the important implication of presenting these young people as personally and socially *deficient* and *incompetent*.
3   significantly, pupils of this type tend to have acquired significant degrees of work experience through part-time and spare-time work and also to possess the social skills of network membership which facilitate grape-vine recruitment (of course, both of these things are affected by local unemployment levels). These issues will be looked at in more detail below. It is important to stress that (a) this type of work experience is precisely that welcomed by employers, and (b) such young people are *socially competent* members of labour market social networks.

Recruitment and the problems of youth
If young people are not deficient in the ways that current rhetoric suggests, then what is the explanation for the high levels of youth unemployment? The view that they lack work experience is contradicted by a substantial body of

evidence. A study by Finn (1987), for instance, illustrates the tendency for non-academic young people to have comparatively more such informal work experience.[3] Lack of conventional school success cannot be seen, in any straightforward way, as indicative of problems in coping with working life. I have suggested elsewhere that difficult behaviour at school can, in fact, reflect a readiness for work and the resentment at having that ambition frustrated (Moore, 1984). Clarke, in a review of the literature on the transition to work, says that it tends to support the view that the 'majority of early leavers adjust fairly painlessly to working life' (Clarke, 1980, p. 10). She concludes a section on young people 'at risk' with the statement that:

> This suggests, rather unpalatably, that apart from bright children who do well at both school and work, it is those children who are apathetic about, or even alienated from, school who adjust best to work. (ibid., p. 11)

The major problem that young people suffer is simply that they are *young*. The re-presented Holland Report data showed how young people are judged to be 'worse' by employers on age-related attributes. Obviously, however much informal work experience young people may have acquired, it cannot compete with that of older workers. However, there is a more significant factor. The Holland Report states that:

> Whilst a little over a third of employers thought there was no difference, those employers who did state a preference were, in almost all cases, more likely to prefer other recruits to young people. This was especially true when young people were compared to up-graded existing employees, those recruited from other firms or women returning to work. (Holland, op. cit., p. 41)

Employers' preference for various categories of older workers reflects, in part, the importance of on-the-job training and experience over that of formal education (especially in relation to recruitment within the firm's *internal labour market*). But it also reflects the fact that older workers are, by virtue of their life situation, *more reliable*. The significance of *attitude* to work has been highlighted by numerous studies. It is important to note that this is not simply to do with naturalistic notions of 'emotional maturity'. Blackburn and Mann, on the basis of their extensive study of the labour market for semi and unskilled labour in Peterborough, say that:

> The ideal worker is male, around thirty, married with small children, related to other employees and with a stable educational and work history. He is not necessarily cleverer than other workers, but his commitments are less likely to make him jeopardise his job. (Blackburn and Mann, 1979, p. 13)

What is significant about the 'ideal worker' has nothing to do with his (the female 'ideal' is usually somewhat different) education *per se*. It is simply that he *is* a married man, around 30, with wife and children, a car, a mortgage (?)

etc., etc. Employers' preferences refer not to personality characteristics developed by a specialized, occupational socializing agency – *the school* – but to *life-cycle characteristics*. The difference between the young and the adult worker reflects their different positions on the trajectories of (common) social career paths. It is not 'the dull compulsion of the labour market' which disciplines the worker through the brute necessities of basic subsistence, but the more developed range of needs and commitments which trap them in, what Blackburn and Mann call, 'the life cycle squeeze' (ibid., p. 108). The ideal model helps to differentiate the workforce (by age, sex and colour) according to how far different groups approximate to the model and can be seen as representing its exemplary qualities of commitment and reliability.

This kind of division in the labour market between youth and adults jobs was also investigated by Ashton *et al.* (1986). In a similar fashion, changes in opportunities reflect the development of the social career.

> Age barriers also served to structure the young adults' experience of the labour market. This was particularly true of the unemployed. They were too old for most of the jobs which provided training and which only recruit school or college leavers, and too young for many of the adult jobs which required recruits to be over 21, and where employers *preferred those who were married, with a family and a large mortgage.* (Ashton *et al.*, 1986, p. 104, my emphasis)

Equally it is the case that the lack of opportunity to participate in employment blocks the development of the social career. Occupational and social careers are mutually facilitating in this respect. Unemployment does not only deny an adequate income, it can create deep crises of social identity.

Recruitment and the Matching Process

Investigation of recruitment strategies indicates that the role of education in occupational allocation is much more contingent than is often allowed. The relationship between qualifications and jobs is attenuated by the complexities of labour market segmentation and this itself is subject to local diversification. The importance of labour market segmentation is emphasized in Ashton *et al.*'s most recent study (1986). This work stresses the fact that there is no simple hierarchy of jobs (matched by a corresponding hierarchy of educational qualifications). The segmentation of the occupational system effectively creates discrete spheres of employment which exhibit radical discontinuities in terms of their structures, processes and possibilities. These in turn are associated with distinctive entry requirements, varying uses of qualifications in recruitment and career development (where career development occurs at all), differing pre and post entry orientations to work by young workers and differential effects by age, sex and 'race'.

Ashton *et al.* also stress the importance of *local* labour markets and argue that their variations can have more significant effects than social class differences. They conceptualize these differences in terms of 'separate local labour market cultures' (ibid., p. 104). A particularly significant feature of these 'cultures' in respect of occupational recruitment is that of *social network* or *grapevine* recruitment. This informal method was found to become increasingly important as individuals moved into second and subsequent jobs. This reflects, the authors argue, an 'increasing awareness of the ways in which employers recruit' (ibid., p. 84). Job-search, on this basis, is seen as 'more efficient, in that it is more closely aligned to employers' recruitment methods' (loc. cit.). At the third job level, between 25 per cent and 60 per cent of recruits found their position through 'word of mouth'.

Granovetter (a pioneer of the study of this dimension of recruitment) has argued that sociologists and economists have seriously neglected this aspect of 'the matching process', i.e. the *actual* process whereby individuals come to get the jobs they do (Granovetter, 1975). He stresses the rationality and efficiency of network recruitment for both employers and prospective employees. It is a cheaper and more reliable way of getting information about jobs or workers.

> Furthermore, my empirical work suggests that the signal chosen in the usual models – education – is not actually the main conveyer of information in labour markets. It is true that most jobs have clear cut educational requirements, such that employers assume workers lacking them to be ipso facto unqualified. This is, however, a crude sort of screen indeed, and if used alone would leave the employer still with a large and unmanageable information problem. On paper, there are few jobs for which large numbers of people are not qualified; in practice, employers use a more refined and differentiated signal than educational qualifications: they use the recommendations of people personally known to them and prospective employees. Similarly, prospective employees know better than to rely on landscaping or other signals put out by employers and attempt, instead, to find out the inside story from their contacts. (Granovetter, 1981, p. 25)

He points out that processes of this type are difficult to accommodate within orthodox economics because they are not amenable to 'costing' in the standard economic sense. Because of this, and despite their obviousness to common-sense experience, they have been excluded from formal analysis.

Granovetter's original sample of *Professional, Technical and Managerial* workers in the Boston (Mass.) area indicates that these processes are not restricted to either élite 'old boy networks' or to tight-knit working class communities such as dockers or printers. The basic rationality principle of their greater efficiency holds across the occupational system. There is, however, a further dimension to network recruitment which goes beyond the basic exchange of information. This has to do with the way in which network *membership* involves possession of the *social skills* and reciprocal relationships which that membership entails.

Grieco, in a fascinating and detailed series of ethnographic studies of working-class networks in this country, has pointed to a number of advantages which workers and employers gain from 'the network':

> Firstly, employee referrals provide the cheapest method of obtaining labour. Secondly, employee referrals provide an efficient screening mechanism. Thirdly, recruitment through employees acts as a form of control since responsibilities and obligations hold between workers so recruited: for if the sponsored antagonizes the employer, the reputation of the sponsor himself will be damaged; thus, the new worker is constrained by the interests and reputation of his sponsor. (Grieco, 1984, p. 30)

A number of significant points emerge from these studies:

1 network membership supplies not only information, but also the *tacit skills* which enable individuals to become competent and accepted members of occupational groups.
2 membership provides a means of social control in the workplace both because those recruited have an obligation to preserve the reputation of their sponsors and also because, in some cases, *family* authority principles can be transferred from the home to the job, e.g. as with a 'dads' lads' recruitment system.
3 membership also provides a source of social support in the workplace while a newcomer learns the ropes and the tricks of the trade, e.g. network members will make up shortfalls in production while the newcomer settles in. People without access to these support mechanisms can be severely disadvantaged.
4 Grieco's work has also pointed to the wider social importance of *women* in maintaining and enforcing the system of network reciprocity, even when not themselves in work. She also stresses the strategic, *collective* role of the network in maintaining employment opportunities *and* a 'family' income. This has important implications for current trends in thinking about the role of the family (and the extended family) in the occupational system of advanced societies and for certain feminist approaches to the issues of women in the labour market which tend to operate from an essentially middle class paradigm of the *individualized* career and salary and the consequent marginalization of women in the domestic context.[4]

Although it is possible to see networks as a mechanism through which workers exercise some degree of control over their labour market, it is important to acknowledge the extent to which they are, by definition, *discriminatory*. Lack of access to network membership can be a major limitation upon employment opportunities and, consequently, a major source of labour market differentiation. As Jenkins and Troyna (and other contributors) have pointed out (in Troyna and Smith (eds), 1983), this has a particular impact upon ethnic minority groups.

First, in an organisation with an all white or largely white workforce, network recruitment will help to ensure that this stays the case, particularly at a time when large numbers of white workers are unemployed and prepared to re-enter the comparatively poorly paid and less pleasant jobs they deserted in the past few years. At best, this will help to ensure that black workers remain in those employment sectors they entered in the boom years of the 50's and 60's. Secondly, and the reasons for this are unclear, there is good reason to suggest that West Indian workers are more likely to use formal or official job-search channels than are whites or Asians, who use informal channels to a comparatively greater extent. (ibid. pp. 14–15)

This indicates a powerful way in which labour market factors can effectively negate *educational* advances, e.g., in changing the pattern of 'racial' or gender inequalities in attainment. It is striking how even when certain minority groups tend to achieve mean levels of attainment above those of the white majority, they still remain heavily disadvantaged in employment terms.

A similar point about the way in which labour market structures and processes limit educational reform can be made in relation to gender. Crompton and Jones (1984) have highlighted the significance of the relationship between *pre-entry academic qualifications* and *post-entry* professional qualifications in shaping the gender inequalities in white collar employment which emerge as occupational careers develop. In their study, young men and women were very similar in their academic qualifications at O and A level at the point of entry into work. As a result of the bi-modal pattern of female involvement in paid employment (reflecting the demands of child rearing), women tend to be absent from work during the period in which men tend to acquire the post-entry *professional* qualifications which are required for promotion.

This points to the importance of the relationship of education to the articulation between social and occupational career paths and to specific labour market structures such as Internal Labour Markets. It also suggests that educational reforms will be of limited success unless complemented by policies such as contract compliance which act directly upon demand-side institutions. A general implication of the material considered throughout has been the limitation of supply-side analysis.

Conclusion

The material reviewed in this chapter indicates that the manner in which educational qualifications are used in employment is both highly variable and subject to a wide range of contingent factors located in labour market structures and processes. Specifically, the following points can be made:

1 Employers have tended to be extremely ill-informed about the content of educational courses and the significance of qualifications.
2 Little direct relationship is seen to exist between specific qualifications and actual job requirements.

3 Qualifications are invariably used alongside other criteria and these usually take priority in recruitment.

4 Employers tend to use a range of recruitment strategies employing a number of devices. Their use and the relative significance and the role of education varies according to sector, size of firm, level of recruitment and local conditions.

5 Given employers' lack of knowledge about qualifications and the relatively arbitrary way in which they use them, it is difficult to give credence to the widespread notion that they are dissatisfied with the educational levels of young workers. The evidence suggests that they are often indifferent to their educational attainment and are interested in only a narrow range of basic skills or in traditional education for the 'high-fliers'. In general, employers seem to be satisfied with those young workers they employ.

6 This is consistent with the findings which indicate that young people tend to adjust relatively easily to working life and that the less academic tend to do so more than others.

7 Young workers are disadvantaged in the labour market mainly by *age* itself and the view that, because of their lack of family commitments, they will be unreliable. Evidence suggests that jobs are often distributed according to age-life cycle criteria.

The material considered emphasizes the importance of labour market structures and processes in mediating the relationship between education and production and between qualifications and work. It also suggests that they create radical discontinuities between the educational and occupational systems which are a major limitation upon the effectiveness of educational reforms. This both attenuates the force of the current occupationalist attack upon the liberal education tradition and suggests that occupationalist objectives will do little more than merely dilute the quality of the education which pupils might otherwise have received.

It also suggests that teachers should oppose their critics on *educational* grounds rather than being forced continually onto the sterile terrain of vocationalism. More generally, it can be suggested that the social reforms which have been pursued through *educational* reform in the post-war period, prior to collapse of the liberal consensus and its political constituency, need to be approached through a direct assault upon the *structural* sources of inequality in *demand-side* institutions.

Notes

1 From Moore, 1983.
2 See *Vocational Preparation* (FEU, 1981) in which it is argued that voc. prep students present a problem for FE colleges because they are neither academic enough to follow a traditional educational course nor destined for jobs of sufficient skill level for a craft type course. The answer is to turn to 'personal development' based in *social and life skills*. This is underpinned by a psychological maturation

theory which presents these young people as immature and, so, actually *requiring* this type of approach.

3   See Finn, 1987. This book is an excellent and strongly argued study of the issues relating to the current education and training situation which places their development in an historical perspective.

4   See Grieco and Whipp, 1984.

References

ASHTON, D. *et al.* (1983) *Youth in the Labour Market*, Research Paper No. 34, Department of Employment, HMSO, London.

ASHTON, D. *et al.* (1986) *Young Adults in the Labour Market*, Research Paper No. 55, Department of Employment, HMSO, London.

BLACKBURN, R. and MANN, M. (1979) *The Working Class and the Labour Market*, Macmillan, Basingstoke.

CLARKE, L. (1980) *The Transition from School to Work*, Department of Employment, HMSO, London.

CROMPTON, R. and JONES, G. (1984) *White Collar Proletariat*, Macmillan, Basingstoke.

CUMIN, D. (1983) *School-Leavers, Qualifications and Employment*, mimeo, Nottingham.

FEU (FURTHER EDUCATION UNIT) (1981) *Vocational Preparation*, HMSO, London.

FINN, D. (1987) *Training Without Jobs*, Macmillan, Basingstoke.

GRANOVETTER, M. (1975) *Getting a Job*, Harvard University Press, Cambridge, Mass.

GRANOVETTER, M. (1981) 'Towards a Sociological Theory of Income Difference' in BERG, I. (ed.) *Sociological Perspectives on Labour Markets*, Academic Press, New York.

GRIECO, M. (1984) *Using the Network ...*, paper given to Development Studies Association Annual Conference, University of Bath.

GRIECO, M. AND WHIPP, R. (1984) *Women and the Workplace*, Work Organisation Research Centre, University of Aston.

HOLLAND, G. (1977) *Young People and Work: Report on the feasibility of a new programme of opportunities for unemployed young people* (The Holland Report), MSC.

JONES, J. (1983) *Interim Report*, British Petroleum, London.

MOORE, R. (1984) 'Further Education, Pedagogy and Production' in GLEESON, D. (ed.) *Youth Training and the Search for Work*, Routledge & Kegan Paul, London.

MOORE, R. (1984) 'Schooling and the World of Work', in BATES, I. *et al.*, *Schooling for the Dole?*, Macmillan, Basingstoke.

RICHARDS, G. (1982) *Work Experience Schemes for School Children: the shape of things to come?*, mimeo, University of Warwick.

TROYNA, B. and SMITH, D. I. (eds) (1983) *Racism, School and the Labour Market*, National Youth Bureau, Leicester.

21

Anti-Racist and Anti-Sexist Education:
Why are Women and Black Students Educational Problems?

Jenny Williams

Introduction

One of the most difficult questions which teachers ask themselves throughout their professional lives concerns the nature of the differences between pupils. How can pupils be categorized and what are the consequences of perceiving, labelling and responding to pupils in certain ways? The processes through which questions such as these are framed and the answers which seem acceptable are already determined by a whole range of social factors outside the control of teachers; by the nature of the social hierarchy, and the distribution of resources in society, by a general set of assumptions current among those who take political and economic decisions, and by the way in which education is institutionalized and so schools are organized. Thus the economic, political and organizational contexts within which teachers work determine which pupil categorizations they take for granted, which they question and dispute, and what those categorizations are.

This social creation of significant labels can be demonstrated by noting how the salience of labels changes over time. Some differences, such as those based on sex, have for decades simply been taken for granted as natural and unproblematic. The majority of teachers in state schools accepted as inevitable that boys and girls would behave differently in school, would find different forms of knowledge congenial, would achieve differently and aspire to differing occupations. The past three decades have seen such assumptions challenged. Sexism is a term used to refer to a whole range of justifications which supposedly make acceptable the inequalities in income, in job statuses, in promotion chances and in access to power, for example, from which women suffer. Differential treatment and discrimination is condoned and made to appear normal.

Attempts to highlight and remove differing forms of sexism, sexual inequalities and discrimination in schools have led to a range of policy statements and strategies from local education authorities and individual schools. These policy initiatives have been variously labelled as Equal Opportunities, Girl Friendly Schooling and anti-sexist programmes (see Arnot, 1986b). The emergence of such policies illustrates the dramatic shift that has occurred within a relatively short space of time in the social interpretation of sexual differences and inequalities.

'Race' and ethnic origin are also accepted labels, attached to pupils to describe who they are, their meaning taken for granted by politicians, administrators and teachers. The emergence of 'race' and racism as political and educational issues and the consequent range of educational policy responses are outlined in the article by Ali Rattansi in this volume. He illustrates the ways in which differing policies, summarized by the terms multi-culturalism and anti-racism, focus upon different dimensions of black experiences and white behaviour. Both policy forms are, however, concerned with inequalities, discrimination, and differential treatment based on colour and the forms of racism which are used as justifications for such behaviour.

Thus inequalities based on sex or 'race', both within the whole social system and within schools, provide the context for the emergence of particular educational policies. This article focuses upon these educational policies. It asks why pupils have been categorized in terms of their sex or 'race', why girls and black pupils have been defined as problems; what is meant by racism and sexism within policy initiatives and it asks what are the consequences for teachers of labelling and categorizing problems in particular ways. In trying to provide some answers to these questions I shall demonstrate the ways in which anti-racist and anti-sexist policies frequently mirror each other in rhetoric and analysis. At the same time they contain both obvious and hidden differences which also need exploring.

Race and Sex as Categories

The emergence of educational policies which focus on the school and college experiences of black and female students necessitates the use of 'race' and sex as significant categories, labelling students in such a way as to highlight both specific aspects of their identity and group membership and particular educational problems. Girls and boys, women and men, black and white students are differentiated and polarized. Girls' educational experiences are shown to compare unfavourably with those of boys; similarly, black students' experiences are contrasted with those of white students, or West Indian and Asian students are contrasted with white students. These are taken-for-granted groupings which assume some form of unity within each category without ever clearly identifying the source of this unity. Is it biological, cultural or material, or is it the result of some aspect of personal and social experiences?

It may appear that male and female students are polarized on the basis of biology. But the emergence of the term *gender* to signify social arrangements consequent upon, but not determined by, biological differences, highlights the complex relationship between biology and culture. The term gender will be used to refer to the social construction of sexual differences. The first task in scrutinizing educational policies, therefore, must be to examine their implicit categorization and labelling. Are they based on some notion of 'inherent' differences? In other words do they assume that biological or cultural categories are unproblematic? Do they suggest a neat and straightforward relationship between biology, culture and differential educational needs? Why and how are these categories used?

Most educationalists, teachers and politicians probably accept that there is no biological basis for the notion of 'race'. Nineteenth century 'scientific racism', with its discrete, hierarchical and inherited categories has been significantly challenged, even if not eliminated, from popular consciousness. Ancestral origins from different geographical regions, however, are still assumed to be important in understanding pupil needs. 'Asians' and 'West Indians', for example, are labelled by their country of origin, even those third or fourth generation resident in this country. They are commonly referred to as belonging to different 'races', and the relations between Asian and West Indian communities and the white British population are referred to as 'race relations' (cf the Race Relations Act). There is, however, little recognition of the cultural origins of such terminology. We conveniently forget that these divisions and the classification of people as 'races', have been historically and politically created. Indeed in post-1945 Britain it is the political creation and solidification of such categories, enshrined, for example, in legislation for immigration control, which provides one crucial context within which educational policies emerge (see Sivanandan 1982, Carby 1982, Troyna and Williams 1986).

How, then, has the acceptance and understanding of racial differences been perpetuated and built into policy discussions during the past 40 years? The most obvious way, clearly demonstrated in educational literature, has been to associate the label 'race' with some notion of cultural unity, encapsulated in the term *ethnic group*. It has become commonplace in educational debates to assert that schools should reflect cultural differences, that the divisions within the school population are cultural ones, represented in different ethnic identities. The confusion between the labels 'race' and ethnicity allows an outmoded biological determinism to be replaced by an implicit cultural determinism. Each ethnic group is portrayed as homogeneous and possessing a culture that is fixed, static and unrelated to the changing social and economic circumstances of their lives. If we are not very careful black and white children in schools are seen as in need of a different education simply because of the culture they are expected to belong to.

But we must question which cultural attributes define groups of people as different. How homogeneous is the culture of white children? How fast are the cultures of different black groups changing? How can schools reflect cultural differences without reinforcing the notion that those differences are unchanging and inherent in particular groups.

A very similar discussion concerning the need for educational reform takes place round the notion of *gender*, though frequently in a less explicit and straightforward form. Again we can ask whether the special needs of girls are attributed to their biology or to a notion of femaleness which implies some form of cultural unity? Gender has been used historically as a basis of the organization of educational provision, whether in terms of separate schools or separate curricula (David, 1980). It was seen as the most 'natural' division given the separate roles of men and women in society. Biological differences were seen to give rise to different needs, interests and abilities. Cultural differences resulting from the division of labour into productive and domestic forms provided a commonsense justification for separate educational provision, focusing for girls on child care and domestic science. Gender divisions were an obvious and convenient division for teachers to use and one that was not contentious during most of the twentieth century. During the 1970s and 1980s the problem became redefined. For some feminists the 'problem' was the masculine culture of mixed schools, which made them problematic for girls (Spender and Sarah, 1980). Within this framework one solution is to incorporate some aspects of the less valued 'female' culture into the curricula. 'Femaleness' has been used by radical feminists as a justification for more co-operative, less competitive forms of learning, as if these were inherent in all female cultures.

One justification, therefore, for using 'race' and sex as significant divisions is that these designate important cultural differences as educationally relevant. Unfortunately, it also encourages the use of a concept of culture which is highly problematic, particularly when used in policy discussions.

An alternative classification, used by some researchers and policy makers, is that which distinguishes pupils on the basis of some aspect of their social and educational experiences. It is suggested that the way women and black citizens are treated in society and in schools provides for a unity among female students on the one hand and black students on the other. Such experiences are summarized in the terms racism and sexism. The ILEA documents (1983, 1985) provide a clear example of this alternative approach. New educational policies take their justification from the experiences of racism suffered by black citizens.

> There are certain routine practices, customs and procedures in our society whose consequence is that black people have poorer jobs, health, housing, education and life chances than do the white majority. (1983, p. 6)

Similarly, girls and women suffer from living in a society in which sexism

> is based on and perpetuates a notion of male superiority. Greater value and

status is more often given to traditional male pursuits and occupations than female ones. This places men generally in a position of power over women, whether at home, at work or through the political, social and economic systems and institutions which govern our lives. (1985, p. 4)

ILEA also brings the issue of race and gender together by stating that 'sex and race inequalities are linked through the experience of discrimination, prejudice, stereotyping and powerlessness' (1985, p. 5). A whole range of examples of sexism within education are given, including textbook biases, differential teacher expectations concerning pupil abilities, differential teacher behaviour with regard to discipline and attention, sexual harassment, assumptions concerning the leadership qualities of males and the monopolization of power by males. This list is mirrored very clearly in discussions concerning racism in schools, where equivalent differential experiences can be found. All aspects of education are included and the experiences of black and female pupils are seen to be qualitatively different from that of white male pupils.

That males and whites are not homogeneous groups, and that many school experiences are similar for all students tends to be ignored. As Lynn Davies (1978) graphically puts it:

it is rather like highlighting the lion's view of captivity, it implies that this is demonstrably different from the tiger's view, and this draws attention away from the significant fact of captivity. (p. 103)

By focusing on particular school experiences, crucial though they are, other differentiating variables tend to be ignored. For example, during the 1950s and 1960s social class inequalities in terms of access to different forms of education, in educational experiences and in educational achievements were documented in sociological studies and Government reports. But recent educational research initiated, or selected as deserving attention, by policy makers rarely allows for ethnic or gender issues to be placed within a social class context. The presentation of educational data, which forms the justification for most policies, is documented in discrete and unrelated forms. In ILEA (1983), for example, social class, sex and 'racial' achievements in education are documented in separate sections. The relationships between the three sets of data are hardly explored. Few references are made to the social class distribution of West Indian and Asian parents found in other studies, and no supporting evidence is offered for the following statement:

our ILEA studies suggest that only about half the difference between reading scores of children from West Indian homes and their white counterparts may be accounted for by socio-economic factors. (p. 17)

There are suggestions that the differences *within* the group labelled Asian are large but here again no details are provided.

The Rampton Report (1981) had used the same processes of data collection and presentation, comparing only overarching ethnic categories such as West Indian, Asian and White with no discussion of sex differences within each. In spite of receiving sharp criticism of this practice from researchers such as Reeves and Chevannes (1981) the Swann Committee repeated this model of data collection. Research by Craft and Craft (1983) which includes a division between middle and working-class black groups is reported in Swann (p. 60) but little interpretive use is made of these data.

What must always have been clear to perceptive teachers, and what is now being documented in some detail in research, is that racism and sexism are experienced in numerous different ways, depending upon the groups concerned and the educational context. Clarricoates (1980), for example, illustrates the relationship between different constructions of masculinity and feminity within the classroom and the social class composition of the school catchment areas. Lynn Davies (1984) describes the ways in which, within one largely working-class comprehensive school, differing versions of femininity interrelate with differing levels of academic achievement.

Racism, similarly, is a complex phenomenon. Not only does the level of racist abuse or harassment vary in different schools and localities, but teacher stereotypes and the labelling of black children vary according to pupil, age, social class, and the demographic distribution of ethnic minority groups. The responses of black students to these different forms of racism have been shown to result in a range of black male and female identities in different settings (see, for example, Fuller, 1982; Riley, 1985; Brah and Minhas, 1985). Initial research suggests, for example, that black students in Further Education colleges may view education in a utilitarian manner, placing more emphasis upon the credentials available within FE than upon their culturally specific or anti-racist provision (FEU, 1985a; Reeves, 1986). Such research emphasizes the importance of defining the experiences of black and female students as multi-faceted, of documenting how they perceive and respond to racism and sexism within society and education in many different ways.

This section has raised two questions concerning pupil categorizations implicit in certain policy developments. The first question concerns the basis of the categorizations. Do policies which focus on girls or black pupils imply, even unwittingly, a biological or cultural unity among females or ethnic minority groups? If this is so, what are the implications of this for practice in schools? The second question concerns the extent to which it is possible and desirable to prevent an oversimplification of the divisions created and reinforced within education. Colour, ethnic and gender divisions interweave with social class and achievement hierarchies in different ways in different geographical areas and institutional contexts. How can this complexity be acknowledged when policies are formulated?

'Race' and Gender as Educational Problems

Built into most policy development over the past four decades, even anti-sexist and anti-racist initiatives, has been the assumption that girls and black pupils are 'problems'; that they either have problems or pose problems that are different from other groups of pupils. In this section I intend to focus on the way four of these problems have become interlinked, namely those of underachievement, the concern over indiscipline, and the need for social integration and the employability of particular groups. Each of these themes can be found in 'race' and gender debates illustrating very clearly both the similarities and differences in the way these pupil groups are defined as educational problems. The 'problem' of underachievement illustrates this particularly well.

As far as female students are concerned:

> Statistics show that girls' academic achievement is at least as good as boys' and that more girls than boys are entered for all levels of public examina-tions. The relative position of girls and boys becomes sharply divided only when we look at two factors behind the generalized statistics: (1) subject choices; (2) post-school experiences. (ILEA, 6, p. 5)

These two aspects of gender differences provide the context within which policy makers frame the discussion of female educational experience and achievement. In particular, attention is focused on girls' differential engage-ment with, and performance in, certain scientific and technical subjects (see, for example, The Further Education Unit, 1985b; The Schools Council Project on Reducing Sex Differentiation in Schools, 1983; Brent LEA, 1982). The Girls into Science and Technology and Girls into Craft, Design and Technology projects and the DES (Orr, 1985) all focused their attention on female subject choice and career aspirations. The MSC in both the YTS and TVEI programmes takes the view that the perpetuation of sex differentiated subject and skill areas is a major problem, at least in those areas where there is a shortage of skilled male labour. At the level of rhetoric much concern has been expressed about female underachievement even if the reference is generally to the experiences of white girls.

Underachievement, however, means something rather different when the focus of educational concern is black pupils. Here the issue is one of general educational failure, as measured, for example, by reading age, CSE and O level passes, entrance to Higher Education, etc. (see, for example, Little, 1975; Tomlinson, 1986; Rampton, 1979; ILEA, 1983; Swann, 1985). The research which underpins current understanding of black underachievement, and the political and professional reinterpretation of it, rests upon ethnic categorizations. 'West Indians' are grouped together and contrasted with 'Asians' and 'Whites'. Avoiding a black/white categorization which might have revealed the impact of racism, this oversimplified ethnic categorization results in an association betwen black educational underachievement and a notion of 'West Indianness'.

The two frames of reference within which the problems of female and black underachievement are located therefore are quite different. The central issue for girls is one of employability within a changing job market where there are specific skill shortages and taken-for-granted assumptions concerning future labour demands. 'Science' and 'technology' cover a very wide range of occupations, and in practice policy makers may have little idea of either the extent of skill shortages or how to redirect girls' energies towards these. Nevertheless, arguments about the current failure of schools are put forward; for example:

> by still preparing many school girls for a sheltered life with the emphasis upon 'suitable' female skills we may 'educate for incapability' – that is, for frustration, unemployment and second-class citizenship in a technological society. (FEU, 1985b, p. 16)

Here the imagery of traditional female occupations contrasted with high status technology is representative of most of the policy documents of gender inequality in education.

The passivity and conformity of girls, their lack of assertiveness and ambition, their refusal to study 'hard', rational subjects are defined as the problem. From such a perspective girls frequently appear as victims of the sexism in education apparent to others (Brah and Deem, 1986). On the other hand, girls' lack of femininity or their 'masculinity' may be seen as more of a problem than that of underachievement. Girls' subject choices, their lack of competition with boys, their restricted career choices, etc. can be interpreted as self chosen, rational (even if misguided) responses to the position of women in society.

In contrast, the problem of black underachievement is almost never interpreted in this manner. The relationship of underachievement with employability is constructed through an assumption that it is the lack of academic achievement which renders black students unemployable (Scarman, 1981). Black pupils need to achieve academically in order to enter the labour market even at the lowest level in spite of evidence that qualifications do not necessarily lead to jobs (see Brennan and McGeevor, 1987, for example). The concept of black underachievement provides an even greater contrast when it is associated with 'trouble', defined as indiscipline and truanting, and results in suspensions and local 'law and order' problems. Teacher assumptions concerning the classroom problems exhibited by 'West Indian' students have been documented for the past 20 years (Brittain, 1976; Rampton, 1981). Key statements in many LEA policy documents show a concern for 'harmony' and 'stability', which is never the case in sex equality policies or statements on girls' education. It is significant that most formal policies on 'race' and multicultural education have been formulated after 1981 when the 'riots' forced the issue of inner city youth on the political agenda (Troyna and Williams, 1986; Solomos, 1986a).

Since the 1950s an association between low school attainment, the problems of classroom discipline, and delinquency has been accepted as a male, white and predominantly working class phenomenon. Now the problems of black male youths in schools have adapted and adopted this 'law and order' language, and its associated imagery of violence, discontent and public concern (Fisher and Joshua, 1982). One consequence of this scenario is that black underachievement is portrayed as meaningless, destructive and irrational (Solomos, 1986b). In contrast with the analysis of female underachievement, there appears to be a refusal to even consider that black underachievement (and disruption) could be a collective, rational, response to a discriminatory social system (John, 1981 is an exception).

It is quite clear from these contrasting analyses of underachievement, employability and disruption, that the differential experiences of black girls are given minimal attention. Stereotypes associated with black girls have been constructed along ethnic lines, and cut across the more general male/female, black/white images (see Allen, 1982; Carby, 1982; Brah and Minhas, 1986; Riley, 1986). As Brah and Deem point out, Afro-Caribbean young women are stereotyped as 'pushy', but achieve better in schools than their male counterparts. Asian young women are seen as passive, meek, ruthlessly oppressed by their families (1986, p. 73), not being allowed to take courses and jobs commensurate with their abilities and achievement. Such overgeneralizations are clearly ridiculous. What they highlight very sharply is the importance of very careful scrutiny of the ways in which girls and black pupils are portrayed as problems.

Explanations of Educational Problems

In order to gain acceptance for their interpretation of educational problems, researchers, administrators and politicians usually find it necessary to 'explain' the problem; to pinpoint the processes which appear to have led to it in such a way as to make the remedy appear obvious. In other words there is little pay off in providing an explanation which implies nothing can be done. (The term 'academic' is often used as a pejorative label to describe such explanations.) Interestingly, the accepted explanations for the problems that female and black pupils pose for schools, and the suggested remedies, are remarkably similar. They follow earlier frameworks developed to explain social class disparities in educational achievements which are summarized by Flude (1974) as (i) cultural deficit (ii) cultural difference (iii) teacher labelling and stereotyping and (iv) discrimination. I shall very briefly consider each set of explanations in terms of 'race' and gender.

(i) Cultural deficit theories
Very many educational reports over the past few decades have portrayed black pupils as having special needs because their cultural background is inadequate (e.g. Rampton Report, 1981). Examples may focus on differences in the structure of their language or parental relationships or the lack of parental knowledge of child development. Schools, therefore, are expected to compensate for these supposed deficits. Interestingly, anti-racist proposals very often assume whites suffer from a cultural deficit, i.e. from racist attitudes which are simply a legacy from imperialism and colonialism (Swann Report, 1985); an

unfortunate ignorance which schools can remedy. Lyn Yates (1985) suggests that this type of deficit approach, which in effect blames the victim, is also the most common approach to girls' schooling. Teachers are asked to develop an alternative female culture of achievement and independence which will compensate for the romanticism, dependency and passivity found amongst women in society.

Theories of compensatory education rest on certain important assumptions. First, deficit cultures are portrayed as irrational, as based on ignorance. There is little, if any, analysis of why particular attitudes and behaviours have developed, of the ways in which cultures are related to and continuously reinforced by the wider structural position of particular groups; the ways in which cultures can be a rational response to the social position of groups at a particular time. Secondly, a change in the overt and hidden curriculum is presented as a solution which will lead to changed attitudes and behaviours, irrespective of other changes outside the control of the school.

(ii) Cultural difference theories

Notions of cultural deficits frequently have been replaced by an emphasis upon differences with apparently no pejorative connotations. It is argued that cultural discontinuities between homes and schools do exist, are inevitable and are to be celebrated. This results in an explanation of gender and 'race' problems in schools in terms of teachers' inability to use these cultural differences. Teachers lack the skills necessary to incorporate and transform ethnic or gender cultures into a form which is educationally relevant. The solution, again, is to retrain teachers, to enable them to understand, interpret and incorporate cultural differences which do exist into their teaching and to reflect these back to pupils in a way which leads to high achievement and satisfaction within schooling.

Again the relationship betwen curriculum and culture is oversimplified. Which aspects of black or female cultures are or could be incorporated into high status knowledge? Some black and female writers can be brought into English literature classes, or O or A level Punjabi can be developed, but other aspects can just as easily reinforce low academic status and perpetuate differences and segregation. Classes on child care, personal health and beauty or African music are currently only likely to be options for those with few alternative examination subjects. We must therefore question very carefully indeed why schools should, and how they could, reflect the different cultures of the local community.

(iii) Teacher labelling and stereotyping

In the third explanatory framework, teachers' attitudes rather than their knowledge are described as crucial. Teachers' expectations, stereotyping and labelling are seen as the mechanisms by means of which membership of an ethnic or gender group results in ethnic or sex disparities in achievements or in particular types of classroom behaviour.

The Rampton Report argued:

> that teachers had stereotyped or patronising attitudes towards West Indian children which, when combined with negative views of their academic ability and potential, may prove a self-fulfilling prophecy. (1981, p. 70)

Stanworth documented very clearly the differentiated assumptions which teachers held about male and female pupils including:

> the implicit assumption that girls' capacities for efficiency and initiative will be channelled into nurturant or subordinate occupations, rather than into other, less traditional, spheres. (1981, pp. 30–31)

The solution, again, focuses upon re-educating teachers, to reduce if not remove racial and sex stereotypes.

Discrimination
The final explanatory framework is quite different. It pinpoints direct and indirect discrimination both within and outside education (Wright, 1984; Spender, 1982). The labels, racism and sexism, are used as summary terms for a very wide range of attitudes, behaviours and institutional processes which result in unequal access to material resources and personal dignity and choices.

Remedial policies again tend to focus upon the school, upon unintentional and institutional discrimination within education. But there are attempts to link educational examples with key political and economic processes in the wider society, such as the institutionalization of racism within the Nationality Acts, with the differential occupational recruitment of women and black pupils, or the lack of child care provision which limits the realistic achievement of female career options. Thus the remodelling of teachers and schools is linked to wider social and political changes.

'Race' and Gender Policies

Stemming from the differing interpretations of the educational problems posed by black and female pupils outlined in the previous section, a range of alternative policies may be introduced into schools. In this article I shall only be able to illustrate the policy consequences of the fourth interpretation, that of discrimination. Most LEAs and schools that have introduced explicit policies to combat sexual and 'racial' inequalities label them as anti-racist and anti-sexist.

The following table illustrates a range of initiatives which occur in schools. Though in this form the list looks a long one, it must be remembered that only a limited number of schools have introduced more than a few changes. It is possible to distinguish three, slightly different, elements within anti-racist and anti-sexist policies. A linked range of innovations focus on white racism

Table 21.1

Focus	Race policies		Gender policies	
	content	*examples of implementation*	*content*	*examples of implementation*
White racism or male sexism	(i) racist incidents – name-calling graffiti attacks, harassment	procedures established for dealing with these as serious offences	(i) sexist incidents name-calling harassment	open discussions with culprits. Sometimes code which states such behaviour is unacceptable
	(ii) attitude change among white students	directly via the curriculum, particularly History, English, R.E., Social Studies	(ii) attitude change among male students	limited curriculum innovations, mainly in Social Studies or tutorial work
	(iii) attitude change among white staff	INSET Racism Awareness Training Curriculum development	(iii) attitude change among male staff	skills-based INSET, limited sexism awareness training
	(iv) monitoring of suspensions	removal of some powers from heads and teachers	(iv) enhancement of teaching skills to promote high achievement of all	INSET analysing sexism in textbooks and syllabi. Persuading girls into science and technology
	(v) monitoring achievement levels and alteration in streaming/setting patterns	little accomplished – checking language policies	(v) teacher expectation, classroom interactions	INSET but little accomplished so far. Revision of teacher-attention techniques
	(vi) curriculum change to remove ethnocentrism	analysis of racism in books, changes in the selection of curriculum materials	(vi) prevention of sexist behaviour by staff	Codes of Practice from Unions and a few LEAs

(vii) teacher expectations and classroom interactions	INSET		
(viii) prevention of discrimination or racist behaviour by staff	code of professional practice – from LEA or Unions		
Institutional policies and wider alliances			
(i) whole school policies, changing ethos and visible representations	staff working parties, school-based INSET	(i) whole school policies	school working parties, Development of Equal Opportunity Statements. Language policies
(ii) community education	involvement of parents, non-teaching staff and students, time and resources to do this	(ii) community education	rare
(iii) institutional support and allocation of resources within the institution	posts of school responsibility, materials available for course development	(iii) changing timetabling option choices	both sexes take core curriculum-limited opting out
(iv) political education within the curriculum	linking anti-racist reforms with world studies, peace studies	(iv) institutional support and allocation of resources within the institution	posts of special responsibility some resources available
(v) staff recruitment and responsibilities	positive action on recruitment, designation of posts to develop anti-racist strategies	(v) curriculum change	analysis of content across all subjects

Table 21.1—*cont.*

Focus	Race policies		Gender policies	
	content	*examples of implementation*	*content*	*examples of implementation*
			(vi) alteration in existing hierarchies of status and authority	changes in allocation of responsibilities with senior staff to include more women/girls' issues as important, emphasis on co-operation, collective work groups
racial equality for black citizens (i)	recruitment, promotion of black teachers	primarily via Section II posts	(i) promotion of women teachers or recruitment to non traditional areas	specialist EO posts, positive action, non-traditional women and management courses. Career development
(ii)	curriculum change	knowledge to fight oppression	(ii) recognition of special needs	single sex counselling, assertiveness training
(iii)	cultural retention within the curriculum	community language options, recognition of different religions	(iii) curriculum change	'herstory' knowledge to fight oppression
sexual equality for female citizens (iv)	other special needs provision	school/community working parties home/school liaison dietary rights	(iv) pupil involvement	consultation of female pupils concerning own needs
(v)	acceptance of community campaigns as part of education	support deportation campaigns	(v) counteracting past discrimination	re-arranging option blocks compulsory common core curriculum alteration in career counselling
(vi)	altering decision-making structures such as governors	local acceptance and support	(vi) links to remove discrimination outside school	links with employers: courses in non-traditional female occupational areas

or male sexism and so introduce school policies which attempt to overcome racist and sexist attitudes and beliefs.

A second type of development sets whole school policies within a wider framework which encompasses the needs and rights of parents and local community groups. The emergence of a set of strategies which encompass the whole institution can be developed at the same time as local links and local issues are given some priority. The third focus sets particular inequalities inside schools within the context of unequal life chances and access to resources generally. The issue of power brings a thread of coherence to what appear to be divergent reforms. Teachers, pupils, parents and community groups all need access to power.

An inspection of the table reveals overlaps between the three trends, and clearly they should not be seen as mutually exclusive. The table simply illustrates the range of policies which have been introduced. It is a useful exercise to look in detail at a particular school with which one is familiar and ask how much of current practice would have to change for the policies listed to be implemented. Could they be introduced as token, surface changes or do they necessitate a fundamental reorganization of the way the school operates?

Comparison of Anti-sexist and Anti-racist Policies

On the surface anti-racist and anti-sexist educational policies are in tune with each other. The early anti-racist initiatives of the 1960s and 70s were school based and developed by teachers drawing their strength and legitimacy from both their professionalism and their identification with local community issues (e.g. ALTARF, 1980, 1984). Anti-sexist initiatives were also likely to be 'bottom-up' developments initially (Taylor, 1985). However, by the early 1980s some LEAs began to adopt more prescriptive approaches, insisting on school policies fostering racial equality within given time limits (e.g. ILEA, Brent), prescribing aspects of headteacher behaviour to ethnic minority parents (e.g. Bradford), making certain forms of racist behaviour a disciplinary offence (e.g. Manchester) or establishing central mechanisms to decide upon school suspensions and so removing power from Heads and Governors (e.g. Birmingham). Similarly a few LEAs stepped up pressure on schools to implement anti-sexist policies, asking for school policies within a particular time limit (e.g. Brent, ILEA) pressuring heads to implement change; organizing inservice courses (Humberside, Brent) replacing text books and appointing Advisers/Inspectors.

There are, however, quite important differences of emphasis. There appears to be far more concern in anti-racist policies to alter the behaviour and attitudes of white personnel, compared with the attention devoted to altering male behaviour in schools. In contrast, the issue of separate provision is suggested by anti-sexist policies, which might prioritize the creation of girls-only classes, women-run support groups, assertiveness training, etc. (Weiner, 1985). It is not a usual part of anti-racist strategies to create black only classes within ordinary schools to prevent unfair competition with white pupils who get more than their share of teacher attention. Black pupils are given more attention by teachers only in terms of discipline and punishment. Black teacher groups are becoming more common, and supplementary schools exist in many cities, but support groups for black students within schools are not usually on the list of policy priorities. Also whilst Women's Studies, particularly in Higher Education, appears to have achieved a certain respectability and is flourishing, Black Studies is on the decline and receives little public support from those concerned about racism. In short, there is no clear anti-racist equivalent of girl-centred schooling, or indeed girl-friendly schooling (see Weiner, 1986 for the distinction between these two approaches).

The creation of specialist hierarchies of teacher advisers, curriculum centres and school working parties is common to both policy arenas. But again certain differences are clear. Sex equality policies are not widespread, yet they do relate to mainstream education practice and funding: for example policies concerned to alter ordinary timetabling processes, counselling systems and resource allocation. The Technical and Vocational Educational Initiative, a nationally funded, vocationally oriented programme, has been able to incorporate some anti-sexist aspects as part of its normal aims and activities, even if the implementation of these aims is limited. In contrast, Section 11 grants available since 1966 to some authorities to provide funding for the special needs of ethnic minority pupils, have tended to marginalize spending on black pupils. The existence of this funding has been the key factor in LEAs' development of specialist appointments and experimental initiatives. The effect on mainstream education and ordinary professional practice has been minimal (Troyna and Ball, 1985).

Single-sex schooling is clearly an issue within the state sector of education. Although the numbers of single sex schools have declined dramatically during the past three decades, girls-only schools have been supported as a desirable alternative to coeduction in some LEAs. Political campaigns have been organized to preserve existing single sex schools when under the threat of closure. In contrast most debates concerning black schools have centred upon voluntary supplementary schools or private religious provision (with one or two exceptions). As far as official policies are concerned, assumptions concerning integration have been based on the acceptance of white majority schools as both normal and desirable. Demands for some form of separatism on grounds of religion, for example, have been perceived as a threat to mainstream education (see Ball, 1986; Swann, 1985). When particular ethnic groups have campaigned to preserve single sex schools, because of compatibility with culutral norms, this has been perceived as a form of cultural imposition and indoctrination and even sexism. Thus separate schooling for white girls, while not generally accepted, is seen as a legitimate demand, linked with high academic achievements, and mainstream educational issues. When such demands become part of a debate concerning black issues, it is marginalized and perceived as a threat to harmony and integration.

Conclusions: Policy Rhetoric and Structural Realities

In this article I have tried to tease out the underlying assumptions of educational policies concerned with 'race' and gender. Two particular themes have guided the analysis. The first is an exploration of the language of explanation and the language of reform and policy change through which particular educational issues come to be debated and understood. The second theme concerns the similarities and differences in these understandings when focused upon 'race' and upon gender.

I have tried to show where explanations and policies are similar and where the rhetoric of analysis reflects similar concerns; but also where there are deep and crucial differences. I have suggested that official LEA policies on 'race' and gender reflect each other and contain similar kinds of rhetoric; significantly local policies in both areas have ignored social class inequalities, and have both tended to isolate education from wider debates concerning inequalities. Policies on 'race' and gender often work within a compensatory model of education. Both also work with polarized categories, black/white, male/female, which by implication if not design, make other forms of inequality acceptable. Thus at this level of problem analysis, of political and administrative policy formation, anti-sexist and anti-racist initiatives appear to mirror each other.

However, behind this surface similarity lie the deeper conflicts and contradictions which have been illustrated earlier. These differences are inevitable given the distinct economic, political and professional contexts of such policy formation.

In general both black and female workers are recruited to the unskilled or semi-skilled area of the economy and are currently suffering high levels of unemployment, particularly among the younger age groups. But the similarities must not be overgeneralized and the differences need to be acknowledged. For example there is a higher chance of a white woman attaining professional or executive position (even if on the lower rungs and with less promotion chances than white men) than a black person of either sex. Sex segregation in the labour market is remarkably resistant to change and most women are channelled into 'appropriate' areas. But these appropriate areas cover the social class range of occupations, so that socially and educationally ambitious girls can be accommodated, at least initially. 'There is ample literature to demonstrate that qualified women have not attained full equality with men, but nonetheless they do have considerable economic and occupational advantages compared with less qualified women' (Bonney, 1986, p. 17). It is later in their careers, when seeking promotion, that direct and indirect discrimination becomes more visible, and women's domestic position impinges most directly on occupational participation, and the monopolization of power by men is starkly evident.

In contrast, discrimination against black students occurs at the initial entry stage into the labour market. The concentration of black workers within manual occupations is being consolidated rather than eroded (Newnham, 1986). The association of colour with particular low status, low paid occupations continues with generations born in this country (see the Swann Report, 1985, Ch. 15 on Liverpool's blacks, for example). The quite different nature of the female labour market means that it is easier to introduce measures in schools and colleges which will improve the initial occupational choices of some female students, particularly middle class or 'academically able' girls. The changing labour market and economic structures therefore allow a certain 'space' for gender reforms even within an overall operation which reinforces existing patterns. The nature of this 'space' is much more limited for black students. Attempts to improve occupational mobility for them may concentrate on a few professional openings where their colour is defined as an occupational advantage (e.g. race relations advisers) or on employers (e.g. local authorities) with positive action policies, or self-employment (small businesses).

Another major factor we need to consider for black citizens in the UK is the way in which black groups have been defined politically over the past four decades. Their presence in this country and the meaning of their citizenship is continually questioned. The Nationality Acts and the revision of entry rules and procedures for example perpetuate the association between blackness and 'alien invaders' bringing unnecessary social problems with them.

Finally, and briefly, the professional contexts within which policies are generated and implemented differ. There are clearly far more women teachers than black teachers, some in influential positions, yet promotion remains limited and the working environment is controlled by men. Therefore it is in women teachers' own interests, as well as those of their female pupils to initiate or support anti-sexist reforms. In a recent study of all Higher Education Institutions it has become quite clear that the main impetus towards Equal Opportunity Policies has come from female members of staff or particular unions representing female members (CRE, unpublished). This is certainly not to argue that all female professionals are active in anti-sexist developments, or that implementation of policy is easy. Many women teachers have faced strong opposition, even ridicule, when attempting to change school policies. Rather the professional context again provides limited space where reforms can be articulated, particularly if their aim is to change one particular institution.

With so few black professionals in post, most pressure for anti-racist reforms has to come from a variety of sources, from white politicians or administrators or black pressure groups working in particular localities in conjunction with anti-racist teachers. It is interesting to note the changing nature of anti-racist reforms and opposition to them when black professionals and politicians gain more influence in particular localities (Brent LEA, for example). Over most of the country, anti-racist reforms within schools have had to rely on the political commitment of white teachers. It is less likely that any significant number of such staff will be persuaded that it is in their own interests to initiate sweeping reforms.

Widespread and gross inequalities and discrimination on the basis of colour and sex, and the beliefs which justify these activities, exist in society and in schools. Policies which address such issues are an urgent necessity. Clearly pupils cannot be treated as identical, assumed to be already equal, as though racism and sexism did not exist. Yet the formulation and implementation of such policies is not an easy task. A careful scrutiny of existing policies and their implicit and explicit assumptions should do two things; it should enable choices to be made at the level of general strategies, as to what is most conducive to equity or equality, it should also enable individual teachers in individual schools to compare their circumstances with those of others and learn which innovations seem to suit what circumstances and to take heart from the struggles and successes of their colleagues.

References

ALLEN, S. (1982) 'Perhaps a seventh person' in HUSBAND, C. (ed.) *Race in Britain*, London, Hutchinson.

ALTARF (1980) *Teaching and Racism*. London, All London Teachers against Racism and Fascism.

ALTARF (1984) *Challenging Racism*, London, All London Teachers against Racism and Fascism.

ARNOT, M. (1986a) 'State Education Policy and Girls' Educational Experiences' in BEECHEY, V. and WHITELEGG, E. (eds) *Women in Britain Today*, Milton Keynes, Open University Press.

ARNOT, M. (1986b) *Race, Gender and Educational Policy Making* E333 Module 4, Milton Keynes, Open University Press.

ARNOT, M. (ed. (1985) *Race and Gender: Equal Opportunity Policies in Education*, Oxford, Pergamon.

BALL, W. (1986) *Policy innovation on multi-cultural education in 'Eastshire' Local Education Authority*, Policy Papers in Ethnic Relations No 4, Centre for Research in Ethnic Relations, Warwick University.

BERKSHIRE LEA (1983) *Education for Racial Equality: Policy Paper 1: General Policy. Policy Paper 2: Implications. Policy Paper 3: Support.*

BONNEY, M. (1986) 'More equal than others', *Times Higher Education Supplement*, 31 October.

BRAH, A. and DEEM, R. (1986) 'Towards anti-sexist and anti-racist schooling', *Critical Social Policy* 16, pp. 66–79.

BRAH, A. and MINHAS, R. (1985) 'Structural Racism or Cultural Difference: Schooling for Asian Girls' in WEINER G. (ed.) *Just a Bunch of Girls*, Milton Keynes, Open University Press.

BRENNAN, J. and MCGEEVOR, P. (1987) *Employment of Graduates from Ethnic Minorities*. Commision for Racial Equality.

BRENT LEA (1982) *Equal Opportunities for Pupils' of Both Sexes* Report No 114/82 of the Director of Education.

BRITTAN, E. (1976) 'Teacher opinion on aspects of school life', *Educational Research*, Vol. 18, pp. 96–107 and 182–91.

CARBY, H. (1982) 'Schooling in Babylon' in CCCS, *The Empire Strikes Back*, London, Hutchinson.

CLARRICOATES, K. (1980) 'The importance of being Ernest. Emma. Tom. Jane' in DEEM R. (ed.) *Schooling for Women's Work*, London, Routledge and Kegan Paul.

COMMISSION FOR RACIAL EQUALITY (CRE) *Equal Opportunity Policies in Higher Education*, unpublished.

CRAFT, A. and CRAFT, M, (1983) 'The Participation of Ethnic Minority Pupils in Further and Higher Education', *Education Research*, 25.1, pp. 10–19.

DAVID, M. (1980) *The State, the Family and Education*, London, Routledge and Kegan Paul.

DAVIES, L. (1978) 'The Girls' View of Schooling', *Educational Review*, 30, 2, pp. 103–9.

DAVIES, L. (1984) *Pupil Power: Deviance and Gender in School*, Barcombe, Falmer Press.

FISHER, G. and JOSHUA, H. (1982) 'Social Policy and Black Youth' in CASHMORE, E. and TROYNA, B. (eds) *Black Youth in Crisis*, London, George Allen and Unwin.

FLUDE, M. (1974) 'Sociological accounts of Differential Education Attainment' in FLUDE, M. and AHIER, J., *Educability, Schools and Ideology*, London, Croom Helm.

FULLER, M. (1982) 'Young, Female and Black' in CASHMORE E. and TROYNA B. Black Youth in Crisis, London, George Allen and Unwin.

FURTHER EDUCATION UNIT (1985a) *Black Perspectives of FE Provision*, London, FEU.

FURTHER EDUCATION UNIT (1985b) *Changing the Focus: Women and FE*, London, FEU.

INNER LONDON EDUCATION AUTHORITY (1983a) *Achievement in Schools*, London, ILEA.

INNER LONDON EDUCATION AUTHORITY (1983b) *Multi Ethnic Education in Schools*, London, ILEA.

INNER LONDON EDUCATION AUTHORITY (1983c) *A Policy for Equality – Race*, London, ILEA.

INNER LONDON EDUCATION AUTHORITY (1983d) *Anti-racist Statement and Guidelines*, London, ILEA.

INNER LONDON EDUCATION AUTHORITY (1983e) *Multi Ethnic Education in Further and Higher Community Education*, London, ILEA.

INNER LONDON EDUCATION AUTHORITY (1983f) *A Policy for Equality – Sex*, London, ILEA.

JOHN, G. (1981) *In the Service of Black Youth*, Leicester, National Association of Youth Clubs.

JONES, C. (1985) 'Sexual Tyranny: male violence in a mixed secondary school' in WEINER, G. (ed.) *Just a Bunch of Girls*, Milton Keynes, Open University Press.

LITTLE, A. N. (1975) 'The Educational Achievement of Ethnic Minority Children in London Schools' in VERMA, G. and BAGLEY, C. (eds) *Race and Education across Cultures*, London, Heinemann.

MILES, R. and PHIZACKLEA, A. (1984) *White Man's Country*, London, Pluto.

MILLMAN, V. and WEINER, G. (1983) *Reducing Sex Differentiation in Schools*, Harlow, Longman, for the Schools Council.

NEWNHAM, A. (1986) *Employment, Unemployment and Black People*, London, Runnymede Trust.

ORR, P. (1985) 'Sex bias in schools: national perspectives' in WHYTE, J. *et al.*, *Girl Friendly Schools*, London, Metheun, pp. 7–23.

RAMPTON REPORT (1981) *West Indian Children in our Schools* Committee of Inquiry into the Education of children from Ethnic Minority Groups, Cmnd 8723, London, HMSO.

REEVES, F. and CHEVANNES, M. (1981) 'The Underachievement of Rampton', *Multiracial Education*, Vol. 10, No. 1, pp. 35–45.

REEVES, F. and CHEVANNES, M. (1983) 'The Ideological Construction of Black Under-achievement', *Multiracial Education* Vol. 12, No. 1, pp. 22–41.

REEVES, F. (1986) *Culture, Race and Education*, Bilston Community College Occasional Paper.

RILEY K. (1985) 'Black Girls Speak for Themselves' in WEINER, G. (ed.) *Just a Bunch of Girls* Milton Keynes, Open University Press.

SCARMAN REPORT (1981) *The Brixton Disorder 10–12 April 1981* Cmnd 8427, London, HMSO.

SIVANANDAN, R. (1982) *A Different Hunger*, London, Pluto.

SOLOMOS, J. (1986a) 'Political language and violent protest: ideological and policy responses to the 1981 and 1985 riots, *Youth and Policy*, No. 18, pp. 12–24.

SOLOMOS, J. (1986b) 'Riots, Urban Protest and Social Policy: The Interplay of Reform and Social Control' *Policy Papers in Ethnic Reliations*, No. 7, RUER University of Warwick.

SPENDER, D. (1982) *Invisible Women*, London, Readers and Writers Publishing Cooperative.

SPENDER, D. and SARAH, E. (1980) *Learning to Lose: Sexism and Education*, London, The Women's Press.

STANWORTH, M. (1981) *Gender and Schooling*, London, Hutchinson.

SWANN REPORT (1985) *Education for All*, Committee of Inquiry into the Education of Children from Ethnic Minority Groups, Cmnd 9453, London, HMSO.

TAYLOR, H. (1985) 'A Local Authority Initiative on Equal Opportunities' in ARNOT, M. (ed.) *Race and Gender*, Oxford, Pergamon.

TOMLINSON, S. (1986) 'Ethnicity and Educational Achievements' in MODGIL, S. *et al.* (eds) *Multicultural Education: the interminable debate*, Barcombe, Falmer Press.

TROYNA, B. and BALL, W. (1985) *Views from the chalk face*, Papers in Ethnic Relations, University of Warwick.

TROYNA, B. and WILLIAMS, J. (1986) *Racism, Education and the State*, London, Croom Helm.

WEINER, G. (ed.) (1985) *Just a Bunch of Girls*, Milton Keynes, Open University Press.

WEINER, G. (1986) 'Feminist Education and Equal Opportunity: unity or discord?', *British Journal of Sociology of Education*, 7.3, pp. 265–74.

WRIGHT, C. (1984) 'School Processes – An Ethnographic Study' in EGGLESTON, J. *et al.*, *The Educational and Vocational experiences of 15–18 year old young people of ethnic minority groups*. Report submitted to the Department of Education and Science, University of Keele, Department of Education, pp. 201–78.

YATES, L. (1985) 'Is girl friendly schooling really what girls need?' in WHYTE, J. *et al.*, *Girl Friendly Schooling*, London, Methuen.

22

Beneficiaries, Benefits and Costs: an Investigation of the Assisted Places Scheme

John Fitz, Tony Edwards

and Geoff Whitty

Introduction

The Assisted Places Scheme announced in sections 17, 18 and 35(4) of the 1980 Education Act was the first significant act of education policy by the Thatcher government, its outlines having already been agreed before the 1979 election in negotiations between representatives of the Conservative Party and of the private sector. This preparatory planning made it possible to proceed to draft specification of the Scheme within weeks of Mark Carlisle's declaration of intent in June 1979. The Scheme was approved in principle by 136 votes to 15 (with 19 abstentions) at the Headmasters' Conference in September, and its outlines were included in the Education Bill presented in the following month. It was then implemented with unusual speed, against strong opposition from the other parties which included an explicit pledge that the next Labour government would end it abruptly. Its coincidence with public expenditure cuts made it politically necessary to scale down the 15,000 places a year, which some of its advocates had intended, to the 5,437 available when it began. Yet it was a considerable administrative achievement that the first pupils to hold assisted places entered their schools in September 1981. By 1985–86, £33.8 million of government money was being paid to 226 English independent schools to reduce or waive the fees they charged to parents of academically able and financially eligible children, and to cover certain incidental expenses arising from the taking up of places.[1] In the fifth year of the Scheme's existence, a total of 21,412 children were receiving such assistance, the amount depending on the 'relevant income' of their parents; about 40 per cent of these held free places, while the average parental contribution for 1985 entrants was £360, and the average DES payment per pupil for fees and other expenses £1,603.[2]

The Scheme has been justified as an extension of parental choice, a restoration of academic opportunities to many children who would not be fully stretched in schools which have to cope with a full range of ability, and as a protection both for those individuals and for the nation's resources of talent against the levelling-down effects attributed to comprehensive reorganization. It has been strongly opposed as an unwarranted declaration by the government that the public sector is incapable of providing for very able children, and as a government sponsored withdrawal of support from schools so evidently identified as being second-best. As portrayed by one independent school head whom we interviewed, assisted places were a means of 'plucking embers from the ashes' of comprehensive reorganization, especially in inner-city areas. As portrayed from another perspective, the same scheme can be seen as part of a policy of 'starving the maintained schools of funds, and then rescuing the brightest children from the surrounding wreckage' (Labour Party, 1980, p. 27).

Origins and Concerns of the Research Project

Our initial interest in studying the Scheme lay in the relationship between certain claims made by its advocates and critics, and its actual operation and effects. Examples of competing claims are given in Table 22.1.

[...] After classifying the claims made about the Scheme into broad categories, we chose to concentrate our attention on the following issues:

1   There were obvious questions about whether assisted places were reaching their intended target groups and about the extent to which the allocation and take-up of places fulfilled the Scheme's objectives as a national scholarship system.
2   In view of claims made about the effects of the Scheme on secondary school intakes and on primary school teaching methods, it also seemed necessary to undertake the more difficult task of studying some of the Scheme's effects both on the schools participating in it and on state primary and secondary schools around them.
3   Another vital issue was the way in which parental choice would operate in the context of the Scheme. At the point of entry to secondary schools, it seemed important to explore whether parents' perceptions of the opportunities it offered were related to the prevailing patterns of state provision in their areas, since the Scheme was initially presented as being of particular significance in inner-city areas with neighbourhood comprehensive schools and without maintained grammar schools.

Table 22.1 *Examples of conflicting claims about the Assisted Places Scheme taken from the public debate surrounding its inception*

Mr Carlisle said that the Labour Party had chosen to attack the scheme on a party political basis, regardless of the fact that it was underprivileged children who would gain most from the Scheme (*The Times*, 8.1.80)	The Scheme is designed for pupils from middle class families who are intent on giving their children educational advantages and privileges over the majority of children in comprehensives . . . (*Labour Councillor*, April 1981)
Able children from our poorest homes will once again have the opportunity of attending academically excellent schools (Boyson, *Daily Mail*, 25.6.81)	Only a very small proportion . . . are likely to go to the sons and daughters of Andy Capp . . . All previous experience . . . suggests that the places will be monopolised by the middle classes (*The Guardian*, 2.2.80)
The government's intention [is] . . . to give priority first to inner city areas without grammar schools (*Times Educational Supplement*, 30.11.79)	The scheme would not only undermine the comprehensive schools but also the grammar schools in the catchment area (Labour Party Information Paper, Dec. 1979)
It is not instantly obvious that the maintained system would be shattered if, say, 5,000 (of the 86,000 two A-level candidates) had been syphoned off to the independent sector (*Times Educational Supplement*, 30.11.79)	Comprehensive schools will lose numbers and in turn some will lose sixth forms, or at least . . . courses, particularly in certain minority subjects (PRISE News, Dec. 1979)
On the income-scale published, the help through the Assisted Places Scheme would go to people who otherwise would be educated in the state system (Carlisle, *Times Educational Supplement*, 15.2.80)	It is sensible to anticipate that parents who seek to use the APS would have been likely to send their children to private schools in any case (Kinnock, Press Conference, 11.12.79)
It helps parents by increasing the degree of parental choice . . . It helps the country by promoting able children (Cobban, *Sunday, Times*, 8.6.80)	Some schools [would] coach their most able pupils for the exams and more teaching resources would be transferred from helping the low and average ability pupils (Labour Party Information Paper. Dec. 1979)
For the sake of the system [critics of the scheme] would sacrifice not only the needs of these children but of a country which is desperately short of graduates in mathematics and modern languages (Maland, *The Times*, 21.3.80)	The Scheme has been endowed with all the condescending virtues of philanthropy, 'pursuit of excellence' and 'moderation', when in reality it means robbing the public purse to support the already affluent whilst pirating scholastic talent from state schools (*The Guardian*, 29.9.79)
The future of hundreds, even thousands of children is at stake. The NEC document speaks much of the viability of schools and the morale of teachers and the size of sixth forms, but says nothing of the needs of individual children. And the prime point we must make in our defence of the scheme is that it is meant to help children, not schools (*Conference*, Feb. 1980)	The Assisted Places Scheme would also prop up private education by increasing the number of places in independent schools and bailing out those independent schools whose recruitment has been flagging (*Labour Weekly*, Feb. 1980)
It is complementary to the provision made by the maintained schools, and indeed it can be fairly looked upon as an extension of the maintained sector . . . (Carlisle, Speech at Harrogate, 24.2.80)	Instead of being bridge it was intended to be between the maintained and independent sectors, it will be a wedge (Newsam, *Times Educational Supplement*, 12.9.80)

4   We also needed to investigate the claim that assisted place pupils would gain tangible relative advantages from being sponsored by the state to attend independent schools. For while advocates of the Scheme have insisted that it 'complements' rather than competes with the public sector by providing academic opportunities difficult to maintain in schools 'catering for the majority', its critics have argued that it represents an unjustifiable expenditure of public money in the absence of any check that the pupils given assisted places needed to move out of the public sector to obtain those opportunities (ISIS, 1981; Rae, 1981, pp. 178–83).

5   Finally, although this is a much longer undertaking, we wanted to examine the claim often made by the Scheme's critics that it would bring about a systemic change in the relationship between the public and private sectors, to the detriment of the public sector and the pupils remaining within it.

These were the main considerations which shaped our decisions about what evidence to collect. In collecting that evidence, we worked at three levels – nationally, in selected areas with high concentrations of assisted places, and in individual schools. Following the example of Connell *et al.* (1982), we have tried to focus down on individual pupils and parents affected by the Scheme, while keeping in view its broader contexts. [. . .]

The Making of the Scheme

[. . .]There is no space here to describe in detail the Scheme's eventual formulation. Instead, we comment briefly on two aspects of it – the selection of the participating schools and the determination of the criteria upon which the eligibility of pupils to receive assistance would be based.

The selection of participating schools
The explicit emphasis on making opportunities available in 'academically excellent schools' made it necessary to select those schools with care. The original [. . .] proposals had been restricted to direct-grant schools, but the national 'network' of schools which the government had promised required much wider participation. The selection of participating schools was bound to be difficult and sensitive. There were understandable suspicions elsewhere in the private sector that the former direct-grant schools would be given undue priority, some prestigious schools might need to be heavily persuaded to take part at all, and some academically undistinguished schools were likely to make unrealistic offers which would have to be refused in the context of a scheme so overtly committed to providing new opportunities for highly academic forms of schooling. As a first step in the sifting process, letters were sent to over 1,100 independent schools in December 1979, inviting them to indicate an interest in offering places. [. . .] The 470 schools which responded were graded 'A', 'B', or 'C' according to the range and the viability of their sixth forms. After the evidently unsuitable had been discarded, a further letter was sent in

June 1980 [. . .] to the schools judged to be both able and willing to participate. The DES letter elicited 291 firm offers of places, and this time they were divided into four categories on the basis of public examination entries over the previous two years, the size of their sixth forms, the inclusion of three sciences and at least two modern languages among their A-level subjects, and the proportion of their pupils going on to higher education. [. . .]

While 214 schools were placed in the top two categories and regarded as entirely acceptable, some academically weaker schools had to be accepted along with them in order to reduce serious inequalities in the provision of places between different regions and between boys and girls. Some schools were so enthusiastic that their offers to take assisted places had to be limited to 50 per cent of their annual intakes, while others were so cautious in committing themselves or (in the case of some boarding schools) so pessimistic about the numbers they were likely to recruit, that an intended minimum allocation of ten places had to be revised downwards to five. [. . .]

The direct-grant schools had enjoyed an 'intermediate status' as 'independent schools which have freely entered an agreement to provide services for the state' (Public Schools Commission, 1970, pp. 47–9), and St John Stevas favoured the revival of that status with LEA representatives returning to their governing bodies (Conservative Central Office, 1977). Carlisle, Sexton and most heads of schools wanted no diminution of full independence. The eventual arrangements were clear. Each school signed a formal 'participation agreement' in which it contracted with the DES to offer a certain number of assisted places. This was intended to protect the schools and their assisted places against a sudden withdrawal of support by a new government. The selection of those pupils was entirely a matter for the schools, subject only to the financial eligibility for assistance of those selected. Since there was to be no return to LEA-allocated places, there was no case for LEA representation on governing bodies. LEA involvement was limited to the right to veto the transfer of pupils to independent schools at 16 where this could be regarded as harming their own sixth-form provision, as a concession to those who deplored the Scheme as a 'pirating of scholastic talent from the state sector' (Neil Kinnock, Labour Party Annual Conference 1979, p. 357). The right was withdrawn in 1983, partly on the grounds that many LEAs were using it without regard to individual circumstances in order to express their general opposition to the Scheme. DES supervision of the Scheme in operation was intended to be slight, and has been so. The main administrative burden, the checking of parents' declarations of 'relevant income' so as to define the remission of fees and other expenses, falls on the bursars of the schools, and even their revenue accounts are unlikely to be called for except when an unusual increase in school fees is being proposed.

Determining the Criteria for Assistance

There were prolonged negotiations [. . .] about the possibility of extending the Scheme to 'needy' pupils who had entered the schools during the period between the phasing out of direct-grant and the introduction of assisted places, and about the appropriate proportion of assisted place holders to be drawn from the public sector. On both issues, official caution prevailed, as did official regard for the rhetoric with which the Scheme was normally defended. Choice of school could hardly be extended by sponsoring children to stay where they were, while any notion of an academic ladder away from 'unacademic' comprehensive schools clearly required that a majority of those with assisted places should be from the public sector. The final Regulations insisted that at least 60 per cent should have been attending a maintained school at the time of their selection, and should have done so for a continuous period which included the whole of the previous school year. [. . .]

The single most important determinant of which pupils would participate in the Scheme was the scale to be used for remitting fees. Defining it was a politically controversial and technically difficult exercise, and the scale which eventually emerged went through a series of revisions. [. . .] The decision in favour of gross income was modified by an allowance (agreed, after consultation, at £600) for each dependent relative, and by reducing parental contributions for a second assisted place holder in the same family. There was also prolonged consideration of how to avoid a sharp cut-off of assistance at the upper end of the income scale. [. . .] The Scheme eventually began with five income bands against which assistance with fees was to be assessed – under £5,000, £5,000–£6,999, £7,000–8,999, £9,000–10,999 and over £11,000. By 1985, the level of 'relevant income' below which families paid no fees at all had risen to £6,376, and five other income bands ended at £12,280. By that time, average tuition fees in the participating schools had risen to £1,886, and the average parental contribution to fees was £360. [. . .]

'Incidental expenses' were allowed for in the final Regulations. These were to cover costs of travel, school uniform and school meals where they were evidently needed, [but not] the costs of boarding education. [. . .] As a result, the HMC schools initiated with their own funds (and with DES encouragement) a limited scheme of assistance with boarding fees, while continuing to press for support from public funds. That support has not materialized, most internal bursaries are small, and the number of boarders in 1981–85 represents only 6.5 per cent of all assisted place holders. These facts illustrate a particularly sharp contrast between the scheme and the majority recommendations of the Public Schools Commission (1968), which saw in the public funding of places in boarding schools the only appropriate and politically acceptable way of 'integrating' the public and private sectors. The limited extent to which academically able pupils with 'boarding need' have been able to benefit from the Assisted Places Scheme has accentuated the already strong bias towards supporting day pupils at schools in urban areas.

The National Allocation and Take-up of Places

Nationally, the distribution of assisted places is highly significant in relation to the overall objective of restoring opportunities for 'real' academic education by creating, more equitably than the direct-grant system had done, a 'network of highly academic schools to which any child regardless of parental income would be free to apply' (Sexton, 1977, p. 87). At least one such school should therefore be within reach of every parent. The distribution of places is also relevant to the more particular claims made at the outset that priority would be given to inner-city areas without selective maintained schools, that the nature of local provision in the public sector would be carefully considered in determining allocations, and that there would be rough equality of provision between regions and between boys and girls. [. . .]

However, our own analysis of the school-by-school statistics made available to us by the DES shows clearly how constrained the Scheme has been by the location of philanthropic activities by individuals and merchant companies long ago.

The predominance of former direct-grant schools in the Scheme was inevitable, given the necessary emphasis on high academic standards and the absence of public assistance towards the costs of boarding education. These schools were well practised in making 'agreements to provide services for the state', and it was no surprise that all those which had chosen full independence in 1976 now entered the Scheme. [. . .] They also took a disproportionate share of the places allocated.

Of the 83 individual schools which offered 25 or more pre-sixth form places in the first year of the Scheme's operation, 67 were former direct-grant schools and seven of the others were former LEA grammar schools. As they saw it, such schools were being enabled to return to selection by academic merit regardless of parents' capacity to pay, and they seized that opportunity despite anxieties about over-committing themselves to pupils from whom a future Labour government would (if it acted on its explicit threat) with-draw financial support at the end of the academic year in which it took office.

As an obvious consequence, there was a heavy concentration of assisted places where these schools are most numerous – in and around the cities of London, Bristol, Liverpool, Manchester and Newcastle – and little or no provision in some other heavily populated areas less well endowed by history. [. . .]

During the negotiations with schools in 1980, there was almost an embar-rassment of offers from some areas while others had to be squeezed and cajoled for whatever was available. Even the upper limit of 50 per cent annual intake imposed on some especially enthusiastic collaborators could not avoid a marked regional imbalance because the paucity of offers elsewhere meant that most schools had to be given allocations for which they asked. Anything like an equitable distribution of places around the country was impossible, short of creating new independent schools, enticing far more voluntarily-aided grammar schools out of the maintained sector than actually made that move, or both extending assistance to the costs of boarding education and creating a much greater demand for it than had been apparent since the 1960s. [. . .]

Marginal adjustments to the allocation of places since 1981 have done nothing to reduce the inequalities. [. . .]

The take-up of places has been consistently high in Liverpool, Manchester and Bristol. It has been relatively low in some areas where few places are available, and where most places are in boarding schools or part-day schools with established boarding traditions. Of the 18 boys' schools which have recruited less than 70 per cent of their quota of places over the period 1981–85, 15 are boarding schools. They include 12 whose heads are members of the Headmasters' Conference. Some of the prestigious 'public schools' whose participation in the Scheme was so energetically sought in 1979–80 – for example, Stowe, Tonbridge and Charterhouse – have had so few of their places taken that their participation can hardly have even symbolic value.

The initially lower allocation of places for girls, though itself much less unequal than seemed likely when the first crop of offers was received by the DES in 1980, has been made more unequal again by lower rates of take-up, which have resulted in girls taking about 42 per cent of assisted places. Neither the costs nor unpopularity of boarding education for girls constitute the main explanation of this difference, since 15 of the 20 girls' schools which have reported less than 70 per cent take-up of places 1981–85 are day schools. And they include 13 former direct-grant schools which have been unable to return to their earlier patterns of recruitment. Yet, a considerable number of schools which have met or exceeded their quotas over that period are also girls' schools. These may be schools with distinctively good reputations in their 'catchment' areas, or schools with less formidable competition from the private sector or from academically oriented comprehensive schools than those which have significantly failed to meet their self-chosen targets. Wall (1986) has made a preliminary attempt to explain differential patterns of recruitment in the case of Girls' Public Day School Trust schools.

While the majority of boys' and mixed day schools have exceeded the minimum quota of assisted place holders who should be recruited from the public sector, at least when permitted virement between sixth-form and other places is taken into account, a significant minority of participating schools have consistently failed to reach it. Although a shortfall in one year can be compensated in the next, repeated failures have brought queries from the DES about whether the allocation of places might not be too high. In some cases, mainly where the problem is compounded by a generally low rate of take-up, the allocation has been quite sharply reduced. There remain, nevertheless, schools where the proportion recruited from maintained schools has remained so much lower than intended that it suggests a concern to keep them in the Scheme at all costs, even though their contribution to achieving its main objectives is almost nominal. Of the nine schools which have recruited less than half their quota over the whole five-year period, seven are HMC boarding schools which are among the educationally enclosed upper echelons of the private sector.

Nationally, the take-up of places has risen from 77 per cent in 1981 to 95 per cent in 1985, which means that the Scheme has been pushing hard against Treasury constraints on the total number of places available.[3] This suggests that, in overall terms, the Scheme has been successful in attracting candidates eligible for assistance. However, 20 per cent of sixth-form places remained unfilled even in 1985 and some two-thirds of those taking sixth-form places were already pupils in independent schools (Assisted Places Committee annual surveys, 1984 and 1985). The overall figure also conceals a considerable diversity between the 85 schools which have filled all or more than all the places allocated to them, and the 36 which have fallen well short. It was the number of schools which were over-recruiting which led to some reallocation of places to them in 1983 and 1984. This was the only way of responding to demand when Treasury resistance to increasing the total was being increased by levels of fee remission considerably higher than had been anticipated when the Scheme began.

Local Studies of Schools and Pupils

[. . .] We want to comment briefly on how we planned and carried out our investigations of the Scheme in operation. It was clear that single LEAs were inappropriate units for a study involving some evidently non-local independent schools. Our initial intention was therefore to focus on two clusters of LEAs, one in the south-east and one in the north-east, where the numbers of assisted places were substantial. However, the refusal of independent schools in one area to provide access to pupils, and of one LEA in the other to cooperate at all, led us to add to the study a further cluster of LEAs in the north-west where the cooperation of both schools and LEAs had already been assured. [. . .]

Within each of the local study areas eventually identified, we interviewed heads of independent and state secondary schools and some senior staff in independent schools who had particular responsibility for selecting assisted place pupils and monitoring their progress. In an LEA with 11 to 16 schools and a tertiary college, we also interviewed the college principal and staff responsible for the recruitment of students. In addition, we interviewed headteachers of primary schools, some of whom were experiencing pressures to prepare children for independent school entrance examinations, sometimes despite an explicit local authority ban on any cooperation with the Assisted Places Scheme beyond that which was required by law.[. . .]

The content of these interviews has been analysed in relation to arguments and predictions identified in the debate surrounding the Scheme's inception.

In the independent schools selected for detailed study (including three boarding schools from outside our local study areas), we interviewed approximately equal numbers of assisted place and full-fee paying pupils from the same year groups, using semi-structured interviews which included questions about their home backgrounds, their reasons for choosing the school, their views of the school, any plans they might have already for higher education and employment, and any contacts they continued to have with friends made at the primary stage who had gone to other schools. The same interviews were conducted with some of their contemporaries in state schools.

[. . .] Where parents agreed to be seen, the interviews lasted from an hour to two hours or more, and extended from precoded items about their own (and *their* parents') education and occupations to open-ended questions about their choice of secondary school for the target child, their objectives and strategies in making that choice, and their more general views about educational and other opportunities in British society.

Among the state schools in which we worked were some which had been available to the assisted place pupils we interviewed, might have been attended by them if the Scheme had not existed, and were attended by former friends from primary school. This component of the research has enabled us to make some detailed comparisons between the characteristics and educational careers of assisted place holders, full-fee pupils in the same schools, and state secondary pupils from the same areas. [. . .]

The Pupils and their Families

[. . .]

The backgrounds of the assisted place pupils

There have been frequent claims that some participants in the Scheme did not 'need' assistance in any accepted sense of need. Our evidence suggests, however, that only a small minority of parents abuse the Scheme financially. Some of these (usually self-employed) seem able by clever accountancy to mislead school bursars just as they mislead the Inland Revenue system. Indeed, concern about such abuses, and the damage they might cause to the Scheme's public image, was expressed in most of our interviews with senior staff in independent schools. Less obvious but perhaps more relevant questions might be asked about the appropriateness of parental income as the criterion of financial eligibility when the parent is cohabiting with an affluent partner (as was evident from several of our home interviews) or where assistance with fees would otherwise have been provided by members of the child's extended family (usually grandparents). We concentrate here, however, on the social backgrounds of those assisted place holders in our sample who legitimately qualify for the assistance they receive. [. . .]

Our initial analysis of the family backgrounds of our sample of assisted place pupils indicates the following:

1 Nearly 33 per cent can be identified from the pupil interviews as coming from single-parent families, almost all of them headed by women. Analysis of responses to more specific questions in the parental interviews points to a figure of 36 per cent. Even the lower figure is in striking contrast to figures of less than 10 per cent among our samples of full-fee paying and state school pupils.

2   On the basis of information provided by pupils, about 9 per cent of fathers and 4 per cent of mothers had occupations classified as working-class on the scale which we employed. While most pupil descriptions were subsequently confirmed in the parental interviews, analysis of the latter suggests that even these low proportions may be somewhat exaggerated. On the other hand, over 30 per cent of mothers were clearly in routine non-manual jobs, some of which critics of the Oxford Study suggest should be reclassified as working-class occupations for women (e.g. Murgatroyd, 1982; Stanworth, 1984).

3   About 50 per cent of fathers and over 20 per cent of mothers were in jobs classified on the scale as service-class occupations, though these proportions were significantly lower than those for the parents of full-fee payers in independent schools, and also of children identified as academically able in maintained schools.

4   About 7 per cent of fathers and 30 per cent of mothers were not in paid employment, though less than 2 per cent of mothers were registered as unemployed.

5   Nearly 58 per cent of mothers had themselves attended academically selective secondary schools, while a further 10 per cent had attended independent feepaying schools. Of the fathers, 40 per cent had attended academically selective secondary schools, with another 10 per cent having attended independent feepaying schools.

6   25 per cent of the siblings of our sample were, or had recently been, at independent schools.

7   44 per cent of our sample qualified for full fee remission while a further 11 per cent paid less than £100 in fees each year. These figures closely match the national statistics produced by the DES. [. . .]

While our evidence supports the claim made in defence of the Scheme that the majority of assisted places are going to children from families with low or 'modest' incomes, it also points to low participation rates by manual working-class families and especially those where the fathers are in semi-skilled or unskilled employment. It has to be noted that children from such families are also not prevalent in our sample of pupils identified as able in comprehensive schools, and they are virtually absent from our samples of pupils in maintained grammar schools and feepaying pupils in independent schools. Compared with these other samples, the parents of assisted place holders are less likely to be in 'higher-grade' professional and managerial positions, and more likely to be in middle-range occupations. Nevertheless, when taken together with more detailed case study evidence from particular families, these findings suggest that a considerable proportion of assisted place holders come from 'submerged middle-class' backgrounds already well-endowed with cultural capital. In broad terms, the social character of our sample of beneficiaries resembles that studied by Douse (1985) in different areas from our own. He found that relatively few assisted place holders came from 'unambiguously working-class backgrounds', that a large minority came from single-parent families or from other families where a low income reflected such 'unusual' circumstances as recent redundancy, and that another large minority were already within what he called 'the independent school frame of reference'. Even the publicly available national statistics are interpreted by Tapper and Salter (in press) as indicating that the Scheme has provided 'real financial assistance to relatively impoverished but educationally aware members of the petit bourgeoisie'.

The direct-grant system had been very vulnerable to criticisms, often made from within the private sector, of directing assistance to many families which did not need it. The Assisted Places Scheme has cast its net with more discrimination, but has it cast it more widely? There was no manifest intention of making the participating schools more socially diverse. [. . .] Yet the Scheme might reach many who needed it financially without necessarily attracting a majority of pupils with no previous family tradition of using independent schools (which was certainly a subsidiary objective) or compensating for the cultural disadvantages of children from culturally disadvantaged backgrounds (which was certainly a major objective for many who supported it). Tapper and Salter (in press) quote from the minutes of a meeting of HMC heads in June 1981 a clear statement that the main purposes of the scheme would be frustrated if too many of its beneficiaries turned out to be 'distressed gentlefolk' – a category similar to Douse's (1985) 'artificially poor' – and they go on to comment on the consistent lack of answers to the question of how many would be too many.

Publicly, however, most supporters of the Scheme have not treated such doubts as constituting a problem, because the 1980 Education Act merely states that the Scheme is intended to help 'pupils who might not otherwise . . . be able to benefit from education at independent schools'. Financial need is therefore the only official criterion, and it is the high proportion of place holders receiving full remission of fees (a rather higher percentage than the government itself initially anticipated) which has been the main evidence used to support the claim that the Scheme has been conspicuously successful in directing assistance to those who really need it. According to Bob Dunn, the junior minister then responsible for administering the Scheme, it had served to open up a third of all the places in participating schools to 'pupils from low-income families who are selected on merit alone', thereby giving 'children from disadvantaged and poor homes an education that they would not normally receive' (see *Hansard*, 6 December 1983 and 15 May 1984).

[. . .] It is clear that the terms 'disadvantaged' and 'poor' were being used here in a rather broader way than is usual within educational discourse, and so obscuring an otherwise notable absence of pupils fitting the more usual definitions of those categories. Douse claims that his own findings do not 'constitute a criticism of the Scheme' because the legislation which created it was never couched explicitly in terms of reaching out to the 'working-class'. Assisting 'bright youngsters' from homes with single parents or where the main wage-earner is unemployed, 'even if the family might reasonably be characterized as middle-class, is certainly not a self-evident misappropriation of funds' (Douse, 1985, p. 217). In our own research, however, which seeks partly to explore the operation of the Scheme in terms of the claims made by its advocates and critics, it is certainly pertinent to ask whether funds are being allocated to the groups originally anticipated. As suggested at the beginning of this section, reference to financial need alone minimizes the significance of a change in the representation of the typical assisted place pupil within the rhetorics of legitimization employed over the years.

While there was certainly little reference to any explicit concept of 'class' in the official justifications offered for the Scheme during 1979–81, parliamentary references being mainly to (for example) 'children from inner-urban areas', or 'academically-minded children of poor parents', or 'children from deprived backgrounds', there can surely be little doubt that these phrases conjured up images of working-class children for whom opportunities for upward mobility through educational success were now being restored. [. . .]

Significantly, this [. . .] argument was used by Rhodes Boyson, speaking now as a junior minister, to justify the Assisted Places Scheme in the week that the first assisted pupils entered their schools:

> Once again the boy or girl from an inner-city area, where the aspirations and achievements of his local comprehensive aren't such that he (*sic*) will be stretched the way he should be, can now once again join the ladders of social and economic mobility, and to me that's part of an open society. And I'm astonished anybody opposes it. (London Weekend Television, 'Starting Out', 11 September 1981)

Though less stridently expressed, a similar view was apparent in our interview with Mark Carlisle, Secretary of State responsible for the 1980 Act. In promoting the Assisted Places Scheme, he had had particularly in mind the opportunities it restored to children from inner-city areas to benefit from the kind of education offered by such schools as Bradford Grammar School and Manchester Grammar School (interview, 16 November 1982). The leading HMC head whom we quoted earlier as characterizing the essence of the Scheme as 'plucking embers from the ashes' clearly shared this view and his own support for research into the Scheme stemmed from a desire to know whether it was in fact reaching the kinds of pupil signified by such images. Yet, despite the considerable optimism displayed by many of the independent school heads whom we interviewed, there is little evidence in our own sample or that of Douse that these pupils are present in substantial numbers. Even though advocates of the Scheme have always been careful to point out that children from inner-city areas are not the only disadvantaged group who might benefit from the scheme, some unease on this point does seem to be indicated by the particular emphasis placed on pupils who do come from manual working-class backgrounds in the annual publicity exercise mounted by both the Independent Schools Information Service and the DES. To this extent, the celebration of the benefits of the Scheme for the 'submerged middle-class' may not be adequate compensation for its failure to reach its core target group, especially when this was predicted by critics when the Scheme was first announced.

Parental orientation towards the independent sector

The evidence is somewhat more mixed in relation to claims that, whatever their social class backgrounds as conventionally classified, the Scheme is assisting pupils who would not have received the same form of education without it. It seems clear that the majority of assisted place pupils in our own sample would not have attended independent schools without this form of assistance, and that the Scheme has introduced into some of these schools a small number of children from social groups not represented among their full-fee payers. Yet, like Douse, we also found a significant minority who claimed that they would have attended either that school or another independent school even if the scheme had not existed. There has always been ambiguity about the extent to which this is consistent with the main purposes of assisted places. As many as 40 per cent of those places can be offered to children already in the private sector. Yet, if a prime objective has been to widen choice by lessening the dependence of entry into that sector at the age of 11 (or 13, or 16) on parents' capacity to pay the fees, then the Scheme seems to have subsidized choice rather than created it for some of its beneficiaries.

Our data on parental and sibling education provide a further indication that involvement with the private sector was not a new experience for many of the families of assisted place holders. Nevertheless, that sample as a whole were much less locked into the 'independent school frame of reference' than were the more traditional clientele of independent schools whom we interviewed. Thus the 25 per cent of siblings of assisted place pupils who were or had recently been in independent schools has to be compared with an equivalent figure of 67 per cent for full-fee paying pupils. However, it is notable that virtually all the siblings of assisted place pupils who attended independent schools were in independent secondary schools. Whereas 56 per cent of younger siblings of feepaying pupils were in private primary schools, the figure for assisted place pupils was only 8 per cent.

This choice of an independent school for children only at the age of 11 provides an important clue to the attraction of the Scheme not just for those families with some prior commitment to the private sector, but also for the majority without that commitment or relevant experience. Our interviews with parents of assisted place holders certainly revealed a general belief that their children were getting a better education than had been available to them in the public sector. They felt this as strongly as did parents who were paying the full fees. Not surprisingly, state school parents were significantly less likely to hold a similarly positive view of the distinctive opportunities in the private sector. Although some of them (and especially some working-class parents in the north) seemed to assume, without any obvious personal sources of evidence, that independent schools were better staffed, better resourced, and uniquely capable of producing self-confident pupils likely to succeed in the world, most state school parents seemed generally satisfied with the opportunities open to their children. [. . .] Many parents of assisted place pupils, especially and unsurprisingly in those schools which formerly had direct-grant status, see those schools primarily, even entirely, as grammar schools. It is their academic selectiveness, not their independence or (at least directly) their social exclusiveness, which they value most highly. In their responses to more general interview questions, 75 per cent of these parents would have liked to see LEA grammar schools retained, compared with 61 per cent of parents of full-fee payers and only 39 per cent of parents of children in state schools.

For many of the parents of assisted place holders whom we interviewed, as well as for some who were paying full fees, their move into the private sector reflected that 'crisis of confidence' in state provision which Fox (1984) describes. They had been driven especially by the conviction that academic opportunities previously available without payment of fees in LEA or direct-grant grammar schools were not available in their local comprehensive schools. Mrs N—, for example, born and bred in a northern town, claimed to have been deterred by local knowledge from sending her son to any of the accessible state schools. For her, the former direct-grant grammar school had been 'part and parcel of her life' and nothing else could replace it. Mrs T—, whose husband had been a 'scholarship boy' at another direct-grant school, had nevertheless had to persuade him that her own determination to apply for an assisted place for her son was more than unrealistic snobbery. Although she had left a secondary modern school herself at 15, she was convinced that the local comprehensive was an 'educational disaster'. Indeed, at the height of an argument with her husband, she had shouted at him, 'I'll dance on your grave before he goes to [the local] comprehensive. I'll knife you in the night and use the insurance money to pay the fees. He'll have a gaol-bird as a mother and a dead father, but at least he'll go to a grammar school.' While such convictions were rarely expressed so colourfully, they were frequently present in many of our interviews.

The crucial question, of course, in terms of the original arguments for an Assisted Places Scheme, is how far such general perceptions about the relative merits of independent and maintained schools are justified. We are therefore looking in some detail at the opportunities available for academically able pupils in the maintained schools in which we worked, and at how those opportunities were perceived by parents in them. The few remaining opportunities for an academic education within maintained grammar schools were diminishing throughout the period of the research. However, within our samples there were pupils who qualified both for assisted places at independent schools and for places at LEA grammar schools. There was no clear pattern to their eventual choices, though the local reputations of the respective schools, the educational experiences of elder siblings, and their parents' financial circumstances were important factors. Overall, our limited sample of pupils from maintained grammar schools suggests that such schools had become even more socially selective than the intake of assisted place pupils to independent schools. Although this phenomenon of middle-class domination of scarce educational resources is hardly surprising (Halsey *et al.*, 1980), it was nevertheless somewhat startling to hear a parent, Mrs V—, justify sending her daughter to an independent school on an assisted place, despite having qualified for a place at the LEA grammar school, on the grounds that the latter was not only too narrowly selective academically but also too 'snobby'.

With regard to the opportunities available for academically able children in comprehensive schools, there is no doubt that there were comprehensive schools in our sample capable of identifying and fostering academic talent. Their academic records and their high levels of parental satisfaction were ample testimony to this. There were also schools whose records in these respects left much to be desired. Yet, the latter were often schools which educationally aware parents found strategies for avoiding and which primary school teachers counselled able children against attending. They were therefore not, by and large, the schools that assisted place holders would have been likely to attend had they opted for the maintained sector. In this respect, and in view of our data about the social class backgrounds of assisted place holders, the slight note of caution about the Scheme expressed in an editorial in the HMC journal *Conference* in February 1980 may have been more prescient than the general tone of optimism amongst most of the heads whom we interviewed. It pointed out that 'a scheme designed to attract working-class children who would otherwise go to a poor neighbourhood comprehensive, may simply attract middle-class children who would otherwise go to a *good* comprehensive'.

Some Potential Consequences of the Scheme for the Educational System

[. . .]

It is clear from the previous section of this paper that, whether or not adequate academic opportunities would actually have been available to assisted place holders within the maintained sector, our own findings indicate that the architects and advocates of the Scheme have had considerable success in mobilizing behind it a constituency of parents who share both their belief in the distinctive education offered by good grammar schools and their doubts about the capacity of some comprehensive schools (or even of any comprehensive school) to extend very able children. In the absence, in most areas, of LEA grammar schools, these parents have come, often reluctantly, to regard independent schools as synonymous with selective schools and therefore with high levels of academic achievement. The presumed association between academically selective schools and academic achievement is, of course, by no means conclusively demonstrated in the literature and the basis of any such association is not necessarily that assumed by such parents (see Heath, 1984). Nevertheless, the strength of their convictions indicates yet again the mammoth task of persuasion which supporters of comprehensive education have yet to accomplish and which the Assisted Places Scheme has made more difficult.

Critics of the Scheme argue that while there is no firm evidence that comprehensive schools are unable to cater for the full range of ability, their chances of doing so are significantly diminished (especially at the sixth-form stage) by that 'pirating of scholastic talent' which the Scheme is said to have encouraged. On the other hand, some advocates of the Scheme have suggested that it will contribute to the effectiveness of state schools, at least in the long term, by exerting additional pressure on them to improve their own standards. This view was certainly not shared by the heads of our sample of maintained schools, and it is difficult to see how such competitive pressure would work. As we have indicated, a large minority of assisted place pupils either come from independent primary schools or would have moved into the private sector anyway, while only a very few of our assisted place holders would have been potential candidates for the weakest comprehensive schools. There is also a distinct possibility that the Scheme may be increasing the academic selectiveness of participating schools, and so enhancing their 'results' beyond what would have been attainable through the operation of 'pure' market forces.

Although there is no evidence in our study to support the view of critics that the Scheme would shore up ailing private schools by filling otherwise empty places at public expense, there certainly were independent schools in our sample which were keen to recruit well-motivated assisted place pupils rather than the new market constituency which the less prestigious schools were being forced to appeal to in the absence of LEA place holders and in a situation of falling rolls. This growing constituency was described disparagingly by one teacher as 'the sons of so-called "company directors" – garage owners and haulage contractors, really, you know – whose knowledge of higher education can be written on the back of a postage stamp'. The continuing opportunity to recruit on the basis of merit rather than capacity to pay is especially relevant to a main factor in the market appeal of most of the schools in the Scheme – the high proportion of their leavers who carry the required A level passport to higher education and (directly or indirectly) to various prestigious occupations (Halsey *et al.*, 1984). Despite the small numbers currently involved, the fact that many assisted place pupils appear to be drawn from a similar constituency to that which provides able pupils in academically successful comprehensive schools means that the Scheme could have negative long-term consequences for the reputation of state schools, and so for their capacity to compete with the private sector. Indeed, as the Scheme was getting under way, the Chief Officer of ILEA warned that eventually it might 'really create a fee-paying grammar school system and a secondary modern maintained sector' by encouraging able children of more affluent state school parents to follow the assisted place holders into the private sector (the statement was made in the same television programme as Boyson's declaration of confidence in the scheme's potential contribution to social mobility for inner-city children, which we quoted earlier in this paper).

More generally, the Scheme has been seen not only as sponsoring a limited though significant withdrawal of able pupils from state schools, but also as a precursor of a large-scale intrusion of private provision into the state sector. It was introduced at a time of strong ideological support for an extension of private provision as part of a new order in which publicly and privately provided services would compete freely for the allegiance of consumers, and improve in quality through having to do so (Anderson, 1980; Harris and Seldon, 1979; Seldon, 1981; Lord, 1984). In this context, it was argued that state schools would only become fully responsive to parents' wishes, and so subject to the discipline of having to retain their active loyalty, when those parents could take their business elsewhere (Boyson, 1975, pp. 148–50; West, 1982; Dennison, 1984). The Assisted Places Scheme has therefore been increasingly seen by some exponents of New Right policies as a preparation for more radical extensions of parental choice rather than merely a traditional scholarship ladder (see, for example, Boyson, quoted in Albert, 1982). Yet while the political climate has certainly become much more favourable to private education, the Scheme itself remains a limited and imperfect expression of the educational policy preferences of a government explicitly committed to reducing the share of national resources taken by the public sector (Joseph, 1984). The 'logical' next steps predicted at its inception have not yet materialized. In particular, the mechanism most favoured by market liberals, that of the educational voucher, has continued to be found 'intellectually attractive' but impractical by the ministers who would be responsible for introducing it, and the high hopes of 1983 that institutional inertia and the vested interests of public sector teachers (and officials) would be overcome have not yet fully revived (Seldon, 1986; Tullock, 1986; Barnes, 1986). This has left the advocates of vouchers unimpressed by a scheme in which a very limited extension of parental choice is itself confined to the parents of academically able children.

Yet the scope of that Scheme reflects clearly its origins and the peculiar nature of private schooling in this country. Where private schools in other industrial countries are widely defended as expressions of religious, ethnic and cultural diversity, their predominant function has been to provide suitable training for high-status occupations within the cultural mainstream (Mason, 1983, 1985; James, 1986). In this English context, it is understandable that the essential defence of the scheme has been that it complements the public sector by offering what its advocates see as a *quality* of provision not readily available within it and which thereby makes a 'real contribution to social mobility' (ISIS, 1981). Furthermore, in relation to objectives defined in this way, it is arguable that the scope of the Scheme was also appropriate – in so far as it offered about as many places as were available in those schools capable of offering a 'demonstrably' excellent academic education to the kinds of able pupils for whom the Scheme was intended.

Proposals to extend the Scheme to a much wider range of pupils and schools, to establish 'Crown schools' and seek private funding for educational experiments in inner-city areas, even to find feasible ways of introducing vouchers wholesale, all remain as potential items on the [. . .] future educational agenda. [. . .] Meanwhile, in that it makes places available to considerably less than 1 per cent of those entering secondary schools for the first time, its effect on the educational system as a whole might well be considered marginal. However, it clearly has practical and symbolic consequences out of all proportion to the numbers of pupils involved. Its direct 'creaming' effects on the maintained sector are certainly of much less significance than its capacity to reinforce belief in the inability of public sector schools to match the quality of private provision or to develop credible alternatives to the type of education which the Scheme has so powerfully sponsored.

Acknowledgments

We wish to acknowledge the support of the Social Science Research Council/ Economic and Social Research Council 1982–1986 for the research reported in this paper (Award no. C00230036). We are also grateful for the assistance given by Dr Mary Fulbrook, research associate on the project from 1982–83, and by Geoffrey Cockerill, honorary consultant to the project from 1982–85. Our greatest debt is, of course, to the many heads, teachers, pupils, parents, politicians and public servants who gave freely of their time to assist us with the project.

Notes

1   The Scheme also extends to Wales, where nine schools had agreed to participate when it began in 1981. A different scheme operates in Scotland, where it is more school-based and is subject to strict cash limits.

2   It is impossible to make direct comparisons with pupil costs in the public sector, as DES officials pointed out during the period of detailed negotiations 1979–80. For what they are worth as a rough indication, the latest available figures from the Chartered Institute of Public Finance Accountants give the net costs per secondary school pupil 1983–84 as £1,836 in ILEA, £1,194 in the outer London boroughs, £1,026 in the metropolitan districts, and £1,071 in the English counties.

3   As noted earlier, the Scottish Scheme is cash-limited. The English (and Welsh) Scheme clearly cannot be, since the total amount paid in remission of fees and other expenses depends unpredictably each year on the relevant income of parents.

References

ALBERT, T. (1982) 'The cheapest way to help the brightest and the best', *The Guardian*, 23 November.

ANDERSON, D. (ed.) (1980) *The Ignorance of Social Intervention*. London: Croom Helm.

BARNES, J. (1986) 'Political pressure and government inaction', *Journal of Economic Affairs*, 6, 4, 22–3.

BOYSON, R. (1975) *The Crisis in Education*. London: Woburn Press.

CONNELL, R., ASHENDEN, D., KESSLER, S. and DOWSETT, G. (1982) *Making the Difference: Schools, Families and Social Division*. Sydney: Allen and Unwin.

CONSERVATIVE CENTRAL OFFICE (1977) *Restoring Direct Grant Schools*. London.

DENNISON, S. (1984) *Choice in Education*. London: Institute of Economic Affairs.

DOUSE, M. (1985) 'The background of assisted places scheme students', *Educational Studies*, 11, 3, 211–17.

FOX, I. (1984) 'The demand for a public school education: a crisis of confidence in comprehensive schooling' in WALFORD, G. (ed.) (see below).

HALSEY, A., HEATH, A. and RIDGE, J. (1980) *Origins and Destinations*. Oxford: Clarendon Press.

HALSEY, A., HEATH, A. and RIDGE, J. (1984) 'The political arithmetic of public schools' in WALFORD, G. (ed.) (see below).

HARRIS, R. and SELDON, A. (1979) *Over-ruled on Welfare*. London: Institute of Economic Affairs.

HEATH, A. (ed.) (1984) 'Comprehensive and Selective Schooling', Special issue of *Oxford Review of Education*, 10, 1.

INDEPENDENT SCHOOLS INFORMATION SERVICE (1981) *The Case for Collaboration: the Independent Schools and the Maintained System*. London: ISIS.

JAMES, E. (1986) "The public/private division of responsibility for education: an international comparison', *American Educational Research Association*, annual meeting, San Francisco, 16–20 April.

JOSEPH, K. (1984) 'Speech to the North of England Education Conference', January 1984, *Oxford Review of Education*, 10, 2, 137–46.

LABOUR PARTY (1980) *Private Schools: a Discussion Document*. London.

LORD, R. (1984) *Value for Money in Education*. London: Public Money (Chartered Institute of Public Finance and Accountancy).

MASON, P. (1983) *Private Education in the EEC*. London: ISIS.

MASON, P. (1985) *Private Education in the USA and Canada*. London: ISIS.

MURGATROYD, L. (1982) 'Gender and occupational stratification', *Sociological Review*, 30, 574–602.

PUBLIC SCHOOLS COMMISSION (1968) First Report. London: HMSO.

PUBLIC SCHOOLS COMMISSION (1970) Second Report. London: HMSO.

RAE, J. (1981) *The Public School Revolution: Britain's Independent Schools 1964–1979*. London: Faber.

SALTER, B. and TAPPER, T. (1985) *Power and Policy in Education: the Case of Independent Schooling*. Lewes: Falmer Press.

SELDON, A. (1981) *Wither the Welfare State*. London: Institute of Economic Affairs.

SELDON, A. (1982) 'West on vouchers', *Journal of Economic Affairs*, 3, 1, 44–5.

SELDON, A. (1986) *The Riddle of the Voucher: An Inquiry into the Obstacles to Introducing Choice and Competition in State Schools*. London: Institute of Economic Affairs.

SEXTON, S. (1977) 'Evolution by choice' in COX, C. and BOYSON, R. (eds), *Black Paper Five*. London: Temple Smith.

STANWORTH, M. (1984) 'Women and class analysis: a reply to Goldthorpe', *Sociology*, 18, 2, 159–70.

TAPPER, T. and SALTER, B. (in press) 'The Assisted Places Scheme: a policy evaluation'. *Journal of Education Policy*.

TULLOCK, G. (1986) 'No public choice in state education', *Journal of Economic Affairs*, 6, 4, 18–22.

WALL, D. (1986) 'The Assisted Places Scheme and its operation in London Girls' Public Day School Trust schools.' Unpublished MA dissertation, University of London Institute of Education.

WALFORD, G. (ed.) (1984) *British Public Schools: Policy and Practice*. Lewes: Falmer Press.

WALL, D. (1986) 'The Assisted Places Scheme and its operation in London Girls'

23

The Role of Parents and Other Adults

John C. Coleman

One of the central themes of adolescent development is the attainment of independence, often represented symbolically in art and literature by the moment of 'departure' from home. However, for most young people today independence is not gained at one specific moment by the grand gesture of saying goodbye to one's parents and setting off to seek one's fortune in the wide world. Independence is much more likely to mean freedom within the family to make day-to-day decisions, emotional freedom to make new relationships, and personal freedom to take responsibility for one's self in such things as education, political beliefs and future career. There are many forces which interact in propelling an individual towards this state of maturity. Naturally both physical and intellectual maturation encourage the adolescent toward greater autonomy. In addition to these factors there are, undoubtedly, psychological forces within the individual as well as social forces in the environment which have the same goal.

[. . .]

In understanding this process it is necessary to appreciate that the young person's movement toward adulthood is far from straightforward [. . .]. While independence at times appears to be a rewarding goal, there are also moments when it is a worrying, even frightening prospect. Childlike dependence can be safe and comforting at no matter what age, if, for example, one is facing problems or difficulties alone, and it is essential to realize that no individual achieves adult independence without a number of backward glances. It is this ambivalence which underlies the typically contradictory behaviour of adolescents, behaviour which is so often the despair of adults. Thus there is nothing adults find more frustrating than having to deal with a teenager who is at one moment complaining of having parents who are always interfering (for example, giving advice) and the next bitterly protesting that no one takes any interest in him [or her] (for example, not giving advice). However, it is equally important to acknowledge that parents themselves usually hold conflicting attitudes towards their teenage children. On the one hand they may wish young people to be independent, to make their own decisions, and to cease making childish demands, whilst on the other, they may at the same time be frightened of the consequences of independence (especially the sexual consequences), and sometimes jealous of the opportunities and idealism of youth. In addition it should not be forgotten that the adolescent years often coincide with the difficulties of middle age for parents. Adjusting to unfulfilled hopes, preparation for retirement, declining physical health, marital difficulties and so on, may all increase family stress, and add further to the problems faced by young people in finding a route to independence which is not too fraught with conflict.

[. . .]

The 'Generation Gap'

[. . .]

In this study [Fogelman, 1976] the parents were given a list of issues on which it is commonly thought adults and young people of this age might disagree. The results indicated a situation which was, from the parents' point of view, a harmonious one. The two most commonly reported areas of disagreement – dress or hairstyle, and the time of coming in at night – are what might be expected, but even here only 10 per cent of parents said that they often disagreed about these things. The views of the parents are illustrated in Table 23.1.

The young people [. . .] agreed that appearance and evening activities were sometimes an issue of disagreement in the home, but otherwise they reported an atmosphere free from major conflict. [. . .]

Table 23.1 *Disagreement between parents and study child (parents' report) (N = 11,531)*

	Often %	Sometimes %	Never or hardly ever %
Choice of friends of the same sex	3	16	81
Choice of friends of the opposite sex	2	9	89
Dress or hairstyle	11	35	54
Time of coming in at night or going to bed	8	26	66
Places gone to in own time	2	9	89
Doing homework	6	18	76
Smoking	6	9	85
Drinking	1	5	94

from K. Fogelman (1976) *Britain's Sixteen-Year-Olds*, National Children's Bureau

Table 23.2   *Family relationships (children's report)* *(N = 11,045)*

	Very true %	True %	Uncertain %	Untrue %	Very untrue %
I get on well with my mother	41	45	8	4	1
I get on well with my father	35	45	13	5	2
I often quarrel with a brother or sister	23	43	10	19	5
My parents have strong views about my appearance (e.g. dress, hairstyle etc.)	15	33	19	27	6
My parents want to know where I go in the evening	27	51	8	11	3
My parents disapprove of some of my male friends	9	19	18	37	16
My parents disapprove of some of my female friends	5	15	18	40	22

from K. Fogelman (1976) *Britain's Sixteen-Year-Olds*, National Children's Bureau

A further important variable is age. [. . .] It is apparent that young people's feelings of conflict increase as a function of age, but reach a peak at different stages for boys and girls. [. . .] It is also important to recognize that the focus of conflict is likely to be different for the two sexes. The results pertaining to age differences are illustrated in Figure 23.1.

[. . .] Smith (1978) draws attention to a further relevant variable, that of social class. He interviewed parents of sixteen-year-olds in Britain, and asked for their views of this age group. He found that middle-class parents expressed much more favourable views than working-class parents. For example, while 31 per cent of working-class parents were unfavourably inclined towards this age group only 18 per cent of middle-class parents responded in this way. [. . .] The working-class group contained a much higher proportion of people who related highly deviant items to most or all teenagers. Thus drink was mentioned by 14 per cent, sex by 14 per cent, drugs by 5 per cent, political demonstrations by 3.5 per cent and violence by 4 per cent. The middle-class respondents, on the other hand, contained a much higher proportion who saw most or all teenagers as considerate to others (43 per cent) and bright and interesting (60 per cent). As Smith says: 'Whilst I am not suggesting that more than a small proportion of working-class respondents see teenagers as being typified by grossly deviant activities, the pattern which emerges does seem to show a distinctly more negative response on behalf of the working class (1978, p. 149).

Figure 23.1. *Proportions of each age group expressing themes of conflict with parents on one item of a sentence-completion test.* (from J. C. Coleman, 1974, *Relationships in Adolescence*, Routledge & Kegan Paul)

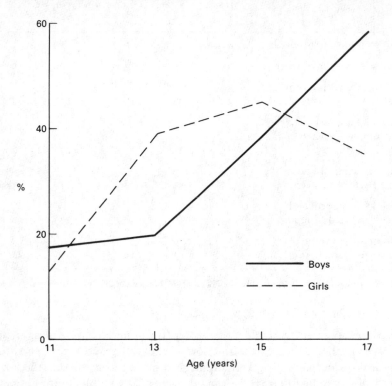

[. . .] While on the one hand the notion of a full-scale generation gap is obviously not sustained by the research evidence, on the other hand it cannot simply be dismissed as a complete fiction. One important reason for the confusion which exists lies in the difference between attitudes towards close family members, and attitudes to more general social groupings, such as 'the younger generation'. Thus, for example, teenagers may very well approve and look up to their own parents while expressing criticism of adults in general. Similarly, parents may deride 'hippies', 'drop-outs' or 'soccer hooligans' while holding a favourable view of their own adolescent sons and daughters. Another fact that needs to be stressed is that there is a difference between feeling and behaviour. Adolescents may be irritated or angry with their parents as a result of day-to-day conflicts, but issues can be worked out in the home, and do not necessarily lead to outright rejection or rebellion. Furthermore, as Conger (1977) points out, too little credit is given to the possibility that adults and young people, although disagreeing with each other about certain things, may still respect each other's views, and live in relative harmony together under the same roof. [. . .] However, to deny any sort of conflict between teenagers and older members of society is equally false. Adolescents could not grow into adults unless they were able to test out the boundaries of authority, nor could they discover what they believed unless given the opportunity to push hard against the beliefs of others. The adolescent transition from dependence to independence is almost certain to involve some conflict, but its extent should not be exaggerated.

[. . .]

Parents as Role Models

[. . .]

It is important to be clear that the likelihood of role decisions or choices being influenced by the parents will be determined not only by the nature of the role model, but also by the degree of identification between parent and child. The topic of identification is a large one, and will not be dealt with in any depth here. [. . .] Suffice to say that the degree of identification, that is, the extent to which the young person incorporates as his or her own the attitudes and characteristics belonging to another person, will depend on a number of factors. Among these the degree of warmth and affection experienced by the child in the relationship with the parents will undoubtedly be of central importance. An additional factor, [. . .] will be the structure of the family, and the child's involvement in decision making processes. Thus it will be apparent that in considering parents as role models we cannot ignore the question of identification. It is this characteristic of the relationship which determines the final impact of parents as models, as will become clear when examining some of the evidence which has accumulated on this topic. [. . .]

Let us first of all turn our attention to the development of sex roles. [. . .] As far as boys are concerned research has indicated that adolescents whose fathers provide a moderately masculine role model, but who are also involved in the feminine caring side of family life, adjust better as adults and experience fewer conflicts between their social values and their actual behaviour. Boys whose fathers provide role models which are at either extreme – excessively masculine or predominantly feminine – appear to adjust less well. To take one example from the experimental literature, the studies by Mussen and others (Mussen, 1962; Mussen *et al.*, 1963, 1974) have shown that although during adolescence those boys with strong masculine role models and stereotyped masculine behaviour seem to be the best adjusted – to be the most popular, to have high self-esteem and so on – when followed up ten years later they appeared to do less well in adulthood than men who during adolescence had more ambivalent role models and more 'feminine' interests. Thus it would seem that for boys at least a rigid adherence to stereotyped sex-role behaviour may be adaptive in adolescence but not so helpful in adjustment to the demands of adult life.

.If sex-role development is complicated for boys, it is certainly just as problematic for girls. There are at least three reasons for this. First, sex roles are usually less clear for girls than they are for boys, second, in many circumstances higher status is accorded to masculine roles, so that girls may face confusion as to which is more preferable; and third, women's position in society is at present passing through a period of rapid change, making it even more difficult for adolescent girls to make personal choices in line with what is or is not expected of them. In Conger's (1977) view, based on research findings, it is perfectly possible for girls, no matter whether they are identified with a mother who is 'traditional' and 'feminine' or with one who is more liberal, independent and socially assertive, to adjust well as women themselves. The important point is that they do have someone positive with whom to identify, someone who has resolved her own problems of sexual identification. It appears to be those whose sex-role behaviour is based on rejection of a not very loving mother, or on identification with a mother who has herself failed to resolve her own identity problem, who have difficulties in adjustment. [. . .]

As far as parents as work role models are concerned [. . .] many of the same things must apply. Close positive relationships are most likely to facilitate the use of the parent as a work role model, although this does not necessarily mean taking the same type of job as the mother or father. Much more important here are the transmission of attitudes to work, and the general area of work interest. Thus the boy whose father is a doctor does not himself need to go into medicine to have seen in his father a positive role model. More important will be a job which requires further education, which has a high professional standing, and which may in some way involve caring for others. In one interesting study by Bell (1969), the effects of father as role model at the ages of seventeen and twenty-seven were investigated. Results showed that those adolescent boys whose fathers acted as the most positive (i.e. highly evaluated) role models at seventeen were likely to adjust best in their future careers. However, interestingly those who, at twenty-seven, still saw fathers as the most positive role models were not likely to be functioning as well in their jobs as those who had, by this time in their careers, sought other non-family role models. In a slightly different study by Baruch (1972), women's attitudes to work were assessed as a function of their own mother's attitudes and experiences. Here results showed that women between the ages of nineteen and twenty-one held attitudes towards work, towards feminine competence (i.e. the ability to hold down a job), and towards the dual career pattern (the combination of motherhood and a career) which resulted directly from their mother's experiences and beliefs. Women whose mothers had not worked devalued feminine competence, and whether a woman was favourable towards the dual career pattern depended directly on whether her mother supported it or not, and if she worked, whether she believed she had suffered as a result of so doing. Thus in different ways both Bell and Baruch indicate how parents play a critical part as role models where work adjustment is concerned. [. . .]

We can learn something of the function of parents by glancing briefly at the studies of the effects of parental absence. [. . .] There is an accumulation of evidence to show that boys from father-absent homes are more likely than those who have fathers living at home to encounter difficulties in a wide variety of areas (Conger, 1977). They are, for example, more likely to score lower on traditional intelligence tests, perform less well at school, and to be less popular in their social group. Interestingly, their intellectual performance differs significantly from that of other boys, in that they are more likely to obtain higher scores in tests measuring verbal ability than in those concerned with mathematics. Such a picture is in direct contrast to the usual male pattern of better performance in mathematics, and closely resembles the typical female pattern of intellectual functioning (Carlsmith, 1964). Furthermore [. . .], boys from father-absent homes are more likely to drop out of school, to be impulsive in their behaviour, and to become involved in activities such as delinquency, which carries with it an aura of exaggerated toughness and masculinity. It should be noted, however, that the incidence of these difficulties, especially delinquency, is closely related to a number of other factors, such as the reason for father's absence (i.e. death or divorce), the nature of the relationship between father and son where divorce or separation has occurred, as well as more general variables such as social class. In spite of this, however, it will be clear that almost all of these differences between boys with and without fathers in the home may be seen to be directly related to the absence of an appropriate role model.

While there have been many fewer studies with girls, much the same conclusions may also be drawn here. [. . .] Hetherington (1972) [. . .] was able to show only too clearly the effects of parental absence on the behaviour of these girls. According to Hetherington, these were, 'manifested mainly in an inability to interact appropriately with males'. In particular the daughters of divorcees spent a large proportion of their time seeking out male company and engaging in sex-related behaviour. While on interview these girls showed no lack of preference for the female role, they were rarely observed in typical female activities. This was explained by the fact that they simply spent so much of their time hanging around the areas where male activities were carried out, such as the carpentry shop, basketball court and so on. In contrast to this group, daughters of widowed women appeared much more likely to avoid contact with male peers. These girls tended to be inhibited and lacking in confidence, and thus to manifest behaviour which was exactly the opposite of that observed in daughters of divorced parents. As Hetherington says: 'it is argued that both groups of girls were manifesting deviant behaviours in attempting to cope with their anxiety and lack of skills in relating to males' (p. 324). [. . .]

In summary we have seen that, at least based on American evidence, the function of parents as role models during adolescence is a surprisingly significant one. It is undoubtedly a popular assumption that, all things being equal, parents have a more important part to play during childhood than during adolescence. Our brief review indicates that this is far from the truth. At a time when role models are necessary to a far greater extent than ever before, it is upon parents above all that adolescents depend for knowledge and example. On their interpretation of such things as work and sex roles will be based the adolescent's adjustment to the choices with which he or she will be faced.

Attitudes to Authority

Changing attitudes to authority are an integral feature of the achievement of independence, and must inevitably form one part of the process of adolescent development. [. . .] Clearly, a number of factors will play their part in such a process. Adults will exercise their authority in different ways, so for example, [. . .] some will attempt to make it legitimate by providing explanations and some will not. Some will wish to share their power with young people at an early stage, while others will keep it to themselves for as long as possible. In addition, adolescents will inevitably meet with a wide range of authority figures, and will experience many different uses of power and influence. They will perceive some as more justifiable than others, and will have different expectations and make different demands on the varying authority figures with whom they will come into contact. None the less a major change will occur at some period between early and late adolescence, a change involving a fundamental reorientation of attitudes towards authority, and it is at this change that we shall now look.

In one of the earlier studies on the subject Tuma and Livson (1960) developed a 'conformity scale', making it possible for them to rank individual adolescents on the degree to which they accepted authority. The five-point scale was as follows:

5   Hectic drive to conform.
4   Real urge to conform, to be accepted, to avoid friction, etc.
3   Occasional assertions of individuality but for the most part accepts regulations, rules, social standards without much wear and tear.
2   Individual tries to sidestep rules and regulations and to avoid conformity. Passive resistance or avoidance of situations where rules or regulations would have to be met.
1   Extremely resistive to rules, regulations and authority. Extreme individualism and non-conformity.

The study itself was a very small one, involving only forty-seven subjects, but it had the advantage of being longitudinal, rating the adolescents for conformity at three ages (fourteen, fifteen and sixteen) in situations at home, at school, and with their peers. Findings showed that conformity was lowest in the home, and greatest in peer group situations, and that, for boys at least, there was a close association between conformity and social class, conformity being greatest among middle-class teenagers. In addition, conformity scores for this group changed very little between the ages of fourteen and sixteen. There was also great similarity between boys and girls, the only significant difference being that at sixteen girls were more conforming than boys in peer group situations.

At first sight these results appear to be in direct contradiction to the contention that attitudes to authority undergo a marked change as a function of age during adolescence. However, let us now look at a rather different piece of evidence. In the author's own work (Coleman, 1974), a sentence-completion test was given at four age levels – eleven, thirteen, fifteen and seventeen. One sentence stem in this test read as follows: '*If someone gives orders to a group* . . . .' Responses were classified according to whether the individual expressed a desire to conform (for example, '*If someone gives orders to a group* everyone thinks he will obey') or whether some challenge to authority was implied (for example, '*If someone gives orders to a group* he is a very conceited and selfish person'). Results are illustrated in Figure 23.2, and indicate that a change in attitude does occur within this age range, but that this applies primarily to the younger age groups. Thus it may be that the results of the Tuma and Livson study are not inconsistent, but simply reflect attitudes to authority in an age span where the major re-orientation has already occurred. However, it should be noted that these studies have major limitations, the first because of the small numbers involved, and the second because we have extrapolated results from only one item of a wide-ranging set of tests. [. . .]

Figure 23.2. *Proportions of each age group expressing acceptance and rejection of authority on one item of a sentence-completion test* (from J. C. Coleman, 1974, *Relationships in Adolescence*, Routledge & Kegan Paul)

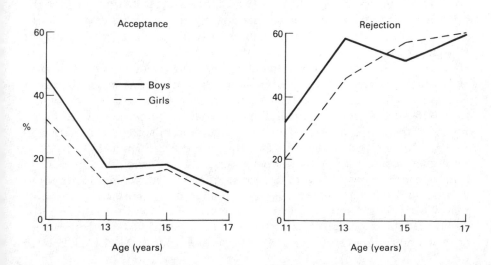

[In] the study by Douvan and Adelson (1966) [. . .] a distinction was drawn between three types of discipline used in the home: physical, psychological (based primarily on verbal admonition) and deprivation (involving the loss of freedom, mobility, finance, etc.) – and these were related to the adolescent's attitude to authority. Girls were shown to be most compliant where physical punishment was in use, and least conforming with psychological types of punishment. Boys, however, while manifesting a similar pattern, showed two further important characteristics which did not apply in the case of the girls. Boys who were physically punished showed a striking resentment of their parents at the same time as being dependent and submissive, and, in addition, appeared under-developed in regard to social behaviour and the internalization of controls. Douvan and Adelson constructed an index indicating the degree of internalized morality. One of the items composing the index was: 'When might a boy break a rule?' Results showed interesting differences between the groups, for those who had been physically punished were most likely to give as examples situations when for some reason authority was not present, while those in the deprivation and psychological punishment groups gave examples of emergencies, accidents and outright rebellion. Clearly, in considering attitudes to authority in adolescence, age and social class are not the only factors to be taken into account, but, as other research reviewed has also shown, the family context is crucial.

[. . .] [A] study carried out by the author in collaboration with Eva Zajicek (1980) [. . .] involved working-class teenagers in an urban environment, and addressed itself to a number of questions, among which were the issues of what young people expected of ideal authority figures, and how these young people felt conflicts between themselves and adults ought to be resolved. In relation to the first question we were keen to look specifically at the issue of how much autonomy adolescents seek in their relationships with adults. The teenagers who took part in the study were between the ages of fourteen and sixteen and the results are illustrated in Figure 23.3. Data are given for the proportions of the total sample mentioning three dimensions – support, control and autonomy – as being features of their ideal authority figures. It will be apparent from the results that, contrary to expectations, these adolescents seem hardly to be clamouring for their freedom. Where mothers and fathers are concerned teenagers would like at least as much control as autonomy, while in the school situation control is of far greater importance than self-determination. This finding is amplified somewhat by the other results of the study – those relating to the adolescent's preferred solution to conflict. In line with Elder's (1963) work we differentiated three types of resolution – democratic, authoritarian and permissive – and asked the adolescents which type they thought most appropriate in conflicts they experienced at home and in school. The results are illustrated in Figure 23.4, and show that while young people appear to feel that they can and would like to be involved in the resolution of conflicts in the home, in the school situation there are many more issues requiring adult intervention. One of the obvious reasons

Figure 23.3. *Proportions of young people mentioning three dimensions as aspects of their ideal authority figures* (from J. C. Coleman and E. Zajicek, 1980, *Adolescence*)

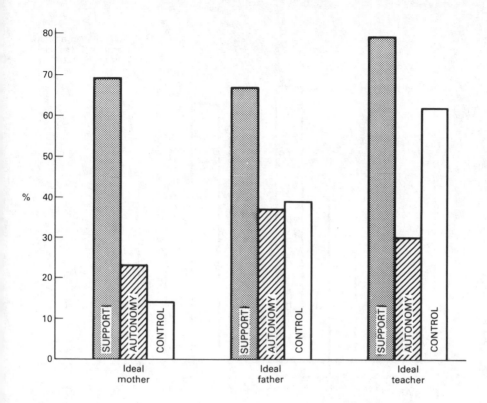

for this difference is the context in which power is exercised. In school it is, by and large, control over others which is at issue, since the conflicts mentioned in this study were almost all to do with delinquent and disruptive behaviour. While the adolescents in this sample wished to have a say in their own activities, they were concerned about the disruptive behaviour of their peers and saw a need for effective authority to control this. In the much smaller family group, however, young people saw themselves as participants in the exercise of power, and here they had a much greater sense of their own ability to contribute in a responsible way to the decision-making process.

[. . .] Perhaps the most important findings are those which show that the family context is critical not only for the provision of work- and sex-role models, but for the whole course of the adolescent transition from childhood to adulthood. Thus, contrary to popular assumption, the role of the parents for teenagers seems likely to be as important and influential as it is during early childhood. [. . .]

Figure 23.4. *A comparison of preferred resolutions to conflicts at home and at school* (from J. C. Coleman and E. Zajicek, 1980, *Adolescence*)

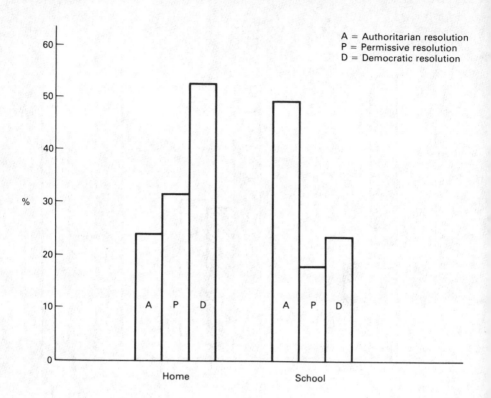

References

BARUCH, G. K. (1972) Maternal influences upon college women's attitudes toward women and work. *Developmental Psychology,* **6,** 32–7.

BELL, A. P. (1969) Role modelling of fathers in adolescence and young adulthood. *Journal of Counselling Psychology,* **16,** 30–5.

CARLSMITH, L. (1964) Effects of early father absence on scholastic aptitude. *Harvard Educational Review,* **34,** 3–21.

COLEMAN, J. C. (1974) *Relationships in Adolescence,* Boston and London: Routledge & Kegan Paul.

COLEMAN, J. C. and ZAJICEK, E. (1980) Adolescent attitudes to authority. *Adolescence,* in press.

CONGER, J. J. (1977) *Adolescence and Youth* (2nd edn), New York: Harper & Row.

DOUVAN, E. and ADELSON, J. (1966) *The Adolescent Experience,* New York: John Wiley.

ELDER, G. H. (1963) Parental power legitimation and its effects on the adolescent. *Sociometry,* **26,** 50–65.

FOGELMAN, K. (1976) *Britain's Sixteen-Year-Olds*, London: National Children's Bureau.

HETHERINGTON, E. M. (1972) Effects of father absence on personality development in adolescent daughters. *Developmental Psychology*, 7, 313–26.

MUSSEN, P. H. (1962) Long term consequences of masculinity of interest in adolescence. *Journal of Consulting Psychology*, 26, 435–40.

MUSSEN, P. H., CONGER, J. J. and KAGAN, J. (1974) *Child Development and Personality* (4th edn), New York: Harper & Row.

MUSSEN, P. H., YOUNG, H. V., GADDINI, R. and MORANTE, L. (1963) The influence of father/son relationships on adolescent personality and attitudes. *Journal of Child Psychology and Psychiatry*, 4, 1–16.

SMITH, D. M. (1978) Social class differences in adult attitudes to youth. *Journal of Adolescence*, 1, 147–54.

TUMA, E. and LIVSON, N. (1960) Family, socio-economic status and adolescent attitudes to authority. *Child Development*, 31, 387–99.

24

Why No Pedagogy in England?

Brian Simon

The term 'pedagogy' is used here in the sense of the 'science of teaching' (OED). The title of this paper is meant to imply that no such science exists in England; the fact that the term is generally shunned implies that such a science is either undesirable or impossible of achievement. And such, it is argued, is the situation. [...]

As an example we may look briefly at the work of the Schools Council, which, after its establishment in 1964, had had the task of stimulating change in the curriculum in an attempt to bring it up to date in the light of modern knowledge and of social and economic change. But the key feature of this effort has been the atheoretical, pragmatic approach adopted (together with the implicit acceptance of the *status quo* in organizational or administrative terms). The technique used has been the funding of teams of teachers and others with the brief of producing 'curriculum reform' plans, syllabuses and packages. These have worked out their own ideas based on 'good practice' implying an emphasis on grass-roots experiences, on curriculum reform from below as compared to reform from above as in the United States and the USSR. [...] The overall approach can hardly be called systematic, and certainly has not been informed by any generally accepted (or publicly formulated) ideas or theories about the nature of the child or the learning/teaching process – by any 'science of teaching' or 'pedagogy'. In particular there has been an almost total failure to provide psychological underpinning for the new programmes proposed.[1] In general the Schools Council approach has reflected a pluralism run wild – a mass of disparate projects. In these circumstances, there is, perhaps, little wonder that the 'take up' in the schools seems to have been vestigial.

This is not intended as a criticism of the Schools Council. No other outcome could have been expected; not so much because of the make-up and constitution of that body itself (revised in 1979) but more because the concept of 'pedagogy' – of a science of teaching embodying both curriculum and methodology – is alien to our experience and way of thinking. There are, no doubt, many reasons why this is so; among them wide acceptance of the unresolved dichotomies between 'progressive' and 'traditional', 'child-centred' and 'subject-centred' approaches, or, more generally, between the 'informal' and 'formal'. Such crude, generalized categories are basically meaningless but expressed in this form deflect attention from the real problems of teaching and learning. Indeed, so disparate are the views expressed that to resuscitate the concept of a science of teaching which underlies that of 'pedagogy' may seem to be crying for the moon. I hope to indicate that it is, in fact, a realistic proposition; that the knowledge base for a science of teaching does exist, and that circumstances urgently demand that the matter warrants serious and close attention.

But first, it may be useful to advance an interpretation as to why the concept of 'pedagogy' has been shunned in England, and why instead our approach to educational theory and practice has tended to be amateurish, and highly pragmatic in character.[2] Relevant here is the practice and approach of our most prestigious educational institutions (historically speaking), the ancient universities and leading public schools. Until recently, and even perhaps today, these have been dominant, both socially and in terms of the formation of the climate of opinion. It is symptomatic that the public schools, in general, have until recently contemptuously rejected the idea that a professional training is in any sense relevant to the job of a public school master. Although toying with the idea in the late nineteenth century, the Headmasters Conference has never adopted a positive attitude to such training, which traditionally has been seen as perhaps relevant and important for an elementary school teacher, but certainly not to someone taking up the gentlemanly profession of teaching in a public school. This was seen, perhaps, not so much as a job anyone from the middle or upper class could do, but as something those who wished to teach, having the appropriate social origins including a degree at Oxford or Cambridge, could learn, through experience, on the job. Certainly no special training was necessary.[3]

The reasons for this are not far to seek. The public schools developed as a cohesive system from the mid to late 1860s serving the new Victorian upper middle class; indeed they played a major role in the symbiosis of aristocracy and bourgeoisie which characterized the late nineteenth century. [. . .]

Socialization, as the major function of these schools at this time, involved little emphasis on intellectual (or cognitive) development. More important, especially in conditions of developing imperialism, was the formation of character, specifically of the qualities embodied in the concept of 'manliness' which, in its late nineteenth century form, involved the religion of games. [. . .]. The burden of the interpretation by modern scholarship of the evolution of the public schools in the nineteenth century focuses on the transition from the Arnoldian ideal of 'Godliness and Good Learning' in the early part of the century to the cult of manliness and games towards the end, the transition having been effected with the aid of 'muscular Christianity' personified by Hughes (*Tom Brown's Schooldays*) and Charles Kingsley.[4]

This is a world far removed from pedagogy – the science of teaching – and from its concerns. Bourdieu's analysis may be relevant here.[5] Teachers and pupils at the public schools, and in general also at the university, came from similar backgrounds and shared a common culture. They talked the same language and were interested in the same things. The schools, in an important sense, were extensions of the home, largely financed by the parents themselves (though the value of endowments should not be underestimated), the products of a close collaboration between parents and teachers. The teacher's pastoral responsibility – in terms of upbringing – was as important, or more so than his [or her] intellectual (teaching) responsibility. In this situation upper middle class culture and attitudes were 'naturally' assimilated and reinforced – the process did not require the application of specifically 'pedagogical' means. Approaches to teaching were traditional, handed down from generation to generation, though here there were exceptions, and certain schools (and teachers) did contribute to new thinking and practice relating, perhaps particularly, to science (Rugby). [. . .]

The (historical) denigration of the value of professional training by the public schools, then, falls into place; it simply did not appear as relevant to the schoolmaster's profession, as defined in terms of public school objectives and practice. And this, of course, implies disdain for the concept of pedagogy – or of a science of teaching – since the function of professional training is, in theory, to lay the basis in science of the practice or art of teaching. [. . .].

The situation is precisely reflected in Oxford and Cambridge, which, of course, have had the closest links with the public school system over the last century. Neither of these universities has, until perhaps recently, contributed to any serious extent to the study of education or to the development of educational theory and practice. [. . .] Cambridge was, in fact, among the last of all British universities to appoint a Professor of Education (in 1948) though, even here, it is ahead of Oxford which still does not recognize the subject in terms of establishing a Chair. [. . .] The low prestige of education as a subject of study, the few resources devoted to it, and the lack of serious experimental or scholarly studies undertaken, all these (and other factors) reflect general attitudes.[6]

The result has been that education, as a subject of enquiry and study, still less as a 'science', has, historically, had little prestige in this country, having been to all intents and purposes ignored in the most prestigious educational institutions. As Matthew Arnold tirelessly pointed out over one hundred years ago, in France, Prussia and elsewhere the problems of education for the middle class were taken really seriously. In Britain, on the other hand, everything was neglected; a *laissez-faire* pragmatism predominated.[7] This situation has, to some extent, been perpetuated. The dominant educational institutions of this country have had no concern with theory, its relation to practice, with pedagogy. This is the first point to establish. [. . .]

The social context of this development has been outlined; its theoretical context is equally important. This is personified – or crystallized – in Alexander Bain's *Education as a Science* published in 1879, reprinted six times in the 1880s, and a further ten times before 1900.[8] Examination of a number of student-teacher manuals, which proliferated in the 1890s, indicates their indebtedness to Bain's approach – or the extent to which they shared common interpretations both of theoretical issues relating to education, and of the practice of teaching. [. . .]

The crucial basis for this approach lay in the theory, announced by Bain as fact, that the formation of associations of ideas in the mind was accompanied by (or was the resultant of) new connections, linkages, or 'paths' formed in the substance of the brain. The process of education since it consisted in the planned ordering of the child's experiences, must therefore have a necessary effect (as Priestley had argued one hundred years earlier), and this, of course, had been the basis of the theory of human perfectibility characteristic of the Enlightenment. This approach not only posited the educability of the normal child, it stressed the 'plasticity', as Bain put it, of brain functioning and processes. Education, then, as again Bain defined it, was concerned with *acquired* capacities and functions. It was about human change and development. [. . .]

It followed from this approach that, to order education aright in terms of the acquisition of knowledge, two things were necessary. First, to obtain a psychological (and physiological) understanding of the growth of human powers through infancy, childhood and youth; and second, to analyse the content of subject matter in terms of its own inner logic. Together these underlay the determination of the curriculum. But Bain was also closely concerned with motivation, discipline, teacher-pupil relationships, moral education, as well as with the mode of teaching the main curriculum areas. Seeing 'education' specifically as schooling, he covered in his book almost every relevant aspect of teaching, learning, and classroom organization.

As suggested earlier, advances relating to pedagogy were an indigenous development from within the elementary school system. This is the case, in the sense that the many manuals for student-teachers published towards the end of the century were written by men working in the teacher-training institutions of the time, all of which prepared students specifically for the elementary schools.[9] The training colleges and pupil-teacher centres involved existed to serve the *elementary* system, or were outgrowths from it. To men working in this field, Bain clearly brought a wider view and deeper knowledge than they were likely to achieve themselves; and, without exception, these manuals reflected what might be called Bain's educational optimism. What is noticeable, particularly to the modern reader, is the stress laid on the extent to which failure to develop positive attitudes, skills, and abilities in the child may be a product of the teacher's own behaviour, or lack of skills, knowledge and method. Later interpretations of failure as the inevitable function of innate disabilities *in the child*, e.g. 'lack of intelligence', do not figure. It can be argued, with Joseph Priestley, that the theory which underlies these manuals – that educational actions have a necessary effect (even if this is not always identifiable) – also underlies the science of education; that is, pedagogy.

Of course the theories, and the practices, advocated by Bain and the authors of these manuals, had their limitations as well as theoretical weaknesses. That goes without saying. But, in the 1890s, the approach was serious, systematic, all-embracing. The pedagogy of this specific decade pointed the way to universal education, and was seen as such by its progenitors. What happened? Why was this embryo pedagogy not systematically developed? What went wrong?

First, the social and political context underwent an abrupt change, as indicated earlier. The development referred to took place within the *elementary* system, but one having for a short period a realistic perspective of organic growth. This was the backcloth, the crucial feature, of this movement as a whole. The administrative and legislative events of 1899 to 1904, almost traumatic in their effects, put a stopper on this, and apart from abolishing the School Boards, confined elementary education within precise limits, setting up a system of 'secondary' schooling parallel to, but quite separate from, the elementary system.

This created a new situation. A positive pedagogy based on scientific procedures and understanding and relevant for *all* was no longer seen as appropriate, or required. Intellectual development in the elementary schools was now at a discount (in parallel with the public schools, but for different reasons). The social-disciplinary ('containment') function of elementary education was now especially emphasized. The soil required to nurture a science of education no longer existed.

However, with the demise of the elementary school as the ground of pedagogy, there now emerged the new local authority-controlled systems of secondary education; it seems to have been into these new systems that the most advanced local authorities put their main efforts. [. . .]

It was the establishment, and rapid development of this new system of secondary schools which underlay new developments in the theory and practice of education. This system insistently required a pedagogy – the development of effective pedagogical means. Thus we find, in the period 1900–14, a renewed concern to develop a relevant pedagogy and it is this that lies behind the great interest in, almost the discovery of, the work of Herbart, and of the Prussian educators who had developed Herbartianism into a system – itself a phenomenon of some interest.

Herbart himself, a philosopher with special interests in psychology and education [. . .] basing himself on associationism in his theory of the 'apperception mass', set out to explain the process of human acquirements, seeing them as the resultant of education, of teaching and learning. [. . .]

It was not until the turn of the century, however, that Herbart's ideas began to make a serious impact in Britain; selections from his writings were first made widely available with the translation and publication of *The Science of*

Education in 1892. By the first decade of the twentieth century most existing universities were developing and expanding their departments of education and a number of chairs in the subject now existed. Several of the new professors of education, for instance, J. J. Findlay, John Adams, J. W. Adamson, pronounced themselves as Herbartians. These and others wrote a number of books for teachers either explaining and interpreting Herbart, or elaborating on his work.[10] Here, if perhaps rather narrowly circumscribed in its context, was a new attempt, at a new level, to establish a science of education – a pedagogy. There was, then, a brief new flowering of pedagogy – a serious concern with the theory and practice of education. But this new, and to some extent hopeful, development was in effect only partial (concerned with secondary schools, and related to their upthrust); and, in the circumstances that developed following the First World War, it did not, and could not, persist.

The reasons for this are complex, and relate both to the structure and nature of the system that developed in the inter-war years and after, and to the movement of ideas and their relation to that system. Briefly, selectivity became the central focus of the whole system, the classification of pupils and their categorization became a main principle of school organization. That system urgently required a rationale – legitimization in the eyes of parents, teachers, pupils and the public generally. Such legitimization was, by the mid-1920s, at hand in the theories (and the practice) of mental measurement, particularly, intelligence testing.

Until then, the rational foundation for pedagogical theories – for the concept of education as a science – had lain in associationist psychological theories concerning learning. These were espoused by Bain, as we have seen, and underlay his whole approach; as also by Herbart and his protagonists (or elaborators). So it was theory and practice based on these ideas which gave rise both to the positive, or optimistic, pedagogics of the 1890s relating to elementary education, and to those of the period 1900–20 relating to the new system of secondary education. But it was just at this period that new approaches came to predominate in the field of psychology which either relegated associationism to the background, or denied its significance altogether.

The two major influences leading to the demise of associationism as a major determinant of pedagogy were, on the one hand, the rise of philosophic idealism which denied the material basis of mind and decisively rejected the model of human formation of the strict materialists of the late eighteenth century (with its emphasis on man as the passive product of external stimuli); and, on the other hand, the triumph of Darwinism with its emphasis on heredity.[11] With the latter is linked Galton's work (*Hereditary Genius* was published as early as 1869), the rise of the eugenics movement with its associated theories (the Eugenics Education Society was founded in 1908), and the work of the Galton Laboratory at University College, London, associated with the names of Pearson, Spearman, and later Cyril Burt. 'No request is more frequently made to the psychologist' wrote Burt in 1921, when he was educational psychologist to the London County Council, 'than the demand for a simple mental footrule.'[12] It was precisely this that the psychologists were now ready to supply.

The demands of the system and the movement of ideas now coincided. In the field of educational theory psychometry (or mental testing) now established its hegemony which lasted over forty years from the 1920s. The triumph of psychometry tied in with a new stress on individualism after the First World War and a kind of reductionist biologism, both of which are central to the thinking of Sir Percy Nunn whose *Education, its Data and First Principles* was the central student manual of the inter-war years.[13] For reasons which will be discussed later, this spelt the end of pedagogy – its actual death. If education cannot promote cognitive growth, as the psychometrists seemed to aver, its whole purpose or direction was lost. 'Othello's occupation gone', as Hayward, an LCC Inspector, once put it.

This, I suggest, is the background to our present discontents. For a combination of social, political and ideological reasons pedagogy – a scientific basis to the theory and practice of education – has never taken root and flourished in Britain. For a single decade in the late nineteenth century in the field of elementary education; for a similar short period early this century in secondary education, pedagogic approaches and analyses flowered – though never in the most socially prestigious system of the public schools and ancient universities. Each 'system', largely self-contained, developed its own specific educational approach, each within its narrowly defined field, and each 'appropriate' to its specific social function. In these circumstances the conditions did not, and could not, exist for the development of an all-embracing, universalized, scientific theory of education relating to the practice of teaching. Nor is it an accident that, in these circumstances, fatalistic ideas preaching the limitation of human powers were in the ascendant. [...]

A Revitalized Pedagogy?

What, then, are the requirements for a renewal of scientific approaches to the practice of teaching – for a revitalized pedagogy?

First, we can identify two essential conditions without which there can be no pedagogy having a generalized significance or application. The first is recognition of the human capacity for learning. It may seem unnecessary, even ridiculous, to single this out in this connection, but in practice this is not the case. Fundamentally, psychometric theory, as elaborated in the 1930s to 1950s, denied the lability of learning capacity, seeing each individual as endowed, as it were, with an engine of a given horse-power which is fixed, unchangeable and measurable in each particular case, irrevocably setting precise and definable limits to achievement (or learning). It was not until this view had been discredited in the eyes of psychologists that serious attention could be given to the analysis and interpretation of the *process* of human learning.

The second condition has been effectively defined by Professor Stones in his helpful and relevant book *Psychopedagogy*.[14] It is the recognition that, in general terms, the process of learning among human beings is similar across the human species as a whole. The view on which Stones's book is based is that 'except in pathological cases, learning capability among individuals is similar', so that 'it is possible to envisage a body of general principles of teaching' that are relevant to 'most individual pupils'. The determination, or identification, of such general principles must comprise the objectives of pedagogical study and research.[15]

One further point may be made at the start. The term 'pedagogy' itself implies structure. It implies the elaboration or definition of specific means adapted to produce the desired effect – such-and-such learning on the part of the child. From the start of the use of the term, pedagogy has been concerned to relate the process of teaching to that of learning on the part of the child. It was this approach that characterized the work of Comenius, Pestalozzi and Herbart, and that, for instance, of Joseph Priestley and the associationist tradition generally.[16]

Both the conditions defined above are today very widely accepted among leading psychologists directly concerned with education and with research into human cognitive development. When Bruner claimed, in a striking and well-known statement, that 'any subject can be taught to anybody at any age in some form that is both interesting and honest', he was basing himself on a positive assessment of human capacity for learning, and deliberately pointing to the need to link psychology and pedagogy. In an essay aimed at persuading American psychologists of the need to concern themselves with education – to provide assistance in elucidating the learning process for practising educators – he stressed his central point, 'that developmental psychology without a theory of pedagogy was as empty an enterprise as a theory of pedagogy that ignored the nature of growth'. 'Man is not a naked ape,' writes Bruner, 'but a culture clothed human being, hopelessly ineffective without the prosthesis provided by culture.' Education itself can be a powerful cultural influence, and educational experiences are ordered and structured to enable people more fully to realize their humanity and powers, to bring about social change – and so create a world according to their felt and recognized objectives. The major problem humanity faces is not the general development of skill and intelligence, but 'devising a society that can use it wisely'.[17]

When writing this, Bruner was clearly concerned with social change, and with the contribution that pedagogical means might make to this, as we must be in Britain in face of the dramatic social challenge that technological change now presents. And in considering the power of education, rightly ordered, to play a central part in this, it may be as well to recall that, while the simplified and certainly over-mechanistic interpretations of the associationist psychologists of the nineteenth century are no longer acceptable in the form, for instance, expressed by Alexander Bain (and his predecessors), the concept of learning as a process involving the formation of new connections in the brain and higher nervous systems has in fact not only retained its force, but been highly developed by neuro-physiologists and psychologists specifically concerned to investigate learning. Among these, perhaps the greatest contribution has been made by A. R. Luria in a series of works relevant to teaching, education and human development generally; but perhaps particularly in his work on the role of language in mental development, and in his theory of the formation of what he calls 'complex functional systems' underlying learning.

It is now generally accepted that in the process of mental development there takes place a profound qualitative reorganisation of human mental activity, and that the basic characteristic of this reorganisation is that elementary, direct activity is replaced by complex functional systems, formed on the basis of the child's communication with adults in the process of learning. These functional systems are of complex construction, and are developed with the close participation of language, which as the basic means of communication with people is simultaneously one of the basic tools in the formation of human mental activity and in the regulation of behaviour. It is through these complex forms of mental activity ... that new features are acquired and begin to develop according to new laws which displace many of the laws which govern the formation of elementary conditioned reflexes in animals.[18]

The work and thinking of both Luria and Bruner (as representative of their respective traditions) point in a similar direction – towards a renewed understanding both of the power of education to effect human change and especially cognitive development, and of the need for the systematization and structuring of the child's experiences in the process of learning. And it is precisely from this standpoint that a critique is necessary of certain contemporary standpoints, dichotomies and ideologies, and, in particular, of the whole trend towards so-called 'child-centred' theories, which have dominated this area in Britain basically since the early 1920s, to reach its apotheosis in what is best called the 'pedagogic romanticism' of the Plowden Report, its most recent, and semi-official expression.

It may be unfashionable, among educationists, to direct attention specifically to this point, more particularly because a critique of 'progressivism' was central to the outlook expressed in the Black Papers in the late 1960s, and early 1970s; but to make such a critique does not imply identification with the essentially philistine and a-theoretical standpoint of the Black Paperites, as I hope to show. Indeed the dichotomies which these and other critics sought to establish, for instance between progressive and traditional approaches, between the 'formal' and 'informal', do not reflect the options now available, nor even contemporary practice as it really is.

The basic tenets of child-centred education derive in particular from the work of Froebel who held that children are endowed with certain characteristics or qualities which will mature or flower given the appropriate environment. The child develops best in a 'rich' environment. The teacher should not interfere with this process of maturation, but act as a 'guide'. The function of early education, according to Froebel, is 'to make the inner outer'.[19] Hence the emphasis on spontaneity, as also on stages of development, and the concomitant concept of 'readiness' – the child will learn specific skills and mental operations only when he or she is 'ready'.

That there is a fundamental convergence between this view and the theories (or assumptions) embodied in Intelligence Testing has been overlooked; nevertheless it is the close similarity between both sets of views as to the nature of the child which made it possible for both to flourish together in the period following the First World War and after. Intelligence Testing also embodied the view that the child is endowed with certain innate characteristics; in this case a brain and higher nervous system of a given power or force – Spearman's 'Mental Energy or Noegenetics' – and that the process of education is concerned to actualize the given potential, that is, to activate and realize the 'inner' (in Froebel's sense).[20] Both views in fact deny the creative function of education, the formative power of differential educational (or life) experiences.

The theoretical, or pedagogical stance of the Plowden Report represents an extension of these ideas. In their re-interpretation of the conclusions derived from psychometry they reject the concept of total hereditary, or genetic, determination. Development is seen as an interactional process, in which the child's encounters with the environment are crucial. Yet Plowden takes the child-centred approach to its logical limits, insisting on the principle of the complete individualization of the teaching/learning process as the ideal (even though, from a pedagogic standpoint, this is not a practical possibility in any realistic sense). In their analysis the hereditary/environmental interactional process is interpreted as exacerbating initial differences so greatly that each child must be seen to be unique, and be treated as such. The matter is rendered even more complex by their insistence that each individual child develops at different rates across three parameters, intellectual, emotional and physical; and that in determining her approach to each individual child each of these must be taken into account by the teacher. The result is that the task set the teacher, with an average of 35 children per class when Plowden reported, is, in the words of the report itself, 'frighteningly high'.[21]

I want to suggest that, by focusing on the individual child ('at the heart of the educational process lies the child'), and in developing the analysis from this point, the Plowden Committee created a situation from which it was impossible to derive an effective pedagogy (or effective pedagogical means). If each child is unique, and each requires a specific pedagogical approach appropriate to him or her and to no other, the construction of an all-embracing pedagogy, or general principles of teaching, becomes an impossibility. And indeed research has shown that primary school teachers who have taken the priority of individualization to heart find it difficult to do more than ensure that each child is in fact engaged on the series of tasks which the teacher sets up for the child; the complex management problem which then arises takes the teacher's full energies. Hence the approach of teachers who endeavour to implement these prescripts is necessarily primarily didactic ('telling') since it becomes literally impossible to stimulate enquiry, or to 'lead from behind', as Plowden held the teacher should operate in the classroom. Even with a lower average of 30 children per class, this is far too complex and time-consuming a role for the teacher to perform.[22]

The main thrust of the argument of this paper is this: that to start from the standpoint of individual differences is to start from the wrong position. To develop effective pedagogic means involves starting from the opposite stand-point, from what children have in common as members of the human species; to establish the general principles of teaching and, in the light of these, to determine what modifications of practice are necessary to meet specific individual needs. If all children are to be assisted to learn, to master increasingly complex cognitive tasks, to develop increasingly complex skills and abilities or mental operations, then this is an objective that schools must have in common; their task becomes the deliberate development of such skills and abilities in all their children. And this involves importing a definite structure into the teaching, and so into the learning experiences provided for the pupils. Individual differences only become important, in this context, if the pedagogical means elaborated are found not to be appropriate to particular children (or groups of children) because of one or other aspect of their individual development or character. In this situation the requirement becomes that of modifying the pedagogical means so that they become appropriate for all; that is, of applying general principles in specific instances.

What is suggested here is that the starting-point for constructing the curriculum, or children's activities in school, insofar as we are concerned with cognitive development (the schools may reasonably have other aims as well) lies in definition of the objectives of teaching, which forms the ground base from which pedagogical means are defined and established, means or princi-ples which underlie specific methodological (or experiential) approaches. It may well be that these include the use of co-operative group work as well as individualized activities – but these are carefully designed and structured in relation to the achievement of overall objectives. This approach, I am arguing, is the opposite of basing the educational process on the child, on his or her immediate interests and spontaneous activity, and providing, in theory, for a total differentiation of the learning process in the case of each individual child. This latter approach is not only undesirable in principle, it is impossible of achievement in practice.[23]

In a striking phrase Lev Vygotski summed up his outlook on teaching and learning. Pedagogy, he wrote, 'must be oriented not towards the yesterday of development but towards its tomorrow'. Teaching, education, pedagogic means, must always take the child forward, be concerned with the formation of new concepts and hierarchies of concepts, with the next stage in the development of a particular ability, with ever more complex forms of mental operations. 'What the child can do today with adult help,' he said, 'he will be able to do independently tomorrow.' This concept, that of the 'zone of next (or "potential") development' implies in the educator a clear concept of the progression of learning, of a consistent challenge, of the mastery by the child of increasingly complex forms – of never standing still or going backwards. 'The only good teaching is that which outpaces development,' insisted Vygotski.[24] Whether the area is that of language development, or concepts of number and mathematics – symbolic systems that underlie all further learning – or whether it covers scientific and technological means can and should be defined, perhaps particularly in areas having their own inner logical structures. In this sense, psychological knowledge combined with logical principles can be established, given, of course, effective research and experiment.

This paper has been strictly concerned with cognitive development, since it is here that technological/scientific and social changes will make their greatest impact and demands. But for successful implementation of rational procedures and planning, in the face of the micro-processor revolution, more than this needs consideration. There is also the question, for instance, of the individual's enhanced responsibility for his own activities; the development of autonomy, of initiative, creativity, critical awareness; the needs on the part of the mass of the population for access to knowledge and culture, the arts and literature, to mention only some aspects of human development. The means of promoting such human qualities and characteristics cannot simply be left to individual teachers, on the grounds that each individual child is unique so that the development of a pedagogy is both impracticable and superfluous. The existing teaching force of half a million have, no doubt, many talents, but they need assistance in the pursuit of their common objective – the education of new generations of pupils. The new pedagogy requires carefully defined goals, structure, and adult guidance. Without this a high proportion of children, whose concepts are formed as a result of their everyday experiences, and, as a result, are often distorted and incorrectly reflect reality, will never even reach the stage where the development of higher cognitive forms of activity becomes a possibility. And this implies a massive cognitive failure in terms of involvement and control (responsible participation) in the new social forms and activities which the future may bring.

Acknowledgment

This paper was originally published as a chapter in a symposium entitled *Education in the Eighties, the central issues*, edited by Brian Simon and William Taylor (Batsford, 1981). The author wishes to thank Dr T. G. Whiston, of the Science Policy Research Unit, University of Sussex, for extremely helpful and stimulating discussions on this issue, as also for commenting on an early draft of this paper. Thanks are also due to Professors E. Stones and J. F. Eggleston for very useful comments on an early draft.

Notes

1 An attempt in 1962 by Nuffield Science project teams to gain assistance from psychologists was entirely negative. At a meeting convened to discuss possible research on the intellectual development of children in areas relevant to the projects, leading psychologists held that little advice was possible since 'so little research had, as yet, been undertaken with British children' on teaching and learning. See M. Waring, *Social Pressures and Curriculum Innovation*, London, 1979, p. 133.

2 The English failure to take pedagogy seriously is stressed in an article on the subject in an educational encyclopedia of a century ago. Interest in pedagogy 'is not held in much honour among us English'. The lack of a professional approach to teaching means that 'pedagogy is with us at a discount'. This, it is held, 'is unquestionably a most grievous national loss.... Without something like scientific discussion on educational subjects, without pedagogy, we shall never obtain a body of organised opinion on education.' A. E. Fletcher (ed.), *Cyclopaedia of Education*, New York, 1889, pp. 257–8.

3 An exception here was R. H. Quick, author of *Essays on Educational Reformers*, 1869, a public school master himself who fought hard for professional training and who appears to have been largely instrumental in setting up the Cambridge Syndicate which organized (prematurely) the first systematic set of lectures on education in an English university; those delivered at Cambridge in 1879–80 (see F. Storr, *The Life and Remains of the Revd R. H. Quick*, Cambridge, 1889, pp. 349–88). For a young teacher's experience of 'learning on the job' in the 1930s, see T. C. Worsley, *Flannelled Fool*, London, 1967, Chapter 1.

4 See D. Newsome, *Godliness and Good Learning*, London, 1961, especially chapter 4; B. Simon and I. Bradley (eds), *The Victorian Public School*, Dublin, 1975, especially chapter 7 by Norman Vance, 'The Ideal of Manliness', and chapter 9 by J. A. Mangan, 'Athleticism: A Case Study of the Evolution of an Educational Ideology'.

5 P. Bourdieu and J-C. Passeron, *Reproduction in Education, Society and Culture*, London, 1977.

6 It is symptomatic that the most recent (and internal) examination of studies at Oxford ignores the topic altogether, *Report of Commission of Inquiry* (the Franks report), 2 vols., 1966.

7 See, for instance, M. Arnold, *High Schools and Universities in Germany*, London, 1874, which devotes a lengthy chapter to the professional training of schoolmasters for the *gymnasia* and *realschule* in Prussia (chapter 5).

8 A. Bain, *Education as a Science*, London, 1879.

9 For instance, A. H. Garlick, 'Headmaster' of the Woolwich Pupil-Teacher Centre, *A New Manual for Method*, London, 1896; David Salmon, Principal of Swansea Training College, *The Art of Teaching*, London, 1898; Joseph Landon, Vice-Principal and 'Later Master of Method' of Saltley Training College, *The Principles and Practice of Teaching and Class Management*, Oxford, 1894; and many others.

10 For instance, the London County Council Inspectors, F. H. Hayward and P. B. Ballard, both of whom were prolific writers on education.

11 G. Murphy, *Historical Introduction to Modern Psychology*, New York, 1938, pp. 109–13.

12 C. Burt, *Mental and Scholastic Tests*, London, 1921, p. 1.

13   Percy Nunn was Principal of the University of London Institute of Education
     from 1922 to 1936. His textbook went through over 20 reprintings between its
     publication in 1920 and 1940; it was required reading for many graduates training
     as teachers. For an acute critique of Nunn's biologism, see P. Gordon and J.
     White, *Philosophers as Educational Reformers*, London, 1979, pp. 207–13.

14   E. Stones, *Psychopedagogy: Psychological Theory and the Practice of Teaching*,
     London, 1979.

15   Ibid., p. 453.

16   This point was clearly and emphatically made by James Ward in the first of his
     Cambridge lectures in 1879–80 (but only published in 1926). Entitled 'The
     Possibility and Value of a Theory of Education', this started by saying that a
     science of education 'is theoretically possible', and that such a science 'must be
     based on psychology and the cognate sciences'. He goes on, 'To show this we
     have, indeed, only to consider that the educator works, or rather ought to work,
     upon a growing mind, *with a definite purpose of attaining an end in view*. For unless
     it be maintained that systematic observation of the growth of (say) a hundred
     minds would disclose no uniformities; and unless, further, it can be maintained
     that for the attainment of a definite end there are no definite means, we must allow
     that *if the teacher knows what he wants to do there must be a scientific way of doing it*.
     Not only so. We must allow not merely the possibility of a scientific exposition of
     the means the educator should employ to attain his end, but we must allow also the
     possibility of a scientific exposition of the end at which he ought to aim, unless
     again it be contended that it is impossible by reasoning to make manifest that one
     form of life and character is preferable to another.' J. Ward, *Psychology Applied to
     Education*, Cambridge, 1926, p. 1 (my italics, B.S.).

17   J. S. Bruner, *The Relevance of Education*, London, 1972, pp. 18, 131, 158.

18   A. R. Luria, *Voprosy Psikhologii*, 1962, 4.

19   F. W. A. Froebel, *The Education of Man*, New York, 1912, p. 32.

20   C. Spearman, *The Nature of 'Intelligence' and the Principles of Cognition*, London,
     1927.

21   The Plowden Report, *Children and Their Primary Schools*, London, 1967, I, paras
     75 and 875.

22   These points are argued in detail, supported by empirical evidence derived from
     systematic classroom observation, in M. Galton, B. Simon and P. Croll, *Inside the
     Primary School*, London, 1980.

23   For a critique of this approach by a psychologist who has worked closely with
     Piaget (regarded as the authority for individualization, for instance, in the
     Plowden Report), see E. Duckworth, 'Either We're too Early and They Can't
     Learn it or We're too Late and They Know it Already: the Dilemma of "Applying
     Piaget"', *Harvard Educational Review*, Vol. 49, No. 3.

24   See L. S. Vygotski 'Learning and Mental Development at School Age' in
     B. Simon and J. Simon (eds), *Educational Psychology in the USSR*, London, 1963,
     and *Thought and Language*, London, 1962, and the Vygotskian Memorial Issue of
     Soviet Psychology and Psychiatry, 1967, 5, 3.

25

Appraising the Teachers: Professionalism and Control

Kieron Walsh

Introduction

The teachers' dispute of 1985–86 was as much about how the teaching force is to be managed as about levels of pay. Local Education Authorities (LEAs) and the Department of Education and Science (DES) were concerned about what would be delivered in return for higher pay, and how they could ensure control over teachers and the teaching process. Appraisal of the performance of individual teachers was seen as crucial in ensuring control, particularly by the Secretary of State for Education and Science and the DES civil servants. The introduction of an appraisal system was made a condition of Government funding of any salary settlement. The Education Act 1986 gives the Secretary of State the power to introduce a national system of appraisal should the LEAs themselves fail to deliver satisfactory schemes. The Bill abolishing the Burnham Committee will give him the power to specify conditions of service, on the basis of which teachers will be appraised.

The pressure for the introduction of performance appraisal for teachers derives from a number of sources, but the most important is the desire for greater central control of education, which has been apparent since the mid-1970s. The Government and the DES are trying to make education conform to new social, economic and political purposes.[1] The centre wishes to see a curriculum that it considers more relevant to the world of work, and to life after school more generally, and that is more fitted to the capacities of students. The present curriculum is seen as too academic, and not sufficiently adapted to the needs either of the most or the least able. As many commentators[2] have argued the DES has, since the 1970s, developed a clear strategy for re-orienting the education system and for asserting its dominance over the LEAs, the school and the teachers. In the thirty years immediately after the

Second World War, the 'partnership' of central government, the LEAs and the teachers controlled education, with no one of the three parties exercising monopoly control. Since James Callaghan's administration the desire of the Department of Education and Science for control over the LEAs and the teachers has become public in white and green papers, in legislation, and in changes to the system of finance. The LEAs, in turn, have been attempting to assert more control over the schools and teachers, and within the school the managerial roles of headteachers and other senior staff have been emphasized. The notion of teachers as independent, autonomous professionals has been eroded, and the importance of management and hierarchical accountability emphasized.

This essay examines one aspect of the development of managerial and employer control – performance appraisal. I shall argue that the development of teacher appraisal has taken two main forms, both deriving from the desire for more centralized control of the education system. The first is the attempt to rationalize teachers' work through influencing both the teaching process, notably through control of the teacher training and in-service training systems, and the content and output of teaching through influence over the curriculum and examinations. The second form is the attempt to formalize the employment relation, by specifying much more closely teachers' conditions of service. Employer and DES control of teachers' work would be limited without control of the employment contract. The teacher-employer relationship is to become one of exchange rather than of trust. In manufacturing industry, and in many service industries, management control can normally be asserted through control of the work process and of the product, as well as by direct surveillance, for example, through the use of technological systems, and the design of work. In teaching, the potential for such control is limited and there is a prior need for the employer to develop control of the employment contract. The changed labour market conditions that confront teachers have allowed the employers to assert a form of bureaucratic contractual control that fits ill with the notion of professional autonomy. I shall argue that there are fundamental weaknesses in the teachers' claim to professional status, which have made that formalization possible.

The managerialism that has come to characterize education in the last decade was made possible by the change from growth to decline that has faced the service in that period. The form that managerialism has taken reflects the balance of forces that operate in education. I shall argue that the teachers' claim to professional status and autonomy is weakly grounded and has become weaker in the last decade. But, as has been apparent in the recent teachers' action, trade unionism is strong in education. In the United States, where teacher unionism is much weaker, states such as Texas have been able to impose rigid forms of appraisal and, in some cases to relate pay to performance. A survey by the American Association of Colleges for Teacher Education found that 44 of the 50 states have introduced some form of standardized test.[3] In Britain, though partnership no longer operates, power is still distributed between the Department of Education and Science, and the Government generally, the LEAs and the teachers. Differences in power and interest have influenced the way that appraisal has developed and the pattern that it has taken. Employers have not simply been able to impose their preferred form of appraisal. But nor have teachers been able fully to assert professional independence and peer control.

The attempt to introduce performance appraisal, is an aspect of the formalization of the employment relation. The employer is to make a more explicit contractual statement of what is expected of the teacher, but there will inevitably be strong elements of discretion in performance, and appraisal can be seen as a means of controlling the exercise of that discretion. In discussing appraisal I shall distinguish between three dimensions:

Focus: appraisal may focus upon the individual teacher or upon the unit within which education takes place, that is at the collective level – the department of the school, or even the whole LEA.

Purpose: appraisal may be used to assess the development needs of teachers, or to pass judgment on their performance, especially in the exercise of discretion (sometimes called 'summative' appraisal).

Form: appraisal may be performed hierarchically by management, or co-operatively, through a process of peer review, possibly involving students, parents and the community.

These three dimensions allow us to distinguish two basic forms of appraisal; managerial, control-oriented appraisal, which is individually focused, judgmental and hierarchical; and participative appraisal, which is collectively focused, developmental and co-operative. Guidelines for the Review and Internal Development of Schools (GRIDS) provide an example of the participative approach. The employers and the DES have been concerned to develop control-oriented appraisal, but the outcome, so far, has been a hybrid of the two basic types, because teachers have been able to resist control, and influence the pattern of appraisal adopted. They have been able to ensure that the systems of appraisal adopted are not wholly control-oriented, but contain elements of the participative approach.

This paper examines the development of teacher appraisal. It first considers the rise of central control. Secondly, it examines the development of the movement for the appraisal of the performance of individual teachers. I shall then develop the argument that the weakness of the teachers' claim to professionalism makes them vulnerable to attempts to develop control-oriented appraisal. At the same time as the nature of the teachers' work makes it difficult to create systems of control oriented appraisal, it also makes it difficult for them to claim the right to independent, professionally controlled, participative review. I shall conclude this article by considering the positive arguments for appraisal, and possible future developments.

The Rise of Control

Political criticism of the standards and relevance of education has been strong since James Callaghan's speech at Ruskin College in October 1976, and has intensified under the present government. The desire to assert more direct control over the teachers, and specifically to introduce performance appraisal, has its origins in the political wish to ensure that the education system carries out national political purposes. The belief that teachers and schools were failing society and the economy, based more in prejudice than in evidence, has led to moves for assessment of the performance of the education service, embodied, for example, in the establishment of the Assessment of Performance Unit, and the publication of examination results by schools and of HMI reports. There has been general pressure for more accountability in education. Financial constraint has led to an emphasis on 'value-for-money' and to financial assessments of performance, reflected in the enhanced role of auditors and the creation of the Audit Commission, which has carried out three specific studies of education.[4]

In the long period of post-war growth, teachers were in control of their own career structures to a much greater extent than had previously been the case. The present concern for central control contrasts strongly with this autonomy that was allowed to teachers or, at least, which the centre was unable to prevent. The expansion of the service meant that teachers could move from school to school and authority to authority with comparative ease. Indeed the DES operated a quota system to try to share scarce teachers out fairly. Career advance and mobility were directly linked. Those who moved most were those who were promoted most. The expansion of the number of scales in the Burnham structure after 1956 increased the extent and range of promotion. Teachers had careers rather than jobs, in contrast to the pre-war period when, as Spooner says, 'there was virtually no promotion ladder but a sudden jump to deputy or head'.[5] It was a sellers' market in which teachers could control their own professional lives and employer power was limited.

The curriculum that was taught in schools also came increasingly under the control of the teachers as education expanded, particularly in the secondary sector. Early Government attempts to gain some influence over the curriculum, through the establishment of the curriculum Study Group, failed because of teacher and LEA resistance. The Schools Council, established in 1964 under the majority control of the teachers, institutionalized their dominating influence on the shape and content of the curriculum. The DES and the LEAs played little part in the control of what was taught, which, in practice, rested with the individual headteacher and teaching staff in a school. As the Schools Council Constitution put it:

> . . . each school should have the fullest possible measure of responsibility for its own work, with its own curriculum and teaching methods based on the needs of its own pupils and evolved by its own staff.[6]

353

The place where curriculum policy was ultimately developed was seen as the individual classroom, and it was this belief in independent control that lay at the heart of the teachers' claim to professionalism. The claim to professionalism was a claim to autonomy in the determination of the form and content of work.

The result of these developments, by the mid-1970s, was a teaching force that was young, largely self-controlling, with good promotion prospects and high career expectations. Studies of teachers' lives have shown that attitudes to careers vary widely, but the post-war development of education had created individual teacher autonomy and self-determination.

Opportunities for mobility and promotion have been dramatically reduced by financial and demographic contraction. Teachers, whose understandings have been shaped by growth, now in the early 1980s face the prospect of becoming old together, trapped on relatively lowpaid scales, with little opportunity for movement. Teachers have lost control of the employment relation and the DES and LEAs and headteachers have gained much more influence over careers.

From the mid 1970s the DES and LEAs were taking more control over the context of teaching. Education was blamed for Britain's long economic decline, the curriculum was seen as insufficiently relevant and vocational, and teaching methods as not rigorous enough. Education was argued not to be accountable for its performance. The evidence upon which such judgements could be based was necessarily limited, given that knowledge about the process of education lay predominantly with the teacher and the school. But this, in itself, was a source of teacher weakness, for, while those who claimed that standards had fallen could cite little evidence, nor could teachers provide evidence to counter the claim. Some mud was bound to stick. The answer was seen as more centralized control of the curriculum, and systematic information on standards. The Assessment of Performance Unit was given a brief to develop criterion-referenced methods of assessment.

From the mid-1970s there was also growing pressure for accountability, which was linked to the concern over standards. Teachers, schools and LEAs were all to be held accountable for pupil achievement and behaviour. The 1977 Green Paper, *Education in Schools* argued that:

> Much has been achieved: but there is legitimate ground for criticism and concern. Education, like any other public service, is answerable to the society which it serves and which pays for it, so these criticisms must be given a fair hearing.[7]

and that:

> growing recognition of the need for schools to demonstrate their accountability to the society which they serve requires a coherent and soundly based means of assessment for the educational system as a whole, for schools and for individual pupils.[8]

Under the Conservative Governments the desire for accountability has become stronger, being expressed in the provisions in the Education Act 1980, requiring schools to publish examination results, the publication of HMI reports and the increased powers of governing bodies. Performance appraisal is part of this movement for accountability and central control, as responsibility for performance has come to be focused upon the individual teacher.

Governments have been concerned to increase their own control of education while weakening the institutional power of LEAs, schools and teachers. The centre has taken an increasing interest in the content of the curriculum. Circulars 14/77, 6/81 and 8/83 have required Local Education Authorities to develop curriculum policies and make returns on the curriculum to the DES. Central government is increasingly concerned to develop a centrally specified core curriculum. Examinations are being developed which embody central purposes. The new GCSE, operating through a simplified system with fewer Examination Boards, must meet both general and specific subject criteria laid down by the Secretary of State. The 17+ examination has been subject to closer scrutiny than previous examinations by the DES. The Government has funded specific curriculum developments directly, notably the Technical and Vocational Education Initiative (TVEI).

The powers of LEAs, schools and teachers have been reduced by a dual process of centralizing and decentralization. The financial powers of the centre have been increased by establishing direct grants for various specific educational purposes, as opposed to funding education wholly through the general rate support grant. A considerable amount of educational finance has been channelled through the Manpower Services Commission. The power of LEAs on governing bodies has been greatly reduced by the Education Act 1986. The power of schools has been reduced by increasing parental rights in choice of school. The teachers' influence has been reduced by the abolition of the Schools Council and its replacement by the Secondary Examinations Council and Schools Curriculum Development Council, which are more directly under the control of the Secretary of State. The Advisory Council on the Supply and Education of Teachers has also been disbanded. Most recently the Secretary of State has announced the establishment of City Technology Colleges, which will be directly funded by the DES and run by trusts independent of the LEAs.

The Education Act recently passed by Parliament radically reduces the power and influence of the LEAs and teachers, while increasing the powers of the centre. The Burnham Committee is to be abolished. Teachers' pay and conditions are no longer to be subject to collective bargaining. The Secretary of State is to set up a small advisory committee on pay and conditions but may set aside their advice if it is not to his liking. The advisory committee will not have to be representative of the teachers or the LEAs. The Act also contains the power for the Secretary of State to vary pay levels in different parts of the country. It will also allow him to specify conditions of service for teachers.

355

It is not only in schools that the development of closer control of the work of individual teachers is leading to increased surveillance of educational work. At the national level government is also introducing procedures that will involve considerations of teachers' performance and the content of their work. The Council for the Accreditation of Teacher Education has been given oversight of initial training and tighter requirements have been laid down for the content of training, and the relation between qualifications, and subjects and age groups taught. The Government is also introducing a specific grant for in-service training, which would require each LEA to:

> ... submit information about its plans for in-service training and making good use of the teachers who had been released to engage in in-service training.[9]

National priorities are laid down for in-service training. The policy has already been partially introduced through the funding for TVEI Related In-service Training which is controlled by the Manpower Services Commission, and involves its own inspection system. Local education authorities are required to submit information on the methods used to ensure that the training offered to, and taken up by, teachers matches their identified needs; what information is available on the in-service training needs of individual teachers; and plans to ensure that training is part of a coherent programme of staff development for individual teachers. A clear line of responsibility and accountability from teacher and school to central government is being established.

The new approach to the closer control of in-service training by central government, implies that individual education authorities and the DES will have more detailed knowledge of what teachers are doing and their standards of performance. The evidence from the development of such policy planning systems, for example Housing Investment Programmes and Transport Policies and Programmes, is that co-ordination quickly becomes control.[10]

The proposal to appraise the performance of the individual teacher, then, is only one aspect of the growing monitoring of the performance of teachers, schools and LEAs. Changes in the nature of educational work in the future may also mean more assessment and appraisal. Eggleston sees the possibility of assessment extending professionalism. He argues that the development of criterion-referenced assessment of pupils will:

> ... make available a far wider range of a child's achievement and of a teacher's work to assessment. ... Such moves, along with other associated techniques such as pupil profiling ... involve the active participation of the profession itself, so extending professionalism. ... Together the new techniques present a prospect of a far more effective appraisal of professional achievement than heretofore – an appraisal that can be made available to the clients.[11]

But assessment may lay the base for managerial control not professional accountability. Closer specification of the nature of teaching – as opposed to the content of the curriculum – may lead to the development of competency based testing, used in some parts of the United States. Competency based appraisal involves specifying single discrete elements of knowledge or skill in professional value positions required of teachers, for example, 'Reinforces and encourages learner involvement in instruction' is a competency specified in one American scheme.[12] While such approaches have had very limited success or impact, they illustrate the possibilities for the formalization and rationalization of the work of teachers. Requirements to be more accountable are also shifting schools towards providing more detailed information on performance, for example, in the case of Croydon LEA, where assessment is performed partly through regular, standardized tests of pupil performance.

Central government has, therefore, pursued control through asserting greater influence over the content of education. It is also attempting to influence the teaching process through control of initial and in-service training. Assessment at all levels is to be a key part of the process.

It is in the context of a weakening of the labour market position of teachers, and growing central control over, and concern for, the curriculum and standards that appraisal must be understood. The debate about teacher appraisal is a debate about accountability, quality, competence and professional autonomy. It follows from a desire to change the nature of educational work, and the employment relation through specifying conditions of service. Given the lack of specific contractual commitments it is necessary, if central control is to be asserted, to develop a more specific contract.

The Development of Appraisal

The early origins of appraisal for teachers lie in the self-critical mood that developed in education from the mid-1970s. There were no immediate moves to introduce formal teacher appraisal as part of conditions of service as a result of the 'Great Debate', but a number of schools and LEAs, starting with the Inner London Education Authority, introduced processes of self-assessment for schools. By 1983 self-assessment was operating in at least 56 LEAs. Such schemes involve schools evaluating their overall performance, normally on an informal basis, though sometimes involving LEA advisers and formal reports. Whole school self-assessment schemes have resulted in the development of individual teacher appraisal in some cases, though normally of an informal sort and with the purpose of development not judgement. James and Newman, in a survey of 233 schools, found that about half would have appraisal schemes by 1987.[13]

Self-assessment procedures are based on a collegial view of the school as professional community. According to Her Majesty's Inspectorate, they have proved invaluable in primary schools because they:

promoted professional discussion among staff; brought frustrations and disagreements to the surface; gave a voice to more members of staff . . .'[14]

In secondary schools HMI found that self-assessment has increased teacher commitment, created a common professional language, and enabled teachers to see their work in the context of the whole school. The forms of self-assessment that have developed embody the participative activity of professional peers.

In the early 1980s the focus shifted to the appraisal of the performance of individual teachers, in negotiations over the reform of the Burnham salary structure, which was almost universally recognized as inadequate at a time of falling rolls. The availability of 'points' for promotion depended upon the size of the school, and as numbers fell there were fewer points. Those in promoted posts frequently had to have their salaries protected as schools lost points. The focus was naturally on the individual, since the problem was the limits that financial and demographic decline placed on the individual teacher's career. But the individual focus fitted the market oriented 'responsibility' ethic of central government under Mrs Thatcher. The decline in promotion opportunities heightened the dissatisfaction of the teachers' unions, which had long been concerned about promotion procedures, and had argued for a systematic approach that would provide objective evidence on teachers' ability for advancement. The Burnham structure no longer provided the basis for the development of teachers' careers or for schools' management structures. It was clear, both to employers and unions, that reform was needed.

From the first the employers saw appraisal as part of any reorganized payment structure. The initial report of a group of officers appointed by the Burnham Management Panel in 1981, argued that pay should be related to performance. There were prolonged negotiations before the employers finally put forward their detailed plans in November 1984, in their document *A New Remuneration Structure for Teachers*. They proposed a three year probationary entry grade, a main professional grade for the classroom teacher, and principal teacher and assistant headteacher posts, forming about 20 per cent of the school establishment, which would have primarily management responsibilities. The proposals involved a threefold process of appraisal. Teachers could only move from the entry grade to the main professional grade by undergoing appraisal. Once on the main professional grade, teachers were to go through a twofold procedure: an annual performance appraisal by 'the senior professional and managerial colleague to whom the teacher is accountable'; every third year there was to be a 'performance review' involving LEA officers or advisers. Pay and performance were to be linked; the proposals stated that:

> If performance appraisal or review demonstrates that the performance of a teacher is unsatisfactory it would make little sense to increase the pay of that teacher. Thus progression to the next point in the teachers' incremental

scale will not be awarded to any teacher unless his or her performance is certified as satisfactory.[15]

A larger salary increment was to follow the three-yearly review as compared with the annual appraisal.

During the period of negotiation between 1981 and 1986, the DES and the Secretary of State were encouraging performance appraisal related to pay. Both the major white papers produced at that time gave it considerable emphasis. *Teaching Quality* argued that:

> the salary structure should be designed to offer relatively greater rewards to the best classroom teachers as well as to encourage good teachers to seek wider responsibilities in senior posts.[16]

Better Schools saw the appraisal of teachers as the 'key instrument' for managing the relationship between pay, responsibilities and performance. So important was it, that the Secretary of State was to take powers:

> to provide [a] national framework in the form of statutory regulations ... it is proposed therefore that the Secretary of State's existing powers for regulating the employment of teachers should be extended to enable him, in appropriate circumstances, to require LEAs regularly to appraise the performance of the teachers. ...[17]

That promise has been fulfilled in the Education Act 1986. The issue was confused by Sir Keith Joseph who gave the impression that the purpose of appraisal was to discover, and dismiss from the service, incompetent teachers. Sir Keith also saw dismissal of incompetent teachers as a means of reducing teacher numbers, which were well above the levels planned by the Government. He made the availability of money from central government to fund any revised salary structure dependent upon performance-related pay being introduced.

The employers' proposals, particularly on appraisal, were unacceptable to the teachers, and talks eventually broke down in Summer 1985. The talks that resulted in the Coventry agreement followed the acceptance by Sir Keith Joseph, that pay and performance should not be linked through appraisal. He had been persuaded, in part, by the Graham Report,[18] which examined various approaches to appraisal in Britain and overseas. The report emphasized the difficulties of appraising teachers' work. The necessary techniques are hardly developed and appraisal will require training especially in classroom observation. The report argued that appraisal was valuable, but that it should not be related to pay:

> We have concluded that the necessary conditions for success do not currently exist in England and Wales. Teachers manifestly believe their salaries to be poor: the criteria for determining a factual base for assessing (a) their classroom performance and (b) their total contribution to the

school community as a whole, are largely undeveloped and in any case exceedingly difficult to construct. In these circumstances the introduction of merit pay for a sceptical and organized teaching force might, we suspect, be self-defeating.[19]

The Audit Commission also:

reluctantly accepts the conclusion of the Graham Report regarding merit pay that the 'necessary conditions for success do not currently exist in England and Wales'.[20]

There is no guarantee that the employers and the DES will not return to performance related pay if conditions become more favourable. Strong teacher unions have been able to resist it. Any major change would require a weakening of the unions. The abolition of Burnham and collective bargaining might be seen as part of a move to weaken the teacher unions. The importance that the employers attach to appraisal can be judged from the costs involved. The Graham Report refers to a total of 8 to 12 hours effort for each teacher appraised. If an additional day of teacher time were allocated for every teacher appraised, the cost would be in the region of forty million pounds. Training costs and the costs of maintaining the system would need to be added to this. Through the Coventry Agreement, the Nottingham negotiations and the ACAS Agreement, the establishment of appraisal has been maintained as a key part of any settlement.

The teachers' successful resistance to the direct link between pay and performance should not obscure the fact that the employers and the DES have gained considerable control over the work of teachers. The settlement of the teachers' pay claim will inevitably involve tighter specification of teachers' duties. The dispute itself illustrated the intimate link between control of work and control of the employment relation, given that little is specified in the teachers' contract. Indeed, in a court case arising out of the dispute, the employers' view that the teachers' contract implies much more than simply class teaching was upheld. The teachers' claim to professional status was used by the judge to undermine their position; he stated in his judgement that:

the contracts are silent on the teachers' obligations on many [other] important matters. This feature of the teachers' contracts does not seem to me a matter of surprise. A contract for the employment of a professional in a professional capacity would not normally be expected to detail the professional obligations of the employee made under the employment contract.

In future duties will be more tightly specified and monitored, and the result will be tighter control of teachers. The formal appraisal system may be developmental, but closer monitoring and the gathering of more information on teachers will also involve judgements on performance.

Whether they are agreed with the employers or imposed by the Secretary of State, teachers' conditions of service will now be specified. While performance-related pay has been dropped for the moment there is no reason why it should not be revived by the Secretary of State in the future. The more hierarchical career structure favoured by the Secretary of State also involves strong elements, of payment for performance, through the promotion process, as he has made clear. Appraisal is not a whimsical notion of the Secretary of State, but a crucial part of the process of control through specifying teachers' work in detailed contract conditions. It is the process that will ensure that central purposes are being fulfilled.

The appraisal of teacher performance is part of a much wider development of assessment, accountability and control. In many types of work greater control and monitoring is possible through technological change and deskilling and fragmentation. Such approaches are much more difficult to adopt in teaching, given the problems in specifying the work, and especially when there is a concern to enhance the skill of the workforce. The approach to gaining control of teaching work has been different from what it might have been in the case of manufacturing work. The politics of the workplace are quite different, because the nature of teaching work is quite different. I shall now turn to an analysis of teachers' work and the implications for appraisal.

Appraisal and Teachers' Work

Littler[21] in his study of the development of work under capitalism distinguishes between rationalization and control of the labour process, of the structure of managerial control and rationalization of the nature of the employment relation. We have argued that, given the particular nature of teachers' work, appraisal of performance is key to the process of rationalization and that reform of the employment relationship is crucial to the process of control. Part of the teachers' claim to professional status is that judgment is part of the educational process because teaching work is difficult to specify. But the teachers' claim to professional autonomy is weak, and given changed labour market conditions they find it difficult to resist change in the nature of the employment relation. More importantly, given their own interest in reform of the career structure and the position inherited from the period of growth, they cannot resist change in the employment relation, only the link of pay and performance.

Appraisal of the performance of individual workers by their employers may be thought to be inappropriate for professionals whose work can only be adequately assessed by other professionals, if at all. Much of teacher resistance to appraisal and to tight specification of conditions of service is based upon the notion that teachers are professionals. The assertion of professional status is typically based on a claim to one or both of two types of knowledge distinguished by Jamous and Peloille,[22] technical knowledge and indeterminate knowledge. The claim to 'technicality' is the claim that one's expertise is based upon theoretical knowledge, which can be codified and passed on through training. In the case of teaching this might be specialist knowledge of one's subject, or theoretical knowledge of the teaching process. The work of

Sikes and her colleagues (23) has shown the importance of the subject base to many teachers:

> ... relating to one's subject rides above the problems, intricacies, pitfalls, and blocked opportunities of the hierarchical structure. It is a countervailing force against bureaucracy, giving one a firm foothold in the semi-autonomy of the subject department, affording status within it and bolstered by a like-minded community.[24]

The post-war period of growth saw a rapid expansion of subject specialisms as the curriculum widened. More recently pedagogical skills have received increased emphasis, for example in the study of teaching styles.

The indeterminacy claim is that there are aspects of one's work that can only be learned through considerable practical experience and which cannot be taught. The extent of indeterminacy is particularly high in teaching because, to a considerable extent, it is done by the teacher alone with the student in the classroom. Teaching is still a private activity, and a skill that can only be acquired in the classroom.

Claims both to technical and indeterminate knowledge as bases for teacher professionalism have become weaker as we have moved from growth to decline, and, to a considerable extent, it has been the circumstances created by growth that have undermined those claims. The technical basis of professional autonomy in specifiable skills will be eroded as management is able to proceduralize such knowledge, and, perhaps, embody it in machines and proceduralized approaches such as curriculum packages. This is much less possible in teaching than in many other types of work, but, as some American experience has shown, can be developed.

The claim to professionalism based upon specialist subject expertise has been seen by Woods[25] as containing the seeds of its own destruction:

> The curriculum has been divided and sub-divided, the areas thus created tending first to ensure their own self-preservation, then gathering strength with a view possibly to some further fission. Thus have teachers become more and more 'expert' as their areas of preserve become increasingly digested in this rationalizing process.

As Buswell[26] has argued, this fragmenting of the curriculum can be the basis of control through the setting of aims and objectives and the development of curriculum packages. Subject hierarchies can form the basis for 'oligarchic control of the institution, through formal and informal meetings of heads of department with the head or principal of the institution'.[27] The expansion of managerial structures in the period of growth created the basis for such oligarchic control.

Expanding career opportunities and control of the curriculum created a strong degree of independence and individualistic self-control. But the growth of specialization and managerial structures worked, implicitly, in the opposite direction. The growth in student numbers and in finance led to a set of managerial structures in schools, which, in a period of decline, could be used for control rather than co-ordination. The increase in pupil numbers and the comprehensive movement, created large schools which made specialization possible. The curriculum expanded because big schools created economies of scale in pupil groupings, and larger teaching staffs made possible a broader spread of teaching expertise. Bigger schools also needed explicit pastoral systems to counter the anonymity that goes with size, and to compensate for the difficulty of maintaining the personal knowledge of, and relationship with, pupils that are possible in smaller schools. Both subject and pastoral structures enhanced career routes for individual teachers, but individual teacher-pupil links, which, along with subject expertise, lay at the base of the claim to professional status, were weakened. The claim to professional status was shifting from the professional relationship of teacher and student to technical knowledge and skill. But the more the professional claim to occupational autonomy is based upon technical skill, the more it is prone to the claim that standards can be checked through appraisal.

Bigger schools with more complex curricula and organizational structures, required more co-ordination and the Burnham structure, with its proliferation of scales, allowed the creation of a range of managerial posts. The approach to management was hierarchical in concept, though, as we have said, the autonomy of teachers that followed from the context of growth limited managerial authority in practice. The school was 'loosely coupled' but the conditions for future hierarchical management that would be able to exert real control had been created. Teachers had come to talk of 'the hierarchy'; in future they would come to experience it. The form of management that developed in the period of growth provides a base for appraisal as the teachers' autonomy is eroded.

Growth led to general teacher shortage, but it has always been difficult to recruit specialist teachers, and the expansion of the curriculum and pupil rolls has led to teachers teaching subjects for which they are not specifically qualified. The Secondary Staffing Surveys of 1977 and 1984 found considerable evidence of such mismatch, especially in English, physical education, mathematics, religious education and physics. HMI reports have continually related poor teaching to mismatch. Changes in the curriculum have weakened some of the traditional claims to technicality as new subjects have been introduced, and as in-service training has been limited. New claims to technical skill have been established in some cases, for example special education. But the growing use of computers, the Cockroft Report, the emphasis on technical and vocational aspects of education, the integration of pupils with special needs and the requirements for multicultural education all serve to highlight perceived inadequacies in the technical skills of teachers.

The claim to autonomy based on indeterminacy is also weak in the face of accusations of declining standards and demands for accountability. The teaching process is complex and there are no standard outputs. It is therefore difficult for teachers to give an account of their stewardship that is adequate and understandable. There is the danger that parents and employers will then fall back on examination results and standard tests. The requirement in the Education Act 1981 to publish examination results is an instance of such a tendency.

Teaching requires skills that are ill-understood even by those who practise them. Hargreaves[28] has argued that:

> most teachers believe[d] teaching to be an intuitive act, one in which skills defy easy analysis and explanation and thus cannot readily be transmitted to the novice. . . .

It is then difficult for teachers to defend themselves against arguments that there are bad teachers and that there is bad teaching, and that the bad teachers should be weeded out.

> . . . certainly there are good and bad teachers but there are very different ways in which one can be good or bad and there are few universally agreed criteria by which teaching can be judged good or bad. Teaching is thus replete with 'endemic uncertainties' about competence.[29]

The privacy of teaching, and the unwillingness to talk about the problems of competence make it all the more difficult to give an account. Sikes[30] argues that it is much easier to talk about problems now than was the case in the 1950s or 1960s, but there are still taboos about admitting problems.

The teachers' claim to professional autonomy is therefore limited by the growth of specialization and hierarchy and by the inability to provide an accounting language. Managerial control rather than peer evaluation is therefore easier to assert, even though it may not be clear how managerially oriented appraisal might be done. Further the claim to and the notion of a right to a career, implicit in much of the recent discussion of the reform of Burnham, is essentially individualistic. The focus is clearly upon the individual teacher, underestimating the role of the school as an organic entity, and the teacher's membership of a collegiate body of colleagues. The work of Rutter and others has shown the importance of the influence of the school and its ethos, and illustrated the limitations of the government's individualistic focus in the development of appraisal. A more collective view would have two implications. First, appraisal of the individual would necessarily involve evaluation of the school. Second, it would imply that any appraisal would be reciprocal and involve all those who go to make up the educational community. As Sayer put it:

> schools and communities are organic. A teacher is responding to demands, pressures and needs among pupils, parents, colleagues, the local community, and personal perceptions of good practice. The response is in a context of a school responding to or creating demands from governors, central and local government and other institutions, including future places of employment or continuing education . . . the collegiality of a teaching

community is not just a matter of style, but of mutual responsibility. Any systematic review of performance . . . has, then, to be mutual if it is not to undermine the spirit of the enterprise.[31]

It is difficult to see how such a process could be used to judge individual teachers, though the Graham Report, while acknowledging the collective nature of the evaluation enterprise, implies that it could:

> . . . provide a vehicle for a cohesive pattern of national education, which in some instances would flow all the way from the Secretary of State through the LEAs to every classroom teacher.[32]

The basis would be laid for management-by-objectives, and centralized influence based upon managerial control-oriented accountability. At each level – DES, LEA, school, department, individual teacher – aims could be specified. A collective orientation could be hierarchical.

Focusing upon the individual teacher also gives a false picture of the teachers' autonomy. HMI, in their paper *Good Teachers*, observe that:

> . . . A successful teacher may rise above some organizational barriers, may bring coherence to a teaching programme where a school or department provides little, and help to compensate for social deprivation or handicap among the pupils. But the contribution of even the best teachers can be limited by outside factors, and appropriate weightings need to be employed in assessing the effectiveness of teachers operating in highly favourable conditions, and those working against a backcloth of severe disadvantage, shortages of necessary resources, or inadequate management. . . .[33]

A strong focus upon the individual may be a means of evading responsibility by those who must provide the conditions within which the teacher must work. Teaching is a constrained activity, and for appraisal of any sort the constraints must be understood and specified.

The developments discussed above all serve to make teaching more public. Professional appraisal may serve to make more open processes that have always been implicit. The British teaching structure, unlike the American seniority based system, has come to contain a high assessment content through the promotion system. But this is essentially based round the individual case.

The individualistic emphasis that characterizes the teachers' claim to professional autonomy, makes it more likely that any attempt at assessment will involve accountability as well as development. It also means that, in practice, assessment of performance and reward are likely to be related. The HMI study of appraisal found that:

> Appraisal was also used to provide evidence of promotability. One head pointed to ten internal and eight external promotions in the previous 18 months. The information gained and the judgements made during the

appraisal process were frequently used as a means of ensuring fuller, more accurate references and this was generally welcomed by the teachers. . . .[34]

There is much more likely to be a link between performance assessment and promotion in a time of decline, when the labour market is much looser and teachers are consequently less able to determine their career progression. Kenneth Baker's proposed hierarchical career structure will, therefore, involve a closer relationship of pay and performance than the more egalitarian ACAS agreement.

As the teachers' unions have argued, the basis upon which evaluation for promotion is made must be questioned. Grace's[35] study of a number of inner city schools has shown that teachers' competence was more likely to be assessed on the basis of features such as personality, relations with other teachers and pupils and bureaucratic efficiency than the ability to teach. Moreover, headteachers frequently claim to know who are the more and less competent members of their staff by a rather unclear, almost osmotic, process of being around in the school.

The individualistic nature of the relationship between teacher and taught has served, according to Lortie,[36] to undermine the teachers' ability to develop a claim to technicality. The consequence, as Becher *et al.*[37] argue, is that the process of assessment moves from teaching to non-class based activities.

> One consequence of classroom privacy and the lack of generally acknowledged criteria for evaluating teaching is that promotion is likely to be based on considerations other than classroom performance. Provided a teacher is sufficiently competent not to have major disciplinary problems it will be his [*sic*] qualifications, his age, his attendance at courses outside the classroom which determines his chances of promotion.

Moving into the classroom presupposes a clear set of criteria on which a teacher's performance in class can be assessed. Such developed criteria do not yet exist.

Conclusion

The teachers are now being subject to two separate processes of control. Developing central control and influence over the curriculum is specifying what shall be taught and how it shall be taught. LEAs, for example, through curriculum staffing, are also exerting stronger central control. Aims and objectives to be met by all schools are being laid down by LEAs and the DES. Second, teachers' contracts are now being more closely specified. Both the content and form of the educational process are therefore being more closely controlled. Teacher appraisal and assessment must be seen in this context. The appraisal process may be judgemental or developmental. In the former guise it is clearly aimed at the control of performance. Implicit or explicit standards established by employers rather than established by the teacher or his or her peers will have to be met. But developmental assessment also has elements of control, for as we have seen, the LEA, the DES and other bodies such as the Manpower Services Commission, will control the planning of in-service training and state priorities for its content. The focus is not an individual, self-determined, development, but controlled development in line with central objectives and priorities. It is worthy of note that one of the key central government priorities is management training.

The ability of teachers to resist these moves towards central control is limited. The labour market is loose, except for certain specialisms like mathematics and physics. Ring-fences and falling rolls limit career mobility, so that teachers are likely to find themselves for long periods in the same authority and the same schools. LEAs and schools can now plan teachers' careers in a managerial fashion. The teachers' own resistance to financial cuts and salary decline has weakened their professional position. By working to a tight interpretation of contract conditions, they have changed the emphasis in their jobs from one of general professional obligation, to specific contractual conditions.

Professionalism is a dynamic concept, changing its meaning according to the claims that occupations generally acknowledged to be professions are able to make. Those professions are strongest in their claims to autonomy that can claim independent self-control both on the basis of technical knowledge and indeterminate, experience-based, skill. Doctors have been very successful in claiming both. Teachers' claims to technical control of the curriculum are no longer accepted, as central government and the LEAs have reasserted control. The claim to indeterminate knowledge has always been weak, because of a neglect in emphasis on the teaching process, and because outsiders have been critical of teachers' methods. The privacy and individualistic nature of teaching has made the development of a collective professional voice difficult.

The development of appraisal systems is part of the development of a more managerial approach to education. A dual process of centralization of control in the hands of the DES, MSC and LEA, and decentralizing of power from the school to the parents and governing body, is eroding the autonomy of the teacher. Schools and teachers are to be held responsible for producing education according to closely specified aims and objectives. The danger is that the result will be the sort of bureaucratization that frequently character-izes attempts at appraisal. Wise has argued in the United States that the result is 'hyper-rationalization' – 'bureaucratic overlay without attaining the intended policy objectives'.[38] Clearly, we have already moved into a cycle of mistrust in which emphasis is laid on contractual obligations and continually enhanced rule-systems to ensure that they are met. We may not have moved as far as some of the individual states in the United States, but we are clearly 'rationalizing'.

Appraisal need not be purely negative and controlling. In laying out various dimensions – focus, purpose and form – along which appraisal can vary, I have argued that appraisal can be either controlling or participative. In the United

States we have seen the development of the control form – with standardized tests and competency-based assessment. Teaching, in such approaches, is broken down into a set of individualized, potentially fragmented skills. By contrast a positive approach emphasizes the 'wholeness' of the teaching and learning experience. Participative appraisal can enhance that recognition of the wholeness of the teaching and learning experience. It can encourage a focus upon the school and its place in the community rather than the individual isolated teacher.

Appraisal may also have a role to play in the partnership-based government of education. It can be a part of the process of involvement of teachers as well as parents and students in the educational process. In that sense it might form part of a reciprocal form of accountability, rather than hierarchical, managerial accountability. Appraisal might then be a process that involved all those that formed part of the school in the community.

Participative appraisal could also help overcome the sort of isolation, uncertainty and loneliness that characterizes a great deal of teaching. In that it could be a part of the learning process in the school. It could be used not to identify the successes and failures of the individual teacher, but the constraints that operated on the school as a learning community. Appraisal might also be part of the process of developing a language in which one could account for education, making possible more rational dialogue on its nature and development. Participative appraisal could contribute to a reassessment of the purpose of education.

Notes

1   See, for example, the discussion by S. Ranson, 'Towards a Tertiary Tripartism: New Codes of Social Control and the 17+' in P. Broadfoot (ed.), *Selection, Certification and Control*, Falmer Press, 1984.

2   See Ranson (Note 1) and the various articles in S. Ranson and J. Tomlinson (eds) *The New Management of Education*, George Allen and Unwin, 1986.

3   *Times Educational Supplement*, 27.6.1986.

4   Audit Commission, *Obtaining Better Value for Money: Aspects of Non-Teaching Costs in Secondary Schools*, HMSO, 1984. Audit Commission, *Obtaining Better Value for Money from Further Education*, HMSO, 1985. Audit Commission, *Towards Better Management of Secondary Education*, HMSO, 1986.

5   Quoted in R. Saran, *The Politics Behind Burnham; A Study of Teachers' Salary Negotiations*, Sheffield Papers in Education Management, Sheffield City Polytechnic, Department of Education Management, 1985, p. 159.

6   Quoted in B. Salter, T. Tapper, *Education, Politics and the State*, Grant McIntyre, 1981, p. 119.

7   *Education in Schools; A Consultative Document*, Cmnd, 6869, HMSO, 1977, p. 2.

8   *Education in Schools*, p. 16.

9   *Better Schools*, HMSO, Cmnd 9469, 1985, p. 54.

10 See V. Karn, 'Housing' and C. K. Skelcher, 'Transportation' in S. Ranson, G. Jones, K. Walsh (eds) *Between Centre and Locality*, George Allen & Unwin, 1986.

11 J. Eggleston, 'Teacher Professionalism and Professionialization' in S. Ranson, J. Tomlinson (eds), *The Changing Government of Education*, George Allen & Unwin, 1968.

12 *Assessment Techniques and Approaches, Better Schools Evaluation and Appraisal Conference*, Birmingham, 14–15 November, 1985, pp. 70–1.

13 Quoted in J. B. Whyte, 'Teacher Assessment: A Review of the Performance Appraisal Literature with special reference to the Implications for Teacher Appraisal' in *Research Papers in Education*, Vol. 1, No. 2, June 1986, p. 154.

14 Department of Education and Science, *Quality in Schools: Evaluation and Appraisal*.

15 *A New Remuneration Structure for Teachers.*

16 *Teaching Quality*, p. 15.

17 *Better Schools*, HMSO, Cmnd, 9469, 1985, p. 56.

18 Suffolk Education Department, *Those Having Torches ... Teacher Appraisal: A Study*, 1985.

19 *Those Having Torches*, p. 9.

20 *Towards Better Management of Secondary Education*, HMSO, 1986.

21 C. Littler, *The Development of the Labour Process in Capitalist Societies*, London, Heinemann, 1982.

22 H. Jamous, B. Peloille, 'Change in the French University Hospital System' in J. A. Jackson (ed.) *Professions and Professionalisation*, Cambridge University Press, 1970.

23 P. Sikes, L. Measor, P. Woods, *Teachers, Careers: Crises and Continuities*, Falmer Press, 1985.

24 P. Sikes *et al.*, p. 21.

25 P. Woods, *The Divided School*, Routledge and Kegan Paul, 1979, p. 254.

26 C. Buswell, 'Pedagogic Change and Social Change', *British Journal of the Sociology of Education*, Vol. 1, No. 3, 1980.

27 B. Bernstein, quoted in S. Ball, I. Goodison, *Teachers' Lives and Careers*, Falmer Press, 1985.

28 D. Hargreaves, *The Challenge for the Comprehensive School*, Routledge and Kegan Paul, 1982, p. 197.

29 D. Hargreaves, *The Challenge for the Comprehensive School*, p. 204.

30 P. Sikes *et al.*, pp. 33–4.

31 J. Sayer, *What Future for Secondary Schools?*, Falmer Press, 1985, p. 160.

32 *Those Having Torches*, p. 10.

33 HMI, *Good Teachers*, HMSO, 1985, p. 2.

34 DES, *Quality in Schools*, p. 29.

35 G. Grace, *Teachers, Ideology and Control: A Study in Urban Education*, Routledge and Kegan Paul, 1978.

36 D. C. Lortie, *Schoolteachers, a Sociological Study*, Chicago, University of Chicago Press, 1975.

37 T. Becher, M. Erault, J. Knight, *Policies for Educational Accountability*, Heinemann, London, 1981.

38 E. Wise, *Legislated Learning*, Berkeley, University of California Press, 1979.

26

Youth and the Transitions into Adulthood

John Clarke and Paul Willis

[. . .]

The conception of youth as a homogeneous group is one which rests on deeply rooted biological and psychological assumptions. They are assumptions about universal patterns of human development and growth to maturity, in which youth appears as the transitional stage between childhood and adulthood. According to this, youth is distinguished by all sorts of biological changes, and a variety of psychological changes and adjustments – the 'Acne and Valderma syndrome'. Youth then, is natural, universal (a 'phase' that we all go through), and inherently unstable (a period of difficult adjustments).

But this disguises two ways in which youth is profoundly social, rather than natural. Youth, as we know it, is the consequence of social arrangements designed to regulate the transition not of child to adult in a universal sense, but of the child to worker and citizen in *our* society, with all the appropriate habits and attitudes that are supposed to belong to such an individual. Youth, in this sense, is a social product which accompanied the rise of mass schooling as a way of regulating and controlling this *social* transition. It is the process by which potential labour-power (the child) is recruited and transformed into actual labour-power (the adult). The 'development' of youth in our society has very specific goals in mind.

Once we understand this social character of the transition, we can follow it to the second sense in which youth is social. Because the transition is not a 'common' process, it is differentiated by the social divisions of British society: by class, gender and race. The transition is differentiated in its starting points, the experience of the transition itself, and in its destination.

Class affects how young people enter it and where they are expected to go when they leave it. Class also shapes the process of transition itself – its length (at what age do people leave it?) and the sorts of institutions in which it is experienced (school; school plus college; school plus university). Gender, too, differentiates the transition. The different destinations assumed for boys and girls structure how they enter it, the sorts of experiences and direction they encounter within it, and the manner in which they leave it. Finally, race impinges on the transition, again partly on the different experiences with which groups enter it and partly on the different destinations presumed for them.

These social divisions, then, produce not a transition from school to work, but a whole variety of transitions. They bear on the process of transition in two ways. First by locating individuals in different starting points and secondly, through the social division of labour, they determine the different destinations to be arrived at: skilled worker, white collar worker, manager, wife and mother, or unemployed.

These points about the social differentiation of youth are not merely part of an abstract academic argument – they bear on everday reality encountered by teachers and the young themselves in the institutions of the state. We have emphasized their importance not because we have somehow 'discovered' them but because they are systematically *not* recognized in official accounts of the confused and contradictory everyday life of institutions. Workers in these state institutions – teachers, lecturers, youth workers and so on – have to face the task of negotiating the gap between the *reality* of the structural and cultural differentiation of the young and the *official accounts* of youth which structure the institutions and programmes within which they work. [. . .]

Bridging the Gap: the Role of the State

In spite of the recent revival of 'classical' free market economics, with its avowal of the importance of supply and demand and with its contempt for government interference, the social reality of youth unemployment is not simply a matter of the market in labour. The state has, throughout the history of British capitalism, always taken an interest in 'surplus labour' – an interest expressed in a diversity of institutions ranging from skill centres to the workhouse. Since the mid-nineteenth century the state has also taken a hand in 'managing' the transition from child to worker – first in schooling, and then in further and higher education. These two concerns have come together in the current crisis . . . a crisis involving not just 'surplus labour', but surplus *youth* labour.

Even under the direction of a government committed to 'rolling back the state' and 'freeing the individual', the state's commitment to managing this broken transition has not only continued but been expanded. 'Thatcherism' (for all its hostility to 'quangos') has maintained and increased the role of the Manpower Services Commission. The MSC's role in youth employment was initially that of 'filling the gap' between the end of school and the arrival of work. To this end, it has provided or financed its own training and education schemes and invested heavily in the Further Education sector, providing finance for suitable courses. At the end of 1982, however, the Minister of Education (Sir Keith Joseph) and the Minister of Employment (Norman Tebbit) announced a scheme to extend the financing of approved courses to secondary education.

This proposal is a logical consequence of two earlier developments. First, it is a development in the career of the MSC as the 'master institution' responsible for both defining and responding to youth unemployment. Secondly, it is a consequence of the attack on the schools' 'failure' to equip young people adequately for their entry to work. Once the 'Great Debate' had identified the failings of the schools, what could be more reasonable than that an organization which 'knows better' should step in with advice (and funds) to improve the situation.

'Work' in the schools

Nevertheless what the 'Debate' and subsequent responses have played down is just how far 'work' has already penetrated the school curriculum. What is startling is not the 'failure' of school to prepare for work, but the extent to which such 'preparation' has been embodied in secondary schooling. The pressure for 'relevance' (particularly for the 'non-academic' strata) has meant that the world of work increasingly has come to be represented in the school curriculum, in the guises of social education, vocational guidance and preparation, social and life skills and so on. The Debate and its subsequent echoes were not the point at which 'work' was suddenly discovered by schools – at best, they accelerated an already well established trend.

Such innovations indicate that the 'pressures from above' on teachers do not remain fixed and permanent. These institutional demands are responsive to the external spheres of economics and politics – although these changing external conditions are always translated into the language of education before they arrive at the teacher. 'Work' – the demands of the economy for particular sorts of labour – may undergo a variety of transformations before its appearance in the classroom. It is translated through the languages of knowledge, values, skills, relevance and pedagogy on its way from the commanding heights. [. . .]

Where to Begin?

We have sketched in some of the main changes in the world outside of the school. Most important is the fundamental and trenchant economic crisis, the various attempts to understand it, allocate blame, and to take steps towards its resolution. These external changes are affecting the school in a number of ways. Indeed, schools are an important battleground between contending interests as these interests try to define the general crisis in a certain way, and therefore offer certain kinds of solution. What are teachers to make of the situation? What are they to do? What are those teachers to do who are involved in the most contested terrain of all – careers? [. . .]

Most basically we try always to bear in mind the perspectives, experiences, and position of pupils in school. Of course, all writing on education purports to take young people as the main stake – it is they who are to be 'helped'. But in most approaches and accounts – never more than now in the age of 'the new realism' – the pupil is taken as an essentially malleable bit of human clay. The child is not anything yet in his or her own right. He or she is only an undeveloped adult. The business of schooling is to mould this adult – hence the argument over the shape of the mould. The argument is over the 'ideal' model of the future adult – honest citizen, good worker, caring family person, critical and informed voter and so on – which the school is then organized and empowered to produce. Currently we can see a clear battle over whether school should produce an 'ideal worker' to help resolve the economic crisis or a 'critical and independent person' who can develop their own capacities to the full. As we shall see, this is often apparently resolved by the former pretending to be the latter.

But this is not the way in which we want to be interested in the pupils. We do not want these ideal constructions. Actually we do not believe that, for the most part, the actual products of our schools ever bore much resemblance to these ideal models. We have tried to keep at the forefront of our minds the *real cultural diversity* of young people and to emphasize that this diversity brings experiences, expectations and evaluations of work to the school [. . .] *specific* social groups who are actively 'knowledgeable' about the world.

We would argue, for example, that most working class children have never been concerned with what the ideal models are supposed to be. Their concern is not with the ideal future worker to solve the problems of capitalism, nor is it with the ideal citizen to solve the problems of democracy, nor is it with the self-developed individual to solve the problems of civilization. Their problems concern survival in scarcity and the need to make material adjustments and plans to cope with their real – and future – situations. Gaining a wage to survive; hoping to enjoy some power as a buyer and consumer through the wage; going through the adolescent sexual dance and setting up the working class home in straitened circumstances; adapting to the strengths and enablements as well as the oppressions of quite strictly policed gender identities – these are the real themes of working class apprenticeship to adulthood in our society. In relationship to this apprenticeship there is often a general and uneasy sense of the *irrelevance* of the school. School is often rejected, rebelled against or treated as a comic interlude before 'real' life begins.

Schools and their ideal models have never really taken into account this *material culturalism* of growing up in the working class. Indeed many of the educational prescriptions do not even recognize how far *their own practices*, and teaching regimes, have less to do with theory than with responding to the *material cultures* of pupils in schools – that is in supervising, controlling and often negotiating with them. This gap between the official and the real – and the problems of managing it – are, of course, the stuff of which the everyday life of teachers is constructed. The tasks of making these two versions of the world match, of managing the antagonisms between them, of controlling unfulfilled expectations, are those around which many of the problems of the classroom centre.

These problems are contradictory ones: a commitment to either the official or unofficial versions of reality encounters the antagonism of its opposite. It is in this sense that one can speak of teachers 'negotiating' these pressures: of trying to hold these tensions and conflicting interests in some sort of balance within the classroom. Containing and handling this situation is often as much as teachers can do – and this is what dictates teaching styles and methods, even though they may be dignified at another level by philosophies of teaching.

Meanwhile, as the 'ideal' models for future citizens miss their mark, we would argue that it is, importantly, from pupils' *own* cultures and experiences, from their *own* struggles actually to make a life, that a connection with the future is made at all. It is here that the transition into work, adult and family life is accomplished, that jobs and functions are filled irrespective of the quality or attitudes deemed ideally to be necessary for these things. Crudely we are saying this: life goes on and 'transitions' are accomplished in all the complexity of normal everyday life, and although this is continuously 'moulded' and 'developed' in part by direct official policy, it is also achieved through experiences, knowledges and cultures of the people involved. The current crisis is also experienced at that everyday level. This is where it is dealt with and suffered. So long as we try to understand this experience only through the school, its constructions, mystifications and specifically 'educational models', we will be lost and confused. The fundamental aim [. . .] is to keep in mind the material experiences and cultures of the pupils and to see how far teachers can respond to *these* problems – rather than to the problems of something called 'the school'.

Whether it was ever accomplished through the intentions of teachers, or actually as an escape from school, the transition into work is a thing of the past. A guillotine has fallen on the traditional couplet school/work – and chopped out an empty chunk of time for most youngsters: five years before their first job, or perhaps before permanent unemployment, or before motherhood, domestic labour and family life intervene anyway. The changed situation can be stated very simply – 'there ain't no jobs'. That is at the heart of the educational crisis and it is not surprising that careers education, and 'work in the curriculum' should be caught up in the storm.

But this central material fact is constructed, understood and acted upon in different ways. Most accounts of why this has come about, and what action must be taken, come from the state or from industrial interests. As we have just said, our approach is to try to see how the crisis is understood and *survived* by the young people involved, and to start from here in trying to work out a relevant curriculum. But the 'problem' of youth and education has actually been massively dealt with by grown-ups, and certain kinds of grown-ups at that. Perhaps the dominant definition of the 'educational crisis' has come from those who represent the power of industry and the power of capital. Of course this has filtered into the 'debate' in a variety of ways and has also now become an educational argument, and even a liberal argument, *apparently* in support of young people. In the new age of international commercial competition and of 'high tech', industry needs better workers – more skilled and especially more loyal and hard working. Just like the Japanese are held to be. If they are not like this, then it is no surprise that the economy is declining – and incidentally that there are no jobs for the young. Industrial interests and those speaking for them interpret changes in 'the transition' in the light of their own problems and therefore propose certain kinds of solutions. The 'mould' for the model pupil here becomes the mould for the model worker – trained, skilled, flexible and above all disciplined. There is no room for reluctant heroes in the sinking ship of HMS UK Plc. In a word, this view wishes to subjugate young people more completely than ever before to the needs of industry and, therefore, to the needs of capital. Youth can only be helped by their *own* contribution towards making a more successful economy and along with it, more jobs. The implications for careers teaching and for work in the curriculum are obvious. The needs of industry, their 'sympathetic' presentation, and production of 'model workers' threaten to carry all before them.

An almost equally powerful 'definition of the problem' comes ultimately from the state and from its problems in maintaining law and order and a peaceful society. In one way more realistic than the industrial view, this perspective accepts that, at least for the moment, youth unemployment will not be spirited away by up-skilling and higher qualifications. The empty chunk of time chopped out of most young people's lives by the guillotine of the recession is also a *social* problem – it might be used collectively to roam the streets, conspicuously colonize shopping centres, to frighten the citizenry or even to riot and directly challenge the social order. It is safe to assume that the riots of summer 1981 helped wonderfully to concentrate the Tory government mind on youth unemployment, and it can be no coincidence that state expenditure on special measures for the young unemployed is one of the things to have escaped the cuts and actually to have been increased dramatically. However the transition into work had been accomplished before, the situation had one over-riding merit – young adults were in work and causing trouble nowhere else. It is therefore hardly surprising that the most immediate – and still dominant – fundamental response has been to keep as many youngsters as possible in something as close as possible to work for as long a period as possible – via YOPs and later YTS. Perhaps no-one will notice the difference! At least they're off the streets!

Of course, many of the YOP and YTS schemes display a combination of the two perspectives. Discipline, compulsory attendance and work experience attempt to duplicate the social discipline of work and also pre-empt alternative and perhaps 'anti-social' styles of consumption, leisure habits, modes of thought and action. The double and partly contradictory aim is to produce people who want and are able to work, but who are also willing to maintain these qualities in suspended animation for a period without letting them deteriorate or allowing the human capacities behind them be turned to other, perhaps dangerous, activities.

In confusing and multi-form ways, the 'industrial' and the 'state' views can combine together in schools to produce a liberal, humane, child-centred view which stresses the individual well-being and development of the child. Indeed, it is to the benefit of the individual child not to be unemployed, not to be locked up by the police. Social and life skills training, and work in the curriculum, can be important and relevant to pupils while still serving also to promote a certain view of society, to promote social control and to offer certain solutions to the problems of the economy. [. . .]

But to repeat, our position is that the variety of student 'moulds' – principally those of 'good citizen' and 'good worker' – do not actually produce very good copies! In a certain sense they are phantoms in the illusions of power that our controllers need in order to make sense of society. The reality of how life and its futures are experienced by the different sections of the pupil population, the actual processes, uncertainties and ambitions which govern how the 'transition' or the 'empty chunk of time' is lived and accomplished, are likely to be quite different. But if the powerful 'definitions' and the solutions which flow from them owe more to phantasm than a serious material analysis of the position of youth, and if they reveal more about the problems which the controllers are trying to solve rather than the problems experienced by youth, they nevertheless have very real effects. They help to give justification to certain kinds of control and to the suppression of other cultures and possibilities within the school. Despite their contradictions, they can also imprint on many student minds certain attitudes and beliefs, even if only to mystify and make less coherent their own views of what is happening to them. Certainly alternative pursuits, alternative styles and types of consumption and behaviour are prevented from emerging or castigated as dangerous or ignorant. Most of all, the weight of the (ironically disappearing) world of work is brought to bear in a certain threatening way which seeks to place the burden of the world on its children. Perhaps the most damaging general tendency is to promote self blame amongst young people – unemployment is the result of *their* lack of ability, skill, capacity and discipline. Individual or collective action or understanding suggesting anything different is anti-social and reflects badly on the moral fibre of those involved.

27

Education Cannot Compensate for Society

Basil Bernstein

Since the late 1950s there has been a steady outpouring of papers and books in the United States which are concerned with the education of children of low social class whose *material* circumstances are inadequate, or with the education of black children of low social class whose *material* circumstances are chronically inadequate. A vast research and educational bureaucracy developed in the United States which was financed by funds obtained from federal, state or private foundations. New educational categories were developed – 'the culturally deprived', 'the linguistically deprived' 'the socially disadvantaged'; and the notion of 'compensatory education' was introduced as a means of changing the status of the children in these categories.

Compensatory education emerged in the form of massive pre-school introductory programmes like Project Headstart (see Ruth Adam, 30 October 1969), large-scale research programmes such as those of Deutch in the early 1960s and a plethora of small-scale 'intervention' or 'enrichment' programmes for pre-school children or children in the first years of compulsory education. Very few sociologists were involved in these studies, because education was a low-status area. On the whole they were carried out by psychologists.

The focus of these studies was on the child in the family and on the local classroom relationship between teacher and child. In the last two years one can detect a change in this focus. As a result of the movements towards integration, and the opposed movement towards segregation (the latter a response to the wishes of the various Black Power groups), more studies are being made in the United States of the *school*. Robert Rosenthal's classic study, *Pygmalion in the Classroom*, drew attention to the critical importance of the teacher's expectations of the child.

In this country we have been aware of the educational problem since the writings of Sir Cyril Burt before the war. His book, *The Backward Child*, is probably still the best study we have. After the war, a series of sociological surveys and public inquiries into education brought this educational problem into the arena of national debate, and so of social policy. Now in Wales there is a large research unit, financed by the Schools Council, concerned with compensatory education. Important research of a different kind is taking place in the University of Birmingham into the problems of the education of Commonwealth children. The Social Science Research Council and the Department of Education and Science have given £175,000, in part for the development of special pre-school programmes concerned to introduce children to compensatory education. There is also the whole educational priority area programme (described by Anne Corbett in 'Are educational priority areas working?', 13 November 1969).

One university department of education offers an advanced diploma in compensatory education. Colleges of education also offer special courses under the same title. So it might be worth a few lines to consider the assumptions underlying this work and the concepts which describe it, particularly as my own writings have sometimes been used (and more often abused) to highlight aspects of the general problems and dilemmas.

To begin with, I find the term, 'compensatory education', a curious one for a number of reasons. I do not understand how we can talk about offering compensatory education to children who in the first place have not, as yet, been offered an adequate educational environment. The Newsom report on secondary schools showed that 79 per cent of all secondary modern schools in slum and problem areas were materially grossly inadequate, and that the holding power of these schools over the teachers was horrifyingly low. The same report also showed very clearly the depression in the reading scores of these children, compared with the reading scores of children who were at school in areas which were neither problem nor slum. This does not conflict with the findings that, on average, for the country as a whole, there has been an improvement in children's reading ability. The Plowden report on the primary schools was rather more coy about all the above points, but we have little reason to believe that the situation is very much better for primary schools in similar areas.

Thus we offer a large number of children, both at the primary and secondary levels, materially inadequate schools and a high turnover of teaching staff; and we further expect a small group of dedicated teachers to cope. The strain on these teachers inevitably produces fatigue and illness and it is not uncommon to find, in any week, teachers having to deal with doubled-up classes of 80 children. And we wonder why the children display very early in their educational life a range of learning difficulties.

At the same time, the organization of schools creates delicate overt and covert streaming arrangements which neatly lower the expectations and motivations of both teachers and taught. A vicious spiral is set up, with an all too determinate outcome. It would seem, then, that we have failed to provide, on the scale required, an *initial* satisfactory educational environment.

The concept, 'compensatory education', serves to direct attention away from the internal organization and the educational context of the school, and focus our attention on the families and children. 'Compensatory education'

378

implies that something is lacking in the family, and so in the child. As a result, the children are unable to benefit from schools.

It follows, then, that the school has to 'compensate' for the something which is missing in the family, and the children are looked at as deficit systems. If only the parents were interested in the goodies we offer, if only they were like middle class parents, then we could do our job. Once the problem is seen even implicitly in this way, then it becomes appropriate to coin the terms 'cultural deprivation', 'linguistic deprivation', and so on. And then these labels do their own sad work.

If children are labelled 'culturally deprived', there it follows that the parents are inadequate; the spontaneous realizations of their culture, its images and symbolic representations, are of reduced value and significance. Teachers will have lower expectations of the children, which the children will undoubtedly fulfil. All that informs the child, that gives meaning and purpose to him outside of the school, ceases to be valid or accorded significance and opportunity for enhancement within the school. He [or she] has to orient towards a different structure of meaning, whether it is in the form of reading books (*Janet and John*), in the form of language use and dialect, or in the patterns of social relationships.

Alternatively, the meaning structure of the school is explained to the parents and imposed on, rather than integrated within, the form and content of the world. A wedge is progressively driven between the child as a member of a family and community, and the child as a member of a school. Either way the child is expected, and his parents as well, to drop their social identity, their way of life and its symbolic representations, at the school gate. For, by definition, their culture is deprived, and the parents are inadequate in both the moral and the skill orders they transmit.

I do not mean by this that in these circumstances no satisfactory home-school relations can take place or do not take place; I mean rather that the best thing is for the parents to be brought *within* the educational experience of the schoolchild by doing what they can do, and this with confidence. There are many ways in which parents can help the child in his [or her] learning, which are within the parents' spheres of competence. If this happens, then the parents can feel adequate and confident both in relation to the child and the school. This may mean that the contents of the learning in school should be drawn much more from the child's experience in his [or her] family and community.

So far I have criticized the use of the concept of 'compensatory' education, because it distracts attention from the deficiencies in the school itself and focuses upon deficiencies within the community, family and child. We can add to these criticisms a third.

This concept points to the overwhelming significance of the early years of the child's life in the shaping of his [or her] later development. Clearly there is more evidence to support this view and to support its implication that we should create an extensive nursery-school system. However, it would be foolhardy indeed to write off the post-seven-years-of-age educational experience as having little influence.

Minimally, what is required *initially* is to consider the whole age period up to the conclusion of the primary stages as a unity. This would require considering our approach, at any *one* age, in the context of the whole of the primary stage. This implies a systematic, rather than a piecemeal, approach. I am arguing here for taking as the unit, not a particular period in the life of the child – for example, three to five years, or five to seven years – but taking as the unit a stage of education: the primary stage. We should see all we do in terms of the sequencing of learning, the development of sensitivities within the context of the primary stage. In order to accomplish this, the present social and educational division between infant and junior stages must be weakened, as well as the insulation between primary and secondary stages. Otherwise gains at any one age, for the child, may well be vitiated by losses at a later age.

We should stop thinking in terms of 'compensatory education' but consider, instead, most seriously and systematically the conditions and contexts of the educational environment.

The very form our research takes tends to confirm the beliefs underlying the organization, transmission and evaluation of knowledge by the school. Research proceeds by assessing the criteria of attainment that schools hold, and then measures the competence of different social groups in reaching these criteria. We take one group of children, whom we know beforehand possess attributes favourable to school achievement; and a second group of children, whom we know beforehand lack these attributes. Then we evaluate one group in terms of what it *lacks* when compared with another. In this way research, unwittingly, underscores the notion of *deficit* and confirms the status quo of a given organization, transmission and, in particular, evaluation of knowledge. Research very rarely challenges or exposes the social assumptions underlying what counts as valid knowledge, or what counts as a valid realization of that knowledge. There are exceptions in the area of curriculum development; but, even here, the work often has no built-in attempt to evaluate the changes. This holds particularly for educational priority area 'feasibility' projects.

Finally, we do not face up to the basic question: What is the potential for change within educational institutions as they are presently constituted? A lot of activity does not necessarily mean *action*.

I have taken so much space discussing the new educational concepts and categories because, in a small way, the work I have been doing has inadvertently contributed towards their formulation. It might, and has been said, that my research – through focusing upon the subculture and forms of family socialization – has also distracted attention from the conditions and contexts of learning in school. The focus on usage of language has sometimes led people to divorce the use of language from the substratum of cultural meanings which are initially responsible for the language use. The concept, 'restricted code', to describe working class speech, has been equated with 'linguistic deprivation' or even with the 'non-verbal' child.

We can distinguish between uses of language which can be called 'context-bound' and uses of language which are less context-bound. Consider, for example, the two following stories which the linguist, Peter Hawkins, constructed as a result of his analysis of the speech of middle class and working class five-year-old children. The children were given a series of four pictures which told a story and they were invited to tell the story. The first picture shows some boys playing football; in the second the ball goes through the window of a house: the third shows a man making a threatening gesture: and in the fourth a woman looks out of a window and the children are moving away. Here are the two stories:

1   Three boys are playing football and one boy kicks the ball and it goes through the window the ball breaks the window and the boys are looking at it and a man comes out and shouts at them because they've broken the window so they run away and then that lady looks out of her window and she tells the boys off. (No. of nouns: 13, No. of pronouns: 6)
2   They're playing football and he kicks it and it goes through there it breaks the window and they're looking at it and he comes out and shouts at them because they've broken it so they run away and then she looks out and she tells them off. (No. of nouns: 2. No. of pronouns: 14)

With the first story, the reader does not have to have the four pictures which were used as the basis for the story, whereas in the case of the second story the reader would require the initial pictures in order to make sense of the story. The first story is free of the context which generated it, whereas the second story is much more closely tied to its context. As a result, the meanings of the second story are implicit, whereas the meanings of the first story are explicit.

It is not that the working class children do not have, in their passive vocabulary, the vocabulary used by the middle class children. Nor is it the case that the children differ in their tacit understanding of the linguistic rule system. Rather, what we have here are differences in the use of language arising out of a specific context. One child makes explicit the meaning which he is realizing through language for the person he is telling the story to, whereas the second child does not to the same extent.

The first child takes very little for granted, whereas the second child takes a great deal for granted. Thus, for the first child, the task was seen as a context in which his meanings were required to be made explicit, whereas the task for the second child was not seen as a task which required such explication of meaning. It would not be difficult to imagine a context where the first child would produce speech rather like the second.

What we are dealing with here are differences between the children in the way they realize, in language use, what is apparently the same context. We could say that the speech of the first child generated universalistic meanings, in the sense that the meanings are freed from the context and so understandable by all; whereas the speech of the second child generated particularistic meanings, in the sense that the meanings are closely tied to the context and

381

would be only fully understood by others if they had access to the context which originally generated the speech. Thus universalistic meanings are less bound to a given context, whereas particularistic meanings are severely context-bound.

Let us take another example. One mother, when she controls her child, places a great emphasis on language, because she wishes to make explicit, and to elaborate for the child, certain rules and reasons for the rules *and* their consequences. In this way the child has access through language to the relationships between his [or her] particular act which evoked the mother's control, and certain general principles, reasons and consequences which serve to universalize the particular act.

Another mother places less emphasis on language when she controls her child and deals with only the particular act; she does not relate it to general principles and their reasoned basis and consequences.

Both children learn that there is something they are supposed, or not supposed, to do; but the first child has learned rather more than this. The grounds of the mother's acts have been made explicit and elaborated; whereas the grounds of the second mother's acts are implicit, they are unspoken.

Our research shows just this. The social classes differ in terms of the *contexts* which evoke certain linguistic realizations. Many mothers in the middle class (and it is important to add not all), relative to the working class (and again it is important to add not all by any means), place greater emphasis on the use of language in socializing the child into the moral order, in disciplining the child in the communication and recognition of feeling. Here again we can say that the child is oriented towards universalistic meanings which transcend a given context, whereas the second child is oriented towards particularistic meanings which are closely tied to a given context and so do not transcend it. This does not mean that working class mothers are non-verbal, only that they differ from the middle class mothers in the *contexts* which evoke universalistic meanings. They are *not* linguistically deprived, neither are their children.

We can generalize from these two examples and say that certain groups of children, through the forms of their socialization, are oriented towards receiving and offering universalistic meanings in certain contexts, whereas other groups of children are oriented towards particularistic meanings. The linguistic realizations of universalistic orders of meaning are very different from the linguistic realizations of particularistic orders of meaning, and so are the forms of the social relation (for example, between mother and child) which generate these. We can say, then, that what is made available for learning, how it is made available, and the patterns of social relation, are also very different.

Now, when we consider the children in school, we can see that there is likely to be difficulty. For the school is necessarily concerned with the transmission and development of universalistic orders of meaning. The school is concerned with making explicit – and elaborating through language – principles and operations as these apply to objects (the science subjects) and persons (the arts subjects). One child, through his [or her] socialization, is already sensitive to the symbolic orders of the school, whereas the second child is much less sensitive to the universalistic orders of the school. The second child is oriented towards particularistic orders of meaning which are context-bound, in which principles and operations are implicit, and towards a form of language use through which such meanings are realized.

The school is necessarily trying to develop in the child orders of relevance and relation as these apply to persons and objects, which are not initially the ones he [or she] spontaneously moves towards. The problem of educability at one level, whether it is in Europe, the United States or newly developing societies, can be understood in terms of a confrontation between (a) the school's universalistic orders of meaning and the social relationships which generate them, and (b) the particularistic orders of meanings and social relationships which generate them, which the child brings with him [or her] to the school. Orientations towards 'meta-languages' of control and innovation are not made available to these children as part of their initial socialization.

The school is attempting to transmit un-commonsense knowledge – i.e. public knowledge realized through various 'meta-languages'. This knowledge is what I have called universalistic. However, both implicitly and explicitly, school transmits values and an attendant morality, which affect the contents and contexts of education. They do this by establishing criteria for acceptable pupil and staff conduct. These values and morals also affect the content of educational knowledge through the selection of books, text and films, and through the examples and analogies used to assist access to public knowledge (universalistic meanings). Thus, the working class child may be placed at a considerable disadvantage in relation to the *total* culture of the school. It is not made for him [or her]; he [or she] may not answer to it.

The universalistic functions of language – where meanings are less context-bound – point to an 'elaborated code'. The more particularistic functions point to a 'restricted code'. Because a code is restricted it does not mean that a child is non-verbal, nor is he in the technical sense linguistically deprived, for he possesses the same tacit understanding of the linguistic rule system as any child. It does not mean that the children cannot produce, at any time, elaborated speech variants in *particular* contexts.

It is critically important to distinguish between speech variants and a restricted code. A speech variant is a pattern of linguistic choices which is specific to a particular context – for example, when talking to children, a policeman giving evidence in a court, talking to friends whom one knows well, the ritual of cocktail parties, or train encounters. Because a code is restricted it does not mean that a speaker will not in some contexts, and under specific conditions, use a range of modifiers or subordinations, or whatever. But it does mean that where such choices are made they will be highly *context-specific*.

This 'concept code' refers to the transmission of the deep-meaning structure of a culture or sub-culture – the 'core' meaning structure.

'Codes', on this view, make substantive the culture or subculture by controlling the linguistic realizations of context critical to socialization. Building on the work of Professor Michael Halliday, one can distinguish four critical contexts:

1 The regulative contexts: these are the authority relations where the child is made aware of the moral order and its various backings.
2 The instructional contexts: here the child learns about the objective nature of objects and acquires various skills.
3 The imaginative or innovating contexts: here the child is encouraged to experiment and re-create his world on his own terms and in his own way.
4 The interpersonal contexts: here the child is made aware of affective states – his own and others.

In practice these are interdependent, but the emphasis and contents will vary from one group to another. I suggest that the critical orderings of a culture or subculture are made substantive, are made palpable, through the way it realizes these four contexts linguistically – initially in the family. If these four contexts are realized through the predominant use of restricted speech variants with particularistic i.e. relatively context-tied – meanings, then the deep structure of the communication is controlled by a restricted code. If these four contexts are realized predominantly through elaborated speech variants, with relatively context-independent – i.e. universalistic – meanings, then the deep structure of communication is controlled by an elaborated code. Because the code is restricted, it does not mean that the users *never* use elaborated speech variants. It only means that such variants will be used infrequently in the process of socializing the child in his family.

The 'concept code' makes a distinction similar to the distinction which linguists make between the 'surface' and 'deep' structure of the grammar (see David Havano. 9 January 1969, and Ernest Gellner, 29 May 1969, on Noam Chomsky's work). Sentences which look superficially different can be shown to be generated from the same rules.

The linguistic choices involved in a précis will be markedly different from the linguistic choices involved in a self-conscious poem. These in turn will be markedly different from the linguistic choices involved in an analysis of physical or moral principles; or different again from the linguistic realization of forms of control by a mother. But they may all, under certain conditions, reveal that speech codes – either restricted *or* elaborated – underlie them.

Now because the subculture or culture, through its forms of social integration, generates a restricted code, it does not mean that the resultant speech and meaning system is linguistically or culturally deprived, that the children have nothing to offer the school, that their imaginings are not significant. Nor does it mean that we have to teach the children formal grammar. Nor does it mean that we have to interfere with their dialect.

There is nothing, but nothing, in the dialect as such, which prevents a child from internalizing and learning to use universalistic meanings. But if the contexts of learning – for example, the reading of books – are not contexts which are triggers for the children's imaginings, are not triggers for the children's curiosity and explorations in his [or her] family and community, then the child is not at home in the educational world. If the teacher has to say continuously, 'Say it again, dear; I didn't understand you', then in the end the child may say nothing. If the culture of the teacher is to become part of the consciousness of the child, then the culture of the child must first be in the consciousness of the teacher.

This may mean that the teacher must be able to understand the child's dialect, rather than deliberately attempting to change it. Much of the context of our schools is unwittingly drawn from aspects of the symbolic world of the middle class, and so when the child steps into school he [or she] is stepping into a symbolic system which does not provide for him [or her] a linkage with his [or her] life outside.

It is an accepted educational principle that we should work with what the child can offer; why don't we practise it? The introduction of the child to the universalistic meanings of public forms of thought is not 'compensatory education'; *it is education*. It is not making children middle class; how it is done, through the implicit values underlying the form and content of the educational environment, might.

We need to distinguish between the principles and operations that teachers transmit and develop in the children, and the contexts they create in order to do this. We should start knowing that the social experience the child already possesses is valid and significant, and that this social experience should be reflected back to him as being valid and significant. It can only be reflected back to him if it is part of the texture of the learning experience we create. If we spent as much time thinking through the implications of this as we do thinking about the implications of Piaget's development sequences, then it would be possible for schools to become exciting and challenging environments for parents, the children themselves and teachers.

We need to examine the social assumptions underlying the organization, distribution and evaluation of knowledge, for there is not one, and only one, answer. The power relationships created outside the school penetrate the organization, distribution and evaluation of knowledge through the social context. The definition of 'educability' is itself, at any one time, an attenuated consequence of these power relationships.

We must consider Robert Lynd's question: 'knowledge for what?' And the answer cannot be given only in terms of whether six-year-old children should be able to read, count and write. We do not know what a child is capable of, as we have as yet no theory which enables us to create sets of optimal learning environments; and even if such a theory existed, it is most unlikely that resources would be available to make it substantive on the scale required. It may well be that one of the tests of an educational system is that its outcomes are relatively unpredictable.

Basil Bernstein

Acknowledgment

The present article is a more spelled-out version of one which forms a chapter in *Education and Democracy*, edited by David Rubinstein and Colin Stoneman, published by Penguin.

References

BERNSTEIN, B. and HENDERSON, D. (1969) 'Social class differences in the relevance of language to socialization', *Sociology*, Vol. 3, No. 1.

BERNSTEIN, B. (1970) 'A socio-linguistic approach to socialization: with some reference to educability' in GUMPERZ, J. and HYMES, DELL (eds) *Directions in Sociolinguistics*. New York: Holt, Rinehart & Winston.

FANTINI, M. D. and WEINSTEIN, G. (1968) *The Disadvantaged: challenge to education*. New York: Harper & Row.

HALLIDAY, M. A. K. (1969) 'Relevant models of language', *Educational Review*, Vol. 22, No. 1.

HAWKINS, P.R. (1969) 'Social class, the national group and reference', *Language and Speech*, Vol. 12, No. 2.

Index

Index

Source Acknowledgements

The editors and publishers would like to thank the following for permission to reproduce material in this volume:

Bristol Classical Press for 'The Whole Experience. Diane Elliott's First Year' by Charles Hannam, Pat Smyth and Norman Stephenson in their book *The First Year of Teaching* (1984); Harper and Row, London for 'Teaching and Learning' by Guy Claxton in his book *Live and Learn: an introduction to the psychology of growth and change in everyday life* (1984); Longman Inc for 'Teaching as a Moral Craft' by Alan R. Tom in his book *Teaching as a Moral Craft* (1984); Open University Press for 'Initial Fronts' by Linda Measor and Peter Woods in their book *Changing Schools* (1984); Open University Press for 'Science: Group Based Curriculum' by John Evans in his book *Teaching as Transition* (1985); Pat Mahony for her chapter 'How Alice's Chin Really Came to be Pressed Against Her Foot: Sexist Processes of Instruction in Mixed Sex Classrooms', *Women's Studies International Forum* 6, 1; Trentham Books for 'School Processes: an Ethnographic Study' by Cecile Wright in J. Eggleston *et al.*, *Education for Some* (1986); Penguin Books for 'Understanding Schools as Organizations' by Charles Handy and Robert Aitken in their book *Organising Schools* (1986); Methuen & Co. for 'House Staff and Department Staff' by Robert G. Burgess in his book *Experiencing Comprehensive Education* (1983); R. N. Deale for his chapter 'Assessment and Testing in the Secondary School', *Schools Council Examinations Bulletin* 32; Harper and Row, London for 'The Side-Effects of Assessment' by Derek Rowntree in his book *Assessing Students: how shall we know them?* (1977); Falmer Press for 'Control and Welfare: Towards a Theory of Constructive Discipline in Schools' by Delwyn Tattum in P. Ribbins, *Schooling and Welfare* (1985); Alun Pelleschi for 'Pastoral Care and Girls of Asian Parentage', *Pastoral Care in Education*, June 1985, vol. 3, no. 2; Open University Press for 'Special Education: the Way Ahead' by John Fish in his book *Major Issues in Special Education* (1985); David J. Gavine for his chapter 'Special Educational Needs—Fact or Friction?', *Scottish Educational Review* (1985) vol. 17, 1; John Head for his chapter 'A Model to Link Personality Characteristics to a Preference for Science', *European Journal of Science Education* (1980) 2; Methuen & Co. for 'Girl Friendly Science and the Girl Friendly School' by Judith Whyte in J. Whyte, R. Deem, L. Kant and M. Cruickshank (eds) *Girl*

Friendly Schooling (1985); Falmer Press for 'Three Curricular Traditions and their Implications' by Ivor Goodson in his book *School Subjects and Curriculum Change* 2nd edition (1987); Nafferton Books for 'The Schooling of Science' by Michael F. D. Young in G. Whitty and M. Young (eds) *Explorations in the Politics of School Knowledge* (1976); Chris Brown for his chapter 'The Curriculum and National Identity' in his article 'National Identity and World Studies', *Educational Review* 6, 2; Falmer Press for 'Contrasting Models in School Geography' by Rob Gilbert in his book *The Impotent Image: reflections of ideology in the secondary school curriculum* (1984); Unwin Educational for '"Political" Differences in English Teaching' by Margaret Mathieson in her book *The Preachers of Culture: a study of English and its teachers* (1975); Falmer Press for 'Change in School Mathematics' by Barry Cooper in his book *Renegotiating Secondary School Mathematics* (1985); The Women's Press for 'Patriarchy in School Textbooks' by Marion Scott in her chapter 'Teach her a Lesson: Sexist Curriculum in Patriarchal Education' in Dale Spender and Elizabeth Saran (eds) *Learning to Lose: sexism and education* (1980); Ali Rattansi for his chapter '"Race", Education and British Society', previously unpublished; Robert Moore for his chapter 'Education, Employment and Recruitment' in his book *Changing Paradigms and Patterns of Provisions in Vocational Education*, vol. 1, Polytechnic of the South Bank; Jenny Williams for her chapter 'Race and Gender in Educational Policies: Why are Women and Black Students Educational Problems?', previously unpublished; NFER/Nelson for 'Beneficiaries, Benefits and Costs: an Investigation of the Assisted Places Scheme' by John Fitz, Tony Edwards and Geoff Whitty, *Research Papers in Education*, vol. 1, 3; Methuen & Co. for 'The Role of Parents and Other Adults' by John C. Coleman in his book *The Nature of Adolescence* (1980); Lawrence and Wishart for 'Why No Pedagogy in England?' by Brian Simon in his book *Does Education Matter?* (1985); Falmer Press for 'Appraising the Teachers: Professionalism and Control' in M. Lawn and G. Grace, *Teaching: the Culture and Politics of Work* (1987); Macmillan Publishers Ltd for 'Youth and Transitions' by Johne Clarke and Paul Willis in I. Bates *et al.*, *Schooling for the Dole* (1984); Basil Bernstein for 'Education Cannot Compensate for Society', *New Society*, 26, 2 1970.